JUDGMENT DAY

NATHANIEL BRANDEN

JUDGMENT DAY

MY YEARS WITH AYN RAND

A MARC JAFFE BOOK

Houghton Mifflin Company

BOSTON

1989

For information about permission to reproduce selections
from this book, write to Permissions, Houghton Mifflin
Company, 2 Park Street, Boston, Massachusetts 02108.

Library of Congress Cataloging-in-Publication Data

Branden, Nathaniel.
    Judgment day : my years with Ayn Rand / Nathaniel Branden.
        p.   cm.
    "A Marc Jaffe book."
    ISBN 0-395-46107-3
    1. Rand, Ayn—Biography.   2. Branden, Nathaniel—Relations with
women.   3. Novelists, American—20th century—Biography.
4. Psychologists—United States—Biography.   I. Title.
PS3535.A547Z56   1989
813'.52—dc19
[B]   89-30396
                    CIP

Printed in the United States of America

D   10   9   8   7   6   5   4   3   2   1

To Devers Branden

The precept: "Judge not, that ye be not judged" . . . is an abdication of moral responsibility: it is a moral blank check one gives to others in exchange for a moral blank check one expects for oneself.

There is no escape from the fact that men have to make choices; so long as men have to make choices, there is no escape from moral values; so long as moral values are at stake, no moral neutrality is possible. To abstain from condemning a torturer, is to become an accessory to the torture and murder of his victims.

The moral principle to adopt . . . is: "*Judge, and be prepared to be judged.*"

— AYN RAND

AUTHOR'S NOTE

In recreating the events of this memoir, I have had the help not only of a keenly vivid memory — made stronger by having recounted the incidents many times — but also by a variety of documents and materials which I talk about in the Epilogue.

In instances where I reproduce conversations that took place many years ago, I am not suggesting that all of the words reported are verbatim, but I am confident they are faithful to the essence of what was said and to the spirit and mood of the occasion. This conviction has been reinforced by those, acknowledged below, who knew one or more of the people about whom I write and who affirm that my characterizations match their own memories of the individual's attitudes, beliefs, behavior, and spoken style.

In the course of this book I recreate a great many conversations with Ayn Rand. Prior to our break, Ms. Rand said publicly and on more than one occasion that I knew her thoughts more profoundly and specifically than any other human being and that I was qualified to speak for her on virtually any aspect of her ideas or convictions. Only the internal logic of my narrative can assure the reader that I am reliable in reporting on the more intimate aspects of our story.

The individuals who read all or portions of this manuscript, shared recollections with me, checked my memory, or offered editorial or other suggestions, include Dr. Joseph Barber, Dr. Roger Callahan, Reva Fox, Florence and Hans Hirschfeld, Jonathan Hirschfeld, Leonard Hirschfeld, Dr. John Hospers, Elayne and Harry Kalberman, Ralph Roseman, Lawrence Scott, and Drs. Lee and Joyce Shulman. I thank them all. I am especially appreciative because I know that for many of them the reviewing of this manuscript brought back painful memories. Thanks also to many former students who helped me recreate details of the atmosphere at the Nathaniel Branden Institute.

Obviously there are facts I write about that no one else is in a position to affirm or disaffirm. I alone am responsible for any errors that may have escaped notice.

The concept and approach of this memoir is a difficult one to convey briefly — it is unconventional in a number of ways — and I shall always be grateful to my editor, Marc Jaffe, for the speed which he grasped my basic intention, and for his sensitivity and insightfulness in helping me to fulfill it.

My greatest appreciation is to my wife, Devers, whose contribution to this book, editorially and psychologically, is truly incommunicable. She provided inspired input through every rewrite. Not only did she encourage me to write freely and openly about my intimate relationships with three other women, but lovingly and mercilessly she challenged me to keep going deeper into self-disclosure. Friends who have read the manuscript say they can feel her spirit on every page. They are right. This book is dedicated to her in love and gratitude.

JUDGMENT DAY

PROLOGUE

ON THE MORNING of March 6, 1982, Ayn Rand died. The author of *The Fountainhead* and *Atlas Shrugged* was seventy-seven years old.

At 4:35 that afternoon, my sister Elayne Kalberman telephoned from New York City to inform me of the death. My wife, Devers, and I were in our home in Los Angeles, and I turned from the telephone to tell her what had happened. Devers reached for my arm, in a gesture of concern, and her eyes searched my face for a reaction. I was aware only of a growing sense of stillness.

For some weeks I had been expecting this phone call. Despite Ayn's efforts to keep the information secret, I had heard a few years earlier of the lung cancer and of the surgery that followed. The operation was successful, but it left Ayn permanently weakened. A subsequent operation for gallstones worsened her condition. I knew that recently her health had been rapidly deteriorating.

When I asked Elayne what precisely Ayn had died of, she answered, "I don't know. We may never know. Leonard Peikoff is in full charge of everything now, and you know Leonard. The Ayn Rand legend must be protected. And sometimes the details of dying are unglamorous."

"Poor Leonard," I said, remembering the shy, nervous boy I had brought to Ayn's home more than three decades ago, with his fiercely intense interest in ideas. Years later, he would be proud to describe himself as the "feudal serf" of Ayn Rand's cause. Leonard Peikoff, who hung on to the end. The man whose job it now was to carry the work forward. I thought of the price he had paid.

Elayne was telling me of a cold Ayn had caught while speaking at a conference in New Orleans some months earlier, and of the cardio-pulmonary problems that had developed. "I imagine," she said,

"Leonard will announce something safely general — like 'heart failure' — and that may even be the truth."

"How are you feeling about it?" I asked.

I had introduced Elayne to Ayn's world thirty years ago. For a long time she had worked for Ayn and me as circulation manager — first for *The Objectivist Newsletter,* later *The Objectivist,* that Ayn and I co-founded and co-edited; and then, after Ayn's and my break, for *The Ayn Rand Letter.* The chief purpose of these publications had been to spread Ayn's philosophical ideas to readers of her fiction. Elayne and I had been estranged for nine years following Ayn's and my break because she had chosen Ayn's side.

"I don't feel much of anything," she said. Her voice sounded tight and controlled. A wave of affection swept through me. I was happy that we had become friends again after so long an alienation. She continued, "Whatever love I ever felt for Ayn vanished a long time ago. I can't feel anything for her accomplishments anymore — I'm too angry at her cruelty, at the harm she caused so many people who cared for her. What about you? What are you feeling?"

Ayn Rand and I had been associated for nearly two decades, and we had lived through extraordinary experiences together. At one time I had been the foremost exponent of her philosophy. We had been as close as it is possible for two people to be. And, in one great explosion, everything ended. Then the questions began, from students, readers, people I encountered socially, strangers in restaurants — from everywhere in the country and from cities around the world: What really happened between you and Ayn Rand? What could possibly have broken you two apart? How could two people who were so close find themselves in such devastating and irreconcilable conflict? For so many years afterward, up to the present, the questions never stopped.

I was seeing myself at the age of fourteen, living in Toronto, reading *The Fountainhead* for the first time. I was recalling the sense of a door opening, intellectually, spiritually, psychologically — a passageway into another dimension, like a summons from the future. Later I would tell Ayn that I felt she had brought me up long-distance by means of her novel. The only rival to that event, some years later, was the experience of reading *Atlas Shrugged* in manuscript.

I had written Ayn a letter early in 1950 while I was studying psychology at UCLA and she was living in the San Fernando Valley, writing *Atlas Shrugged.* In it I asked her a number of philosophical questions stimulated by *The Fountainhead* and by her first novel, *We the Living.* My letter intrigued her and she invited me to her home. Later we would speak of the "shock of recognition" at our first encounter. I was twenty years old, she was forty-five, that spring.

Over the next eighteen years our relationship went through many transformations: from student and teacher to friends to colleagues and partners — to lovers. Ultimately we became adversaries. Our association came to an emotionally violent end in the summer of 1968.

And now, while my sister Elayne was waiting for me to say something, I could hear the voice of my first wife, Barbara, at the time of the break, crying to me, "You've got to defend yourself! You've got to fight back! You've got to understand that Ayn is intent on destroying you! You've got to understand that *Ayn wants you dead*!"

"What are you feeling?" Elayne asked again.

I struggled to find the words that would accurately describe my state. "No particular sense of loss and not much sadness either. For me, Ayn died a long time ago. Maybe what I'm feeling now is just a kind of quietness, and a sense of waste, of shame, for both of us, for the stupidity of those years, the lack of dignity in the way we dealt with each other." I did not know, until Devers told me later, that I had tears in my eyes.

In a few minutes, the telephone rang again, this time on the office line, and I allowed the call to be put through because the caller claimed an emergency. It was a man from Virginia whom I did not know. He introduced himself in a gentle voice, explained that he had been an admirer of Ayn's and mine for many years, and then told me of Ayn's death.

"On Monday evening," he continued, with a touch of formality that disclosed a tightly disciplined suffering, "that's March eighth — from seven to nine o'clock — at the Frank E. Campbell Funeral Home at Madison Avenue and Eighty-first Street — there will be an opportunity for people to pay Miss Rand their last respects." He paused, but I did not respond. "I thought you might want to come."

"Why, no," I said, as kindly as I could. "I don't."

"I know, sir, that you and Miss Rand have been . . . separated . . . for a long time. You were like a father and mother to me. You both contributed so much to my life, to the lives of so many of us. You gave inspiration and courage. It's been hard for me to understand how two people who shared so much could have a conflict they couldn't resolve." I told him that Ayn's and my conflict really didn't matter and that what did matter was whatever he had learned from us that was of value to him. "I know that — intellectually. It's very hard to feel it right now." His voice sounded hollow and muted.

There will be so much pain of his kind in the next few weeks and months, I thought.

"She was a great woman, wasn't she?" he asked. The meaning of his plea was unmistakable.

"She was a genius," I answered.

"You haven't changed your mind about that?"

"No. Not about that."

"She was a great novelist and a great philosopher."

"Yes."

"People will be mourning her all over the world."

"Yes, I would think so."

The next call came on my private line. It was Barbara Branden, my first wife. Had I heard the news? she wanted to know.

We talked about our reaction to the death. She projected an air of wistfulness, a kind of subdued, dreamy tragedy that suggested someone a good deal younger than her fifty-three years.

"Even though I expected it, I feel stunned," Barbara said softly. "You must be feeling something like that, too."

"Not stunned. Just . . . contemplative."

"It's the end of an era."

"The era ended a long time ago, Barbara," I said gently.

She sighed. "I know, but still . . ."

I very much wanted to feel a warmth I was unable to feel. If we had once shared a common context, having lived through so much together, the sense of a common context was precisely what was lacking now, as it had been lacking for many years. I could not escape the thought that we inhabited totally different worlds.

I had met Barbara when I was eighteen and she was nineteen. We were married when I was twenty-two; too young for both of us. My feelings for her had been a good deal stronger than hers for me. The marriage had lasted thirteen years; the on-again, off-again friendship that followed, roughly another decade. But that was behind us now and we both knew it.

Our last meeting, some months ago, had ended uncomfortably. Barbara was writing a biography, *The Passion of Ayn Rand*, and I had agreed to come to her apartment to answer a number of questions about my relationship with Ayn. I explained that since, as she already knew, I had decided to write a memoir, there was a good deal I would not discuss; I wished to reserve it for my own book. I knew that in declining to help Barbara in detail, I was putting myself at risk with regard to what she might write; I would not be able to correct any possible inaccuracies; but I could not involve myself in her project. I had mentioned the concept of my memoir to her two years earlier, before she began work on Ayn's biography. I saw our purposes as very different and I wished her well. During our meeting, she questioned me, as she had before, about the projected publication date of the memoir. I assured her that she could easily publish before me, if that was her concern, because there were other books I planned to write first. Up until this point, her manner had been reasonably friendly, although some sense of strain was always present; but now, suddenly, her voice took on a disorienting note of ruthlessness: "Just keep out of my way." Keep out of your way with what? I wondered. My own life? I looked at her through a moment of silence, to give her time to hear her own statement. I did not care to express what I was feeling in that moment. I said, "You don't have anything to fear from me, Barbara." Then I left.

Now, on the telephone, she was saying, "It somehow feels natural that we should be talking today — I mean, fitting. I had to call."

I understood. Her words reached me. I had once loved her and now, in this moment, I was seeing the two teenagers who had walked in the snow in the first months of our meeting, talking of the books we would write and the things we would accomplish. I saw our years with Ayn Rand and what we had lived through together and survived — the times of incredible happiness we had had with Ayn and the nightmarish times of anguish. I saw not only the ways Barbara and I had hurt each other in that world but also the ways we had helped each other — and I was able, for a moment, to feel the sense of a connection that had eluded me earlier.

Then she asked me if I knew about the evening at the funeral home. Did I want to go? I was astonished at the suggestion and I said so. Had time really stood still for her? What did that event in New York have to do with her or me? "Well," she answered, "I still love Ayn — I know, I know all the things you could say — but I do. And I'd like to say good-bye to her."

I thought of past conversations, for many years following the break with Ayn, when she had tried to persuade me that I was naive or misguided in not seeing Ayn as "evil." On occasion she spoke as if Ayn had ruined her life; she was adamant that Ayn had obstructed her development as a writer. At that earlier time my chief concern was to understand my own role, and my own responsibility, in the terrible events that had led to the final explosion. Over the years I cautioned her many times against seeing herself as a victim. Now, it seemed, I was the one to be perceived as cold and Barbara as transformed benevolence.

I said, "Leonard will never allow you into that event. He's the keeper of the faith now, and you're 'the enemy.' "

"I'll send a message, through someone, that I'd like to come, and see how Leonard responds."

"All you will accomplish is to give Leonard the pleasure of refusing you."

She answered that I was probably right and that she didn't care.

I spent the next several hours talking with Devers about Ayn's death, about its likely effect on various people I knew, about the past, and about the future impact of Ayn's work — trying, as I had done many times before, to capture for Devers and for myself the unique quality of the world I had lived in for so many years. "If I could have known, at nineteen, what I was setting in motion when I wrote Ayn that first letter —"

Devers smiled. "You would have gone ahead and done exactly what you did."

"I would have done some things differently. I wouldn't have kept Patrecia waiting for so long, or put her through what I did."

"Of course. I meant, apart from that —"

"Apart from that, it was a great experience I am glad to have lived."

"I'm glad you acknowledge that," she said.

I knew what she meant. Early in our relationship, during a period when we were telling each other about things we had done in the past, I would sometimes muse about the possibilities I might have missed in life. One day she laughed at me and said, "Nathaniel, you've missed nothing. You've created exactly the kind of life you wanted for yourself. You've had it all. You like drama. Look at what you have been living since you were eighteen years old." I knew that she was right.

I nodded my head now in affirmation. I felt almost light-headed, as if reality would not stay in focus. My perspective kept shifting so that I felt quietly solemn one moment and cheerfully buoyant the next. This did not astonish me. I knew about the strange and complex ways in which the mind processes events of this kind. I had had to deal with a death before — one that had been incomparably devastating. That, too, was part of my context today.

I allowed myself to think of her — of Patrecia — for a moment, and of the role she had played, through my love for her, in bringing the world Ayn and I had created crashing down. The thought swept me into a far deeper level of pain, mixed with gratitude, and after a moment I let it go.

Later that day I spent some time alone in my study, writing in my journal, making notes on the afternoon's conversations, and trying to go deeper into my reactions. At some point I stopped writing because a part of my mind had drifted. I heard myself saying to Ayn: You didn't have the facts right at the time of the break and now you've died still not having them right. You never did know what really happened or what any of it meant. And if you were to read the story I'm going to write, and have the whole context spread out before you, would you understand then? Would you allow yourself to understand? I doubt it.

I tried to remember the first moment I thought of writing this book, but I knew it was the sum of many moments: the first time Devers pointed out the dramatic aspect of my experiences; the afternoon when, in an effort at self-understanding and self-healing, still struggling to absorb Patrecia's sudden, accidental death, I began writing an intimately detailed journal that was to draw my thoughts deeper and deeper into the past; the day I saw that in my personal life I had faced, in one way or another, most of the major issues I wrote about as a psychologist; and that this memoir offered the challenge of a more dangerous self-confrontation and self-exploration than any I attempted before.

Turning the pages of my notebook, I stopped at one of my earliest efforts to formulate the concept of the memoir early in 1980.

> If I proceed with this, if I tell Ayn's and my story, set in the context of my relationships with Barbara and Patrecia, it will be a new opportunity to write about love, different kinds of love — from love of persons to love of ideas to love of causes — and the extraordinary things love sometimes leads us to do. Additionally, an opportunity to write about a brilliant, innovative thinker — an exalted and tortured woman. And to write about the psychology of intellectual movements and why and how even the best of movements can bring out the worst in people as well as the noblest. More personally, it will allow me to explore the process of individuation, the drama of growth and evolution, as it has worked out in my own life. There is something frightening in this — underneath every truth there always seems to be a deeper truth, *and that is the appeal and the incentive.*

I got up from my desk and walked into the living room. Our home is near the summit of a very high hill. The living room is a large rectangle made almost entirely of mirror and broad sheets of glass, overlooking a garden, trees, and beyond that, the homes and offices of Beverly Hills, and beyond that, the surrounding curve of Los Angeles, and beyond that, the Pacific Ocean now slowly disappearing into night. Flames of yellow, gold, and red stretched like beacons in all directions, as rays of countless lights hit the wall of glass in front of me. Every minute or two I could see one of the lights moving across the sky at the rising or descending angle of an aircraft, so that the sparkling expanse below looked like a vast landing field.

I thought, This is how we were back then, Ayn and I and all of us — detached from the world — intoxicated by the sensation of flying through the sky in a vision of life that made ordinary existence unendurably dull.

On Monday morning, I received a telephone call from the *New York Times*, the first of several such calls from newspapers across the country. The reporter said she wished to check her understanding of certain aspects of my relationship with Ayn Rand. Prior to the opening of Nathaniel Branden Institute, the organization I had created to teach her philosophy, Miss Rand had been known exclusively as a novelist, had she not? I told her that was correct. It was the Nathaniel Branden Institute, founded in 1958 and closed in 1968, that effectively launched the Objectivist movement — and generated widespread awareness of Miss Rand as a philosopher? It was. Could one state that America's third largest political party, the Libertarian party, was an important part, a consequence, of the influence of Ayn Rand's work and that of the institute? Yes.

Then I told her that Ayn Rand's most important long-term influence would be in the universities, among teachers and professors whose thinking has been significantly affected by her work. "In political philosophy?" the reporter asked.

"Yes, but more fundamentally in ethics. And epistemology."

"Can you condense her overall philosophy in a single sentence?"

"Reason — enlightened self-interest — the supreme importance of human ability and achievement — individual rights — political and economic freedom."

She asked if I was aware that there was considerable speculation concerning the nature of my friendship with Ayn Rand and the reasons for our break. Would I comment? No. Did I know about the event tonight at — ? Yes, I did.

On Tuesday, March 9, the *Times* reported:

Ayn Rand's body lay next to the symbol she had adopted as her own — a six-foot dollar sign [a floral arrangement, sent by an admirer]. Outside the funeral home, her followers, some in jeans and some in furs, stood in the cold waiting to pay her tribute.

From 7 to 9 o'clock Monday night, 800 admirers of the novelist and philosopher passed through the Frank E. Campbell Funeral Home. Some wept as they spoke of her in hushed tones, and some glowed as they described how she changed their lives.

Those who came to the funeral home to pay their respects reflected Miss Rand's influence in political, economic and intellectual spheres. They included Alan Greenspan, chairman of President Ford's Council of Economic Advisers; Robert M. Bleiberg, editorial director of *Barron's* magazine; many of the leaders of the Libertarian Party; and

professors of philosophy, business management and psychology at
schools from Vassar College to York University in Toronto.

* Later I was to learn that the word had been sent out that anyone
was welcome — friends and enemies alike — with only two exceptions: Nathaniel Branden and Barbara Branden. There were men close
to the door, I was told, to keep us out. I regretted that Barbara's request had evidently resulted in the assumption that I wished to be present.

In the weeks that followed, I received press clippings from around
the world, announcing Ayn Rand's death and discussing the influence
of her work. Some came from places as far away as Israel and Australia. Some of the pieces were laudatory; others were savagely hostile,
as if Ayn were still alive and her attackers dared not relent for an instant. Perhaps the extraordinary and continuing sales of her books
worldwide inspired this response: an author whose readers continue
to number in the millions *is* alive as an intellectual force. In this country, William Buckley wrote a graceless piece, the intent of which, evidently, was to persuade his readers and possibly himself that Ayn
Rand was truly dead. None of this was surprising, neither the adulation nor the animosity. I had seen it all before.

But the news stories did awaken memories of a time when I, and the
other members of Ayn's New York circle, seemed to live in a moving
fortress that was advancing against ignorance, cowardice, conformity,
and prejudice. The exhilaration of those years, and the pain, seemed
to dwell in that part of the psyche which contains neither past nor
future, only a timeless present. The exhilaration had to do with the joy
of fighting a battle that was supremely worthy, supremely important;
the pain, with what I learned about people in the process.

I was still in my twenties when the learning began, and I was
shocked and dismayed by the misrepresentations of Ayn's ideas in the
media. Ayn was a philosopher who taught that thinking is the highest
virtue, who celebrated consciousness as the source of all meaning and
glory, and whose fictional characters manifested the highest spiritual
integrity — and she was denounced as a "materialist," an apostle of
"mindless greed." She was a philosopher who taught the inviolability
of individual rights and who argued for a world in which no one would
be empowered to enforce his vision of the good on other human
beings — and she was accused of advocating a dog-eat-dog world. She
was the most passionate and consistent champion in the twentieth century of the rights of the individual against the state — and she was
smeared a "fascist" (a strategy originated by communists to discredit
their critics and adopted by unthinking "liberals" against any oppo-

nents of the welfare state). I was stunned by the gross misrepresentations. At the time, it was not easy for me to admit how hurt I was.

The pain did not involve only the psychology of opponents. The psychology of allies and supporters, and of my closest friends, and of Ayn herself, were all to come into focus, in ways that were to change everything: how I saw myself in the world, how I saw the culture and the battle in which we were engaged — and ultimately, how I saw human life.

A few weeks after Ayn's death, I realized that while I was still deliberating consciously about the pros and cons of writing the memoir, I had already made a decision: I had made it within minutes of my conception of the project four years earlier. But I was in the early stages of writing *Honoring the Self*, the distillation of nearly three decades of thinking about the psychology of self-esteem. Not until the spring of 1986, having completed for the time being my commitments in psychology, did I feel free to begin the project that, it now seemed to me, I had been moving toward since the age of fourteen.

So you want your future to be a great adventure, said an inner voice to my fourteen-year-old self. *You want to experience everything, to burst through the boundaries of normal feeling — into ecstasy. Well, then, listen carefully. . . . One day the world of* The Fountainhead *will open and you will enter. You will meet its author. She will be twenty-five years your senior, but you will become friends. She will come to see in you the embodiment of the very traits of character she celebrates in her writing. You will fall in love with each other and you will become lovers. You will become a warrior — a warrior of consciousness. And then you will meet a woman who will shatter your world. Your closest friends will become your enemies. Your idol will plot your destruction. You will know greater pain than you can imagine — and greater happiness. Your end will be your new beginning. But listen, even that is not all, because then . . .*

PART
ONE

ONE

" 'I want to sleep with you. Now, tonight, and at any time you may care to call me. I want your naked body, your skin, your mouth, your hands. I want you — like this — not hysterical with desire — but coldly and consciously — without dignity and without regrets — I want you — I have no self-respect to bargain with and divide me — I want you — I want you like an animal, or a cat on a fence, or a whore.' "

The girl who was reading these words aloud to her friends was trying, it seemed to me, to contain and deny her excitement. I was puzzled by her unconvincing attempt, just as I was puzzled by the slightly nervous laughter of the other two girls. The book to which they were reacting was clearly an object of their intense fascination.

One of the girls was my oldest sister, Florence, aged twenty-one, seven years older than I.

That summer afternoon in 1944, far from Toronto, Canada, where we lived, wars were being fought; human beings were killing and dying. In Paris, German troops were surrendering to French and American forces. In the Pacific, General MacArthur was unleashing devastating bomb attacks against Japanese shipping. To me, it was all rather remote.

This afternoon the radio and newspaper reports did not capture my interest. Nothing seemed able to capture it.

I sat in a large armchair in our living room, my legs stretched over the side, gazing off into space as usual. I did not expect my sister Florence or her two friends to pay any attention to me, and they didn't. I had wandered into the room a few minutes before, in response to the mysteriously hushed and excited sounds of their voices. With nowhere to go and nothing to do, I listened, thinking that there was something silly about such behavior from twenty-one-year-olds. At fourteen, I felt detached and faintly superior.

A few minutes later, without saying a word to me, they walked out of the room.

They had left the book behind, lying on a coffee table.

I walked over a little disdainfully, picked it up, and glanced at the title. *The Fountainhead,* a novel by Ayn Rand. I read the dust jacket and gathered that the book's central idea was that the ego, meaning the independent mind, "is the fountainhead of all human progress." I was intrigued. I studied the photograph of the author on the back of the jacket. Nothing about the face reminded me of anyone I had ever seen. Perhaps it was the dark, perceptive, intense eyes, conscious in some heightened way, that imparted a glamorous, even exotic cast to the face.

I vaguely recalled the boy up the street mentioning the book to me months earlier. I tried to recall what he had said — something about an architect with a very unusual philosophy of life. I turned to the first page.

"Howard Roark laughed." That was how it began.

There are extraordinary experiences in life that remain permanently engraved in memory; experiences that represent turning points; moments, hours, or days after which nothing is ever the same again.

The writing had the most marvelous purposefulness and clarity. I had the sense that every word was chosen with excruciating care; the book seemed absolutely devoid of the accidental. This was stylization of a kind I had never seen before, and it was maintained consistently down to the smallest detail. The author's ability to provide an experience of visual reality was instantly evident, and it was visual reality of the highest level of luminosity and precision. Years later the analogy that would occur to me was that it was like stepping into a painting by Vermeer.

The author's constructions, images, rhythms, all took hold of me in some profound way. The style reflected a manner of processing experience, a way of being conscious, which I had never encountered before and yet that seemed intimately familiar.

Six years later, at one of my early meetings with Ayn, I told her, "My excitement wasn't just at the stylization of the writing — your particular way of seeing and re-creating reality, which runs through everything — it was like being in a *stylized universe.*" She clapped her hands in appreciation of this image and later referred to it many times.

The first chapter of the novel establishes the basic character and context of Howard Roark, a young man passionately committed to becoming an architect, who has just been expelled from school for designing buildings that represent a total break with tradition. Unmoved by the expulsion, he knows he will not be stopped. His direction comes not from the opinions or values of others but from his own inner vision and convictions.

The novel covers nearly two decades in Howard Roark's life. The plot-theme of *The Fountainhead* is the battle of a great innovator, an architect of genius, against a society geared and committed to tradition and mediocrity. In terms of its abstract theme, the novel is a dramatization of the morality of individualism.

Every work of art is an act of psychological self-disclosure. An artist declares to the world: "This is what I think is important; important for me to project and for others to perceive." By the same token, an intense response to a work of art is also psychological self-disclosure. More often than not, the roots of our responses lie deep in our subconscious, but our values, philosophy, and sense of life are necessarily engaged when we encounter a work of art and fall in love.

I was aware that Ayn Rand had reached me in some unique way, and that in the cardinal values of the novel — independence, integrity, love of one's work, and a sacred sense of mission about one's life — I had found a world more interesting, more energizing, more challenging, and in a way more real, than the world around me. I experienced it as more relevant to my growth and development than anything I was hearing from my elders. To me, at fourteen, the vision offered by *The Fountainhead* was a great and inspiring gift.

I was what psychologists call an "alienated adolescent." Certainly I felt radically different from everyone I knew, to the point of sometimes feeling that I had almost nothing in common with anyone. At times I felt almost unbearably lonely. However, the concept of alienation is a somewhat troublesome one. To some extent, any thinking person experiences alienation as a by-product of independence, although I do not for a moment believe that independence was the only factor involved for me.

And yet my memories of childhood are primarily happy ones: climbing trees, being carried on my father's shoulders, visiting the animals in the zoo, riding a bicycle as if it were a horse or a spacecraft, running down the street in an explosion of exuberance — and wondering only occasionally why all grown-ups and most children seemed sad.

By my teenage years, my sense of distance from other people had grown stronger. My memories of those years are not so much unhappy ones as questioning, searching ones. What I wanted, without the words to name it, was a world that would somehow match what I had felt as a child running down the street, a place of laughter and challenge and high-energy excitement. I wanted to find heroes. What I saw instead was a world in which life was perceived not as an adventure but as a burden, and in which growing up was equated with giving up.

My feelings of progressive isolation and estrangement provided the psychological backdrop for the events that were to follow — even events twenty or more years in the future.

Living in the predominantly Anglo-Saxon city of Toronto, my parents were Russian Jewish immigrants who had never really assimilated themselves into Canadian culture. A sense of rootlessness and disorientation was present in our home from the beginning. I had no sense of belonging, in Toronto or anywhere else, nor was I even aware of what a sense of belonging would mean. To me, the void seemed normal.

I was aware that neither of my parents felt effective in practical matters. My mother was by far the more this-worldly of the two, an action-oriented woman with no outlets for her energy, with a sense that life is to be "taken" but with no sense of how to seize it — and with rage against my father because he did not know either. My father, more passive, was a dreamer whose favorite recreation and escape from my mother was his garden, where he loved to work, especially when Mother was yelling that he come and deal with some matter of family business.

My mother's greatest preoccupation was, What will people think? Reality for her was only what others believed it to be. In retrospect I can see that she existed in a chronic condition of anxiety.

However, she provided the minimal grounding that existed in our home. Father's contribution, apart from supporting us, was of a different order: he brought music and literature into our lives — the voice of Caruso and the plays of Shakespeare, for instance.

My father owned a men's clothing store in a blue-collar suburb of Toronto. I was obliged to work there most Saturdays, which I disliked, wanting more free time for myself. He evidently believed that leisure time, music and literature aside, was only for small children and perhaps for girls; a man *worked*.

I can remember times when he attempted to be physically affectionate with my mother; I cannot remember a single occasion on which he was not rebuffed. They fought a good deal, chiefly over my father's tendency to disappear mentally, to start talking about birds or flowers, when Mother wanted to discuss some matter of money or family.

If Mother suffered from an anxiety disorder, then my father was passive-aggressive. I did not feel close to either of them, although at times I felt sorry for what I perceived to be the joylessness of their lives.

Once, when I was sixteen years old and had failed to do a chore, my father, frustrated and angry to the point of fury, struck me with his open hand. We stood looking at each other. He appeared bitterly forlorn: he could not control his family; he could not win respect from his wife or children; he could not even get his son to perform satisfactorily a simple task. I felt neither pain nor anger. To resort to a physical blow seemed like a confession of impotence, and, in that moment, I felt older than my father. It was not a happy feeling.

As the only son, I received many messages to the effect that all important family expectations centered on me: I was the one who was supposed to achieve something noteworthy in life. On the other hand, I also received messages to the effect that I might be a failure, since I did not seem interested in money, business, or most things the "world" regarded as important.

I did not take seriously the accusations of impracticality. I thought that if practicality meant anything, it meant knowing how to create a happy life — and my parents and other relatives had clearly failed at that.

One of my earliest impressions of grown-ups in general, was that they were liars, saying not what they thought or felt but rather whatever they believed would serve some particular purpose. When I was very young, this sometimes distressed me. As I grew older, I tried to understand it, believing, implicitly, that understanding is protection, understanding is power. Often, it seemed to me, they themselves did not know what they thought or felt and just made up explanations as they went along. I felt starved for the rational and the straightforward — as well as for the sight of joy. I grew up very slow to trust.

I loved physical activity — bicycling, treeclimbing, archery — but it was almost always as solitary as my reading. I rarely admitted to myself how much I longed for human companionship. I wanted to like and admire people, but I was indifferent to the values and concerns of my contemporaries: winning love from mother or father, being popular, or cloning oneself in the image of whatever was currently fashionable. I suspect that others my age probably thought my indifference was an affectation.

I knew no one to whom I could talk about what most mattered to me, no one who felt as strongly about the importance of ideas or the great questions of life. With the exception of two or three girls to whom I felt attracted for a while, there was no one my own age who seriously interested me.

Occasionally I would meet someone with whom I might have several exciting conversations. I would think I had found a friend, but at some point either I would decide that this person was not really "serious," or the person would drift away, evidently losing interest in our high-intensity discussions.

Also, and this puzzled and troubled me, the people who did seem serious were typically depressed. I was the only person I knew whose interest in ideas felt joyful, and apart from differences in our outlook, it was happiness far more than suffering that estranged me from other people.

From time to time I would have interesting conversations with my cousin Allan Blumenthal. Allan was an A student, a model son, the very essence of decorum in just about every conceivable respect. Years later, as an adult, he would mock himself: "Mother could put a white suit on me on Monday and it would still be clean on Friday. I hated that. And sometimes I hated you, because you were so different. I used to think, enviously, that if your mother put a suit on you, any kind of suit, you would probably have torn it — swinging from a tree or something — within half an hour." The irony was that while my mother wished I was more like Allan, his mother expressed the wish that Allan would be more like me, because of my aggressiveness; he and I would joke about that. Two years older than I, Allan would sometimes drop pompous rebukes to the effect that I should be more family-oriented and "more conventional," meaning more compliant; at such moments, he would show puzzling flashes of irritation. But he was intelligent and we could talk about such subjects as why people believed in God and whether there were grounds for free will. Allan introduced me to a novel by Romain Rolland, *Jean-Christophe,* which deals with the life and struggles of a musician of genius. It reinforced a conviction already forming in me, especially after reading *The Fountainhead,* that a hero is one who perseveres. The novel was very meaningful to Allan because he dreamed of becoming a concert pianist. His parents' intention was that he become a physician, and a physician is what he eventually became, and after that, a psychiatrist.

During those years I lived in a void, but, without a comparison, I did not always recognize it. So it was easy, at times, to be equally oblivious to signs of hostility or of friendship. My protection was my exuberant conviction that it was great to be alive and my hope that someday in the future I would find my kind of people.

Between the ages of fourteen and eighteen, I read and reread *The Fountainhead* almost continuously, with the dedication and passion of a student of the Talmud. It was the most important companion of my adolescence. When I opened its pages, I was transported into a world where the issues I cared about really *mattered.*

There were particular scenes I returned to again and again, like favorite pieces of music. One such scene occurs at the conclusion of Part I. At a time when he is struggling and destitute, Roark receives an enormously important commission, one that could virtually make his career, on one condition: that he agree to modify the unconventional design of his building. Roark explains why it is as important for a building as it is for a man, to have integrity, why it cannot borrow pieces of its soul. They concede that he may be right, but in practical life one can't always be so consistent. They give him an ultimatum: " 'Yes or no, Mr. Roark?' " After a long, agonizing moment, Roark says, " 'No.' " Appalled, one member of the board of directors cries, " 'You need the commission. Do you have to be so fanatical and selfless about it?' " Pressing his architectural drawing to his body, Roark answers, " 'That was the most selfish thing you've ever seen a man do.' "

In first reading this, I knew immediately what Roark meant. Maintaining the integrity of his own convictions, values, and commitments above fame, worldly success, or money was not an act of self-sacrifice but a supreme expression of selfishness in the noblest possible meaning of that word. If he had perceived his action as self-sacrificial, it would have lost all moral grandeur.

Everything I had ever heard about the virtue of self-sacrifice and selflessness became preposterous and irrelevant. It missed the point of what life — and greatness — demanded. Not to sacrifice the self but to remain true to it at all costs — that was the heroic vision *The Fountainhead* offered.

"That was the most selfish thing you've ever seen a man do." I pondered those words as one might meditate on some esoteric saying containing a treasure of secrets. If self meant consciousness, thought, judgment, creativity — how could it be evil? How could people think self-surrender was noble? I asked these questions of everyone — from people on the block to visitors in our home to almost anyone who professed to take ideas seriously. I was not satisfied by the answers I received which ranged from "Everyone knows it's evil to be selfish," to "Wait until you grow up."

To keep faith with the best within yourself was clearly *selfish* and clearly a *virtue*. I knew what a break from the beliefs of the people around me this way of seeing things represented and I welcomed that.

Another scene of great personal meaning to me was "the boy on the bicycle scene" at the beginning of Part IV. A young man, newly graduated from college, is wheeling his bicycle through a forest, thinking about his future. He wants to love and admire others, but he is most happy when he is alone. This saddens him because he longs for the sight of human joy and achievement as fuel and inspiration. He comes to a clearing and stands overlooking a valley; he sees a series of breathtaking structures, a magnificent symphony in stone. Lost in contemplation of this answer to his longing, he finally notices a man sitting alone on a rock, looking at the same sight. Who built this? the boy wants to know. " 'I did,' " the man says. " 'What's your name?' " the boy asks, and the man answers, " 'Howard Roark.' " The boy thanks Roark and walks away. "Roark looked after him. He had never seen that boy before and he would never see him again. He did not know that he had given someone the courage to face a lifetime."

There was one scene in *The Fountainhead* that I reread a hundred times. For one sentence only, this one scene was more important to me than any other in the book. Peter Keating, a parasitic yet successful fellow architect, asks Roark to design the government housing project, Cortlandt Homes, and let him, Keating, take the credit. Years earlier, Keating graduated from architectural school with honors on the day Roark was expelled. Later, when they were both in practice — Roark struggling desperately, Keating rising to the top of his profession — Keating went to Roark again and again for help with his work. Keating is the "second-hander," the man without independent values or judgment, the man who lives through and by others. Roark, the innovator, the egoist, the man who lives for his own sake and by his own mind, has fought a battle of eighteen years against the society around him. Now his architectural ideas are beginning to win; clients are coming to him in increasing numbers. Keating, having ridden for years on a prestige he had not earned, is now slipping. Roark, inspired by the challenge of Cortlandt Homes, agrees to design the project for Keating on one condition: that it be built exactly as Roark designs it. In a rare, pathetic groping for honesty, Keating struggles to understand Roark's motive. " 'Everybody would say you're a fool. . . . Everybody would say I'm getting everything. . . .' " Roark answers: " 'You'll get everything society can give a man. You'll keep all the money. You'll take any fame or honor anyone might want to grant. You'll accept such gratitude as the tenants might feel. And I — I'll take what nobody can give a man, except himself. I will have built Cortlandt.' "

To me, aged fourteen, fifteen, sixteen, seventeen, eighteen, those words, " 'I will have built Cortlandt,' " were like a hymn or a battle cry, celebrating an almost reverential feeling for the activity of creative work and the self-sufficiency of the creative process. This feeling has never changed.

Many years later, in an introduction to the twenty-fifth anniversary edition of *The Fountainhead*, Ayn said that her novel is a confirmation of the spirit of youth. My own experience quite supports this assessment. A confirmation of the spirit of youth — and a confirmation of the conviction that joy is possible to human beings, that doom and defeat are not our inevitable fate.

I cannot discuss the impact of *The Fountainhead* upon me without discussing the much-debated climax of the novel — Roark's blowing up of Cortlandt Homes. How many discussions — how many arguments! — among how many readers must that event have inspired! On my first reading of the novel, and at each successive rereading through my teenage years, I was inspired by the integration of the various characters and their conflicts at the climax, and by the story's final resolution.

Ellsworth Toohey, the architectural critic who secures the government commission, Cortlandt Homes, for Peter Keating, is Ayn Rand's first major literary portrait of evil. Toohey is a socialist who preaches self-surrender, self-sacrifice, and collectivism as a means to power over other human beings. Now, after years of plotting and scheming, he is at the height of his fame and influence; his goal at present is control of the Wynand newspaper chain for which he works as a columnist. His boss, and the target of his manipulations, is Gail Wynand.

Gail Wynand is projected as the great tragic figure of *The Fountainhead*. Having succumbed in his youth to the belief that virtue and integrity have no chance in human society, he concludes that one's only choice is to rule or be ruled — and chooses to rule. He pours his energy and genius into the creation of a vast newspaper syndicate that does not express his own values or convictions, but panders to the lowest values and tastes of the mob. With the exception of the *Banner,* his New York paper, Wynand finds only two passions in life: Dominique Francon, whom he marries — and Howard Roark, whom he first attempts to corrupt and later virtually worships. Roark is the embodiment of the impossible: a man of integrity. But the realization toward which Wynand is moving is that if Roark can be practical *and* successful on his own moral terms, then there is no justification for his, Wynand's, life.

Wynand does not know that Dominique and Roark are in love. Dominique had left Roark years earlier, before she met Wynand, because she could not bear to witness the destruction to which she felt certain he was doomed. Like Wynand, she believes that the good has no chance in human society, but she does not seek any values from a world she despises. She marries Wynand, her symbol for evil, in a deliberate act of self-destruction, seeking to kill her own ecstatic sense of life. Then she witnesses Keating's disintegration, she sees Roark winning his battle, she observes Wynand's helplessness before him, and she begins to grasp the impotence of evil.

The book dramatized for me, and no doubt for many young people seeking a rational view of life, the idea that the moral and the practical are not in conflict, provided one knows what is, in fact, moral. This was hardly what I was hearing from my peers and elders.

When the first building of Cortlandt Homes is completed, Roark discovers that it has been totally disfigured. The government officials have used Roark's structural and engineering plans, without which the project would have been impossible, but they have drastically altered the design, for petty and personal reasons. No legal recourse is available to Keating or Roark: the government bureau cannot be sued or forced to honor its contract.

Roark dynamites Cortlandt and waits at the scene of the explosion to be arrested. The storm of public indignation against him, led by Ellsworth Toohey, emphasizes Cortlandt's status as a housing project for the poor. Roark has no right to a motive.

Peter Keating, who has made a final, desperate effort to save his career by another act of parasitism, is brought to public disgrace and to the full realization of his own emptiness and mediocrity. From my teenage perspective, Keating's characterization illuminated the conventional mentality I found so inimical. He was the quintessential "good boy."

Gail Wynand attempts to use the *Banner,* for the first time in his life, for a cause in which he believes: his defense of Roark. His readers desert him — and Wynand learns that it is not he who has directed public opinion, but public opinion that has controlled and directed him. To save his newspaper, he finally joins the voices denouncing Roark, but recognizing the futility of his career, recognizing that his pursuit of power has delivered him to slavery, he finally closes the *Banner.* He sees that a man cannot sacrifice his values all his life and expect to escape the consequences. " 'You were a ruler of men,' " he tells himself. " 'You held a leash. A leash is only a rope with a noose at both ends.' "

A leash is only a rope with a noose at both ends — how I treasured that sentence with its masterly, elegant way of conveying the self-humiliating and self-defeating nature of the quest for power over other human beings. In my later teenage years, I would have many arguments with people who accused Ayn Rand of being a Nietzschean. By the time I knew who Nietzsche was, it seemed obvious that the character of Gail Wynand was intended to be an indictment of Nietzsche — a conviction that Ayn would subsequently confirm. "A true and consistent egoist," she would say, "would never seek power over other human beings. He would be too independent for that. And power-seeking always means dependency." To me, this could not have been clearer.

The dynamiting of Cortlandt puts Dominique to the severest test possible: her highest value, Roark, is in far worse danger than he has ever faced before. But she is not afraid for him; she knows that he is right, that he has won — no matter what happens. She makes peace with her love for him, and joins him.

I found the character of Dominique the most troublesome in the book; I could not really make sense out of her psychology. She must be read very abstractly, symbolically. Once, Ayn rather bluntly acknowledged, "If you take Dominique literally, she's quite stupid. You have to see her more as the projection of a certain attitude, taken to an extreme — an idealist paralyzed by disgust." But what nonetheless attracted me was Dominique's passion and her spirituality, a priestess run amok, as it were, and certainly more interesting than the "normal" girls I met in Toronto.

Dominique's love for Roark focused another issue that influenced me profoundly: the supreme importance of admiration in romantic love, as contrasted with the mixture of affection and contempt that seemed to pass for love with so many people. This total dedication, I thought, is what I want to feel for a woman one day and what I want her to feel for me.

At his trial, Roark's statement to the jury is a summation of the novel's philosophy: that all progress and achievement come from the independent mind; that altruism, the doctrine that self-surrender in service to others is the highest ideal, is a device for controlling and ultimately enslaving productive men and women; that a human being is not a sacrificial animal, but has a right to exist for his or her own sake; that society depends on the work of the creators and has a right to that work only on the creator's terms. Roark is acquitted.

I listened to the boys on the block talk about girls and popular songs and baseball; I sat in class while teachers talked about geography and social studies; I listened at family dinners to my parents arguing with each other or lecturing my sisters or me — but what I was seeing and hearing were the events and characters of *The Fountainhead,* the ecstatic laughter of the book's sense of life.

This, of course, is precisely the inspirational power of Romantic art. Contrary to the claims of Naturalism, a young person does not require descriptions of the people next door but an escape from them to a wider view of life's possibilities.

The Fountainhead was for me an invaluable aid to psychological survival. Not many novels have that power.

·   ·   ·

Although my three sisters liked and admired the book, each in her own way, Florence and Elayne sometimes teased me about it. Florence, who was then a socialist, was intrigued by the book but insisted it was intended to provide an ethical justification for capitalism. I, who did not really know what capitalism was, told her she was crazy. While she was not correct, literally, her observation disclosed a perceptiveness for which, years later, Ayn complimented her.

My youngest sister, Reva, four years older than I, seemed most touched by the book emotionally, and occasionally we would try to talk about it. We were both a little shy and inhibited about sharing our intimate feelings, even though at that time I was closer to Reva than to anyone else in our family.

All four of us seemed to inhabit private worlds, and were all preoccupied with different goals and concerns. In that summer of 1944 when I first discovered Ayn Rand, Florence was employed in an office, Elayne was preparing to study nursing at the University of Buffalo, Reva was about to enter the University of Toronto, and I was approaching my second year of high school, impatient to know my future.

Sometimes I would look in the mirror, trying to decide if my inner self was visible in my appearance. I was on my way to being tall, I was slender, and I wondered if it was desirable to look so intense, not that there was anything I could do about it. My face stared back at me, as if challenging me to make up my mind about what I saw. Then I would fling myself into a book or jump on my bicycle and forget about it.

That fall, my mother noted my obsession with *The Fountainhead* and although she had not read it — unlike the rest of the family, she did not read books — she became slightly alarmed. She wanted an outside opinion and invited Selena Herman, a teacher of Hebrew studies and an "intellectual," for dinner and a discussion of *The Fountainhead*. The evening was to have extraordinary consequences for my future.

I welcomed the opportunity to discuss the book with someone who might be genuinely interested. As Selena had not read the novel, I proceeded to synopsize the story; then I handed her the novel and waited silently while she read Roark's courtroom speech.

"Well, there's nothing new in this. This is a very well known philosophy. It is called anarchism."

The next day I skipped school, later forging a note from my mother saying I had been sick. I went down to the Bloor Street branch of the Toronto Public Library and discovered Bertrand Russell's *Proposed Roads to Freedom,* an examination of socialism, anarchism, and syndicalism. I read the book in its entirety that day and confirmed my judgment that Selena had been wrong. Ayn Rand's message in *The Fountainhead* was a different one entirely, primarily ethical and psychological. But I did become interested in anarchism and in philosophy. I began reading other books by Russell, then by other philosophers.

As for politics and economics, I never did discover capitalism, or the Founding Fathers' concept of government as the protector of inalienable rights, or the idea of a free-market economy. I decided that if coercive power over other human beings is evil, anarchism is the only defensible political philosophy. I wondered if Ayn Rand would agree with me.

I kept skipping school, forging excuses from my mother, and spending my days at the library. It was as if I had been set loose in a candy store.

Eventually a book on psychology fell into my hands. I recall looking through it, slowly grasping the kind of issues and questions psychology addressed. What causes our emotions? Are any of our choices truly free? What are the origins of genius? It was the beginning of a lifelong passion.

In the fourteenth year of my life, I made two decisions: I wanted to be a psychologist and I wanted to be a writer — a psychologist, because of the things I wished to understand; a writer, because of the desire to give objective form to the things I felt, believed, understood, and envisioned.

In that same year, I failed to get passing grades in high school. I had skipped too many classes, spent too much time reading books absolutely unrelated to my curriculum.

I did not feel the slightest bit guilty about how I had chosen to spend my time, but the idea of failing in school nonetheless rankled. I convinced my mother to let me enroll in a special school that offered four years of high school in one year. At this school, there were no sports, no social activities, and many of the students were adults. Everyone was treated with the respect due a grown-up. We were there for one purpose only, which everyone understood: to learn. It was the most satisfying school year I had ever known and I graduated with the highest marks I had ever earned.

My extracurricular studies did not stop; they were merely confined to evenings and weekends.

In *The Fountainhead* there was a reference to a playwright Ayn Rand obviously admired — Henrik Ibsen. So I went to the library and discovered drama. I would borrow my sisters' library cards so I could take ten or twelve books of plays home at one time. I once estimated that between the ages of fifteen and seventeen I easily read two thousand plays. I wrote several plays of my own. It was as if *drama* had disclosed itself to me as a separate category of existence more stimulating than any other.

I tried to share my reading interests with a boy up the street with whom I had become friendly. Wilfred Erikson's family were socialists and often tried to convert me, but I frequently found my visits there entertaining because at least the Eriksons talked about ideas.

However, I was far more interested in philosophy and religion than in politics. I had been an atheist since the age of twelve when one day, walking down my street, I looked up at the sky and had an electrifying experience. I had a sudden sense of the universe as a total, and I thought: if God is needed to explain the existence of the universe, then what explains the existence of God? If God does exist, he's at least as marvelous and impressive as the universe — and no less in need of an explanation. But then who created whatever created God? Isn't it more reasonable to accept the existence of the universe as the starting point of everything? Whatever stages of development it may go through, whatever its forms at different points in time, in an ultimate sense *the universe is.* We begin there. I felt a great rush of exhilaration and, looking at the blue sky overhead, at the green of the trees on our block, at people and cars and children playing, I felt a love of a kind I had never experienced consciously before: a love for being. A love for existence itself. I felt a great sense of serenity.

Of course I announced my discovery that evening at dinner.

"The smartest men believe in God!" my mother yelled at me. "*Einstein* believes in God! How can you not believe in God?"

I countered, "But *why* do people believe?"

"They're brilliant men. They must know."

I had heard the same kind of argument at school: "Do you think you're the only one who knows what's true — and everyone else is wrong?" I began to think that most people believed in God only because others did, rather than because of any perception, knowledge, or experience of their own. I wondered if this might not be the ground for most of their beliefs.

I decided that nothing was more important than to protect the sovereignty of my own mind — against family, teachers, anyone who might try to get me to see the world their way rather than the way it appeared to my own eyes. "That's why *The Fountainhead* meant so much to you," Ayn later said to me. "You were already on the track of its basic premise."

The way I applied the idea of independence was far from entirely positive, however. In encounters with other people, I screened out too much. I prevented myself from learning things from my teachers that could have been helpful to me, for example. In later years, I often struggled to reinvent the wheel.

And there was another way in which I misconstrued the idea of independence. I began, after reading *The Fountainhead*, to reproach myself for my loneliness. I told myself it was a weakness. I imagined that an ideally evolved man could enjoy people without suffering pain over the absence of satisfying relationships. I struggled to repress my desires for human companionship. Interestingly enough, it was Ayn who helped me to understand the nature of my error. "I can see how you could have gotten that idea from *The Fountainhead*," she would say to me. "But it's a mistake." It was a mistake, I learned later, that a great many people had made.

One consequence of my repression was that sometimes I failed to see that girls I liked returned my feelings. Signs of interest or warmth could pass right over my head. Once, in my twenties, I remarked to Ayn, "As a teenager, I was not a great success with the opposite sex. Perhaps I was too serious. Anyway, I don't think girls liked me." She stunned me by the insightfulness of her response: "Would you have known if they did?"

The kind of woman I admired was not so much like Dominique but like Kira, the heroine of Ayn's first novel, *We the Living*. Kira struck me as far more rational, far more psychologically healthy — a young woman of "purposefulness, contempt for the inconsequential, and furious innocence." She is committed to work, love, and personal freedom, and she is completely unconfused about these issues. That, I understood.

The plot-theme of *We the Living* is the struggle of three young and talented people to achieve life and happiness in Soviet Russia, and the manner in which the system destroys all three of them, not in spite of, but because of, their virtues. When I first read the book, I did not know that Ayn Rand had emigrated to the United States from Soviet Russia.

"Can you imagine what it was like to read your novel," I said to Ayn some years later, "while hearing people talk about Soviet Russia as a 'noble experiment'? " Ayn answered, "Can you imagine what it was like to *write* it, having *come* from that hell, and hear Americans talk about Russia that way — with absolutely no understanding of, or appreciation for, their own country?"

At the same time that I found *We the Living*, I discovered another earlier work of hers, *Anthem*, a novelette written a few years prior to *The Fountainhead*. In *Anthem*'s world of the future, the word "I" has disappeared from language and the concept of "ego" has vanished. An individual refers to him- or herself as "we" and to another individual as "they." The hero's struggle to identify and name the concept of "I" is developed with such tension that when, after pages of "we," I saw the opening line of the climactic chapter, the emotional experience was one of unsurpassable violence and power: "I am. I think. I will."

I related this struggle to my own, not in political terms, but in psychological terms — the struggle, so acute in adolescence, to carve out a sense of identity and a view of life unsurrendered to the opinions and values of others. To me, Ayn Rand was the ultimate champion of autonomy, and therefore a shield against the world to protect the process of my own growth.

No one can understand the appeal of Ayn Rand to youth — or to readers of any age — who does not understand how profoundly she speaks, on many different levels, to the quest for individuation, autonomy, and self-actualization.

One of the most meaningful memories of my adolescent years concerns a conversation I had with my sister Florence, one evening when we sat talking about what we wanted from life. This was a rare occasion. Ordinarily, we did not have much contact and would have said we shared few common interests.

"What I would like to find, someday, is a great issue, a battle, a crusade . . . something really worth fighting for . . . something that would require and demand everything I am and everything I've got to give . . . something *important,* something that would really be challenging."

Florence, who could be very protective of me, observed thoughtfully, "In battles people sometimes get hurt."

A battle worth fighting; that was precisely what I was destined to find in the world of Ayn Rand — the fulfillment of just that longing I struggled to express to Florence. But real battles, I would discover, are very different from the battles of our dreams.

In 1948, at the age of eighteen, I knew *The Fountainhead* so thoroughly that if someone read me any sentence in the book, I could recite the gist of the sentence immediately preceding and following. One of the things this meant practically, which would assume so much importance later, was that I had become intimately familiar with the workings of Ayn Rand's consciousness: it was as if there were a direct line from her psyche to mine. I was two years away from our first meeting.

After high school, I spent twelve months in Winnipeg, Manitoba, working in the jewelry store of my uncle, David M. Copp. While my father had remained at his usual detached distance, my mother had begged me to forget about psychology and accept the opportunity her younger brother offered me to join him in business. Uncle Dave had become wealthy in his jewelry business and in real estate. He had no children of his own and was prepared to offer me a virtually guaranteed future if I would live and work with him in Winnipeg.

"You do have brains," Uncle Dave said. "And you have a good gift of gab." I think he also enjoyed my energy and assertiveness. When I thanked him for his generosity and explained that I had other ambitions, he was kind and gracious. He did not push, in spite of his obvious disappointment. He told me that if I wanted to go to college, to become a psychologist or anything else, and my parents found the expense difficult, he would take care of it. My mother had implored me to work in Uncle Dave's store for a year before making a decision. I agreed, knowing that at the end of a year I would proceed precisely as I had planned.

In the fall of 1948, when I was just settling into Winnipeg, I met Earl Hyman, a passionate reader whose father had a splendid library. I enjoyed visiting their home, where we all talked about books. One day Earl said to me, "I've been thinking. There's an old friend of mine you've got to meet. She's nineteen years old and she's in college. She wants to be a writer and she talks about *The Fountainhead* the way you do. Her name is Barbara Weidman."

Initially, he had difficulty setting up the meeting. Barbara was rather elusive. Later she would tell me, "He talked so much about how brilliant you were that I pictured you as maybe five foot two, with thick glasses, and very, very sensitive — you know, an 'intellectual.' I really wasn't very curious."

Earl prevailed. We drove to Barbara's home, which was on one of the "best" streets in Winnipeg, and we were greeted at the door by a slender girl with blonde hair, hazel eyes that flashed intelligence, a warm, somewhat shy smile, and a quality of innocent vulnerability that I found appealing.

"Barbara," said our friend, "I want you to meet Nathan Blumenthal."

T W O

BARBARA AND I sat in her den, mutually assessing each other, mutually intrigued. I felt more adult and male than I had ever felt in my life. I spoke about my reasons for being in Winnipeg. She spoke about her studies in college and her desire to be a writer. She mentioned her love for Thomas Wolfe, whom I had not read; I liked the quiet enthusiasm with which she spoke of him. I looked at the books on the shelves and was pleased to learn that most of them were hers. I told her I thought she would enjoy *Jean-Christophe*. She asked me if I liked Oscar Wilde. Our friend Earl sat beaming, as if he were at an enjoyable play.

I had absolutely no idea that my life was about to change in an irrevocable way. At most I might have guessed that I was on the verge of an interesting romance. Barbara was a year older than I, and I found that appealing. I somehow gathered that she had had more experience with men than I had had with women; a part of me found that appealing too.

I liked her voice: warm and musical, it promised a depth of feeling she might not yet know how to express. I liked the slenderness of her body and the fluidity of her movements; they, too, hinted at passion underneath her somewhat formal manner. With her light hair and eyes, she evoked fantasies of a lovely ice-maiden waiting to be melted.

When she talked about books or ideas, she did so as if they mattered, with a childlike earnestness incongruously combined with an obvious effort to look and sound sophisticated. I was very impressed when she told me that she intended to major in philosophy. Her glasses heightened both her intellectuality and vulnerability.

The three of us drove off to an afternoon cultural gathering. Barbara and I were acutely aware of each other. I thought I sensed some muted, distant sadness within her, which in no way impeded the excitement rising within me. I felt exhilarated, challenged in a way I had not experienced before.

Later, when I asked her about *The Fountainhead,* she remarked, simply, that she liked it very much. Our conversation on this subject was rather restrained, so that our enthusiasm was manifested chiefly by the exaggerated casualness of our statements. Perhaps we were testing each other.

However, the next time we met for a date, our reticence began to melt. "What do you think of Dominique?" "How do you interpret her?" "Isn't Steven Mallory a terrific character?" "What do you say when people want to argue about Roark blowing up Cortlandt Homes?" "I wonder what Ayn Rand is like as a person."

Throughout December, we saw each other frequently, and our encounters became more and more intimate. We were clearly going to have an affair. It would be my first.

Since my own mother and father were rarely in my thoughts, I was rather surprised that Barbara spoke so frequently about her parents. Her father had no grasp of her dreams and ambitions and failed to defend her when she clashed with her mother. Her beautiful, glamorous mother rarely had time for her except to rebuke her, and clearly preferred Barbara's older brother, who was handsome and far more socially adept. While I could not help wondering at times why a nineteen-year-old girl would still have so much energy invested in her mother's and father's approval, I certainly understood the phenomenon of frustrating parents and I listened compassionately, agreeing that life would really begin for Barbara when she got out of Winnipeg and was on her own. At that time I did not know how to hear the true significance in what she was telling me — or how profoundly relevant it would be one day to understanding her choices and behavior with Ayn Rand and me.

She spoke about her previous relationships with boys and about her desire for someone who would not try to change her. I could not see why someone would want to change her, I said. She spoke of having had one sexual relationship in her life, which had ended a few months ago; she suggested that the young man had been too conventional for her and expressed some pain over the intensity of her past feelings for him.

Our actual affair began on an evening in January — when Barbara appeared at my apartment, out of a subzero winter night, bringing with her a transparent smile and the scent of perfume.

When a man makes love to a woman for the first time in his life, he feels aligned with the forces of the universe in a new way, and aligned with the internal energies of his own maleness. The connection feels cosmic. I felt a deepening sense of integration and power. Sensuality and spirituality fused into an experience of shattering force. When the first experience of sex is a happy one, as mine was, it is an experience of waking up, of enlightenment, of the birth of a new self. Through the act of sex I discovered my own body, as if only now had it fully come into existence.

The intensity of my feelings — for Barbara, for sexual intercourse, for the exquisite miracle of a woman's body — were almost overwhelming: irresistible and yet disorienting. I was flung out of my isolation — and out of control. A few days after our first sexual encounter, driving through streets piled high with snow, I announced to Barbara in a matter-of-fact voice, "I want you to know that I am not in love with you."

When we mentioned this incident to Ayn, a few years later, Ayn shook her head and grunted, "Emotional repression." Barbara laughed and said, "That was when I knew he was in love with me."

I rarely went to sleep without telephoning to say good night. Sometimes I would call her, in high excitement, to read her some poem I had found and liked. We met frequently for lunch, and when I saw her walking toward me through the snow, smiling, carrying her textbooks, bundled in boots and fur coat, with sunlight reflected off her glasses, I laughed in unbearable happiness. I did not think about our future. The present was a magnificent gift, an end in itself, and it seemed to me that of all of nature's blessings, the phenomenon of woman was the greatest.

If we sometimes had small clashes or disagreements, they were resolved swiftly, gracefully, effortlessly — or else dismissed as unimportant. "What do couples fight about?" I once asked Barbara wonderingly, and added, "You're so easy to get along with." And she would remark, "Don't you ever have moods? Aren't you ever grouchy or on edge?" I would answer, "No, I'm happy."

Very rarely would some small piece of behavior I did not understand trouble me. She might occasionally avoid eye contact, while telling me something important, for instance. She might respond with unexpected sharpness when I questioned some action of hers, or fall into puzzling fits of sadness, or reminisce with strange dreaminess about some former boyfriend, or look at me as if she expected to be reproached when no such thought was in my mind. When I saw this apprehension in her glance, I told myself that she had been hurt and needed time to learn to trust me. A moment, an hour, or a day later she would be so warm, loving, and joyful that I almost believed none of it had happened. "God, life is wonderful," we would say, melting into each other's arms.

Barbara claimed passion as her highest value. She would say that one of the things she most appreciated about me was how intensely I felt about things, about life, about myself, about her. She was very moved by *Tristan and Isolde.* "I know it's tragic, but who cares? They *felt* things." I never quite thought we were aligned on this issue. I knew that I was a good deal less receptive to tragedy than Barbara, but that was only part of it. There was something more, something that concerned our view of passion itself. I did not identify passion with tragedy; at some level Barbara did.

Whatever our differences, we agreed on the most important thing: there was nothing in the universe to compare to *The Fountainhead.* Like the skyscrapers it celebrated, it rose above everything.

Since I saw her as a child of *The Fountainhead,* like myself, I was puzzled by her sexual shyness. I could not reconcile this with the independence and freedom of spirit I took for granted she possessed. It did not yet occur to me that, while she may have been shy, she was also less attracted to me than I was to her.

Further stifling my efforts to understand her sexually, Barbara initiated a discussion of a favorite book, Somerset Maugham's *Of Human Bondage,* and went on to say that she had read the book for the first time when she was thirteen and immediately had identified with the hero, Philip, in his uncontrollable passion for the mindless and somewhat vicious Mildred. She hinted at an inner part that seemed at times to betray her, as Philip's passions betrayed him, giving rise to guilt.

I brought her my copies of *We the Living* and *Anthem,* which she devoured with great enthusiasm. The hero of *We the Living* is called Leo, and when Barbara said to me, " 'Leo' is not an Ayn Rand name. I can't explain how I know that, but I know it," I agreed with her. Then she went on, "I'll bet that Leo is the name of some man Ayn Rand actually knew and probably cared for, perhaps was in love with." Later, when we met Ayn, she told us that Barbara had been right and expressed astonishment at such perceptiveness.

At the age of eighteen, it continued to feel like a miracle that I was having such discussions with a girl, in an erotic context. Watching her as she spoke, her eyes alive with an intensity that was almost enraptured, her gestures delicate yet firm and decisive, I thought her feminine, sexual, intellectual. At such times, my faint doubts and misgivings seemed unreal.

One evening we met two male friends of hers in a restaurant. One of them, Wilfred Schwartz, several years older than I, was a former boyfriend of Barbara's. He was also an admirer of *The Fountainhead*. Sitting with them in the restaurant, I remembered Barbara's recounting of their stormy relationship, which she had broken off, "because I was always made to feel guilty." It was obvious that whatever they had once meant to each other had not died. Most of Wilfred's comments to her conveyed an undertone of sarcasm. Barbara remained warm and friendly, but I sensed an underlying hurt and helplessness. His good opinion matters to her enormously, I thought.

Wilfred and his friend were curious about the new man in Barbara's life. One moment they were polite toward me in a guarded sort of way, the next moment one of them would say something outrageous. I laughed and remained cordial.

When we were alone again, I asked her, "Are you really such a heartbreaker?" She answered sadly, "In this case, perhaps I was. He really cared about me." A little while later she made a remark that I thought extraordinarily revealing. She wondered aloud how Wilfred would explain her and my relationship, since this time she was with someone he would have to respect. Again I noticed her search for approval.

If approval was what she wanted, for once she had it from her mother who enthusiastically supported our relationship. Usually they fought over Barbara's taste in young men.

I slipped once, badly. We were out somewhere and she pointed out a former boyfriend. I prided myself on seeing a lot when I looked at a person and I didn't like anything about what he projected and foolishly said so. I was not without jealousy; I simply could not bear the idea of anyone else touching her. But I lacked the wisdom — or the courage — to say so in plain language. Subsequently she told me that she had been deeply hurt by my remarks.

One night, lying in my arms, she suddenly whispered, "Don't judge me. Just love me." My whole system went on alert; at the same time I felt myself pulling away emotionally and reproached myself for it. Had she been hurt that badly by her mother's rejection and by Wilfred's continuing disapproval? Holding her tightly, I felt alone, helpless, and miserable. A person who is proud of herself is not afraid of another person's judgment.

But when we made love, all of these concerns vanished. My hunger for union after so many years of isolation could sweep everything else out of my consciousness. Through the act of sex I shattered the walls of an invisible prison. I became connected, not only to this human being who had become so precious to me, but to nature, to the world. These were not the words in my mind, but the feelings in my body. I was not yet able to express myself through work, but here, with Barbara, my love, my excitement, my sense of power, my life-force, had an outlet. I was eighteen years old and in the egocentricity of my joy it did not occur to me to wonder what the act of sex meant to Barbara.

I felt only that she was desperately important to me — and that, for reasons I did not understand, we were in danger.

Wilfred and I remained curious about each other and met a couple of times on our own. He seemed more intelligent and serious than at our first meeting and I was liking him more. Also, I could not help but be touched by his pain over Barbara. Whatever their story was, he had loved her, and that gave us a kind of bond.

One day he invited me to join him and a friend for lunch. They were already seated and stopped talking when I arrived. After a half hour of casual conversation, prompted, no doubt, by demons of his own, Wilfred suddenly asked me, "Has Barbara ever told you about her great love affair with ———?" He named the young man Barbara had pointed out to me, about whom I made some negative comments. She had told me they had never slept together. Now, Wilfred was saying — what was Wilfred saying? I struggled to follow his somewhat oblique and rambling discourse. This, I gathered, was the man to whom Wilfred felt he had lost her — the first of several, he stressed. But Barbara told me she had only one lover. Assuming Wilfred was telling the truth, why hadn't she been straight with me?

I walked back to work sick with confusion, disorientation. I felt caught in a situation absolutely without dignity. I had no choice but to tell Barbara what had happened.

Her response was devastating. "I knew Wilfred would try to turn you against me," she said sadly, looking at me with wounded eyes. Whether I recognized it or not, she chided, I was very puritanical, and before she could safely talk about her past experiences I needed to know her better.

In her face I saw a child with a painful fear of being condemned — and all my protective impulses were activated. I did not know whether or not she was right in saying I was puritanical. I had standards of personal conduct — was I expected not to have them? Somehow she had maneuvered the conversation around to the point where I was wondering if I, perhaps, was guilty — of causing Barbara suffering. I persuaded myself that I was strong enough, and that our love was strong enough, to carry us through this episode. I pulled her into my arms.

Spring was coming — and we continued to take walks and drives and make love and talk about books and life and the future. We made plans to go to Los Angeles in September, to UCLA — she to study philosophy, I to study psychology. But something had changed between us, and we both knew it. The ease and serenity of our beginning had vanished.

The fact that she had had a few affairs was not the problem. What was hardest for me, and ultimately most damaging, was not her "promiscuity" but the guilt that lay behind it.

One of the human qualities that I associated with my ideal woman was spiritual innocence, the purity of high self-esteem. At times Barbara manifested the innocence of someone very young, but that is a different thing entirely.

Fairly early on in our relationship she began to drop remarks to the effect that at times she felt something was wrong with her, that her mind and body were split. At first I did not take her seriously, or imagined that in my presence problems would magically dissolve. But part of Barbara projected that she was a "bad girl." Further, she projected that she expected disapproval. Often I felt the need to reassure her, but if I tried to question her, wanting to understand, she often became gently defensive, or soulfully tragic, or so confused and forlorn that my heart would melt and I would feel self-reproachful or else retreat in frustrated silence. What is apparent to me today is that attitudes such as hers do eventually turn into self-fulfilling prophecies.

One day she suggested we visit her sixteen-year-old cousin, who was very troubled about his life; perhaps I could help him by supporting his interest in ideas and encouraging his self-confidence. I met a nervous, high-strung boy, gloomy and in doubt about virtually every aspect of himself. But he had read and liked *The Fountainhead,* and he became more animated as we talked about it. He obviously found the book inspiring; it seemed to give him hope that he might create a satisfying future for himself. He told me he was going to study medicine; his father was a prominent physician in Winnipeg; discussing medicine, his spirits seem to drop again. I wondered why Barbara's first cousin looked so frightened and unhappy and what would become of him. His name was Leonard Peikoff.

By late April Barbara was finding reasons to see less of me. She swung between intense demonstrativeness and mystifying withdrawal; hurt and bewildered, I responded by pursuing her more vigorously. During sex, Barbara had never been particularly active, but now she was becoming more and more passive, and less and less inclined to have sex at all. The frequency of our quarrels escalated — about dates, about sex, about her friends. In some way I could not define, I felt as if her allegiance was switching to something unnamed but utterly alien to me. Our times together left me with the taste of despair.

Then, in the midst of it, I contracted a form of pneumonia and was advised to take a month off from work, go home to Toronto, and convalesce. I spent most of May in Toronto, lying around the house, or in the backyard under a blanket when it was warm enough, consuming endless quantities of my mother's chicken soup, reading books, daydreaming about the future, talking to Barbara on the telephone and writing her letters, trying to determine whether the tone of her voice or of her letters signaled any shift in her feelings, never being certain — and missing her to the point of physical pain.

In June I returned to Winnipeg. When I telephoned Barbara she said, softly and ominously, "I have to talk to you." She arrived at my apartment twenty minutes later with the following story.

She had met a man while attending the opera in Minneapolis. He had invited her out for a drink and she had accepted. They were attracted to each other, but he solemnly explained that he was often impotent. If Barbara was willing to risk disappointment, he wanted to try, anyway. They made love, and the man was fully potent. It was an exquisite experience. Could I understand and forgive her?

Even in my pain and rage, part of me wanted to laugh. I — who was supposed to be far less worldly than Barbara — would have bet almost anything that that man had used his particular line before and would do so again. What was there to talk about now? Barbara knew the impact on me would have to be devastating — and this mattered less to her than the value she found in her sexual encounter. She was crying and insisting that I was the most important man in the world to her; there was no one like me and never could be; didn't I know that?

I was nineteen years old and I felt defeated. I knew that my adversary was not another man; it was something in Barbara beyond my power to understand or cope with.

We lasted through the month, with the abyss between us growing wider each day. Formally, we had reconciled; but the sense of doom permeated our every meeting.

It was warm in June, and one day we went swimming. There was a long pier, stretched over the water, where everyone spread towels. Barbara waved hello to various people she knew. I sat quietly, finding conversation difficult. A few yards away we saw the young man with whom Barbara had broken off shortly before she and I met, the one she had described as "too conventional," but for whom she had had such strong sexual feelings. He was doing handstands, then diving into the water. I watched Barbara watching him. I saw the veiled emptiness in her eyes when she glanced at me.

One night, near the end of June, sitting in a parked car a few feet off the highway, we agreed that it was over. The initiative for the breakup was Barbara's. I did not argue with her; I knew it was useless.

"I would give anything to know *why*," I said. "If only I could understand *why*."

Barbara was not interested in questions of this kind; not at the moment; and perhaps she was right. "I will always love you in my own way," she said solemnly, as if she were reciting a line from a play. And yet, at some level, I believed her.

We drove home in silence.

Two weeks later I learned that she was back with the young man I had seen doing handstands on the pier.

During July and August, my last two months in Winnipeg, I dreaded weekends. Monday through Friday I had the distraction of work; in the evenings, I could force myself to go to bed early. But the weekends were especially difficult: hours of time stretching before me in which there was no escape from my thoughts and feelings.

If someone had asked me whether I loved Barbara, I do not know what I would have said. Could love endure when so much else had gone? But the void created by her absence made time move with unbearable slowness. I would lie in bed, or walk the streets, remembering the joy we had shared and wanting to cry out at the insanity of what had happened. In any universe I could understand, love and desire followed the path of affinity and admiration: our *values,* our personal sense of what was important in life, were what determined who we chose for companionship, sex, or love. How was one to explain a passion that bore no relation to anything one professed to value? The "human bondage" of which Barbara had spoken, and which her behavior now appeared to be manifesting, was worse than sickness to me — it seemed like a violation of reason itself. The shout *why?* became a point of torture throbbing relentlessly in my head.

There was another torture, even worse: the images I could not dispel of Barbara with another man. I walked the streets of Winnipeg for hours, trying to exhaust myself into mental emptiness, so as to have a respite from my imagination.

I went to movies and walked out in the middle; I could not concentrate. I forced myself to go on a few dates and found this harder than being alone. Only reading offered any kind of relief, when for a few minutes or for a few hours I could become sufficiently absorbed in some book to forget about missing Barbara.

One powerful symbol of a rational universe remained: Ayn Rand. On an impulse, motivated perhaps by a desire to give my life some other focus, I decided to write her a letter, care of her publisher, inquiring about her political convictions. What did she believe in? "Certainly not capitalism," I wrote her confidently. I received no answer to my letter.

Finally, in early September, my stay in Winnipeg came to an end, a little more than two months after the breakup with Barbara. I was eager to fly to California, to begin my studies at UCLA.

Uncle Dave drove me to the airport, wished me luck, and said good-bye. Approaching the boarding area, I saw Barbara, departing for Los Angeles on the same flight, as we had previously arranged. We smiled at each other, with unexpected affection. In that moment, without any discussion, we became "friends."

Shortly after arriving in Los Angeles, we enrolled at UCLA. It was impossible not to feel excitement at the start of this new life. The brilliant sunlight on the UCLA campus seemed a symbol of unlimited possibilities. I was in the United States. I was beginning college. I felt more like an adult than I ever had. Who knew what might happen now? Who might I meet? And what might yet happen with Barbara?

Although we saw each other frequently at school, talked on the telephone, and sometimes went to a movie or for a drive together, we did not date and were not physically intimate.

The problem, and it was a serious one, was that I continued to feel that I was moving on a planet of strangers, whose language I did not speak, and Barbara was the only one who spoke English. True, she did not speak it all the time — she kept mixing it with that other tongue — but there was nonetheless some sense of kinship, a bond I was reluctant fully to relinquish. To a much lesser extent, she seemed to feel that, too. Sometimes I thought she hated me for the bond she felt.

During the preceding months in Winnipeg a connection had evidently been forged that was now showing unexpected strength. We were no longer lovers, we could not really be friends, yet we could not let go of each other. To me, Barbara represented a battle I could not accept having lost. Further, there was no one in my new environment with whom I felt I could share my inner world, although there were people I met and liked.

On Barbara's part, my esteem mattered to her greatly. To maintain it, she needed to preserve our contact and to sustain my sense that she was a participant in my dreams of Ayn Rand's world. If I began to drift away, she would subtly reach out to bring me back, evoke that sense of our special intimacy, even hint at the presence of unspoken sexual feelings. Some part of me was waiting. Somehow I knew the ending to our story had not yet been written.

On arriving in Los Angeles, I had renewed contact with my sister Elayne who was working as an operating room nurse at Cedars of Lebanon Hospital; she was now twenty-four. We decided to take an apartment together, in order to have a larger place than either of us could afford alone.

As we approached the end of 1949, I thought of writing Ayn Rand another letter. Perhaps my previous one had not reached her. I wrote asking if she had any works in print other than *We the Living, Anthem,* and *The Fountainhead* which I might have missed.

A couple of months later, I received a brief note from her with the information that those were the only books she had published. She added that she could not say when she would complete her next novel. Then she asked me if I was the gentleman who had written her from Canada, asking about her political convictions. If I was, she hoped I had learned that she believed in laissez-faire capitalism.

This response inspired me to write a longer letter, asking her a number of questions about *We the Living,* the nature of free will, and capitalism. As she later told me, although the letter impressed her, she was deeply engrossed in writing *Atlas Shrugged* and had no time for non-essential correspondence — and too many times her "fans" had disappointed her. It was her husband, Frank, who felt there was something special about the writer of the letter and urged her to respond. When her letter arrived — several pages, single-spaced — I was delirious with excitement. The letter was cool in tone, intellectual in content, but direct and personal, concluding with an invitation to further correspondence and even suggesting the possibility of a meeting.

I shot over to Barbara's to show her the letter. Suddenly there were no conflicts between us, no other men in Barbara's life, no abyss separating us, nothing else that mattered but the bond we shared in what Ayn Rand meant to us.

I fired off a lengthy answer, included my telephone number, and waited. On an evening toward the end of February 1950, I was tired and had gone to bed early. The phone rang a few minutes before 9:00, waking me up.

"Mr. Nathan Blumenthal?" said a woman's voice with a thick Russian accent. I could not imagine who this was.

"Yes."

"How do you do. This is Ayn Rand speaking."

THREE

ON THE EVENING of March 2, 1950, I drove my old La Salle down Mulholland Drive and into the San Fernando Valley, heading toward Chatsworth and an address that had been the target of my thoughts for a week: 10,000 Tampa Avenue. There were no freeways or super-markets in that area then, just a few scattered structures in a small, sleepy California village. I had the sense of being in a country environment far removed from the city of Los Angeles an hour's drive away.

For the past week I had shifted between two perspectives. On the one hand, this meeting felt like the impossible, like a miracle, or a dream. On the other, and this response was stronger, the meeting felt natural, normal, logical, as if life for once was as it ought to be, and the unreal had been almost everything else up to this night.

I found my way to a dirt road lined with trees, and stopped when I saw the modern glass and aluminum-covered steel house that looked incongruous in this rustic setting, yet absolutely appropriate for its owner; it was somehow an elegant statement of self-assertion, so that at second glance it seemed to transform the setting into a perfect back-ground.

The house was set back about two hundred feet from the road, and I followed the straight driveway down to the entrance. I saw a small moat curving around the front of the house, with flowers floating in the water. The property was actually a modest-sized ranch, but the land beyond the house faded into the evening mist. The beams of my headlights disappeared into shadows.

I felt as if ordinary reality had been left somewhere behind and I was entering the dimension of my most passionate longing, and I knew that the abnormal calm of my body meant an excitement so enormous that stillness was its only possible expression. I got out of the car but did not immediately ring the doorbell, because I wanted to freeze this moment in my memory forever.

"Would eight o'clock be convenient?" she had asked me in that phone call a week ago, and I had willed my voice to relaxation when answering, "That would be fine."

I reached for the doorbell, knowing without words and with irresistible certainty that nothing was ever going to be the same again.

Within a moment the door swung open and a tall, slender man in his early fifties stood facing me. I thought: he looks like the kind of man she writes about — gray-blue eyes set wide apart, high cheekbones, hair the color of dark sand, swept straight back, long legs, and a simplicity of manner that somehow combined friendliness and detachment. He wore slacks and an open-collar shirt. I liked him on sight.

"Mr. Blumenthal?" he said, holding out his hand. "Frank O'Connor. Come in." I walked ahead of him into the living room. "Ayn will be down in a minute."

A single large painting hung in the room — a magnificent portrait of Frank O'Connor set against a jungle background. It endowed him with a quality of subtle power that he himself did not project; his gentle assurance did not match the larger-than-life certainty of the portrait. I wondered if the artist had revealed an aspect of Ayn Rand's husband that was not readily visible. "This is marvelous," I said to him. I heard a note of relaxed authority in my voice, the ease in pronouncing a value judgment, and I felt how simple everything was, how free of doubts, hesitancies, or complications, in the universe I had now entered.

The dominant colors of the living room were green, turquoise, and peacock blue. The room held a few pieces of oversized furniture that looked custom-designed, and large plants that threw dramatic shadows against the walls. Frank stood watching me study the room, his smile good-natured, as if he somehow knew what all this meant to me. I smiled back at him, willing to be transparent.

And yet, looking around the room, I was aware that I had imagined something more theatrical or futuristic, more fantastic. The room looked almost too comfortable, too "California."

Then I heard the sound of steps coming down the stairs and I turned. She was walking toward me, wearing a simple straight skirt and blouse, with a helmet of dark brown hair, bobbed in the style of the twenties, and the most penetrating eyes I had ever seen, large, dark, and luminous. She was not as slender as she looked in the photograph on the jacket of *The Fountainhead*, nor as elegant — she was a little stocky and rather more "Russian" than I had imagined — but the intensity was there and so was the consciousness that was like a searchlight.

I felt myself standing in the path of that light and I liked the experience and I knew she knew I liked it. There are timeless moments, suspended between seconds, in which it is possible to know these things. That was the first connection between us, the first link. Later she told me, "That first night, you were not afraid of whatever I might see. I knew that immediately. You were not afraid."

"How do you do, Mr. Blumenthal," Ayn Rand said a bit formally but not without warmth. As we shook hands I felt more comfortable than I had ever felt with another human being. I saw myself as having walked into the world of *The Fountainhead*.

Frank stretched out on a chair, instantly relaxing, while Ayn sat on the enormous sofa, leaning forward intently, and I sat facing them, completing the triangle, my glance shifting back and forth to absorb them both.

For the next several hours she and I talked while Frank listened attentively but more or less silently; he disappeared once and returned a few minutes later carrying a tray with coffee and cookies. "Food for the body as well as the mind," he said, smiling.

She began by wanting to know how I discovered *The Fountainhead*, and when I told her the story of Florence and her girlfriends reading from the scene when Dominique first speaks of her desire for Roark, she chuckled with amusement. I began to talk about what *The Fountainhead* meant to me and what my favorite scenes were and my reactions to the various characters, and I knew I was under very careful scrutiny from both Ayn and Frank, and I enjoyed that very much. It was as if their combined glances were challenging me to take a false step, but I knew that was not possible, not this night.

I felt simultaneously the exhilaration of operating at a very high level of consciousness and in the dreamy state of a somnambulist — much like an athlete who has been in training for years for one event, and this was the event and there was no longer anything to hesitate about or doubt.

Ayn's Russian accent was very strong, which at first I found a bit disorienting; it did not seem to go with the author of so streamlined, so American a novel as *The Fountainhead*. At some point she mentioned that she was forty-five years old and had come to the United States when she was twenty-one. "I turned twenty-one on the way over here, while passing through Berlin," she remarked. I wondered if one of the consequences of her extraordinary independence was a failure to absorb the sounds of American pronunciation.

Ayn asked a few questions about my background: my childhood,

my parents, my interests as a boy growing up in Toronto. We talked
a little about *Jean-Christophe* and Romain Rolland, whom she disliked both as a literary figure and as a thinker. She disapproved of his
kind of literary "realism" and of his sympathy for socialism.

I was somewhat surprised by her interest in my adolescent years.
"Were there no adults you admired when you were growing up?" she
inquired at one point.

Wanting to communicate the support I had found in books, I said,
"Perhaps this will strike you as weak, but the characters of Howard
Roark and Jean-Christophe helped me, gave me strength, inspiration,
and I have to say I needed that."

I was astonished by the protectiveness I heard in her response. "You
foolish child! Of course that's not weak! We all need that fuel. That's
what art is for."

To be spoken to so compassionately, to be given such understanding, and then to hear the intimately personal tied to the philosophical,
was to feel nurtured and cared for in a uniquely satisfying way. In one
breath Ayn had addressed multiple levels of need.

She went on to talk about Aristotle's view that literature is of greater
philosophical importance than history; whereas history reports things
as they are, literature presents things "as they might be and ought to
be." This was the principle of her writing, she explained, "the projection of man as he might be and ought to be." "Might be" implies realism, she explained, as contrasted with mere fantasy; "ought to be"
implies ethical judgment, a moral vision.

"I call this approach to fiction writing, 'Romantic Realism,' " she
said. " 'Romantic,' taken by itself, can mean values divorced from
reality, you know, just a sea of emotion, or gushy sentimentalism, and
'realism' taken by itself can mean 'naturalism,' just the description of
things as they are, the folks next door, which doesn't interest me in the
slightest. If the folks next door bore me in real life, why would I wish
to write about them? But the unusual, the exceptional, the strong, the
heroic, that which shows man at his best, at his highest possibility,
does interest me and that's what I chose to write about." She chuckled
and added, "And that's why you're here — because that's what interests you."

I listened, intoxicated.

She said that if our relationship was to develop successfully we
would need time to establish "a common vocabulary" so as to allow
each of us to learn how the other used words; otherwise needless mis-
understandings would occur. This statement stunned and thrilled me
because I had not permitted myself to assume I would have more than
this one meeting.

Love affairs can begin in many different ways. Ayn's and mine began with discussions of epistemology, metaphysics, and ethics. The initial steps of our courtship dance were formal, cerebral, philosophical — while another kind of drama was playing at the edges of our awareness, two souls shocked in mutual recognition, as the testing and probing continued.

Ayn said that there were three questions she wanted to ask me, questions that touched on the essentials of how one saw human existence. What did I think of reason? What did I think of man? What did I think of life?

Ayn Rand was interested in what I thought about reason, man, and life.

From that point on I could not stop talking. I assumed she wanted to know my stand on reason versus revelation, so I spoke at length about respect for evidence, facts, logic, proof, and about my disbelief in any form of faith or supernatural claim to knowledge. In my enthusiasm, I jumped up, I paced, I gestured — I came very close (as she told me later, laughing) to lecturing her.

She wanted to know what I thought about "the mind versus the heart," thinking versus feeling, and did I agree that feelings by themselves were not a reliable guide to action? Of course I agreed. I thought of Barbara, whose life seemed so largely ruled by feelings she could not account for, and an idea and a hope began to germinate in my mind. I suddenly wished she were in the room to share this experience with me.

Most of Ayn's and my conversation that first evening was abstract, fairly impersonal. Intellectual discussion, after all, is what I had come for. And to Ayn the most important thing about a person was his ideas. Yet we were intimate that evening, in a subtle and indirect way. Everything had a subtext; a separate, silent dialogue ran counterpoint to whatever we discussed explicitly. We were falling in love; not romantically, but intellectually.

Ayn was saying, "Because of *The Fountainhead,* people think that the most important issue in my philosophy is individualism versus collectivism, or egoism versus altruism, but these are derivatives, not the starting point. The most important issue, the most fundamental, is reason versus mysticism — the premise that knowledge is based on logic and the evidence of the senses versus claims to some sort of nonsensory, nonrational knowledge."

I said that I had always taken reason so much for granted, as an unquestioned principle, that it never occurred to me think of it as in any way controversial. I had not yet really grasped the philosophical significance of the issue. Of mysticism I actually knew nothing. To me, the basic issue had always been independence or autonomy versus conformity, that is, seeing the world through your own eyes versus uncritically accepting the beliefs of others. What was wrong with people, it seemed to me, was that they didn't think for themselves.

"That's true enough," she said, "but it doesn't go deep enough. Psychologically, that idea is very important, but philosophically, it isn't where you begin."

"When you ask me what I think of man," I said, proceeding to her second question, "I'm not sure I know what you mean." She explained that she meant, did I think man was evil by nature or good? I found the question odd: I did not believe either. I thought that we were born with a potential for evil or for greatness. I did not believe in original sin and I did not believe in original virtue. Frank broke his silence to laugh at this. She said she agreed with me, but this was not what she was asking. Did the concept of "human being" or "man" evoke a positive response in me or a negative one? "Put that way, I would say a positive one," I responded. Did I see man as depraved by nature? Of course I didn't. Did I see him as heroic, at least potentially? "*Oh, yes.*" This satisfied her.

As to what I thought of life, this meant: did I see life as malevolent or benevolent? Again, I thought the question strange, explaining that I thought of life as neutral and as containing both malevolent and benevolent possibilities. But I did not think of existence as intrinsically evil? Ayn asked. "Of course not." I did not think that the universe was such that man was doomed to defeat and tragedy? "No." Did I think that life was such that success and happiness were in principle possible to man, if man acted rationally and realistically? "*Of course.*" This is what she meant, she explained, by the concept of a benevolent universe. "The benevolent universe premise," she called it.

"I hate the idea," she said in her thick accent, "that the essence of life is frustration, futility, and tragedy. It's very Russian, you know. That's one of the reasons I love America. In the American sense of life, happiness is normal. With all its flaws and contradictions this is a pro-life culture. In spite of the guff about religion, I believe it's also pro-reason and pro-man, in its deepest 'instincts.'"

Then she added, leaning forward with smiling assurance, "With you it's not 'instinct.' You're pro-reason, pro-man, and pro-life, *consciously.*"

I felt as if I had been knighted. I felt appreciated, recognized, seen to a degree that I never had before in my life. No woman my own age could have given me what Ayn was giving me. I had left the sphere I shared with Barbara and was now in a different world entirely; somewhere inside I knew that, but not its full significance, not what it implied about the limitations of Barbara's and my relationship. Later I would understand that one of Ayn's special talents, one that she could use with a surgeon's precision, was the ability to evoke such feelings of unique visibility. Watching her mesmerizing impact in personal encounters over the years I had many opportunities to see this skill in action.

When she asked me about the kind of writing I wanted to do, I answered, "Novels; perhaps plays; books on psychology certainly, as my knowledge develops. I'm not certain how to do it all, but these are the things I think about."

"Don't imagine that you have to confine yourself to one kind of writing," she said eagerly. "Don't think you have to be as single-tracked as my heroes. I myself struggle between fiction and philosophy, each of which is really a career in itself. Perhaps you'll learn to integrate fiction and psychology, to combine both. Why not?"

I was struck with the matter-of-factness with which she discussed my ambitions; there was not the slightest suggestion that they might merely be passing dreams. What she projected was the sense of unlimited possibilities, conveyed in the way she said, "Why not?"

We had been talking for several hours and were approaching midnight before I raised the subject of capitalism. This, "officially," had been one of the chief reasons of our meeting: for me to learn about capitalism and its relation to her individualist philosophy. I told her how impressed I was by the books she had recommended and how much I was beginning to understand.

"It was a revelation," I said. "I truly had no idea what capitalism is — and neither does anybody else I know. I would love to see Hazlitt's *Economics in One Lesson* made required reading in the schools." I spoke with enthusiasm about what I had learned from reading Isabel Paterson's *The God of the Machine,* and we agreed that, notwithstanding Paterson's unconvincing attempt to tie capitalism to Christianity, the book was a masterpiece of politico-economic thinking. I gathered that the two women had been personal friends once and were now estranged, which in no way diminished Ayn's appreciation of the book.

Most people, she explained, think capitalism is the system we have in America today, but what we have today is a mixed economy, part free, part controlled — *nominal* private ownership with a good deal of regulation by the government — a kind of fascism, in effect.

"If you care to do the research," Ayn said, "and I can give you an excellent reading list, you will discover that virtually every evil ascribed to laissez-faire capitalism is in fact the result not of laissez-faire but of government intervention, government controls, the betrayal of laissez-faire. For example, capitalism is blamed for scarcities that are created by government price controls. Or the government, not the market, establishes monopolies that forbid competitors to enter a particular field, and when high prices result, again capitalism is blamed. What capitalism? Most people are shocked when I tell them this; they think it can't be true. But let them check the facts for themselves — in non-Marxist textbooks and histories. Remember, capitalism means laissez-faire, not government controls in favor of business but rather no government controls — *hands off* — a totally free market."

She went on to say that pure laissez-faire of the kind she advocated had never existed, but the United States in the nineteenth century came closer to it than any other time or place in history, with spectacular results. American capitalism had transformed the world.

Rather sheepishly I mentioned my interest in anarchism, and she said to me, "You thought anarchism was the right system because you understood the evil of ruling men through physical force and you thought that was intrinsic to all government — and where were you going to learn that a system existed, at least in principle, that had solved this problem? At college? Most of your professors are leftists. From the conservatives? You'll discover they don't know that much about capitalism either, they merely favor different controls than the liberals, and when you hear them prattle about God and tradition, you'll be tempted to run to the Marxist camp, if only because it's more intellectual. In my philosophy the government's only proper job is to protect individual rights against violence by force or fraud — to provide courts for the protection of property and the peaceful settling of contractual disputes — and a military for protection against foreign invaders. . . . The greatness of the Founding Fathers was how well they understood this issue and how close some of them came to understanding it perfectly."

As she talked she waved her cigarette holder in the air to punctuate what she was saying. Her hand movements struck me as feminine and graceful, in contrast to the masculine sternness with which she sometimes spoke. She smoked through most of the evening, but even when she was not smoking she kept the holder in her hand, like a conductor's baton.

"In any event," she was saying, "what really interests me is the job of providing a moral or ethical foundation for capitalism, which we've never had and badly need. That's one of my goals in the novel I'm writing now. But the essence is already in *The Fountainhead*. Let me show you how."

I noticed that although she was functioning in the role of teacher, there was no hint of condescension or disrespect in her manner. She spoke from the premise of absolute equality, the equality of two minds in search of the truth.

She asked, as if preparing to present a syllogism, "Do you believe that man has the right to exist?"

"Yes. Yes, of course."

"Do you understand that that means he has the right to exist *for himself?*"

"Sure. If he has a right to exist only if he serves others, or does whatever others want, that isn't a right."

"You understand that already? Good. You're fast. What my philosophy teaches is that a human being is an end in himself, not a means to the ends of others, which means he has a right to exist for his own sake, neither sacrificing himself to others nor others to himself."

I did not yet have the historical context necessary to appreciate how radical this idea was, although at some level I knew it. At the same time I thought that this idea surely was self-evident to any reasonable person. "I agree completely," I said.

"You would have to, if you understand *The Fountainhead.*"

I drew myself up and assured her politely and confidently, "Miss Rand, I do understand *The Fountainhead.*" Playing back this moment in my mind, so many years later, I can hear a note of youthful pomposity in my voice I was quite oblivious to at the time.

I was enjoying the obvious fact that she liked the way I talked to her. There was a spontaneity and freedom from the very beginning. I was enormously impressed by her and yet absolutely happy about being myself. I felt I was in a place where no harm could possibly come to me.

"If you understand that a man's life is his own, that he's not a sacrificial animal, nor the property of the collective — that he has rights that are not to be sacrificed — then you understand that no person, no group, no government, has the right to force him to act against his own judgment."

And then I saw clearly the relation between the theme of *The Fountainhead* and the advocacy of a free market. I experienced a great rush of excitement, as if a new continent had been disclosed to me. At the edge of my consciousness I saw her noting and approving of my excitement, which she would interpret to mean that I was a person who took ideas seriously.

"Capitalism is the only *moral* system," she was saying, "because capitalism, in its pure, consistent form, is the only system based on the inviolability of individual rights."

I knew I would need time to digest everything she was saying, to reflect on it and assess it, but there was a clarity and internal consistency to her ideas that was instantly appealing. What I had always wanted was an older person I could respect and from whom I could learn. This was the need that was being fulfilled in this encounter. More important to me by far than the content of what I was learning was the experience of learning itself, of listening to a rational voice speaking in intelligible language about issues that mattered.

When I became aware that it was approaching two o'clock in the morning, and that Frank was beginning to drift in and out of sleep in his chair, I stood up apologetically. "I'm sorry for keeping you both up so late. I'd better be going."

"Not if you don't want to," Ayn said brightly. "But perhaps you're tired?"

I laughed incredulously. "Right now I don't know what being tired means."

Ayn spread her hands in a broad, expansive gesture. "Then sit down, Mr. Blumenthal. Or may I call you Nathan?"

"Of course."

"You may call me Ayn if you wish."

We went on talking, about her books, about my experiences at UCLA, about my enthusiasm for the plays of Ibsen, until I finally asked her the question that interested me most: "Can you tell me what your new novel is about?"

Her dark eyes flashed with excitement; I could see that this was the most important subject in the world to her, and that her desire to talk about it, tightly controlled at the moment, was fully as powerful as my desire to listen. Looking to Frank for permission, she asked him with unexpected girlishness, "May I tell him a little?" Frank grinned and nodded.

"The novel is called *The Strike*," she began slowly, "although probably I'll change the title. . . . The background is the world of business, heavy industry, specifically railroads and steel."

I felt the smallest stab of disappointment. "Will the novel be philosophical? Can you make businessmen romantic and interesting?" I asked.

My question seemed to delight her. "Wait and see."

"Come on." I grinned pleadingly. "Tell me something more."

"It's a mystery novel, not a detective story, of course, but there's a mystery —"

"A mystery about what?"

"About what's happening to the world."

There was an air of suppressed excitement about her that was delightful and intriguing; she was like a child with a marvelous secret she was bursting to tell. Again she turned to Frank: "Don't let me say too much." Her deference struck me as a bit strange: I couldn't imagine anyone stopping Ayn Rand. "Would you like to know the hero's name?" she asked provocatively.

I nodded eagerly, gesturing for her to speak.

"John Galt. You don't meet him till the last third of the book. Oh — I shouldn't have told you that!"

"Why not?"

"That's part of the mystery."

Next I asked her, "What's his occupation?"

"He's an inventor."

I did not know what was proper or improper to ask, but I could not contain myself. "Can you tell me what the climax of the book is?"

"A scene in which the hero is being tortured by the villains."

I took a moment to consider this, then asked, "Do they want to force him to reveal the secret of some invention of his?" Even as I asked, this did not sound right, not original enough, not for the author of *The Fountainhead*.

"No," she said, deliberately pokerfaced, the humor in her glance felt rather than seen. "They want to force him to become dictator of the country."

I burst out laughing. "Oh God," I said happily.

Whatever I had wanted out of life — ever — I was experiencing at this moment.

Their faces were glowing as they looked at me, as if they knew what I felt and were feeling it too. Beneath everything we were discussing, like background music to the entire evening, I felt the presence of that exhilarating connection among all three of us, as I had felt it from the beginning of the evening. The words in my mind were, *I'm home, I'm home, I'm home.*

I had arrived at 8:00 and left at 5:30 in the morning. "You'll come back," Ayn said as we stood up. "But if there are philosophical issues you would like to discuss in the meantime, you can phone me."

"I can?"

"Certainly."

"When?"

"Whenever you like."

I was not shy. There were times when I had been shy with young girls, but there was not one moment when I was shy with Ayn Rand. "Do you mean tomorrow?"

"Tomorrow by all means," she said.

When I turned to Frank, he took my hand in both of his and held it for a long moment with a friendliness and affection that touched me deeply.

The roads returning to Los Angeles were thick with fog as I made my way around twisting curves at fifteen miles an hour — while feeling that I was flying weightlessly through unobstructed space.

Where are you and what are you doing with some other man? You should have been with me tonight. It was as if I was hearing these thoughts from some great distance inside my mind. I realized I was addressing Barbara.

I imagined reciting the events of the evening in detail to her, going over and over the lines of dialogue in my mind, never wanting to relinquish them, wanting to hold them for the rest of my life. Everything was going to change not only for me but also for Barbara. I knew it.

Next day, when Barbara asked me what Ayn Rand was like, I hesitated for an instant, then answered, "Mrs. Logic." Then I went on to recreate for her, as fully as possible, this incredible night, and to describe my vision of this extraordinary personality. "She's more than anything I could have imagined." Did my stature seem to be growing in Barbara's eyes — and if so, what were the implications of that?

In the years that followed, Ayn and I reminisced over that first night many times, quoting each other's lines, delighting in the speed and depth of the connection that formed between us.

"Walking into the living room, seeing you for the first time," she would tell me, "I thought, 'He's got my kind of face,' and then I told myself, 'Don't start that again,' meaning, 'Don't start hoping.' I'd met too many alleged admirers who seemed intelligent and serious in their values, and who turned out to be phonies. But, you see, this time it didn't end in disappointment. This time I was right."

When I returned a week later, I brought Barbara with me.

I had spoken to Ayn on the telephone several times that week and on one occasion had said to her, "May I bring someone? I have a close friend who feels about your work as I do." "By all means, bring him along," Ayn had said. I had answered, "It's not a 'him.'" She had laughed. "Fine. Bring her along."

Driving to the ranch, Barbara was more nervous than I had ever seen her. Feeling very much the hero of the occasion, I urged her to relax, and she looked at me as if I were mad to suggest that anyone could be relaxed under the circumstances.

During the evening she was visibly enthralled but relatively silent. She listened avidly, but seldom spoke except in answer to Ayn's questions. But when she did express herself it was with precision and clarity; she knew what it meant to talk philosophically. "How does one determine what one can legitimately call an axiom?" she wanted to know. Later she remarked to Ayn, "How I wish my professors could explain issues the way you do."

When Ayn began discussing the idea that all emotions are the product of a person's conscious or subconscious premises, and reflect conscious or subconscious value judgments, I saw that this was a principle of enormous importance to her. It was tied in her mind to the supreme importance of reason in human life.

"*Emotions are not tools of cognition,*" she said; she would say it often, always with great intensity. I deliberately drew her out on this subject, even though what she was saying was clear to me. My hope was that she might accomplish what I could not: a reorientation of Barbara's psychology with regard to thinking and feeling. I imagined that I might be the beneficiary of such a reorientation.

I watched Barbara's face as Ayn spoke, taking pleasure in the eager attentiveness of her expression, feeling as if every value I cared about was sitting in this room.

"When you abandon reason as your standard," Ayn said at another point in the evening, "there's no peaceful way for people to settle their differences — and you open the door to every kind of evil, every kind of atrocity. Look at Hitler, with his hatred for 'bourgeois reason' and 'bourgeois science,' or the communists with their claim to a special 'proletarian logic' that justifies every sort of contradiction, irrationality, that justifies lies, torture, and murder. In both cases, *reason is the enemy.*"

This was a new idea to me and I thought it of the highest importance. I recognized the same awareness in Barbara. When we glanced at each other, we smiled in the intimacy of shared excitement.

Waving her cigarette holder, Ayn went on, "And of course this issue applies in more personal situations as well. . . . I remember once being at a party and talking to a man who was praising me for *The Fountainhead,* and he said, 'On your tombstone it should read, "Ayn Rand, Individualist." ' And I said, 'No. It should read, "Ayn Rand, Rationalist." ' And he answered, 'Oh, I was afraid of that,' and when I asked him why, he answered, 'Because if I go to the doctor and he tells me I have cancer, if I go by reason I have to take him seriously. I have to believe it. But if I'm not bound by reason I can deny it, can go on my way as if it isn't true.' I despise that man's mentality. In my philosophy nothing is more important than respect for reality."

Seeing the glow of eagerness in Barbara's eyes as Ayn spoke, I felt as if Barbara and I had no conflicts. Wasn't it obvious that this was the world in which we both belonged and whatever had gone wrong before was only a senseless mistake? How could anything or anyone compete with what we were now experiencing? What I did not allow myself to think consciously and in words was: How could anything or anyone compete with me, the engineer of this event?

We jumped from one subject to another, eager to explore everything at once. We were rather more interested in philosophy, psychology, and literature than in political economy, and we talked about the latter as something to be clarified and gotten out of the way so that we could discuss more enjoyable subjects. And yet, learning to understand the nature and workings of a market economy was intensely stimulating; for Barbara and me the experience was *grounding* — it connected us to the world.

I brought up the subject of military conscription, certain that Ayn would share my opposition to it; she did. "The draft is a good example of our mixed political system, and of what's wrong with it," she stated. "Military conscription contradicts the basic principle of a free society: a man's right to his own life. It's sickening how many conservatives favor the draft, while pretending to be champions of freedom. The bastards."

We went on to talk about Freud, who Ayn had never read and knew only from secondhand reports, but nonetheless detested. "Freud sees emotions, for all practical purposes, as primaries, as givens, rather than as proceeding from premises."

We talked about logical positivism, which seemed to be the dominant influence in the philosophy department at UCLA, and against which Ayn gave us intellectual ammunition. "Let me show you some of the contradictions in that so-called scientific philosophy. It's complete nonsense, you know, but vicious nonsense."

We talked about Ayn and Frank's house, which, Ayn told us, had been designed by the renowned modernist architect Richard Neutra and had belonged to Marlene Dietrich and Josef von Sternberg. "Do you want a tour?" she asked.

We were led, first, to the modest office in which Ayn worked, overlooking a garden. There we were introduced to Oscar and Oswald, two stuffed lion cubs that had been among Frank's first gifts to Ayn, many years ago, and who evidently were important members of the family, to be brought out with their red and green hats on all festive occasions. "Oscar and Oswald are our symbols of the benevolent universe," Ayn remarked wryly. Then we walked to the long, narrow kitchen, which inspired Ayn to a brief monologue on her hatred of cooking; for her, cooking evidently required a form of concentration she found particularly onerous. Finally we were led to their bedroom on the upper level, which was made intimate and erotic, as I recall, by the amount of mirror and glass and by a bidet set down not in the bathroom but in the bedroom. "I believe that was Dietrich's contribution," Ayn joked. "It was not in Neutra's original design."

Downstairs again we somehow fell into a discussion of our religious antecedents, and Ayn mentioned that she was Jewish by birth and that Frank was Catholic, although they were both atheists and felt no tie to religion of any kind. "What matters," Ayn remarked, "is what you accept by choice, not what you are connected with through the accident of your ancestry."

Then she proceeded to tell us with obvious pride how Frank had been taken to church as a young boy, had heard the priest expound on the doctrine that all human beings are born in sin, had thought this idea preposterous, and had rejected Catholicism then and there. Frank listened silently.

"I became an atheist at thirteen," she said. "For two reasons. First, because there were no rational grounds for believing in God. And second, and terribly important to me, because God was held to be the greatest entity in the universe, that made man inferior — and I resented the idea that man was inferior to anything." She paused thoughtfully for a moment, and then added, "If you were to put a title over everything I have written, or ever will write, it would be, 'To the Glory of Man.' "

I loved seeing Barbara in the living room of this house, sitting with Ayn and Frank. I felt that she too had at last come home, that whatever she had hoped to find when she was a young girl growing up in Winnipeg was now here before her. I did not mind her relative quiet that first night. Let her take it all in, I thought; let her discover that everything we talked about in our happiest times together is possible. I felt pride that I could lay all this before her.

Had her passion and enthusiasm for Ayn's world been less than it was — had I not believed that this was the world she wanted — I would have let her go. I would have released her internally, not without pain, but I would have done it, accepting the fact that I had failed to understand our differences. Without our shared love for Ayn Rand, I would not have imagined that Barbara and I were actual or potential soul mates. I did not recognize how much more than a mutual passion of that kind was needed to make two people right for each other.

When Ayn learned that Barbara and I had met over *The Fountainhead,* she was delighted. "Good fiction," she called it, meaning that that connection between the three of us was the kind of event one might put in a novel.

Driving home from that first meeting, Barbara was radiant. Now that we were alone words poured out of her. She felt as if here at last she was going to find the answers to all her questions. "You can ask her *anything*," Barbara exclaimed. She was overwhelmed by Ayn's sensitivity, clarity, dazzling intellect, and benevolence. "Is it really possible?" she asked. "Is this really happening?" And she struck my arm with excitement. "Are we really here?" she wondered, as we drove through the night, with dawn only a couple of hours away. And I answered, "We're here."

Years later, reflecting on their first meeting, Ayn said that Barbara's combination of fragility and strength made her think of Dominique. "You were very quiet, and so your personality did not come immediately into focus, but it was obvious that you were highly intelligent.

The comparison to Dominique had occurred to me long before Ayn mentioned it. Was not Dominique a heroine in spite of her conflicts? I saw a justification in my fight for Barbara and my hope for a happy outcome. But for the time being the hope was to remain unvoiced and the fight was to be abstract. I clung to the dream of a victory that would eventually occur by dint of my brains, character, perseverance, and by what I imagined to be the natural logic of things. I did not yet know that there are victories more terrible than defeat.

FOUR

I DID NOT RECOGNIZE it immediately, but the four of us were on our way to becoming a family. For me it felt like the first family I ever had, my first sense of roots. Not that I perceived Ayn and Frank as mother and father figures; that would have been very remote from our situation. Rather it was family in the sense of intellectual clan. As part of this experience, my sense of a bond with Barbara deepened.

I would visit Ayn and Frank every Saturday night and talk with Ayn almost every evening on the telephone, sometimes for several hours, chiefly about philosophy but sometimes about my growing up. Chatsworth was a toll call and I remember my sister Elayne's concern in light of my rather limited budget. I did not care; there was nothing of comparable importance for me to spend money on. When she thought of it, Ayn would suggest that I hang up and let her call me back.

Although Barbara did not initiate phone calls to Ayn, she usually would join me on the Saturday night visits, and often on other visits as well. I encouraged Barbara to contact Ayn on her own, rather than route the entire relationship through me, but she never did so; she said she was too shy, which disappointed me. I wished she were more assertive.

"I don't want you to think of Barbara as my appendage," I once said to Ayn. She answered, kindly, "But, realistically, for the time being, how else can I think of her? I don't really know her as I know you." Her interest sparked when Barbara mentioned that she wanted to become a novelist.

Once Ayn and I were talking about our childhood heroes and ideals and the role they played in our development, and I told her, "When I was six or seven, my hero was the Lone Ranger. Then, at about eight or nine, it was Superman. When I was twelve I discovered the novels of Baroness Orczy, and my ideal became the Scarlet Pimpernel." As an aside I remarked, "Interesting, isn't it, that all three were in a sense invisible? Their true identities were not known to people." I went on, "So how do I translate what I admire in these figures into the terms of twentieth-century reality? That question felt supremely important. I had no interest in rescuing French aristocrats from the guillotine, but there was something in those adventure stories I was in love with and didn't want to let go of. I wondered how I could apply it to my life in the modern world. Then at fourteen I read *The Fountainhead* — and discovered the answer. The adventure of creative work. Individualism as a moral battle."

Ayn became enthusiastic. "Don't you see?" she exclaimed. "You kept the same values — daring, audacity, independence — but you kept adjusting the form of their expression to your growth and developing knowledge. You stayed integrated. A more conventional man would have left it all as a daydream that had nothing to do with his adult life. And observe that you weren't literal-minded: you didn't decide to become an architect like Roark. You responded to the *abstraction* — passion for one's work — and translated that into terms relevant to your own goals." She added, "Of course you're right: it is significant that all three childhood heroes were masked or disguised — invisible men. That would strike a chord in your own feelings of isolation."

Gratefully and cheerfully I answered, "I'm not feeling invisible now."

In my first year at UCLA I was taking as many courses in philosophy as I was in psychology. But college could hardly compare with the intellectual excitement of my contact with Ayn; no professor ever conveyed as Ayn did that the ideas being discussed were matters of life-and-death importance. I tended to find philosophy courses relatively more stimulating, because my introductory courses in psychology, with their strong emphasis on laboratory experiments, psychophysical measurement and the like, seemed very distant from what had initially captured my imagination. I would be more intrigued by my classes on personality theory and the nature of neurosis, still a year away.

The two dominant schools of psychology, with which I was somewhat familiar from my own reading, were psychoanalysis and behaviorism, and I was impressed by neither. So many of their assertions struck me as arbitrary. I did not believe in psychological determinism, nor in domination by alleged instincts, nor in Freud's theory of psychosexual development, nor in any reductionist stimulus-response model of human behavior, as propounded by Watson, Hull, and Skinner. I began to think that historically psychology was approximately where philosophy was at the time of Thales in ancient Greece: a science waiting to be born.

As to my own understanding of behavior, my strong philosophical inclinations, reinforced by Ayn's beliefs and attitudes, disposed me to think about emotion and motivation in purely cognitive terms — that is, to explain feelings and behavior primarily in terms of a person's ideas or premises. Understanding a person ultimately meant understanding the conscious or subconscious conclusions he or she had formed about life and human existence. In addition, there was the principle of free will, which Ayn had defined as the freedom to think or not to think — to exercise consciousness or to suspend it. This was a view I found persuasive and illuminating.

Psychology was not our primary focus in those early months. Many of our most exciting discussions centered on issues in epistemology and metaphysics that had arisen at school, and questions about the nature of knowledge or the nature of reality were never dry to us; they were of the very stuff of life.

How do you justify the validity of sensory perception? What is the basis of the laws of logic? What were the historical consequences of Descartes's treatment of the mind-body relation? How do you refute Hume's "refutation" of causality? These were the kind of questions we would hurl at Ayn.

At times it felt like hitting balls across a net to a player who, with a relaxed kind of intensity, never seemed to miss her stroke. I cannot recall her ever saying, "Let me think about this." She always had an instant answer.

"This is *so much fun*!" I would exclaim at 7:00 in the morning, after one of our all-night sessions. Ayn could not relate to my use of the word "fun," but she would laugh and blow Barbara and me a kiss good-bye.

One of our most memorable visits during this period was an evening when Barbara brought *The Rise of Scientific Philosophy*, a textbook from one of the classes we were taking together. The course was given by the author, Dr. Hans Reichenbach, a famous exponent of logical positivism, which held that the laws of logic are ultimately arbitrary, the senses are unreliable as sources of information about the world, nothing can be known for certain, and that any statement made about the nature of reality is meaningless. We enjoyed him as a teacher because of his humor and liveliness but disagreed with almost everything he said. The conversation that followed was extraordinary.

Ayn had never heard of Reichenbach. She picked up his book and read the first two or three pages, then forecast what Reichenbach's position would be on any number of issues, then waited for our confirmation that she was right, then began to teach us how she had done what she had done, and, more generally, how to read far-reaching implications into the simplest choice of words. We were astonished by what she was able to know about him, based on what seemed to us to be almost no evidence at all.

"When you speak, when you write, when you read, *watch the implications*," she said. "Pay attention to the implications of your own statements — and the statements of other people." That was one of the first philosophical lessons she drummed into us.

Never was our energy and enthusiasm greater than that of this woman who was twenty-five years our senior. Sometimes when we arrived at the ranch she would be visibly exhausted from a difficult day's writing, but once the discussion began to flow and her mind became engaged, it was as if she had tapped into some universal energy source: the lines of tiredness vanished and her face took on the brightness of early morning. She conveyed a passion for ideas that was inspiring and electrifying. The best of our professors seemed drained and worn out by comparison. She was the apotheosis of the philosophically dedicated mind. In future years we would hear her in discussions with any number of professors, and I cannot recall one who did not comment on this trait of hers, this burning commitment to the importance of ideas.

She gave inexhaustibly of her time and energy to Barbara and me. I was puzzled by her generosity. "Surely," I said to her, "you must have contemporaries who share your intellectual interests?" She replied, "Friends, or more often acquaintances, who share my interest in politics. Conservatives, mainly. Not philosophical thinkers." I remained puzzled. "But Barbara and I haven't accomplished anything in life yet." She chuckled. "You will. Are you concerned about receiving something you don't deserve?" I hadn't quite thought of it that way, but answered, "Well, I suppose so." She said, "Don't be. You and Barbara *know how to think*. No one had to teach you that. One day you'll understand how important that is — and how unimportant differences of age are by comparison." We held versions of this conversation not once but several times. As we came to know each other better, her perspective seemed more and more natural to me.

At UCLA I tried to engage some of my professors in the kind of issues I talked about with Ayn. When I tried to persuade a psychology professor that the doctrine of psychological determinism contained insuperable contradictions, he replied, "Don't get philosophical on me." When, in a logic class, I tried to argue that reality was knowable to the human mind, I was told, "No enlightened person believes he can know anything." When, in an obligatory course on government, I challenged a professor who spoke glowingly of Soviet Russia, he informed me, "You're just prejudiced against dictatorships."

I tried to find friends among my fellow students. I looked for opportunities to exchange ideas. "How can you *not* be a socialist?" I was asked. Or, "You don't *really* believe in laissez-faire capitalism, do you?" Or, "You're an admirer of Ayn Rand? Great, so am I. I wouldn't really want to live that way, but it's exciting to read about, isn't it? Of course, in the real world, integrity just isn't practical. What I would like to be is a *nice* Peter Keating." Or, "Gosh, you're kind of serious, aren't you?"

I tried dating girls, but the ones I met seemed empty, conventional, frivolous, passive, too "dreamy," hopelessly nonintellectual. I was very serious, probably too serious. I made myself go out occasionally and fought against feelings of boredom. I was not indifferent to pretty faces or attractive bodies, but I felt as if I were watching them from some great distance, where no action but contemplation was possible. Occasionally in the campus cafeteria I might flirt, but I had little energy for the endeavor and somehow I communicated this. The conversations I managed to initiate never caught fire. I still wanted what I had always wanted: a heroine.

In Barbara I saw a *longing* that elevated her above other girls I knew: some version of the same longing I recognized in myself — for the extraordinary, the challenging, the ecstatic, a life that would be *important*. In a strange way, that was her theme as a person: longing — as if her identity was her aspirations.

When we went out together, as we did occasionally — to the beach, or to a movie, or for a drive along the coast — we had a good time, notwithstanding an undertone of tension. We would talk about Ayn and the things we were learning, about capitalism, about our courses at UCLA. I liked the intense earnestness she always brought to discussions of ideas; this was the girl I had fallen in love with.

Our relationship was not sexual; by Barbara's choice there was no physical intimacy. Neither was it quite nonsexual; it hung in a strange limbo, punctuated by instances of seductiveness on her part, as if she wanted to reassure herself that my feelings toward her had not changed. Or did I only imagine that my constancy had some value to her?

One Sunday afternoon we went to Saint-Saën's opera, *Samson and Delilah,* and for a moment in the half-darkness our glance met, our breath stopped, and I could see a spark of sensuality in Barbara's eyes as she moved closer toward me; then she sat back, her eyes returned to the performance, and the moment was gone. Incidents like this occurred from time to time and my hopes fed on them.

Sometimes Barbara suggested that she "should" feel greater sexual passion for me in light of how much she admired me and felt an affinity with me. When she reproached herself I had no idea how to respond. I did not like her nonresponsiveness but I did not like her guilt either. All I knew how to do was wait. No one else attracted me, except, perhaps, in the most transitory and superficial way.

What I wanted in every aspect of my life was a "stylized universe," the world of *The Fountainhead*. It seemed so right that Barbara should join me in that world on every possible level. Why could she not feel that?

With Ayn I shared my feelings of boredom and impatience with other people. She smiled a little sadly but she nodded in understanding.

In later years there were many discussions of what Ayn did or did not recognize that first year. She would say, "I don't think I would have permitted myself to know, at first. The situation was impossible. Being that unaware of my feelings is out of character for me, isn't it? I was not evading — I would not evade knowingly — but I suppose it was a kind of suppression, or repression, or something. I knew you had my kind of face, and that you were my kind of person, and had the best mind of anyone I'd met, but I never allowed myself to think further than that. But if I were to read it in a novel, I would certainly have suspected. The dramatist in me would have been on the alert." She admitted to great caution in approaching our relationship. Her inscriptions in my copies of *Anthem, We the Living,* and *The Fountainhead,* were, for example, perhaps unusually reserved. Ayn said of these early inscriptions, "I was so cautious in the beginning. So concerned about what was appropriate to say on paper. And yet, wasn't I already feeling . . . almost everything?"

Not long after we met Ayn and Frank, Barbara said to me, "I wonder what their social life is like." I replied, "It's hard to imagine them in ordinary social settings, isn't it? I mean, you know, with ordinary people?" Over time we met a number of their friends.

One of these friends was a young screenwriter, Albert Mannheimer, who was working on the screen adaptation of Garson Kanin's *Born Yesterday*. Ayn had converted him from Marxism. She had been amused by the fact that he had proposed to convert *her*; she appreciated his intelligence and his seeming enthusiasm for ideas. Under her influence he became an enthusiastic advocate of laissez-faire.

We learned that Albert was struggling with painful personal problems, involving a good deal of anxiety and depression, and Ayn was attempting to help him, chiefly with philosophical discussions. She seemed very fond of him. One of his conflicts was the pull between the values represented by Ayn and those associated with Hollywood. By way of explaining, in part, her "tolerance" for his problems, Ayn mentioned that years earlier when she and Frank had been financially desperate Albert had sent her a check for five hundred dollars, which had been of enormous help to them. She spoke of her gratitude. "I can't forget his help to us when our situation was so bad." I was surprised because I had heard her declare, in the presence of a number of people, that during her years of financial struggle, no one had ever helped her; years later, she would repeat this claim to the whole world on the About the Author page of *Atlas Shrugged*. But I did not question her about this evident contradiction and dismissed it from my mind.

None of us appreciated that what Albert needed was not abstract discussion of his "premises" but competent psychotherapy. Among other things, he needed the freedom to explore the roots of his feelings and to say anything that came into his mind without fear of censure, which would hardly have been possible with anyone as given to moralizing as Ayn. Of course I did not call it moralizing then; I called it moral passion. In any event, Ayn was unable to help him.

One day she announced that she had become very disenchanted with him. Lying on her sofa in miserable depression Albert had uttered something to the effect that he did not care about ideas, that philosophy did not matter to him. To Ayn this was anathema. In light of the convictions she thought they shared, she found Albert's utterance incomprehensible. Telling us about it, she projected an almost childlike quality of having been betrayed. She appeared both hurt and angry, and their relationship deteriorated from that point.

Ayn had specific expectations of those she regarded as friends; the closer the friendship, the higher the expectations; and if those expectations were not met, her response could be ruthless. When Albert did not pull out of his depression, when he permitted his "psychology" to get the better of his "philosophy," he lost Ayn's friendship; she did not break with him explicitly, but he lost all stature in her eyes.

I fluctuated between feeling sorry for Albert while thinking Ayn had been too severe, and feeling unconcerned about Albert and sorry for Ayn; but the latter response prevailed. The collapse of their friendship struck me as rather sad because her other relationships seemed cordial enough but clearly less intimate. There was Dr. Borroughs (Buzzy) Hill, a cancer researcher at UCLA, and his wife, Ruth Beebe Hill, who would later become well known as the author of *Hanta Yo*. There was the economist Henry Hazlitt and his wife, Frances, who Ayn had met and worked with while employed as a reader for Paramount Pictures more than a decade earlier. The Hazlitts lived in New York, and when they visited Los Angeles Ayn and Frank gave a party for them, where I had an opportunity to tell Henry Hazlitt how much I admired *Economics in One Lesson*. There was Leonard Read, whose small firm was responsible for the first American publication of Ayn's novel, *Anthem*, and who founded and guided The Foundation for Economic Education, an organization dedicated to the ideals of individualism and political freedom. There was William Mullendore, president of Consolidated Edison of California, an older businessman of great integrity who lectured throughout the country on the merits of a free market and for whom Ayn had exceptionally high esteem. Other friends included the actress Janet Gaynor and her designer husband, Adrian, whose rather theatrical clothes Ayn loved and wore on all dressy occasions; and Morrie Ryskind, who wrote *Of Thee I Sing*.

It was exciting to meet people in Ayn's home and to feel that we were almost being shown off, not as Ayn's children — there was nothing of the maternal in Ayn's manner — but as products of her philosophy. "Certainly not," she said, a little indignantly, when someone asked if she felt like our mother; then she added, "They're not *my* children, they're the children of *The Fountainhead*." She felt a need to stress the intellectuality of our relationship. I felt happily comfortable with this.

It was exciting to see Ayn moving among her guests with great charm, warmth, and even humor; to see Frank sitting in a corner with someone, talking with surprising animation, perhaps about his activities on the ranch; and to know that, after all the guests had left, Barbara and I would remain for the postmortem on the evening, which could go on for another six hours, while we shared our thoughts and impressions.

"They all seem very nice, very intelligent," I remarked to Ayn, "and they all seem to admire you. But" — I felt hesitant and was not certain how to express myself — "do they actually share your deepest interests and values?" Ayn shrugged. "That's a good question. To answer literally: possibly yes in one or two respects and definitely no in a good many others."

Had I asked that question from some impulse of inappropriate possessiveness? When I conveyed my concern, Ayn laughed. "If you did," she said, "I approve. It's what I would have done in your place. That's what I call the 'Dominique premise' — not wanting to share your values with anyone. As a young girl, I hated it when someone said he liked the same books or music as I did. I wanted my values to be my private possession. In effect, I felt that no one else was good enough to share them. If that's how you feel about me, darling, I'll take it as a compliment."

I was amused by her use of "darling," which I noticed she said frequently — to me, to Frank, to Barbara; it was her one touch of Hollywood.

In this moment I heard only her cheerfulness and warmth; I was oblivious to other implications in what she was conveying, the subtle encouragement of estrangement from the world.

Barbara and I gathered that many brilliant and celebrated people visited Ayn and Frank's home. Yet I agreed with Barbara when she observed, "Have you noticed that they are not really that close to anyone? There's always that distance." My agreement contained a trace of pride because I felt no such distance between Ayn and Frank and us.

Ayn made it clear that she preferred the informality of just the four of us sitting around and talking. "I'm not really good at gracious living," Ayn said many times; by 'gracious living,' she meant anything above the most primitive amenities of *social* living. We noticed that she looked most comfortable with her hair barely combed, snags in her stockings, a casual blouse and skirt, and hastily applied lipstick — as if material reality, like cooking, was a boring distraction from writing and intellectual discussion.

Notwithstanding the passion she conveyed for the physical world in her writing, there was a good deal of the ascetic, or the absent-minded professor, about her. One felt that her appreciation of physical reality was very abstract, like contemplating the beauty of a distant horizon. As a writer she was a master at recreating sensory reality — sight and sound and motion — and many of her descriptions of nature are almost reverential in their lyricism. Moreover, most of her heroes and heroines are masters of managing the physical. But as a person, she herself lived almost entirely in a world of ideas.

Locks that jammed, toasters that malfunctioned, blouses with missing buttons, dresses with falling hems — all seemed to be malevolent adversaries whose sole intention was to frustrate and thwart her. I was sometimes astonished at the intensity of her angry exasperation over such trivia.

An example of Ayn's estrangement from physical reality was the fact that she never learned to drive an automobile. She was entirely dependent on Frank for transportation, which she professed to hate. He was not a good driver, and Barbara and I witnessed more than one incident of harsh words when Ayn became agitated and impatient with him. In view of Ayn's independence and her admiration for technology, I couldn't understand how she could not learn to drive. When I told her so, she said, "Oh, Frank tried to teach me, but it didn't go well, and Frank is afraid I'll be thinking about writing and not have my mind on the road, and he's probably right." I had the sense that she was trying to romanticize the situation, and I dropped the subject, mystified. I felt that her self-concept did not include being able to drive a car: that simply was not her relationship to the material world.

There may have been another reason for her not driving. She was so much more powerful than Frank in virtually all other respects that she may have elected, consciously or otherwise, to remain dependent on him in the matter of driving, whatever the inconvenience; perhaps that was her way of protecting their relationship.

Although we rarely discussed it, Barbara and I found Ayn's and Frank's relationship puzzling. We wondered about what they had in common. He never participated actively in our discussions, did not read books, was clearly not an intellectual, did not match her energy or passion. They had met when he was a struggling actor. Now Frank was operating their thirteen-acre ranch, which he had reconditioned and landscaped, growing flowers and citrus trees as a commercial enterprise. He was most alive and talkative when discussing his ranch activities.

"I never miss acting, never think about it," he told me cheerfully. "I love the ranch."

"Frank believed in me, saw who I was and what I would become, when no one else did, when we were both young and struggling and had nothing," Ayn told us. "We have the same sense of life. But Frank is too disgusted with people to share what he is with the world."

Frank would listen silently to such statements, almost like the painting on the wall. Once I found myself wondering why, since Frank was not "disgusted" with Ayn, Barbara, or me, he was so silent during our meetings. He had great natural dignity, considerable charm, and always projected enormous benevolence, and I felt much affection for him; and yet I found his lack of ambition incomprehensible, given that he was "Ayn Rand's husband." For another man, operating the ranch would have been a perfectly legitimate occupation. But when Ayn spoke of work and career she spoke of changing the world, of having an impact on history. "I could never love anyone who was not a hero," she said; literally, a hero meant someone who excelled in moral virtue high above the average, but it also usually connoted, in the contexts in which she used the term, someone with a range of vision and ambition far beyond anything Frank suggested. I recognized that there was something between them I did not understand.

Yet I made no particular effort to get to know Frank. I would ask an occasional question about his ranch activities or admire the beautiful peacocks he raised or observe that he looked a little tired. But within moments my attention swung irresistibly back to Ayn. She was the great light that leaves everything beyond it in darkness. She and Frank both seemed to regard this state of affairs as natural. Most people who I saw at the ranch treated Frank as I did. He was the man who wasn't quite there.

At this time I had absolutely no intimation of trouble between Ayn and Frank. Ayn told me, much later, that those years on the ranch had been very bad for them. They were quarreling a great deal. She was bothered by his passivity and nonintellectuality. Then she confided that in the entire history of their relationship, not once had he initiated sex; it was always she who began it; after that, she said, everything went fine, he was very involved and uninhibited; but it was not difficult to imagine how that would leave her feeling. Then, there was the plain fact of their enormous intellectual differences — not merely the issue of intelligence but also differences in how their minds worked. She understood only pure, linear, sequential reasoning; he was almost totally intuitive; and although he could appreciate her cognitive style, she was never really comfortable with his. She said that she had been thinking of divorce but wanted to wait until the novel was finished because she dreaded the interruption of her work. Work came above everything. Years later she told me that she could not live without him. He was, in his own sad way, her rock.

Ayn loved to talk about the beginning of their relationship. When they met for the first time, they were both in their twenties. Having arrived in America only a few months earlier, she had come to Hollywood, hoping to find work writing scripts for silent films while she acquired the mastery of English she would need for her future novels. By an extraordinary stroke of good fortune she fell into a conversation with Cecil B. DeMille, who saw her staring at him near the gate of his studio. "Why are you looking at me?" DeMille had asked, and she had answered in a daze of excitement that she had just come from Soviet Russia and was happy to see him. She greatly admired his films, she told him, and wanted to write for the movies. Charmed and intrigued, he invited her to watch the daily shooting, so she could learn how films were made, and he gave her a job working as an extra in his current production, *The King of Kings*. Frank had a bit part in the film.

She had seen Frank earlier that day on a streetcar headed for the DeMille studio in Culver City. "I took one look at him," Ayn told us, "and, you know, Frank is the physical type of all my heroes. I fell instantly in love." On the streetcar she was terrified that he would get off and she would never see him again. On the set, determined to attract his attention, *she tripped him,* which led to them talking for a while and exchanging names. "I couldn't think of any other way to make contact," she said smiling.

Frank did not mention to her that this was his last day on the set. When shooting was finished, he simply vanished. He had found her interesting, it seemed, but he had not been very aggressive about it. He had planned to wait for her, but someone offered him a lift and he took it. I thought there was a faint hint of resentment when she mentioned this. "Why couldn't you have waited for me, that first day?" she asked Frank in mock reproachfulness. For nine months she dreamed — and despaired — of finding him again. "You can't imagine how miserable I was," she remarked.

During those nine months Frank was her obsession. This fascinated me in view of how little she knew about him. Frank's appearance and manner obviously spoke to a private, inner vision, a male archetype existing within her psyche. When this happens, when we meet someone who seems to embody the traits of our opposite gender archetype, we can be flung instantly into the experience of romantic love. If our perception of the other is realistic, if more detailed knowledge supports our initial impression, love can flourish. If on the other hand, we are merely projecting our own needs and longings, we step into a dream — or a nightmare — from which we may not ever choose to awaken.

One day, while working for DeMille as a junior screenwriter, she wandered into a public library and saw Frank. He looked up and recognized her, and they went out to walk and talk, about writing and acting and life, and both were hit by an instant sense of profound affinity. It did not take them long to decide — or for Ayn to decide — that they were "soul mates."

Ayn said, "When Frank began to talk about movies, I could see how much alike we were in our values. He hated the conventional. He loved the daring and the heroic."

"One of the most striking things about her," Frank reminisced, "was the absence of any trace of deviousness. The total honesty. If she liked something, she liked it violently. If she didn't like something, she would communicate that violently, too. She never wondered if she was going to succeed. The only question was how long it would take."

"Frank seemed completely unaffected by other people," she said. "It was as if he existed alone in the world. Like Roark."

Listening to her tell the story of their beginning, I enjoyed her openness; she spoke like a young girl, and I thought that that was how a woman should speak about the man she loves. The women in her novels projected the same attitude of hero worship. It did not matter that I could not fully understand Ayn's worship of Frank. What mattered to me was her capacity to experience love that way.

What Frank projected was affection and admiration rather than passion. I took this to be a matter of form rather than essence, assuming that at the core their feelings for each other must be of the same order. There was so much I did not grasp.

I gathered that she saw in her kind of hero worship the essential meaning of femininity, and one day I asked her, "Don't men worship women? I mean, the women they love?"

"Oh, I suppose so, but that's not how I would think of it. By 'worship,' I mean our highest capacity for admiration, reverence, looking up. I see man as superior to woman, and —"

"Oh, Ayn," I protested. "You don't. You're joking!"

"I am not joking," she answered seriously.

"Superior in what? Intelligence? Creativity? Moral worth?"

"No, of course not. In spiritual or intellectual matters the sexes are equal. But man is bigger, stronger, faster — better able to cope with nature."

"You mean, at a purely physical level?"

"The physical is not unimportant."

I would return to this issue many times across the years. I did not feel fully comfortable with her point of view. Yet I would discover that many of the most independent, strong-minded women I met shared it.

Ayn would smile good-naturedly at my evident bafflement. Once she said to me, as if to make the matter clear once and for all, "Don't you understand that a truly strong woman *wants* to see man as stronger? Certainly *her* man." When I asked why, she answered, "For the pleasure of surrendering."

I persisted, "So in a way the issue is sexual?"

She laughed. "Of course." Then she added, "And beyond that, the pleasure of being helpless at times, of laying down the burden of strength. In a way, that also is sexual. A woman can't do this with a man she doesn't look up to. Nathan, be honest. You understand me perfectly. This is exactly how you expect a woman to feel about you."

"Maybe so," I conceded reluctantly, "but I wouldn't try to defend my position philosophically."

"I would," she said brightly.

On one visit I acquainted Ayn with the nature of Barbara's and my situation — the difference in the strength of our feelings for each other. I said that while my feelings for Barbara were romantic and sexual, hers for me were not. "What kind of men does Barbara like?" Ayn wanted to know. I muttered something to the effect that Barbara claimed to be confused and, in effect, in transition. I knew Barbara would not have appreciated a more precise answer.

While conveying respectful sympathy toward Barbara, Ayn made it clear that she found Barbara's psychology difficult to understand. In Ayn's view our sexual desires are the product of our deepest values, and if Barbara's values were the ones she professed and seemed to hold, how could she not be in love with me? I felt acutely uncomfortable listening to this, yet I could not deny that I felt much as Ayn did. Subsequently, in a private conversation, she conveyed her perspective to Barbara, who later reported it to me, a little sadly. I was torn between embarrassment, gratitude to Ayn, pity for Barbara — and misery.

One day I visited Barbara in her apartment. She'd had some kind of quarrel with her current boyfriend and looked confused and unhappy. She flung her arms around me, pressed her face against mine, and whispered, "Don't give up on me." She had such a look of innocence and vulnerability and childlike goodness that I felt a rush of tenderness; I also felt uncertainty. Was this merely a mood or was she genuinely trying to tell me something? Next time I saw her, she was cheerful again, and it was as if the moment had never happened.

During those first months I looked for opportunities to draw Ayn out on the subject of love and sex, hoping to gain insights that might illuminate my relationship with Barbara. Ayn told us that she was developing her theory of sexual attraction in her novel and that in fact it was very important to the plot. The theory is dramatized through the character of Hank Rearden, primarily at the level of conscious philosophical convictions, which was the level at which Ayn tended to think — and which imposed a severe limitation on the theory. Her view of sex, I grasped only years later, was badly oversimplified. And yet her core idea is one that many psychologists today recognize as valid: that our deepest vision of self, as well as our most intimately personal values and our underlying sense of life, inevitably will be manifest in our sexual-romantic responses — above all, in who we fall in love with.

In the spring and summer of 1950 the chief result of Ayn's theory of sex was to worsen Barbara's guilt for not being romantically in love with me. I did not think this was Ayn's intention and she was doubtless unaware of her impact. In her own way she was laying a foundation for Barbara's and my eventual reconciliation, by treating as more and more self-evident the idea that I was, in some sense, "a hero."

I could not have conceived that a day would come when Ayn's theory of sex would be used not against Barbara but against me.

That summer, Barbara's cousin Leonard Peikoff, and my cousin Allan Blumenthal, both re-entered our lives, but in very different ways.

Leonard, who was then seventeen years old, came from Winnipeg to visit California. He was as high-strung as I remembered him. He was eager to meet the author of *The Fountainhead* and we had promised to take him. One evening we drove together to the ranch. Within a few minutes of arriving, he plunged into the philosophical questions he had come prepared to raise, which we all found delightful.

One question was especially important to him. "Is Howard Roark idealistic or practical?"

Barbara and I smiled, no doubt feeling a little superior, because we both knew what Ayn's answer would be.

"Do you assume that if Roark is idealistic he can't be practical, and if he's practical he can't be idealistic?" she asked.

Leonard replied that he had always assumed that it was one or the other. "That's what everyone says."

"Well," Ayn proceeded encouragingly, "is your own firsthand judgment that Roark is idealistic?"

Leonard answered yes, observing that Roark refused to sacrifice his principles; he had integrity.

"And does he seem to you to be practical?" Ayn persisted.

Leonard answered, "Well, in a way he does. He has a hard time of it, but he succeeds. That's what's confusing."

"He succeeds both professionally and personally. And men like Peter Keating and Gail Wynand — who are what the world usually calls 'practical' — fail, are defeated in the end."

Leonard said that was what he was attempting to understand. He needed to know for his own life, for his future. Was it better to be moral or practical, idealistic or successful?

"If your ideals are rational," Ayn said, "if your moral principles are based on reality, there's no conflict. The moral *is* the practical. Roark is totally practical — and totally consistent in the principles he lives by. That's why he succeeds."

Barbara added, "Not that success is ever automatically guaranteed in life. Of course it isn't. But if your values are right, and you have integrity, you have the best chance possible."

It is only an irrational morality, Ayn went on, a morality in contradiction to man's nature and to the nature of reality, such as the kind of ethics typically taught by religion, that creates a conflict between the moral and the practical. If you believe that self-sacrifice is a noble ideal, if you believe that happiness, sexual enjoyment, personal profit, and self-assertion are evil, then there *is* a conflict between the moral and the practical. She developed this idea for Leonard in great depth, anticipating many of his possible questions and answering them.

"Whenever you think you have a conflict between the idealistic and the realistic, check your premises about what you've accepted as 'idealistic,' " said Ayn.

This, for Leonard, was not merely an important idea but a totally revolutionary idea, one that went against just about everything he had ever heard. He was euphoric.

Some months later he wrote that he had decided against a career in medicine, in defiance of his family's expectations, and was going to major in philosophy. In his letters he seemed very happy. "Good for him," I said.

One day during that same summer I received an unexpected letter from Allan. We had not been in contact for some time. Allan was now in medical school, in acquiescence to his parents' wishes. With no context to prepare me for it, his letter was a bewildering attack on my behavior as a son; he took particular offense at what he perceived as my indifference to my mother.

Allan was twenty-two years old at the time, but in his letter he sounded like a prissy old lady. I was utterly perplexed. What did Allan imagine he was up to? It seemed I did not telephone home often enough, in Allan's opinion; furthermore he felt that I thought too highly of my own opinions, didn't appropriately heed parental advice, caused my mother to worry about my future because of my indifference to "the practical," and was generally much too much of a nonconformist. I was flabbergasted, not only because I perceived my relationship with my parents in rather more benevolent terms than he did, but also because I could not grasp what would inspire him to lecture me on a subject that was none of his concern.

I showed his letter to Ayn, wondering what she might make of it.

She said in the tone of an infallible pronouncement, "This is the most malicious letter I have ever read. This person is filled with envy. Keep away from him."

I did not know what to think. *Allan?* Was she talking about my cousin *Allan?* When Ayn saw my reluctance to accept her assessment, she questioned me like an expert attorney, drawing from my memory those occasions across the years when I had been puzzled by Allan's sudden flashes of resentment. "Watch out," she said. "You will see, sooner or later, that I am right. I know how to read implications in what people say — and especially in what they write."

Echoing Ayn, Barbara declared, "Allan hates you for your virtues."
"Be careful," Ayn insisted. "He's jealous of you."

As the months passed and our friendship with Ayn and Frank progressed, we learned more details of their past — where they had been born, their relationship with their families, and a little about their early struggles.

Ayn was born on February 2, 1905, in the city of St. Petersburg (subsequently called Petrograd and eventually Leningrad), which is the setting of *We the Living*. "Ayn Rand was not my original name," she told us. "My first name was Alice. I adopted the name Ayn from a Finnish writer and I adopted the name Rand soon after coming to America — from my Remington-Rand typewriter! I never tell anyone my original family name because if I still have relatives living in Russia, they'd be endangered." Many years would pass before I would learn that her original name had been Alice Rosenbaum.

Discussing her first novel she said, "*We the Living* is not autobiographical, except in the intellectual sense, but it does give you a good picture of St. Petersburg — Petrograd — in the years following the Revolution. Kira's mother is somewhat patterned after my mother, and Kira's uncle Vasili after my father, a strong, silent, retiring man but intensely anticommunist, unable to adapt, a self-made man now in an impossible situation. Self-made men were unusual at that time in Russia, and my father had been very proud of having his own business; he was a pharmacist. Many occupations were closed to Jews, of course, so he chose to become a chemist. The character of Leo was inspired by a man I was in love with. Nothing ever happened between us, just a few dates, certainly not an affair, and when he stopped calling me I suffered horribly. In some ways that was the most painful experience of my life. Much later I heard that he ended up in a very conventional marriage. What I saw in him, what he meant to me, is what I gave to the character of Leo in the novel."

In response to a question about her mother, she remarked, "My mother and I didn't get along. She was always encouraging me to do physical exercise, which I hated. 'Make motions, Alice,' she would say, 'make motions!' And she was very social, very people-oriented, which I also disliked. She was totally not my kind of person."

I could not help but notice the detachment with which she discussed her parents, even her father, of whom she was to grow fonder during her adolescent years. But her distance seemed entirely normal to me — I related it to my feelings about my own parents.

On another occasion Ayn told us, "I would say my childhood was happy, although I really was not close to anyone. I always received

enormous recognition for my intelligence, not just from my parents
and relatives, but also from my teachers. I was always first in the class.
I was special — unusual — and everyone seemed to know it. So that
kind of recognition, I got."

"I was always asking questions," Ayn said proudly. "I drove adults
crazy — I always wanted to know 'why' about whatever anyone
said."

If any adult had ever cuddled her or told her she was pretty or
treated her in any real sense as a little girl, she did not mention it; and
somehow I felt certain that no one ever had. Or perhaps it was simply
that she remembered only the kind of nurturing that paid tribute to
her intelligence. It was only of this last that she ever spoke.

This did not strike me as unnatural either. Had I myself not wondered on many occasions why people insisted on taking their child-
hoods so seriously? It would have been quite beyond my understanding to hear a child's isolation and loneliness in her words. To have
understood this aspect of her, I would have had to understand it within
myself.

On yet another evening she spoke of the pleasure she took in family
summer vacations, usually in the Crimea, and of her excited discovery
one summer of what she called "tiddlywink" music, by which she
meant music that was bright, aggressively cheerful, defiantly non-
tragic. This included certain marches, songs like "It's a Long Way to
Tipperary" (one of my father's favorites, which I often heard him
sing), certain German and American popular tunes, and, as she grew
older, some selections from operettas by Lehár, Kálmán, Millöcker,
Offenbach, and the like. She loved Rachmaninoff, Chopin, and a few
other classical composers (or a few of their compositions), but not as
she loved her tiddlywink music.

Sometimes, when Barbara and I would arrive in the evening, we
found Ayn listening to this music, dancing around the room and waving a bamboo stick. It was as if she wanted to laugh at all the suffering
she had ever endured, to proclaim that these joyful sounds were the
actual essence of life.

In contrast to such moments, on one of our visits she talked about
the horrors of the civil war and about the communist takeover and
about her reactions to communist ideology. I recall the implacable severity of her voice as she told us, "I was twelve years old when I heard
the slogan that man must live for the state — and I thought right then
that this idea was evil and the root of all the other evils we were seeing
around us. I was already an individualist. And, you know, hearing
what the communists were saying, it wasn't just the idea of sacrifice,

which would have been evil enough, but the sacrifice of the highest to the lowest, the intelligent to the mediocre, the exceptional to the substandard, which is the ideal they were really preaching . . . and, for years, up to the present day, all the torture and all the slaughter and all the blood doesn't stop people from calling it a 'noble ideal' . . . and I saw what it really was when I was twelve."

Then, with that particular brightness she exhibited whenever she could link the personal to the intellectual, she said, "When I saw that my father felt as I did, and he saw my interest in political issues, that was the beginning of a kind of bond between us."

She was convinced, no doubt rightly, that if she could not escape, she would be killed. Adjustment to the Soviet system was out of the question for her. In 1926, during a period of temporary loosening of travel restrictions, she obtained permission to leave the Soviet Union for a visit to the United States.

"I have to give my mother credit," she said almost reluctantly, "for saving my life. Father was apprehensive about my fate abroad, but Mother knew I had to get out. Mother was the one who got things done. She contacted relatives in Chicago and they invited me for a visit." Her family understood that her "visit" would be permanent.

For a few months she lived with her Chicago relatives, about whom she had almost nothing to say except that they were kind to her. Later, in *The Passion of Ayn Rand*, they were quoted as saying that they were fond of her and admired her but found her self-absorption more than a little dismaying. She typed on the kitchen table noisily, late into the night, oblivious to the ruinous effects on her relatives' sleep; neither did she appear to be interested in anything else about their lives. They were very nice, she once told Barbara and me, very kind, "but we had very little in common; they were not really my kind of people."

Ayn moved to Hollywood, where she met Frank and subsequently married him, which allowed her to become an American citizen. "That was why I married her," Frank joked.

Between difficult periods of unemployment she worked as a movie extra, waitress, newspaper subscription salesgirl, and studio wardrobe clerk.

She wrote short stories, outlines for movies, film scripts, none of which were remotely about the folks next door or in any sense in the spirit or style of the times, and none of which, evidently, aroused anyone's interest sufficiently to allow her career properly to begin.

When she felt ready, she began working on her first novel, which dealt with the subject of "man against the state" and whose central characters were young people "because I knew I could not yet handle the kind of fully mature adults I wrote about in *The Fountainhead*." She added that she wanted to get Soviet Russia out of her system; when *We the Living* was completed, she felt she had achieved that.

After a number of publishers rejected it, *We the Living* was published in 1936. It was attacked for its unsympathetic portrayal of Russia. This was the "Red decade" in America, when sympathy toward Soviet Russia and communism was at its height, especially among intellectuals, the literati, and show business personalities. The book did not sell well. By the time word of mouth had caught on and sales began to climb, the publisher had destroyed the plates, and the novel went out of print. She told us these facts in a dry, uninflected voice; there was no hint of self-pity.

During the same year a play Ayn had written, *Penthouse Legend*, enjoyed a moderately successful Broadway run under the title *Night of January 16th*. This helped for a while, financially, but she knew that the real mountain she had to climb — attaining success as a novelist — still lay ahead. Her ambition was to make enough money to be able to write full time, without having to support herself by other kinds of work. She described her experience in the theater as "ghastly," chiefly because of endless fights with a producer who was trying to change her material.

When she wrote her novelette *Anthem*, she was unable to obtain a publisher in this country; the book was published in Great Britain. Nearly ten years went by before *Anthem* was published in this country in 1946, when Leonard Read discovered it.

"To understand how I felt," Ayn remarked, "you have to know what kind of books *were* being published in the thirties, and hailed as serious literature."

She spoke of the continuing financial difficulties and intellectual isolation through the years of writing *The Fountainhead*. After being rejected by twelve publishers as "noncommercial" and "too intellectual," *The Fountainhead* was published in 1943, when Ayn was thirty-eight years old. The novel achieved spectacular success and brought her worldwide fame. Nearly half a century after its original publication, it continues to sell more than one hundred thousand copies a year.

Ayn often declared that it was Frank who sustained her through her struggle. "No matter how desperate I was feeling, he would smile and say, 'Nothing that a little writing won't cure.' There was one night when I really wanted to give up, I felt nothing for the world but paralyzing loathing, and it was Frank who pulled me through. I had never seen the sense of dedicating a book to a particular person; I always felt that books were dedicated, in effect, to whatever readers were worthy of them. But that night I decided that *The Fountainhead* would be dedicated to Frank."

Frank (Charles Francis) was born on September 22, 1897 — he was eight years older than Ayn — in Lorain, a small steel town in Ohio. His father was a steelworker, a passive, unambitious man — warm, gentle, and kind, according to Frank — for whom Frank conveyed quietly restrained love. It was obvious that his mother had been the central power in their family, and what Frank expressed, when Ayn prompted him to talk to us about his childhood, was adoration. We gathered that she had been aristocratic in appearance and bearing, ambitious for her sons, strict in their upbringing, determined that they be "gentlemen."

When his mother died, Ayn informed us, Frank was devastated; he was fifteen years old at the time. "I think the subject is still painful to him," Ayn stated. Frank did not contradict her. I wondered what to make of Ayn's remark, since Frank was now in his fifties.

Frank felt himself drawn to motion pictures ever since the first two-reelers came to Lorain. With his older brother, Nick, who would later become a newspaper reporter, he organized theatrical productions in the basement of their home. Every aspect of theater interested him: acting, directing, writing, set design. As he grew older, he gravitated specifically toward acting. I say "gravitated" because, listening to him talk about his early years, I never heard that sense of single-track purpose so evident in Ayn. Unlike her, Frank never saw himself as a person with a destiny. In the telling of his life his words lacked force. And in the living of his life, I could not help but wonder if the man also lacked force.

As he grew older he held many odd jobs on the way to New York City, where he hoped to find work as an actor. He obtained work from time to time as an extra, and did several bit parts. Eventually he found his way to the D. W. Griffith Studio, and got a job as an extra on *Orphans of the Storm*. He admired Griffith and hoped for more roles with him, but they failed to materialize. In 1925, when Frank was twenty-eight years old and still struggling on the fringes of a career, Griffith moved his studio to Hollywood, just as the other movie studios were doing. Frank followed. Not long after, he got a bit part in De Mille's *King of Kings,* and met Ayn. In the years that followed, he landed a few larger parts but never broke through.

He showed no anger or bitterness in speaking of this; it was as if it had all happened in another lifetime. He had put thoughts of acting behind him; I caught myself thinking that it was success he would have found astonishing, not defeat.

Frank is not meant to deal with people, I thought; he's meant to deal with physical nature with his peacocks, his flowers, his cyprus trees — that's why he's at peace now. And his helplessness with people is part of why Ayn loves him. "Let me be the one the world batters," I had heard her say. I remember also thinking that it was as if by some tacit understanding they had agreed that she would be the man and he the woman. She was the ambitious, aggressive one, out to conquer the world, and he was the loyal companion, the emotional support system, far more passive regarding the world.

Ayn spoke of their hardships only rarely and rather reluctantly. It was as if she did not want to grant importance to suffering. Barbara and I wished she would have told us more. To us, her struggle was inspiring. What we were given in those first months was only the roughest of sketches. Much more was still waiting to be disclosed.

On September 22, 1950, Frank turned fifty-three, and Barbara and I were invited to a candlelit dinner at the ranch to celebrate. In honor of the occasion Ayn did the cooking herself, making what was to become one of my favorite dishes, beef stroganoff; my number-one favorite was chicken kiev, also introduced to me by Ayn. "You've given me a new appreciation of Russian culture," I told her. Looking from face to face, from the table to the flickering candles to the luminous intensity of Ayn's eyes, I felt drunk with joy.

"The thing I want you to understand," Ayn said, "is that no matter how hard the battle, it can be won. You can break through. So long as a society is semifree, you have a chance. Maybe, when your turn comes, it won't be as hard for you. And if I can make it any easier, I would like that."

At such moments as this, my feeling of family was at its strongest. I felt: here is my home; here is my space; here are my roots. I was conscious of my longing for a sense of roots and I welcomed it.

Swept by gratitude I said, "We're so fortunate to have you at the very beginning. You do make everything easier. Whatever happens later, we will have no right to complain about difficulties, because you've paved the way." I felt as if I had broken free of gravity, as if I dwelt in an unobstructed universe where anything was possible, as if all obstacles could be overcome, all problems could be solved, and no pain need be taken too seriously.

A month earlier Barbara and I had begun reading the manuscript of Ayn's new novel. This was background to everything I was now experiencing.

I had entered the world of *Atlas Shrugged*.

FIVE

FOLLOWING THE PUBLICATION of *The Fountainhead*, Ayn briefly considered writing a nonfiction treatise on the morality of individualism but quickly found she had no enthusiasm for the project. Isabel Paterson, author of *The God of the Machine* and a close friend at that time, made the mistake of trying to argue Ayn into writing the book on the grounds of her duty to mankind: "Your message is so important for people." If readers didn't find enlightenment in *The Fountainhead*, Ayn wanted to know, if they did not understand its message, why should she wish to help them further? Because people *need* it, Paterson insisted. To which Ayn replied, "Oh, they do? What if I went on strike? What if *all* the creative minds of the world went on strike?" She added, as an afterthought, "That would make a good novel." When she hung up the telephone, Frank said, "It *would* make a good novel," and they stayed up all night discussing how the idea might be developed.

By morning she had decided to make "the mind on strike" her next project — "an action story, a stunt novel, no new ideas beyond what I had presented in *The Fountainhead*, just a dramatization of the importance of freedom to the creative mind" — not yet grasping the enormity of the assignment awaiting her. But her casual, throwaway remark to Isabel Paterson became the catalyst for the vision of John Galt, an inventor-philosopher who, in rebellion against the growing statism and collectivism of American society and its underlying morality of self-sacrifice, leads a strike of "the men of the mind."

During the period of her research for this project she was working six months of the year as a screenwriter for Hal Wallis Productions. She had come back to Hollywood to write the film script of *The Fountainhead*, but the project was delayed because of the war. She wrote two highly successful adaptations — *Love Letters* and *You Came*

Along — but as she became more deeply immersed in the new novel she found this division of her time increasingly intolerable and she persuaded Wallis to release her from her contract. For many years to come, far longer than she had imagined, her life would belong entirely to the book that she would regard as the fulfillment of her life's purpose.

Atlas Shrugged is most certainly a philosophical novel, expressing all of the author's key ideas in dramatic form. As Ayn herself said at one point, it has all the elements of a mystery, which keeps building as the story progresses. Initially we are presented with a series of events that appear inexplicable. We see these events chiefly through the eyes of the heroine, Dagny Taggart, Vice-President in Charge of Operation of Taggart Transcontinental, the nation's largest and most powerful railroad. The world seems to be moving toward destruction, in a manner neither Dagny nor anyone else can understand. A brilliant industrialist, Francisco d'Anconia, the first man Dagny ever loved, appears to have abandoned all purpose, as well as every character trait that Dagny had admired in him; he becomes a worthless playboy. A great composer, Richard Halley, renounces his career, after years of struggle, on the very night of his triumph. Businessmen who have been single-tracked in their devotion to their work — Midas Mulligan, Ellis Wyatt, and Ken Danagger — retire without explanation, and disappear. A pirate, Ragnar Danneskjöld, once a brilliant student of physics and philosophy, is loose on the high seas, attacking and robbing government relief ships. The world's most distinguished philosopher, Hugh Akston, once Francisco and Ragnar's teacher, leaves his university position to work as a cook in a diner. The remnant of a new type of motor that could have revolutionized the economy is abandoned on a scrap heap in the ruins of a factory. And in the growing darkness of a crumbling civilization, in moments of hopelessness, bewilderment, and despair, people are crying, "Who is John Galt?" — without knowing what the question means or where it came from.

Ayn had told me the first night we met that John Galt, the inventor of the motor and the man who set all these events in motion, would not appear until the last third of the book. Yet his presence is felt from the beginning, so that ultimately he dominates the entire book. The question "Who is John Galt?" — asked by a nameless bum — opens the novel. We quickly grasp the emotional meaning of this slang expression: it is a cry of despair and a plea for help. It reflects the ominousness that permeates the atmosphere, the sense of impending doom.

At first Ayn said she would allow us to see only Chapter One, "just to give you a sense of the novel." Then, because our excitement and enthusiasm were so high, she agreed to show us Chapter Two the following week. Then, the week after that, she showed us Chapter Three. Then all pretense was dropped, and we read all that she had written thus far, which was a little more than half the book.

No one had seen any of it, she told us, except Frank and Archie Ogden, her editor on *The Fountainhead* at Bobbs-Merrill, who had read some of the book during a visit from New York. "How can I resist two readers who react as you do?" Ayn asked happily. She remarked that after working on the book for five years, essentially in isolation, she enjoyed being able to expand the world of her writing to include the two of us. I felt privileged, honored, ecstatic.

Although I admired the literary style of *The Fountainhead,* I gathered within a few pages of the new novel that Ayn was now writing at a much higher level of mastery and control. Thus, for example, when we are introduced in the first chapter to a New York City that is strangely unlike the New York City of the present, and the mood must prepare us for what is happening to the world, I read:

> The clouds and the shafts of skyscrapers against them were turning brown, like an old painting in oil, the color of a fading masterpiece. Long streaks of grime ran from under the pinnacles down the slender, soot-eaten walls. High on the side of a tower there was a crack in the shape of a motionless lightning, the length of ten stories. A jagged object cut the sky above the roofs; it was half a spire, still holding the glow of the sunset; the gold leaf had long since peeled off the other half. The glow was red and still, like the reflection of a fire: not an active fire, but a dying one which it is too late to stop.

I lifted my head and looked at Ayn, feeling as if I literally had been hit by these words — "like an old painting in oil, the color of a fading masterpiece" and "not an active fire, but a dying one which it is too late to stop" — feeling myself quietly, irresistibly carried into the atmosphere of a collapsing civilization that precedes the birth of a new one — and wanting the expression on my face to disclose to Ayn the nature of her effect on me and knowing that she saw it, that she understood. I went on reading and there was no reality but this room and these pages.

Dagny Taggart, an engineer-industrialist, is the first fully realized portrait of Ayn's concept of the ideal woman. Dominique clearly was not; she was torn by paralyzing inner conflicts. Kira dies at the end of *We the Living,* before she achieves full adulthood. Dagny, "the woman who runs a railroad," passionate, creative, a hero-worshiper of exactingly high standards, was Ayn's personal ideal.

Dagny, Ayn once said, is Kira if she had grown up in America: self-confident, independent, ambitious, action-oriented, highly intelligent and energetic, and totally feminine, totally at peace with herself as a woman.

Here is Ayn's description of Dagny, on the day that Hank Rearden falls in love with her:

> He saw a girl standing on top of a pile of machinery on a flatcar. She was looking off at the ravine, her head lifted, strands of disordered hair stirring in the wind. Her plain gray suit was like a thin coating of metal over a slender body against the spread of sun-flooded space and sky. Her posture had the lightness and unself-conscious precision of an arrogantly pure self-confidence. She was watching the work, her glance intent and purposeful, the glance of competence enjoying its own function. She looked as if this were her place, her moment and her world, she looked as if enjoyment were her natural state, her face was the living form of an active, living intelligence, a young girl's face with a woman's mouth, she seemed unaware of her body except as of a taut instrument ready to serve her purpose in any manner she wished.

This was one of my favorite scenes in the novel, one that spoke to me at the most intimate level. It addressed my deepest longings.

"Dagny is a man-worshiper," Ayn remarked, "as any heroine of mine would have to be. For Dagny, Dominique, and Kira, man is the ultimate, just as he is for me — and I don't have to tell you how important my work is to me or how important Dagny's work is to her."

On another occasion Ayn stated, "Dagny is myself, with any possible flaws eliminated. She is myself without my tiredness, without my chronic, slightly antimaterial feeling, without that which I consider the ivory tower element in me, or the theoretician versus the man of action." I thought it typical that she did not say *woman* of action. I also thought it typical that she spoke of tiredness as a flaw. "Dagny is myself without a moment of exhaustion."

Ayn would make statements of this kind quite often and I was always surprised in that, as a total human being, I thought her Dagny's superior. Dagny was beautiful; Ayn was not. But Ayn was a genius, a cosmic force so powerful that thoughts of physical beauty rarely entered my mind in regard to her. The only exception were those infrequent moments when I thought how Russian-Jewish she looked; she could have been a family relative, a cousin, say, of my parents; but this was a thought I quickly dismissed because it did not fit my vision of her. No, she did not have Dagny's appearance, nor Dagny's ease with the material world, nor Dagny's tireless energy — although I never thought of Ayn's energy as less than awesome — but she was Dagny's creator, she was the source from which Dagny and Francisco and Rearden and all the characters flowed, and in my eyes that placed her above them all.

When I attempted to convey this perspective to her, she became strangely modest, almost humble, as if she did not *want* to think herself superior to her own characters because as long as she could look up to them she felt relief from her aloneness. She said, "A man, conceivably, could adjust to the knowledge that he was at a higher level than those around him, although no rational man could possibly enjoy that perspective; but to a woman it would be unbearable."

Ayn did have two striking physical attributes: dark, enormous eyes, alive with consciousness and passion, and beautiful legs, in scale with her height, which was about five two or three. She was very proud of both these features, but apart from that she did not like her appearance. Dagny was the incarnation of Ayn's physical ideal and frustrated yearnings: tall, slender, with long legs and a sculptured face. "I see Dagny more or less as Katharine Hepburn looked in her thirties," Ayn told me.

To see a woman in heroic terms seemed very natural to me — I had never been impressed by conventional notions of femininity like passivity or weakness — and Dagny did strike me as an exciting projection of woman at her highest possibility, in effect as a kind of goddess of the industrial revolution, a supremely American kind of woman.

Just as the characters in the *The Fountainhead* were completely real to me and were the true companions of my adolescence, so the characters in the new novel instantly became important figures in my life, to be discussed as one would discuss intimate friends. Barbara, Ayn, and Frank spoke of them in the same way. Our "family" now consisted not only of Ayn, Frank, Barbara, and myself, but also of Dagny Taggart, Francisco d'Anconia, Hank Rearden, John Galt, and the others. When Barbara and I would meet for lunch or dinner or go for an ocean drive, or, on rare occasions, go to a nightclub, we talked about Ayn's characters as people we would be getting together with on Saturday night.

Throughout most of the novel, until Galt entered the story, I could not decide whether Francisco d'Anconia or Hank Rearden was my favorite character. I kept switching back and forth, as did Barbara. "Rearden is definitely my favorite," Barbara would laugh, voicing my own reaction, "until Francisco enters the story. Then Francisco is my favorite — until the next scene with Rearden." But certainly Francisco, Galt's closest friend, is the most colorful figure Ayn ever created.

A brilliant intellect, a financial and productive genius, he is a man whose personal theme is pure gaiety and an unclouded capacity for the enjoyment of life. He is the first person to join Galt in the strike — and he assumes the persona of an irresponsible woman-chaser, indifferent to achievement and to d'Anconia Copper, so that the world will not know that he is deliberately and systematically destroying his fortune and all his industrial properties.

"In a sense," Ayn remarked, "I created Francisco in the tradition of the Scarlet Pimpernel — or Zorro." Part of what she meant by the "stunt" aspect of *Atlas,* which delighted her so much, was just this adaptation of elements from popular literature, even from Saturday afternoon serials, recast in high intellectual and literary form.

Ayn remarked, "Francisco is the philosophical expression — the concretization in a human character — of what I heard in the operetta music I fell in love with in my childhood. Francisco symbolizes the enjoyment of life on earth." She went on to say that the drama of his character is that he experiences the most terrible losses — he loses Dagny and he destroys d'Anconia Copper — as the cost of fighting his battle and masquerading as his exact opposite, and yet his sense of life remains untouched by tragedy. "I suppose Francisco is about as un-Russian as you can get," I remarked. "Exactly," Ayn said, beaming. For me personally, Francisco was an inspiration, a role model, a source of spiritual fuel.

When Ayn told me that of all her characters Francisco was the one I psychologically resembled the most, I felt both flattered and uncomfortable: flattered because of how much I admired Francisco, uncomfortable because I felt I had a long road to travel before I could hope to equal that ideal. When I voiced my uneasiness to Ayn, she answered, "Yes, but you have a lightness in you that's like him." In later years I wondered whether Ayn helped or harmed me with such compliments.

In the character of Hank Rearden, the leading industrialist in the novel and the highest representative of the kind of person Galt and Francisco wish to avenge and liberate, Ayn created a hero different from her other heroes in that he struggles with inner conflicts. Other Ayn Rand heroes all appear to have sprung out of the brow of Jupiter, fully grown and formed. "What I like about Rearden as a character," said Barbara, "is that he is *not* perfect. He makes terrible mistakes. You see him anguished, bewildered, torn, divided against himself — trying to understand what is right. He's a human being." Out of a misguided sense of duty and honor, Rearden chooses to remain married to a woman he does not love or respect. Out of a failure to understand his own sexuality as an expression of his mind, spirit and values, believing instead that it represents the dark side of his nature, he condemns himself for his passion for Dagny, who is the first and only woman he has ever loved. Out of naiveté and mistaken generosity, he remains blindly tolerant of persons who are plotting his destruction. His personal integrity, sometimes at the cost of his own agony, is absolute. "Rearden is meant to be the American businessman at his best," Ayn said, "self-made, inventive, resourceful, unself-pitying — and much too innocent for his own good."

The plot developments in the first two-thirds of the novel are integrated around the relationship of Dagny and Rearden. We see through their actions the kind of intelligence, courage, and integrity which underlies industrial innovation and achievement; we see the heroism of that achievement as well as its spiritual foundations; we see their impossible battle against power-hungry bureaucrats and envious, fascist-style business rivals who seek to defeat them (or harness them) by means of government decrees and regulations; we see, one by one, the brains of the country quitting and disappearing, industrialists, engineers, scientists, artists, philosophers, persons who have one attribute in common: ability. The gates of factories are closing, conveyer belts are stopping, roads are growing empty, buildings are crumbling, weeds are crawling over the abandoned ruins of great industries. Dagny and Rearden fight to preserve a world that no longer exists, too much in love with their work and possessing too much strength and endurance to accept the perspective that Francisco is slowly disclosing to them, unready and unwilling to "shrug" and go on strike.

Rearden was Ayn's most detailed study of masculine psychology, and I marveled at her insight, especially about sexual issues — not so much Rearden's sexual conflicts as the healthy and dominant side of his passion. "How do you know all that?" I once asked her, and she answered, "It's very simple. I know what I want as a woman, and I believe that a woman's desires and a man's are complementary — it's a rational universe — so I created Rearden and my other heroes out of what I want to feel, see, and experience as a woman." She added, "You're mistaken if you think that every man would respond to Rearden's psychology as you do."

Again she began to pay me the kind of compliments that made me uncomfortable, not because I lacked self-confidence, but because I felt that comparisons to her heroes had to be earned and that this was not possible for a young man of twenty; or at any rate, that I had not yet provided an objective demonstration, whatever my future possibilities.

The conversation about Rearden, like most of our conversations, took place in the presence of Barbara and Frank. If there was a subtext to the discussion that had to do with building bridges of sexual understanding between Ayn and me, none of us openly perceived it.

In retrospect it strikes me as obvious that through discussions of her novel I was disclosing more and more intimate details of my own emotions to Ayn and at the same revealing my understanding of her psychology — while Ayn was doing the equivalent with me. Those discussions continued the courtship we had begun the first night we met, in a way that was safe, legitimate, invisible even to ourselves.

In the fall of 1950, when we were reading the novel as Ayn was writing it, Galt had not yet appeared in the story. Early in our reading I spotted his unidentified presence, to Ayn's astonishment and delight. The scene involves one of the lesser characters. Eddie Willers is Dagny's childhood friend and personal assistant. He is meant to represent the best of the average man, honest, conscientious, hardworking, bewildered by the irrationality of the world around him. Eddie, the "feudal serf of Taggart Transcontinental," a title he adopts proudly when it is flung at him as an insult, often takes his meals in the employees' cafeteria where he has acquired the habit of sitting with a nameless worker who seems to share Eddie's intense interest in the railroad. We never hear this worker speak; he is merely a silent presence with whom Eddie thinks aloud and shares his concerns. In their first scene together, I felt an odd chill run through me when I read these lines:

> Yes, we have Diesels on order, at the United Locomotive Works, but we've waited for them for two years. I don't know whether we'll ever get them or not. . . . God, do we need them! Motive power — you can't imagine how important that is. That's the heart of everything. . . . What are you smiling at? . . . Well, as I was saying, it's bad.

I stopped, read these lines again, then looked up at Ayn and announced, "The worker Eddie is talking to is John Galt."

Ayn almost screamed with excitement: "*How did you know?*"

I grinned. "I know you," I answered. "I know the way your mind works. It was the juxtaposition of Eddie's statement about the importance of motive power with his question to the worker, 'What are you smiling at?' "

"My God!" Ayn exclaimed. "You really do know me! No one is intended to guess this soon in the book. Galt works at Taggart Transcontinental — that's one of the ways he keeps track of what's happening in the economy and also how he acquires information about Dagny. At this point the reader is intended to think the worker is just a literary device to facilitate exposition, not an integral part of the plot."

"You wouldn't use a literary device just for that purpose. It would be too ordinary, too unimaginative."

"You understand that too?"

It was such moments, multiplied many times by similar incidents, that tightened the bonds between us.

Bonds were also tightening between Barbara and me. "There's no one else I can talk to as I talk to you," she said many times. "That never changes."

It seemed at moments as if she were absorbing some of Ayn's perspective, from the way she sometimes looked at me, a special glance of appreciation. Was it a signal to Ayn? *See? — I'm your kind of person — I share your values."* I made no attempt to conceal my desire for a renewal of our affair. Occasionally we would embrace with brief but awkwardly feverish intimacy, stopping short of sexual intercourse. "Not yet," Barbara insisted. Not *yet?* Did that mean — eventually? I did not know what Barbara was thinking or feeling, but something was changing. Whatever her other relationships were giving her, she did not seem happy about them. She said that these other relationships were not affairs; she stressed that. I waited.

Neither of us especially liked Los Angeles. I found the place too vacationlike, too lacking in energy. It was not, in my eyes, a "serious" city. I wanted to live in New York. I had not yet visited there — Barbara had — but Ayn's writings had made it the focus of my dreams. Barbara had fallen in love with New York from reading Thomas Wolfe. In my mind moving there became associated with a final step into adulthood, as if New York were the "real" world.

Ayn herself spoke of longing to move back to the East. She had lived in California since her return to Hollywood in 1943, when the film production of *The Fountainhead* was delayed. Then, settled in at the ranch, she did not want to interrupt the writing of her new novel with another move. She would return to New York, she said, the minute the novel was completed. "New York is the *only* city," she told us.

I wondered if Frank would miss the ranch. I watched his face while Ayn was speaking; it revealed nothing. Frank too hated the West Coast, Ayn assured me. "Frank is as eager to return to New York as I am." He listened but did not comment.

One day Ayn took Barbara and me into her study to show us some of the notes she had made in preparation for writing her novels. I was very excited at the prospect of such intellectual intimacy. Ayn's notes on *The Fountainhead* revealed a portrait of Roark which struck me as highly spiritual. I had not yet become acquainted with Zen Buddhism and so did not think how Zen-like this portrait was.

I wondered if I would ever attain the kind of serenity Ayn was describing. But right now that did not seem important; not when it was possible to feel this alive, not when I was standing in Ayn Rand's study being given a guided tour of her writer's mind.

I was reading, in her sharp, angular, European handwriting, some of her notes for the new novel. She believed her most important task, as a novelist, was the development of an all-encompassing "rational morality." I remarked that by the time she had written this she must have gone beyond her original notion of simply writing an action novel to dramatize the importance of political and economic freedom to the creative mind. She agreed and said that she had seen that in order to tell the story properly she was obliged to work out her moral philosophy in comprehensive detail on the one hand, and on the other, to create a plot-structure that would properly dramatize it.

In a novel, she said, nothing is more important than the plot, and in a philosophical novel nothing is more important than the way ideas and actions are integrated. "I despise novels like Thomas Mann's *The Magic Mountain*, in which characters merely sit around and philosophize about life. And that's why I admire Dostoevsky so much, in spite of his mysticism and his malevolence: he's a master of integrating philosophy, psychology, and action. There's no one better at it. Read *The Possessed*; it's a masterpiece. If you want to write philosophical novels, your events have to really dramatize and illustrate your ideas — integration is everything — just as a rational human being is integrated, just as mind and body, theory and practice, need to be integrated in a proper existence."

I had not yet identified the fact that one of the characteristics of nineteenth-century Russian novelists was that they tended to create characters on the basis of an individual's ideas — in contrast, for instance, with English novelists, who tended to characterize on the basis of social class considerations. And so I did not yet recognize how typically Russian Ayn was in this aspect of her literary approach. She told me explicitly that she created characters out of philosophical abstractions, and neither of us was aware of the psychological limitations this imposed. But I was aware of her animus against treating her heroes from a developmental perspective when I read her notes for the character of John Galt:

No progression here. . . . He is what he is from the beginning — integrated . . . and perfect. No change in him, because *he has no intellectual contradictions and, therefore, no inner conflict.* . . . His important qualities (to bring out): *Joy in living* — the peculiar, deeply natural, serene, all-pervading joy in living which he alone possesses so completely in the story (the other strikers have it in lesser degree, almost as reflections of that which, in him, is the source); all-pervading in the sense that it underlies all his actions and emotions, it is an intrinsic, inseparable part of his nature . . . it is present *even when* he suffers . . . [I want to show] the worship of joy as against the worship of suffering, [and his] magnificent innocence — the untroubled purity — a pride which is serene, not aggressive — "the first man of ability who refused to feel guilty."

Growing up, I was bewildered by the unhappiness of most people; it had never been acceptable to me or logical that such could be the nature of life. Ayn's emphasis on joy had powerful meaning for me. I stood at her desk, looking down at these notes, while she stood on one side of me, Barbara on the other. I was at the center of a universe from which pain had entirely disappeared.

"Tolstoy," Ayn remarked during one of our many discussions about literature, "said that a good writer, after watching a street fight, should be able to describe a military battle. I've had to do a lot of research for this novel but perhaps not as much as you might think. It's an issue of grasping the essence, of observing the street fight. Of course, Tolstoy is not my kind of writer, although I can appreciate his skill. He's too much of a naturalist, or a 'realist.' "

"I wouldn't exactly call Dostoevsky a romantic," I commented. By now I had read most of his novels. "Unless you want to invent a special category, a 'negative romanticist,' who focuses on what might be and *ought not* to be."

"True. He writes with magnificent contempt and indignation about human irrationality. You would never call him a naturalist; he has too passionate a moral vision, even if it's one we wouldn't agree with."

There was no theme to the discussion, we were merely drifting, almost associationally, Ayn stretched out at one end of the enormous sofa and I stretched out at the other. Barbara was sitting opposite, her eyes glowing, like a child in a roomful of toys, and I imagined that Winnipeg felt very far away to her. Coffee and pastry, served as usual by Frank, rested on the low table in front of the sofa.

I was content to listen silently while Barbara began voicing her impressions of a novel of Dostoevsky she had recently read. "The sheer intelligence of the man, never mind his neuroses, the sheer intelligence of his observations of people, of human psychology . . . and then his unexpected humor, his irony . . . and the way he takes you inside the mind of irrationalism, makes you feel it, gives you that perspective . . . it's wonderfully lucid and insane all at once." My glance swung between the two women, as if contemplating a scene that I had staged.

Occasionally Frank and I would smile at each other, in unspoken understanding.

Ayn asked if we had ever read Henryk Sienkiewicz's novel *Quo Vadis?* We hadn't. She began to extol its virtues, describing it as perhaps the finest historical novel ever written — "from the point of view of the integration of plot and theme. It deals with the moral bankruptcy of the declining years of the Roman Empire, when Christianity is first emerging. The recreation of the period, the development of the plot, the way all the elements are tied together, are magnificent. Of course Petronius, 'the arbiter of elegance,' is my favorite character."

We talked about Victor Hugo, the novelist she admired above all others, whom she had discovered as a young girl in Russia. "It was the grandeur of his vision that inspired me." She was captivated by his larger-than-life characters, the extraordinary inventiveness and imaginativeness of his plots, his superlative sense of drama. The first Hugo novel she read was *L'Homme qui rit,* followed by *Les Misérables,* then everything of his she could find. She was fascinated with his sense of life — the vision of human existence as supremely important and the vision of man as a hero. "Even his villains are heroic. Hugo couldn't create a true villain without stature. Which I think says something about his own psychology. He was a giant."

She went on to talk about her favorite play, Rostand's *Cyrano de Bergerac,* again stressing the plot-structure, the dramatic inventiveness, the beauty of the writing. "*That* is theater," she said, "which is why I can't stand to look at the junk they put on today. It's one world or the other."

When she told us that she had cried the first time she read *Cyrano,* I wondered if her dislike of her own appearance caused her to identify with the hero. I shared her judgment of the play's greatness.

We eagerly consumed whatever books or plays she recommended and enjoyed them so thoroughly that if it had occurred to us that we were in any sense being tested for the purity of our premises, we would have dismissed the thought as irrelevant. What did we care? Were we not all becoming closer and closer soul mates?

Evenings such as these were fairly typical. But occasionally a note of tension would enter our discussions, when it seemed to Ayn that Barbara or I was being seduced or deluded by "alien values." In the case of Barbara, a focus of Ayn's concern was Barbara's enjoyment of Thomas Wolfe, whose novels Ayn thought without literary value.

First Ayn elicited Barbara's agreement that the essential elements of a novel were plot, theme, characterization, and style. She did this in the flat, unrevealing manner of a district attorney leading a witness to an inexorable conclusion. Then she began reading from *Look Homeward, Angel,* analyzing Wolfe's defects in virtually every key area of fiction. "It's all adjectives and overblown emotion," Ayn pronounced.

I felt torn. On the one hand, I agreed with Ayn: she had helped me to articulate many of my own misgivings about Wolfe; literary inadequacies apart, I found him intellectually and spiritually empty. On the other hand, beneath Barbara's quietly gentle exterior I knew she was suffering and that something was being dimmed within her.

To me Ayn said, "I give Barbara enormous credit because of how much reason means to her. But her sense of life is very malevolent, very unhappy." She mentioned, as evidence, Barbara's enthusiasm for *Tristan and Isolde.* "She won't be at her best until she frees herself of that sense of tragedy."

I had a similar experience with Ayn regarding *Jean-Christophe,* but it was a good deal milder: first, because I was already disenchanted with Rolland; and second, because Ayn's assault was more philosophical than literary and I experienced no conflict in agreeing with her; and finally, because she was more easygoing about *Jean-Christophe* and did not press with the quiet, deadly ferocity she had brought to the novels of Thomas Wolfe. Still, I felt pushed along a particular path faster than I would have moved at my own speed. I did have my moments of resentment at the pressure she could generate to win my agreement. But, like Barbara, I told myself that Ayn was in the right. Such moments seemed a small price to pay.

There was a world beyond the ranch and I was not uninterested in it; but it did not inspire admiration in me. I entered it when I had to, then quickly returned to the world I cared about most.

In 1950 Great Britain recognized Communist China. The Soviet Union and Communist China signed a thirty-year pact. Chiang Kai-shek resumed the presidency of Nationalist China. Communist China's forces occupied Tibet, Tibet appealed to the United Nations, and China rejected the UN appeal for a cease-fire. Senator Joseph McCarthy advised President Truman that the State Department was riddled with communists and communist sympathizers. Alger Hiss, a former U.S. State Department official, was sentenced for perjury. And on the campus of UCLA, through the fall of 1950 into the winter and spring of 1951, there was increasing talk of "red-baiting," hysteria about communism, and the persecution of professors whose politics were liberal or left-wing.

This last puzzled me a good deal because in my classes on government, economics, political philosophy, ethics, or indeed on any other subject, I heard much abuse of capitalism, the free market, the American political system, and American culture in general.

The professor who had mocked me for being "prejudiced against dictatorships" made continuing sarcastic comments about business, businessmen, and anyone misguided enough to speak in their defense. An economics professor was so openly contemptuous of anyone who did not share the premises of Keynesianism that I was compelled to stand up one day in class and ask him point-blank, "Is it possible for a student who believes in laissez-faire to pass your course?" A professor of art history spoke glowingly of the "idealism" of Soviet Russia, as contrasted with the "materialism" of America. A psychology professor blithely announced that anyone who was not a socialist was suffering, intellectually and morally, from arrested development. Students who had never read a word of Karl Marx were spouting Marxist platitudes. And in classrooms, in the university cafeteria, on campus lawns, Barbara and I were encountering every kind of vituperation, every kind of hostility, from students who gathered that we thought well of capitalism. We could only look at each other in astonishment when we heard a professor announce, preposterously, "No one to the left of the Republican Party is free to speak his mind in America any longer."

We did encounter conservatives on campus and we liked them, as a group, no better than the liberals. We shuddered when we heard the expression "atheistic communism," as if the worst thing to be said about communists was that they did not believe in God. "We're atheists," we announced cheerfully, and laughed at the question, "Then why aren't you communists?" Atheism, we would say, is not grounds to condemn communism, and "loyalty to the faith of our fathers" is not grounds to champion capitalism.

Our dominant impression of liberals was of sanctimonious self-righteousness, fanatical hostility to anyone who did not agree with them, ignorance of economics — and lack of respect for a rational argument. Our dominant impression of conservatives was of moral weakness and confusion, fear of intellectuals, fanatical hostility to anyone who did not agree with them — and lack of respect for a rational argument. Sometimes we met individuals from one camp or the other who seemed more reasonable but sooner or later most of these relationships broke down over the "extremism" of our own position. If they shared our opposition to mysticism and supernaturalism, they turned out to be logical positivists or pragmatists, certain that no one could be certain of anything. If they agreed with us about the power of reason, they were appalled by our advocacy of enlightened selfishness, convinced that we were hell-bent on riding over widows and orphans. If they professed agreement with our ethics of rational self-interest, the relationship broke down over our advocacy of laissez-faire: "What? You don't believe in minimum wage laws? Or protective tariffs? Or military conscription? *You don't even believe that the telephone company should be a legally enforced monopoly?*" The exceptions, and they did exist in both the conservative and liberal camps, were those we succeeded in persuading entirely to our viewpoint.

"Boy, is our work cut out for us," Barbara said gleefully.

I was becoming a crusader and I loved it. I was the Lone Ranger riding the plains of UCLA, six-guns blasting at the forces of intellectual savagery.

Barbara, too, enjoyed this battle. "Give me a barricade!" she shouted. "I'm at home on a barricade!" It seemed to me that in such moments her eyes said we were indeed meant to be together, comrades-in-arms, fighting for the glory of man, for the supremacy of reason, and the sanctity of an individual life.

As time went by we delighted more and more in mastering the intellectual arguments and communication skills that made it possible to turn around someone who began as an adversary and ended as a friend. One such person was a young businessman named Harry Kalberman who, some years later in New York, married my sister Elayne.

Through Ayn I had discovered the works of Ludwig von Mises, one of the founders of the Austrian school of economics, a brilliant scholar, a lucid thinker, an intransigent defender of capitalism. Highly esteemed in Europe, he was at this time still relatively unknown in America. I began studying his books, such as *Socialism* and the recently published *Human Action,* with great enthusiasm. I also read *The Road to Serfdom* by Friedrich von Hayek, Von Mises's student, who would later be awarded a Nobel Prize for his work in economics. I was astonished to learn how thoroughly the case for socialism had been refuted — and how ignorant just about everyone on campus seemed to be of that fact.

"Are you familiar," I would say to people, "with Ludwig von Mises's proof that in a pure socialist society, without any outside markets to refer to, *economic calculation is impossible?* They did not know who Von Mises was; but they could recite, as it if were the last word in profundity, whatever they had read most recently in the pages of *The Nation* or *The New Republic.*

"Of course part of the problem you're fighting is the current intellectual fashion," Ayn said to me, "but the problem goes deeper than that. What you're really fighting, darling, is a thousands-of-years-old tradition that equates morality with self-sacrifice. That means you're

fighting altruism. According to altruism, man has no right to exist for
his own sake, and his prime duty is to place others above self, sacrificing his interests for someone's idea of 'the common good.' Altruism
and capitalism are incompatible. Capitalism rests on the recognition
of individual rights. If man has no rights, if his life belongs to others,
if self-interest and the profit motive are evil, then capitalism is evil,
never mind how productive it is — and communism is noble, never
mind how much blood it spills. The battle for capitalism can't be won
by proving its practicality; that's been done. What the world needs —
and what capitalism deserves — is a moral defense."

"It needs your new book," I answered.

"Yes, I think so."

"When I tell people I'm opposed to altruism, they go crazy. They
think it means I'm opposed to kindness, charity, benevolence, and respect for the rights of others — and yet altruism means none of those
things — and what people miss is what it actually does mean. Just the
same, at a deeper level they accept its premise: self-sacrifice to others
as the highest good."

"Which is precisely the idea Auguste Comte intended when he
coined the term: altruism means *others above self*. Comte was a total
collectivist, a total advocate of dictatorship. I wonder what those people would think if someone told them that imprinted on Nazi coins
was the slogan, 'The common good above the individual good.' No
one spoke more passionately than Hitler about the nobility of the individual sacrificing himself for the tribe — only he called it the 'race.'
That's why the basic issue is an individual's right to his own life. That's
where the battle has to be fought."

In the spring of 1951 Barbara took a course in political philosophy
from a Dr. Hans Meyerhoff, a Platonist and a socialist. We were Ar-
istotelians, in that basic sense in which everyone is said to be either a
Platonist or an Aristotelian; Aristotle was the one and only philosopher to whom Ayn acknowledged an intellectual debt. Barbara found
Meyerhoff intelligent, stimulating, even charismatic, and was intrigued when he exhibited interest in Ayn Rand. When Barbara let it
be known that she and Ayn were friendly, Meyerhoff made it plain
that he would love to be invited to meet her.

"Why not?" Ayn had chuckled. "Bring him along, if you think he's
intelligent. We'll see what kind of mind he has."

It was clear that Dr. Meyerhoff considered himself a brilliant de-
bater and expected to dazzle us all. That was not what happened. Riding home with us many hours later, he seemed dazed, like a man who
could not grasp what had taken place. "She's amazing," he kept mut-

tering, as if talking to himself. "She's incredible. She has an answer for everything. She knows Hegel and Marx, she knows history, and she knows logic. She's like no defender of capitalism I ever met. She's blown holes in almost every belief I ever held." At the end of the evening Ayn had said to him, smilingly, "Would you like to come back and continue this?" And he had answered with apparent sincerity, "I would love to, Miss Rand. This has been an outstanding intellectual experience. You've given me a great deal to think about." Watching his face as we drove home together, I doubted it. I saw anger in his eyes, perhaps because he had been defeated in front of students. I saw something hard and cold waiting for a chance to explode.

The chance came shortly thereafter. A prominent Harvard scholar committed suicide, and though his note declared that his motive was despair over the state of the world, there were stories that his affiliation with the Communist party was in danger of being publicly exposed and that he found the pressure unbearable. An editorial in the UCLA *Bruin* spoke compassionately of this scholar and excoriated the anticommunist atmosphere that had possibly caused his death. I immediately responded by writing an answer, asking why there should be sympathy for an apologist for communism but none for communism's victims. Had he not helped create that very state of the world he decried? Why should he not bear responsibility for the results of his own teachings? Barbara asked to sign the letter as co-author. What we did not know was that this man was an idol of Hans Meyerhoff. Within a few days of the publication of our letter, Meyerhoff broke a well-established precedent — professors did not interfere in student debates — and wrote a blistering, highly personal attack on us. Students who did not share our convictions were shocked by the tone of his letter and told us so. In his political philosophy class he began making snidely abusive remarks, unsupported by any pertinent context, about Ayn Rand and anyone who shared her ideas.

One of the most important tenets of Ayn's philosophy, the foundation of her political theory, was that no individual and no group, including the government, has the moral right to *initiate* physical force against anyone who has not resorted to its use; force, she held, may be used only in self-defense, only in retaliation; this is the principle that protects individual rights, against the state and against other human beings. In class this day Meyerhoff was decrying the "antisocial" and "unprogressive" nature of this viewpoint, throwing little asides, as digs, at Barbara. After a while, no longer able to remain silent, Barbara responded. "By what right?" she demanded of Meyerhoff. "By what right do you seek to impose on others, by physical coercion, your vision of the good?"

I was auditing the class with her that particular day, intrigued by the drama of their conflict, and I sat beside her, delighting in the sound of trumpets. I loved confrontations of this kind and was good-naturedly envious that this one had to be all Barbara's.

"My God," Meyerhoff began impatiently, "ever since Plato it's been understood that —" Her voice rising, Barbara responded, "Plato was an advocate of dictatorship! Do you deny that?" Meyerhoff answered, not by talking about Plato or about ideas, but by ridiculing Barbara's naiveté, her narrow-mindedness, her unmodern approach to life, her strange choice of friends.

She went to Meyerhoff's office to protest his behavior. His response was to observe that if she planned to take a postgraduate degree in philosophy — this was her final undergraduate year — she would be well advised to seek out some other university.

"I cannot see myself approving any thesis you might choose to write," he told her with matter-of-fact candor. She had always been an A student and prior to Meyerhoff's meeting with Ayn she had received an A on her midterm in his course; but for her final grade of the semester Meyerhoff gave her a C. What astonished us was the lack of any effort to conceal his hatred.

Early in 1951, some time before this experience with Meyerhoff, I went to meet Barbara for lunch in Westwood, at a restaurant near UCLA. Barbara and I were now closer than we had been at any time since our first months in Winnipeg.

I saw her walking toward me with an odd look of determination and purposefulness. I felt my heart expanding in my chest; she seemed so desirable. I did not wonder if there was any significance to her having proposed lunch today.

She sat down, looked straight into my eyes, and said, "Will you marry me?"

I recall very clearly the first thought that entered my mind: Oh, God, she's playing Dominique.

I felt almost annoyed, as if my feelings were being toyed with, out of some incomprehensible whim. To leap from our context, with all its conflicts, to a proposal of marriage? I immediately answered, "No," then added, a little more gently, "Come on. What is this about?"

"I'm afraid," Barbara said, and I saw there were tears in her eyes. "I'm afraid of what's happening to me." I knew that she meant the other men in her life and that I represented some kind of anchor. "I know you're the person I belong with. In my heart I love you. You know that."

We talked for a long time. Part of me thought: Don't be a fool; don't wait; marry her now. But another part knew that would be short-sighted and self-destructive: if we were to be married, it had to be *real*, it had to be because Barbara loved me; not because, through me, she might "save" herself, or have a passkey to Ayn's world.

We agreed that we would commit ourselves to a relationship; we would see if we could make it work. We were too young to get married now, anyway, we said. We would resume our affair. We promised sexual exclusivity. Barbara wanted to know if I would demand that she cease seeing her male friends, with whom she was not, she assured me, sexually involved. No, I would not demand it.

There was little elation or joy in this discussion. It was earnest, intense, muted. There was only, for me, the sense of the possibility of future joy, against a background of uneasiness and agitation.

I wondered about Ayn's influence in bringing Barbara to this moment. By now we had read nearly two-thirds of the new novel and were thoroughly acquainted with her theory of sex, which she had sketched at our early meetings. We had read the incredible scene between Francisco d'Anconia and Hank Rearden, neither man knowing about the role of the other in Dagny Taggart's life. Francisco says:

> A man's sexual choice is the result and the sum of his fundamental convictions. Tell me what a man finds sexually attractive and I will tell you his entire philosophy of life. Show me the woman he sleeps with and I will tell you his valuation of himself. . . . He will always be attracted to the woman who reflects his deepest vision of himself, the woman whose surrender permits him to experience — or to fake — a sense of self-esteem. The man who is proudly certain of his own value, will want the highest type of woman he can find, the woman he admires, the strongest, the hardest to conquer — because only the possession of a heroine will give him the sense of an achievement, not the possession of a brainless slut. . . . There is no conflict between the standards of his mind and the desires of his body. . . . Love is our response to our highest value — and can be nothing else.

I found this a provocative and intoxicating idea. If it represented an oversimplification of a complex psychological issue, I was not aware of it. Nor was Barbara. She and Ayn had a number of private discussions about love, sex, and relationships. For Barbara, Ayn's theory was a trap she felt compelled to enter — in the name of reason, she would have said; in the name of self-esteem.

One night we lay in bed together after we had made love; the love-making was intense on my part, compliant on Barbara's. We were silent for a while and I did not know whether Barbara was still awake.

Dropping the discipline I usually felt compelled to maintain with her, I surrendered to a feeling of unbearable loneliness. Too often, when we were together, I felt myself fighting ghosts. Barbara would look at me with veiled eyes, mysteriously remote one moment, warmly affectionate the next, but rarely straightforward about her inner experience. "I love you," she would say, but it was not a kind of love I understood. It was not the kind of love I wanted. I stirred in the half-darkness and Barbara opened her eyes. "What's the matter?" she asked urgently, in response to whatever she saw on my face.

"Sometimes," I whispered, choking, "this whole situation is very, very hard." She did not say anything, just took my hand and pressed it. Years later she said to me, "I was paralyzed. All I could feel in that moment was guilt about my sexual psychology."

That night she did not speak of guilt; she began talking, after a while, about how upsetting it was for her to see me in pain. "I always think of you as being able to handle anything. I know this is terribly unfair, but when you look like you're suffering, I take that to mean weakness. When there are tears in your eyes, I don't know what to do, I want to run, and I know that's not right. It's ridiculous to expect you not to have feelings. But if I'm to be honest, I would have to admit I lose respect for you."

I could not speak. I did not feel hurt. I did not feel misunderstood. I felt an icy sense of withdrawal.

She's a child, I thought. She's a child. Then what are you doing with her? Get out. Get out.

I did not know what Barbara was aware of in that moment, or what she sensed from me, but she threw her arms around me and clung tightly. Feeling the warmth of her body, and the hunger of my flesh for contact — and some stubborn refusal to lose the hardest battle I had ever fought — I heard myself answering: Get out? What are you thinking of? Now — when she says she's determined to make things work? You've got to hang on — and give her time.

The thoughts I had tried to dispel had not been extinguished; they had merely been submerged, gone underground, until such time as I would be ready to hear them. By that time, we would be married.

April 9, 1951, was my twenty-first birthday, and the following Sunday Barbara and I had been invited to spend the day at the ranch. Since Ayn usually wrote seven days a week, often from early morning to well into the evening, we did not spend many full days with her. "I'm taking the day off in honor of your birthday," she announced.

When we arrived I could see that she and Frank were smiling in some special way, as if about to spring a surprise. After we were seated, they disappeared into Ayn's study and returned a moment later with their arms full of books, which they proceeded to spread out on the coffee table. It was a beautiful leather-bound set of the complete works of Ibsen, red, gray, and gold, and I was stunned into speechlessness. "Happy birthday, darling!" Ayn said brightly and kissed my cheek, and Frank stepped forward, put his hand on my shoulder, and said with surprising feeling, "Happy birthday, Nathan."

I was moved beyond my power to explain; I reacted as if I had never before received a gift from anyone. I felt lifted out of myself in gratitude and euphoria. I did not feel twenty-one; I felt five years old.

"I never knew, until I looked at these volumes," Ayn said, "that early in his career Ibsen wrote a whole series of Norwegian sagas, very romantic in style, quite unlike the later plays for which he became known. I've never read them. You'll tell me about them. Also, notice that most of the volumes contain Ibsen's notes for the plays in that volume, sometimes rough drafts of specific scenes, so one has a chance to see his mental processes at work. You'll like that."

Later the four us went for a walk and, seeing how affected I was by the gift, Ayn smiled, "What's the matter? Didn't you really believe we were friends?"

Barbara and Frank were walking ahead of us, and Ayn made a statement that was typical of her in regard to whatever might evoke an aesthetic response: "Don't they look attractive, walking together?"

A week or two earlier, Barbara and I had gone dancing; some time before that, bicycling. I thought of how glamorous she had seemed to me on the first occasion, how much like a carefree schoolgirl on the second. Now, seeing her walking with Frank, I thought how naturally she blended into this world and how complete I felt when the four of us were together.

"I never before felt I belonged anywhere," I said. "I would have said it didn't bother me, either. Now I know it must have — because of what I'm feeling right now. I don't remember ever being this happy."

"Frank likes you very much. He likes you both. That's unusual for him: he doesn't like most people. Without Frank having felt there was something special about your letter, we wouldn't have met. I would have felt, why bother? I've had too many bad experiences. But this only proves why one shouldn't make collective judgments."

Later, when Barbara was walking with Ayn, and I with Frank, I said to him, "This is really so wonderful of you both."

"You don't know what you're doing for Ayn," he answered.

"You don't know what Ayn is doing for me."

"Oh, yes, I do," Frank said, suddenly very wise and very assured. "When you're young, you can't know what you are yet, not fully, you can't know what you've got — but an older person can see it and help you to see it. Ayn gives you that. She helps you to appreciate yourself. She can see your future."

"What's my future?" I asked eagerly.

Frank chuckled and did not answer. For a few minutes we walked in silence. Then, unexpectedly, he remarked, "You and Barbara will work things out."

"Do you think so?"

"She's a good girl. And Ayn will help you."

"By all means go to New York," said Ayn. "Barbara can't possibly remain at UCLA — not after what that bastard Meyerhoff told her. And you two shouldn't be apart, not now. But God, I'll miss you both! Terribly!"

It was not an easy decision. When I thought of being in New York with Barbara, making a fresh start together, not knowing anyone there, not having any of her old boyfriends to contend with, I felt optimistic, excited, confident that the last barriers between us would dissolve. When I thought of separating from Ayn and Frank, I felt pain; more than I expressed to anyone.

Barbara was a year older than I and two years ahead in college; she had already earned her B.A., and would be working toward her M.A. in philosophy at New York University while I completed my undergraduate degree. In retrospect, it is not easy for me to recreate the context in which moving to New York — leaving Ayn — seemed an appropriate action to take. Looking back, I find my own decision astonishing; it only underscores for me how desperately I wanted my relationship with Barbara to succeed.

We all consoled one another by talking about exchanging letters, phone calls, even visits. "And, anyway," said Ayn, "the moment the novel is finished, Frank and I will move back to New York." She had now been at work on the book for six years. "It will only be a year or two; two at the most. I don't dare interrupt the work sooner. I'm coming to the chapter where John Galt enters the story!"

One day she said to me, "I'd like to have a copy of that letter you wrote to the *Bruin*, that triggered the Meyerhoff incident. It's your first published writing. I want it as a historical memento." When I brought the piece to her it was Father's Day, and when she asked me to autograph it, I wrote, laughing, "To my father — Ayn Rand." One day I would realize that I wrote more aptly than I knew.

On an afternoon near the end of June we drove to the ranch for the last time. Barbara seemed sad to leave but not as sad as I. Many years later she would acknowledge that part of her was eager to be away from this environment, away from Ayn's influence, free and on her own.

Ayn and Frank seemed so unhappy to see us go that I found it difficult to stay connected with my own feelings; I concentrated on projecting an air of calm and restrained cheerfulness, seeking to dispel any hint of tragedy.

When we embraced good-bye, all four of us had tears in our eyes. We wiped them away, grinning, trying to cheer one another up.

"It's only for a little while," said Frank, echoing Ayn. I thought of Frank having told me that the best years of his entire life were those he had spent on the ranch.

In spite of my sadness and my hesitancy about leaving, I felt the exhilaration of embarking on a new adventure: *I was going to New York* — the greatest city in the world, the center of *The Fountainhead* and of the new novel, the heartbeat of Western civilization, a place of drama and challenge and unlimited possibilities. Through Ayn's writing, and through my relationship with her, I had fallen in love with America. I felt connected to this country as I had never felt connected to the country of my birth. Ayn had a European's appreciation of the United States and a keen understanding of its historical uniqueness, and she had transmitted her vision to me. Now I was moving to the city that was, for the entire world, the symbol of America.

We drove up the long driveway to the road that would lead us through Chatsworth, back to Los Angeles. I stopped to wave good-bye one last time. We were too far away to see their faces clearly. I would not know until a long time afterward that as they waved to us tears were streaming down Ayn's face.

S I X

THE FIRST FEW MONTHS in New York turned into a nightmare. Later I would wonder why Ayn was so intent on saving the relationship, given the nature of Barbara's problems. If someone had asked me that question then, I would have answered that surely it was because Ayn knew the relationship was important to me. Only much later did a different explanation occur to me.

On leaving California, Barbara had spent a couple of weeks with me in Toronto, then went on to Winnipeg. We planned to meet later in the summer in New York. We were not yet engaged, but we were "engaged to be engaged."

I was uneasy over the separation. Our relationship was tenuous; I did not know who Barbara might meet or what former boyfriend might re-enter her life; I knew only that no foundation of confidence had yet been built between us; there had not been enough time for that. I thought it would take very little to blow apart the fragile structure we were trying to build.

We remained in constant contact by letter and by telephone. When we spoke, I heard a disquieting mixture of warmth, strain, intimacy, distance, affection, elusiveness, and anxiety. But a phone call or two later, she would be loving and euphoric, eager for our future together, and I would tell myself not to be "malevolent."

The uncomplicated happiness of my relationship with Ayn stood in sharp contrast, even though I defined the relationship as being of a very different order. With Ayn everything was simple, natural, easy. I wrote to her every three or four days, sharing my experiences in Toronto: my efforts to convert my family to our philosophy, my struggles to write a new novel, an unexpected series of encounters with Allan Blumenthal, and my concerns about Barbara.

Writing those letters gave me a sense of being connected to a living intelligence I could trust — and to a rational universe. I was not alone in the world. Barbara might be problematical but Ayn was as firm and reliable as the law of gravity.

I did not say these things to Ayn. I did not convey what she meant to me in emotional terms; her natural language was the language of philosophy, of abstract ideas, and it was easy to follow her lead, to relate intellectually, to talk around my need of her and my appreciation, but never to name it fully, never head-on — using humor, at times, as a mask for my deeper feelings. She responded in kind, totally open on the surface, and yet with volumes left unexpressed.

"It was too much," she said to me years later, at the time of our affair. "What I felt was just too much — and I mean much more than romantic love — and I had no words for it then, I who have words for everything." And I would answer, "We both hid behind philosophy, and literature, and, God help us, economics."

So I wrote about economics and my arguments with people and my often unsuccessful efforts to remain calm in political discussions — especially with my sister Florence and her husband, Hans Hirschfeld, a businessman, both of whom I was intent on converting.

Florence, now twenty-eight, and Hans, thirty-eight, initially were rather adversarial, especially about issues pertaining to political economy. Gradually, however, they began to give way. But the process of conversion would nonetheless take years. I do not think it was complete until they read *Atlas Shrugged*.

Discussing my encounters with Florence and Hans in a letter to Ayn and Frank, I wrote:

With Florence, her own intelligence is my best ally. I've got her on the immorality of initiated force. She tells me that each time she thinks about just "one last control" she'd like to hang on to, the flaw becomes obvious to her — both economically and morally. I am discovering the power in the argument against the initiation of force; it seems to bring many decent people to their senses.

Hans is approaching the end of *The Fountainhead* and is, he claims, more impressed with every page he reads. . . . He can't get over how someone from another country could have written such a fundamentally "American" novel. . . . At this point, he and Florence are dying to meet you. . . . Neither one of them is 100% with us, by any stretch of the imagination, but their hearts are very much in the right place. . . . Hans still thinks that while *he* can get along in a free society, the "little guy" can't. . . . In regard to *The Fountainhead*, he said to me: "You don't know how much I'm emotionally in sympathy with this — no matter what I say to the contrary."

Elayne and Reva, now twenty-six and twenty-five, respectively, who had no particular interest in politics, were relatively open and receptive to my ideas regarding reason, individualism, enlightened self-interest, capitalism, and romantic realism in art.

I wrote to Ayn and Frank about Reva returning from her honeymoon with her new husband, Sholey Fox, an architect, and about Reva's desire that I "educate" him, since she was ahead of him in her acceptance of Ayn's ideas. The discussions with Sholey were not always easy, and with Reva looking on, expecting me to deliver, I sometimes felt a bit stressed. Barbara took over from me, spent a good deal of time talking with him, and was successful in bringing him into our philosophical orbit. I liked him, and our encounters made me feel closer to Reva. "He really has a great many excellent qualities," I wrote, "foremost of which is total honesty and independence." What I did *not* say to Ayn was: you see? I will be your champion. I will justify your confidence in me.

It would not have occurred to me to mention in my letters that I was pleased by the fact that these intellectual discussions were a means of my connecting with my sisters and, in the case of Reva and Florence, their husbands. I would not have acknowledged this thought even to myself: what did it have to do with the great issues of life?

That one of the consequences of my friendship with Ayn was greater contact with my family seems ironic, but that was clearly the case. One day it would result in a much closer relationship with my father, who now seemed more baffled by me than ever; like my mother, he was still wondering why I had turned my back on a career in business. Eventually my father would come to understand me in a new way; it seemed to me that my sisters had already begun to. "I've always felt," I said to Ayn, "that my family sees me as a bit odd — eccentric, or erratic, or both. No doubt they still do — and yet somehow I have the sense that who and what I am is beginning, slowly, to come into focus for them." I knew that they spoke to me with a new respect.

That summer I had begun work on a novel, and I was going through agonies — writing and tearing apart, writing and tearing apart. It dealt with the world of modern sculpture, and I wrote to Ayn about all this in great detail.

In her answers to my letters, Ayn seemed to possess, at an instantly accessible conscious level, all the knowledge I longed for regarding fiction writing. She was consistently encouraging and spoke highly of my potential. Eventually I dropped the project, as I had dropped an earlier attempt, because I recognized that what I was trying to do was much too ambitious for my knowledge and experience. I was aware of my inclination to place excessively high expectations on myself. I was not aware that Ayn's sometimes extravagant praise — to say nothing of the shining example of her own genius — was encouraging me further in this direction. But she had the wisdom to say to me once, "Nathan, I could not have written *The Fountainhead* in my young twenties."

I sent Ayn and Frank one postcard, from New York City, where I went for an interview at New York University. I was seeing the city for the first time, and I thought of Ayn's description of Roark's walk through these same streets. Dreams and reality flowed into each other. The postcard contained a magnificent photograph of the skyline. My whole message read: "Good God!"

A few weeks later, in a letter dated August 19, 1951, I wrote as if trying to break a barrier: "I miss you terribly and think of you always. The one consolation to the fact that we may not see each other for a year, is that with both of us in the east, we'll have the rest of our lives together to solve the mysteries of the universe." The letter began, "Dear Ayn and Frank," but it read like a letter written solely to Ayn.

Again, in a letter dated August 21: "Ayn, I don't know whether it's love or what — but as each day goes by and I look at your picture on the mantelpiece near my typewriter, you seem immeasurably better-looking." And as an aside to Frank, I wrote, "Frank, my offer is still open to trade the picture for the real thing. I've got the best picture of Ayn framed in a leather case and placed on the mantelpiece of my study — but I could easily mail you the leather case and put Ayn on the mantelpiece. What do you say?"

I have no memory of any conscious effort to be flirtatious; I thought I was being funny.

While in Winnipeg, Barbara wrote Ayn a long letter of agonized self-analysis that distressed me when I first read it, but very quickly I gave her credit for it, taking it as a sign of her honesty and conscientiousness.

She identified herself as believing in "a kind of mysticism" — rationalizing behavior she knew to be wrong by telling herself that, in effect, there was "another reality" in which her behavior made sense, or didn't matter. She evidently felt that both her adolescent boyfriend Wilfred and Thomas Wolfe had somehow contributed to this irrationalism, that they had infected her with it; I do not know if I was ever clear on how. She said that her desire to date other men represented, in part, her desire to escape from the world of Ayn and me, in which everything was "important," and to enjoy the greater security of a more conventional life. The fact that she was "bad" in some way undercut her motivation to be "good," and this explained some of her sexual behavior. She spoke of growing feelings of anxiety, even of panic, over some of her actions — and of her firm resolve to transform herself.

Before she wrote this letter, Barbara had called to tell me about a brief infidelity with a former boyfriend in Winnipeg, over which she now seemed to be suffering intense remorse. Her apprehension and despair were so acute that I felt as if there was no room in my consciousness for the personal impact of her announcement. She said she was coming to understand herself as she never had before, would be writing Ayn a long letter about it, and would send me a copy.

"How do you feel about all this?" Ayn wanted to know when she received Barbara's letter. She had telephoned me at once, concerned.

Like screaming, a voice within answered. Instead, I replied, "Oddly hopeful. To me, her anxiety is actually a sign of moral health — her inability to live with lies. She's fighting. I think she'll win. I hope so."

If a feeling of numbness was moving through my body, if something at my center was growing colder, I had no desire to know it; not when I needed all my resources to think clearly and stay in control.

The part of me that was most adult was struggling to be "philosophical." But internally pain — and rage — were building.

During the summer I resumed my friendship with my cousin Allan Blumenthal.

He was now twenty-three years old, of medium height and slight build, with light hair and blue eyes, a bit effeminate, perhaps, in the manner of an English schoolboy — as "correct" as ever in demeanor.

His family lived a block from mine and inevitably our paths crossed. When I mentioned his strange, reproachful letter to me, he dismissed it summarily, a little embarrassed, saying something like, "Just a mood I was in that day — I don't know why I do these things — can we just forget it?"

"Sure we can," I answered. There was no way for me to be angry: he looked too distressed, and I did not know about what.

He was curious about Ayn Rand and obviously impressed that I knew her. He wanted to know what she and Frank were like, where they lived, what we all talked about, and did she really mean the things she had written in *The Fountainhead*? Looking at me as if he had never quite seen me before, he said, "And you've become a friend of hers? Who would have thought?"

When I visited him a few days later, he began talking with a kind of driven candor about some painful personal problems. I was on fire with the concept of ideas being able to explain emotions and behavior — and with the possibility of changing emotions and behavior by changing the ideas that gave rise to them. I was able to help him, for which he thanked me earnestly.

His other problems aside, I knew Allan still dreamed of being a concert pianist. I urged him not to relinquish this aspiration. "Who cares what your family wants? It's what you want that's important." Then I added, "You see? This is why Ayn Rand stresses that to be selfish in the rational sense, as contrasted with the petty sense, takes courage and integrity. It's anything but easy. Never mind what people tell us."

In late August, Barbara and I met in New York, to register at New York University and to begin a new life together.

Barbara moved into a modest walk-up on Twenty-ninth Street, a few yards from Fifth Avenue, and I took a room in the Carteret Hotel on Twenty-third, two blocks west of Fifth.

Our favorite activity was walking, looking at buildings, watching the people and automobiles streaming past, the sights and sounds merging with everything we had ever read about New York. We told each other that Ayn was right, this was the only city, the center of the universe — and wouldn't life be perfect when Ayn and Frank were here with us?

In September Barbara confronted me with another tearful confession of a recent affair. Again I was devastated. However, after a painful explosion, I struggled to regain a foothold on serenity, optimism, and benevolence. I told myself I was tough, resilient.

On another September evening I answered the telephone to hear Ayn's exuberant voice. "Well, darling, how would you like to see us? I can't stand California any longer. We're moving back to New York. We'll be there in three weeks."

I would not let her off the phone. "Wait a minute! This is wonderful. But — how come? What changed your mind?"

"When I finished the chapter in Atlantis, when Dagny meets Galt and discovers the secret of the strike, I thought, Why am I sentencing myself to exile? Who knows how long I will need to finish the book? I want to be in New York. And naturally, darling, I miss the two of you. Anyway, that's my explanation. Frank would answer a little differently." She chuckled. "I don't know if I should tell you what he said." Her voice sounded abnormally alive. "He says I've become a hopeless dependent and can't live without you!"

I chuckled in answer. "I like Frank's version better."

When I ran to Barbara's apartment to share the news, she seemed as happy and excited as I was.

·   ·   ·

To make the waiting more bearable, I continued writing to Ayn. September 27, 1951:

Dear Ayn . . . I must say Barbara is trying very hard, and seems to be making major strides. . . . When you come back, you will naturally be talking about her problems with her, and there's something I want to suggest. In the past, when Barbara presented a difficulty, you would analyze all the issues involved, deliver a comprehensive lecture on the subject, and if she said she understood and agreed, you let it go at that. Well, what I have learned is to talk as little as possible, to 'lecture' only when it seems urgently necessary, and instead to have her do all the thinking that she can. This accomplishes two purposes. First, it assures that this time she really understands — and second, the fact that she does the crucial work herself, with her own brain, helps to restore her self-confidence, which is in a bad way at present. . . . It is not easy to be a calm, objective 'psychologist' in these circumstances — anybody but me should be having these conversations with Barbara — but I don't seem to have any choice. Maybe I am helping. What's most important is that for the first time she appears totally rational in facing everything.

October 4: "A bright spot in Barbara's life at school. Her political science professor wrote on the blackboard: 'The two fundamental philosophies of the last 2500 years.' And then he had two columns, one reading, 'Platonism, Irrationalism, Collectivism,' and the other reading, 'Aristotelianism, Rationalism, Individualism.' So, life at NYU is looking hopeful! . . . *Hurry up!*"

There was a quality of intellectual seriousness about the professors at NYU that somehow seemed different from what, for the most part, I had experienced at UCLA. I even liked the fact that NYU at Washington Square had no real campus, but consisted of a group of structures that looked like rather old office buildings. The atmosphere was almost grim: no lawns, no playing fields, no terraced banks of flowers, nothing to distract from the life of the mind. There were bookstores everywhere, in the streets surrounding the university and scattered throughout Greenwich Village, and I spent hours in them, drunk on how much was there for me to learn. I wrote about this to Ayn and Frank, as I wrote about everything important in my life. Each letter ended with a "Hurry up!" or a "Why aren't you here yet?"

During the third week of October, Ayn and Frank arrived in New York, and moved into an apartment their lawyer had arranged — on 36 East Thirty-sixth Street. "Easy walking distance from my hotel!" I shouted.

·   ·   ·

And then the four of us were together again, in Ayn and Frank's apartment, talking about the chapter Ayn had recently finished, "Atlantis."
Barbara and I were laughing and interrupting each other, and Ayn was
saying to me, "Nathan, you're impossible. Please let me finish a sentence." Such interruptions were her biggest complaint against me in
the first year or two.

Ayn appeared vibrant, intense, inexhaustible, as if the introduction
of Galt and the establishment of his character in the story had charged
her with renewed vitality; when she spoke of him, her eyes glowed
with love. Frank and she had motored from Los Angeles to New York,
and Frank, who of course had done all the driving, looked happy and
pleasantly tired. "It's good to see you two." He smiled. Barbara, too,
looked happy, with only the faintest reflection of anxious tension in
her eyes, and I brushed my awareness of it aside because I did not want
it to be part of this occasion.

As we sat around talking about Ayn's new chapter — Barbara and
I had insisted on reading it that night — John Galt felt present among
us, a spiritual presence of overwhelming reality.

We talked about how Ayn saw Galt, relative to her other two heroes
in the novel, Rearden and Francisco, and Ayn said that she did not
intend Galt to be perceived as their superior in any important way,
"merely more serene within himself, and of course free of any conflict." Rearden has conflicts, she said, but at his core he is on the same
level as the other two men. Francisco, she declared, was totally on
Galt's level; he, too, had no internal conflicts, and the differences between them were differences of style, not essence. Dagny falls in love
with Galt, she explained, because *in form* he is a more complete
embodiment of her personal values as an adult woman. Did we
think readers would find that difficult to understand? Ayn wanted
to know. "I don't find it difficult to understand," Barbara stated,
"but I think readers might." We talked about what might be said in
the novel to make the issue clearer, but our efforts trailed off inconclu-
sively.

Next evening, after rereading the chapter, I suggested that perhaps
Galt, as presented, was a bit abstract and needed a few more personal
touches, more indications of his feelings at a simple human level. Ayn
agreed, and in the final version of his characterization Ayn added "hu-
manizing" elements not present in the first draft we read. When, for
example, Ayn showed me a reference Galt makes to his pain over
abandoning the motor he has invented, she announced, "I put that line
in for you, darling." Galt remains, however, the most abstract of her
heroes. Ayn offered this explanation for her characterization of him:
"One does not approach a god too closely — one does not get too

intimate with him — one maintains a respectful distance from his inner life."

Atlas Shrugged has about it the quality of a great myth — *all* the characters, major and minor alike, are touched by it. But in her portrayal of Galt, Ayn had shifted to the highest level of abstraction, perhaps because in him she wished to focus most clearly the underlying spirituality of her vision of the human ideal. "Galt," she once said to me, "is definitely presented as man as a god. To some extent that's true of all my heroes, but in Galt it's most pronounced." I added, "In essence, we see him only as Dagny sees him. He's written exclusively from an external perspective, from the perspective of woman as man-worshiper." Somewhere, dimly, the thought occurred that Ayn's approach to the characterization of her heroes, Galt in particular, would have to exact a cost in diminished psychological realism. At the time the thought did not really register.

One evening Barbara cheerfully announced, "I've solved the problem of who is my favorite — Rearden or Francisco?" "How?" I asked. She answered, "Galt is my favorite."

My joy at Ayn and Frank's return to New York lasted about two or three weeks. Then Barbara's new confessions began.

The three of us were sitting in Ayn's apartment — Ayn, Barbara, and I. Frank had gone off somewhere. Barbara and Ayn sat at one end of the room and I at the other. I stayed apart to stress my nonparticipation; I thought this might make talking easier for Barbara. She was conveying to Ayn some of her confusions about the realm of emotion, about love, sex, and human relationships; and she spoke about her feelings of anxiety.

My mind was half drifting when, to my surprise, in a quietly purposeful voice, Ayn asked Barbara if she had slept with a young man with whom she claimed to have a warm but platonic relationship, during the period that she and I were purportedly "committed." Barbara's answer was vague but gave me the impression that she had not. Then, a few minutes later, in the same tone of voice, Ayn asked the question again. I was puzzled: what was the matter with Ayn? Barbara had already answered that question. Had I missed something? Then, in a low, husky voice, I heard Barbara answer yes.

I sat without moving, in shock, trying to force my brain to absorb this new information. The sound of their quiet voices continued, a distant background to the upheaval that was tearing at my insides, flinging me into a state like none I had ever experienced before. The pain felt physical and it was excruciating. I reproached myself for my reaction. Had I not heard two previous confessions in the past four months? What right did I have to be shocked now? All I could think was, I had tried to trust and I had been proven wrong; her protestations of love had meant nothing; I no longer knew what was real and what was unreal.

Looking back, I have thought many times that that was the night my relationship with Barbara should have ended (if not much earlier). But in my mind she had acquired the status of "my woman." She had become the repository of too many of my projections and dreams. I loved her, or at any rate I felt bonded to her; and there were times when I was incredibly happy with her; and the wrong kind of ego involvement forbade me to simply acknowledge defeat and walk away; and I do not doubt I had rescuer fantasies. And then, there was the strange, unexpected response of Ayn.

There was no sound of reproach in Ayn's voice, just a gentle, persistent probing, encouraging Barbara to explore and voice her feelings. I could not stand to listen. I needed to escape, to be alone. I got up and went into the bathroom. It was as if there was some great pressure building up internally, pushing against the wall of my chest and stomach. I bent over, holding myself. I fought not to cry out. I finally regained sufficient calm to return to the living room.

I was confused by Ayn's benevolence and warmth toward Barbara. Given the moral ruthlessness that was more typical of Ayn, this was unusual. She stressed that while she did not approve of what Barbara had done, she continued to believe in her goodness. I felt almost angry, as if Ayn were unconcerned with the impact on me of Barbara's actions. As if she could read my thoughts, she turned and said to me, "I know this is terribly hard for you, Nathan. But everything is going to be all right. We're going to solve this, once and for all." Her calm in that moment projected an almost supernatural certainty.

Later, when Barbara was out of the room for a moment, Ayn said — and the look on her voice told me how foolish I had been to imagine that she was unconcerned about my feelings — "You went into the bathroom so you could be alone with your suffering." I nodded, and she went on, "Darling, I'm so sorry. This is terrible for you."

"What made you think of asking about that fellow?"

Ayn smiled. "What else would Barbara have to be so anxious about?"

The next day, when we were having lunch, Barbara said, her voice trembling, with the look of a frightened child facing an angry parent, "That's not all. There's more." Then she proceeded to recount additional affairs.

We had one more such meeting in which, in escalating terror, she told me about relationships she had "forgotten" to speak of earlier.

Ayn continued to be warmly supportive of both of us, undisturbed by Barbara's revelations, compassionate toward me — and almost incomprehensibly serene.

Sometimes my anger was ungovernable. Once, in my hotel room, I spent half an hour shouting insults at her, driven to greater and greater fury by the sight of her nodding her head, agreeing with everything I said, as if she was welcoming the abuse. In a complex mixture of rage, pain, hatred, and desire, I initiated "lovemaking," very aggressively, and was astonished by the intensity of her responsiveness. Barbara and I became reconnected sexually — and I determined anew to persevere in my struggles to rescue our relationship.

"What you are doing is not easy," Ayn said to me one evening. "I admire your strength. If you believe she's the woman for you, you don't let go."

"I'm afraid," I answered, not certain of how to explain what I meant. "I'm afraid of what's happening inside, to me, while all this is going on. Something is happening — something is going wrong with me — and I don't know how to tell you what it is."

"What do you mean?" Ayn asked, with puzzling detachment, as if I, for once, was incomprehensible to her.

"There's too much pain I don't know what to do with, and too much rage. I don't like feeling this angry — this is not how I've ever seen myself. All I can say is, I feel something . . . happening . . . inside of me; something is wrong."

Ayn looked perplexed. "But surely it will pass and none of it will matter — if you succeed, if Barbara comes around. You're not going to start believing it's a malevolent universe, are you?"

I did not fight harder to make myself understood. I withdrew, feeling strangely let down, looking at Ayn as from a great distance. What I told myself consciously was: don't dramatize; don't indulge in self-pity; Ayn is right.

"You could do me one favor," I said to her. "You talk to Barbara; you try to help her."

"Of course I will, darling."

We continued to read — and reread — the new novel. We even had a small influence on its content, beyond my suggestions about the characterization of Galt.

One of the most imaginative lesser characters in *Atlas Shrugged* is that of the philosopher-turned-pirate, Ragnar Danneskjöld. He, Galt, and Francisco are close friends — and when Ragnar lands his plane in the hidden valley of the strikers, he briefly greets his wife, whom he has not seen in eleven months, then departs for breakfast with his two friends. "Ayn," I protested, "this is impossible. I don't care how close the three men are — or how important their ritual breakfast of June first of every year — any man in his right mind, and certainly any hero of yours, is going to have his wife as his first priority. Otherwise, it would be damned strange." Ayn sighed and said, a little reluctantly, "I suppose you're right."

It was Barbara who was responsible for Ragnar being married. For certain literary and philosophical reasons, Ayn had made Ragnar shockingly beautiful. When Ayn mentioned a minor character in the story, Kay Ludlow, an exquisitely beautiful actress who joins the strike, Barbara suggested that two such individuals aesthetically belonged together. Ayn had chuckled — and agreed.

"It looks," I was now saying to Ayn, "like you haven't fully accepted that you married those two characters." She asked, "Suppose I have Ragnar arrive in the valley the night before — would you then accept him being gone for an hour in the morning, for breakfast?" And that is the way the final version of the novel reads. Ayn joked, "Barbara saw to it that Ragnar got married and Nathan saw to it that he was a good husband."

Kay Ludlow has only a walk-on role. I once teased Ayn about the absence of significant female characters in her novel, with the exception of Rearden's wife, Lillian, who is thoroughly despicable. Ayn's eyes sparkled with gaiety and she answered, "This is my fantasy. What do I need other women for?" Then she added, "I suppose, as a writer, I'm not really interested in women, except in relationship to the men. It's man I wanted to write about — the ideal." I responded, "What about woman, the ideal?" This was an old argument between us. She said, "Dagny is that." I persisted, "But you show several versions of the male ideal, not merely one." She shrugged. "You write about women. It doesn't interest me." I would not let the subject go. "But Ayn, *you're a woman.*" Again, her eyes sparkled with amusement. "And glad of it, too. I've never wanted to be a man; not for a moment. Do you know why? Because then I'd have to be in love with a woman."

I gave up. I did not know how seriously to take Ayn's antiwoman remarks. Her earnestness and her humor both seemed authentic. I wondered what any of this meant in terms of her own self-concept. I did not realize that it would have been worth my while to have pursued this issue more vigorously.

The writing of the novel was proceeding more slowly than Ayn had anticipated. She worked long hours every day, pushing herself to the point of exhaustion and beyond it, and while she was happy with the final result, she was not happy with the time needed to achieve it. "If only I wrote more 'inspirationally' — but, you know, with me *every-*

thing has to be conscious. That's why the work is so laborious. Of course I use my subconscious — one has to — but part of me resents that, fights it, and my resistance slows me down."

Some evenings I sat in Ayn's living room, waiting for her to emerge from her study, and through her open door I would hear her reading her work aloud, searching out the smallest failure of appropriate rhythm or balance, or an inexact word, or a missing adjective. She demanded of every sentence and every paragraph the perfection of poetry. When I observed that there was something profoundly musical, which I did not quite know how to identify, in the quality of her writing, she answered, "*The Fountainhead* was written in notes. This book is written in chords. Much harder; much more demanding. Sometimes I feel my brain is going to crack open." She often complained of excruciating tension pains in her neck and shoulders.

We would talk about my favorite passages — Dagny and Rearden's train ride on the "John Galt Line" in Part I, climaxed by the start of their affair; or Dagny's airplane pursuit of John Galt at the climax of Part II — about Ayn's extraordinary ability to communicate the sensory reality of motion, or her ability to shift between descriptions of physical action, inner emotional experience, and broad philosophical meanings, or her artistry at manipulating implication and indirection to evoke the most profound feelings in the reader.

"If you want to obtain the strongest emotional response," she said to Barbara and me one evening, "then you write between the lines, never on the line, you write around the feeling, you don't spell it out explicitly." Barbara had some resistance to this idea; she seemed to prefer a more Wagnerian approach to writing. "What's wrong with stating the emotion or whatever directly? What's wrong with being explicit?" Ayn answered, "Because if you tell the reader everything, if you don't leave spaces for his mind to fill in, if you don't engage his consciousness by giving him something to do — if, in effect, you try to do it all for him — then you leave the reader passive, his consciousness is not engaged as it could be, and so *he's not that involved emotionally.* "In this issue, Thomas Wolfe is my exact literary opposite. He thinks if he shouts his feelings at you, that will make you feel something. It doesn't work that way." Barbara sighed. "It works for me," she said. For the flash of an instant I saw anger in Ayn's eyes. "Well, darling," she replied in a gentle, satin-and-steel voice, "it's just not good writing."

The sessions between Barbara and Ayn continued, and Barbara and I slowly, tentatively, grew closer and happier. Once mysterious and elusive, Barbara shifted radically in the opposite direction: she now reported to me the smallest details of her activities, far beyond anything I had requested. When I asked her why she felt the need to give me such specifics, she answered, "I don't want any more lies between us, or any omissions, not even over unimportant things. Whenever I say anything that isn't quite exact, my anxiety flares up." I felt sadly touched by this — and grateful, because, whatever her motives, her compulsive honesty was, in our context, healing. I really do love her, I told myself.

"Barbara," Ayn said to me, "has a genuine longing for integrity. She was not really meant to have made the kind of mistakes she made." She said it with the authority of royalty. When she spoke this way I felt torn: part of me wanted only to believe her; another part felt uncomfortable about her way of putting things — as if she were the supreme arbiter in all matters pertaining to the condition of a human soul.

Whatever this way of speaking signaled, I was already beginning to hear it in myself when I handed down my own opinions and moral judgments. With Barbara, my pain and anger were slowly surfacing in the form of moral condescension and arrogance.

An unquestioned absolute during this difficult time was Barbara's devotion to Ayn's work and to Ayn herself. "This is very important," Ayn said more than once. "It shows her basic character." I heard nothing strange in this observation; it sounded utterly reasonable.

The idea of marriage became increasingly appealing. Marriage was a lifetime commitment. I imagined it would help provide Barbara and me with the structure and security to protect and nurture the growing closeness between us. Our respective families were providing us with a monthly allowance — $250 each — and they both agreed to maintain it until we graduated and became self-supporting. We did not ask for or expect more than that; neither of us believed it was anyone's obligation to subsidize the marriage. If our families expressed any negative reaction, it was only about our lack of interest in having children. Both of us liked children, but neither of us desired to be parents; we wanted a life organized around our work.

We continued to enjoy NYU more than we had enjoyed UCLA. We felt intellectually stimulated and challenged. I think, for example, of two philosophy professors — Sidney Hook, a pragmatist and a socialist, and William Barrett, an existentialist — two men poles apart from each other and still further apart, intellectually, from us. Barbara took several courses with Hook; I had one or two with Barrett. We laughed at our classroom discussions, our fights, the statements our professors uttered that we thought preposterous, the questions hurled at us which sent us searching for answers — and we would interrupt each other telling our stories to Ayn and Frank.

Usually, we talked philosophy, in part because that was where Ayn had most to say. Sometimes she would remark, "I really don't know much about psychology. I leave that sewer to you, Nathan."

She was constructing a philosophical system and yet, by her own statement, knew almost nothing about psychology. It did not occur to me that this lack was dangerous to her intellectual efforts, as well as to Barbara and me. Her attitude was, in effect, that rational minds do not require psychology; philosophy is enough; psychology is essentially for pathology — that is, for the irrational. I argued with her about this and she would always concede that I was right: "Yes, of course, Nathan, we all have a psychology, and the operations of mind do need to be studied, but . . . " And a week or two later she would say, "Oh, how I hate your profession, Nathan, how I hate the irrational, how I hate having to deal with it or struggle to understand it."

Sometimes Barbara and I played hooky from school, went to Times Square, and, moving from theater to theater, saw perhaps four films in a single day. It was our favorite form of recreation. In the darkness of the theater, we held hands. But Barbara was shyly reluctant to hold hands on the street, especially if we were anywhere near NYU. "What would Plato think?" she would say jokingly. I found this shyness utterly mystifying. She was willing to challenge the beliefs of the whole world, yet she worried what people would think if they saw us holding hands? I interpreted this as some strange remnant of conventionality that surely would pass. And meanwhile, the sense of solidarity between us was growing. We had fun together — with Ayn and Frank, and away on our own. When our budgets allowed it, we loved to go dancing. "You see?" said Ayn. "It's a benevolent universe."

I was reluctant to discuss with Ayn one problem that persisted — the disparity in Barbara's and my desire to make love. Barbara said no at least as often as she said yes. I imagined that this was a problem marriage would somehow automatically solve.

I had not been able to maintain my decision to leave psychology out of my dealings with her, in that discussions of our relationship overlapped inescapably with discussions of her problems. "I'm caught in a trap," I complained to Ayn. "To involve myself at a psychological level seems wrong, and not to involve myself seems wrong." But whatever we were doing, the strategy seemed to be working in that Barbara looked happier, said she was happier, spoke more of loving me, spoke less of feelings pulling her in other directions.

I was becoming progressively more interested in psychotherapy as a profession. I saw it as a doorway through which to enter and explore the human psyche. However, to write remained the deepest and most enduring of all my career goals. Nothing seemed more natural or compelling than the process of taking whatever most mattered to me and making it real by putting words to paper. I thought of writing as a semireligious act, and this was one of the bonds between Barbara and me. She would say to me, "I can't understand why anyone would want to do anything except be a writer."

In the summer of 1952, Barbara and I decided the time had come. We set a wedding date for the following January.

"What would I have done," I said to Ayn, "if you had not been here to help?" She answered, "You're going to have a very happy life together — and both of you will have earned it."

Hired limousines carried Barbara and me and members of our families to the home of Barbara's aunt and uncle in White Plains, New York. I remember almost nothing of the final months leading up to this event, except that there were doubts, insecurities, conflicts, almost to the end.

I remember the gently implacable sound of the tires rolling over the snow and ice as we moved like a caravan through a night filled with stars, with white mist rising from the car windows, and icicles hanging from tree branches along the way, reflecting the fire of our headlights.

I was now twenty-two years old; Barbara was twenty-three. The challenges of my career still lay ahead, but tonight was my celebration of a battle fought and won.

With Ayn and Frank standing behind us, matron of honor and best man, their eyes and faces glowing with a happiness that was like a blessing on this event, Barbara and I took our vows. I felt powerful, effective, sure of myself. I felt that I loved Barbara. I did not think to ask myself whether or not I liked her.

There was a dinner party following the ceremony. Scattered throughout the room, in addition to family, were a few friends, the nucleus of a group we had just begun to form — young people who admired Ayn's work and were keenly interested in her philosophy.

Later that night we returned to our apartment — a single room on East Thirty-fifth Street — to find that Frank had decorated it with flowers in a stunningly imaginative way, transforming it into the intimate setting of a beautiful country inn. I was gratefully touched by his thought and effort, and by his superlative artistry. His virtuosity at manipulating visual elements displayed a side of him I had not been aware of before; his dramatic floral arrangements had the impact of sculpture.

Then Barbara was standing before me, wearing a pale nightgown that stressed the slenderness of her body, she was smiling at me in the half darkness, her blonde hair fell to her shoulders, and her hazel eyes projected a kind of innocent vulnerability that promised total surrender.

This was my wedding night. This was my wife. Tonight there could be no question of our making love. With that thought as reassurance, I took her in my arms.

SEVEN

"WHEN YOU WERE COMING to meet me for the first time," Ayn asked me one evening that spring, "were you at all concerned that I might disappoint you — might not live up to your expectations?"

I was sitting on the floor of her living room, playing with the gray and white kitten she and Frank had brought with them from California; he was named Frisco, after Francisco d'Anconia. Ayn could not look at him without smiling affectionately. She would stroke him, talk to him, whisper words of adoration; it was as if he tapped into the softest, most nurturing side of her nature.

"No, I wasn't concerned at all," I told her. "I didn't even consider it. I knew that the author of *The Fountainhead* was not going to be something less in person. And I was right, wasn't I?"

She seemed pleased. "Amazing. I would have been so fearful of disappointment, if our roles had been reversed."

"How can you know? You've never met anyone who wrote a book like *The Fountainhead*."

"True. Everything I've liked has had some inconsistencies, some contradictions. *The Fountainhead* hasn't any." This was said impersonally, with no implication of boasting, but merely as a self-evident fact. I had grown accustomed to hearing her discuss herself and her work this way. "Still," she went on, "I admire your benevolence. You know, my biggest goal is not to let any disappointment or setback affect my sense of life. I hate bitterness. Do you see any bitterness in me?"

"No," I said, looking at the mouth I had seen twisted in anger many times when discussing other people's "irrationality." I wondered what the truth was and if she really wanted to hear it and whether I had the courage to name it. I was vaguely aware that there were signs of the most terrible bitterness; but superimposed on them were images of her eyes laughing when she was happy with the day's writing, or of her face softening when she held her head against Frank's chest, or of her body dancing around the room to her tiddlywink music — and I told myself that this was her core, this was her essence, and nothing else mattered.

She said, expressing a concern she often had, "I don't want to be touched by any malevolence." She began to speak about early experiences that had hurt or disappointed her — from her rejection by Leo, to her failure to get writing jobs in Hollywood, to her experiences with *We the Living, Anthem,* and *The Fountainhead.* I was surprised that Leo was still so important to her. I assumed that if one was happily in love, old wounds automatically faded away. Yet she spoke of her pain over Leo as if it were brand-new, and there was an edge to her voice that did not fit my view of her. Perhaps what made me uncomfortable was not the hurt but the hint of anger after so many years. Speaking of her experiences in Hollywood, she seemed much more detached; this part of her life did seem truly behind her. When she spoke of the struggles involving her novels, she projected a strange kind of pride — as if to say she had personally suffered almost everything she had ever written about. This evoked empathy and protectiveness in me.

I was keenly interested in her reminiscences and never tired of them, even when I had heard many of the stories before. Every word she uttered was important to me, every small detail, even every pause or arrhythmical intake of breath or faint tightness in her voice, because I wished to penetrate every corner of her consciousness, to absorb everything, to know her and be connected with her in that special way that is sometimes true of identical twins. This was tied in my mind to the process of thoroughly grasping her way of seeing and apprehending the world — of understanding everything within her from which *The Fountainhead* and *Atlas Shrugged* had sprung. I wanted to know her "secrets," her uniqueness. Perhaps this desire was a form of love, but it felt like an expression of my need for mastery and control — not over her but over my own life, over whatever I regarded as important. I was committed to the idea that life is conquered through understanding.

"You know," she was saying, "when I'm writing, I'm living in the world of the novel, not 'ordinary reality,' and there's always that sense of shock when I come back to the world at the end, when the job is finished. I was not fully satisfied literarily with *We the Living,* I was not yet in control of my style, but I was completely satisfied with the plot, with the structure, and with the climax. I can't tell you exactly how many publishers rejected the book, but there were a great many. The chief criticism was that I was too intellectual, too concerned with ideas. Then there was the opposition from all the people who were indignant because I criticized Soviet Russia. I wasn't 'open-minded' enough, I wasn't 'tolerant,' I didn't appreciate the 'noble experiment.' It was hard. There were times Frank and I had almost nothing to eat. Finally, the book was accepted by Macmillan — against the violent objections of Granville Hicks, an editor there, and also a member of the Communist party and an editor of *New Masses*. The book was not supported by Macmillan, not in ads, not in any way. They did nothing for it. I expected attacks from the critics, of course, and there were plenty — political much more than literary; literary criticism would have been much easier to take at that time. There was no way for the book to find its readers. It did not do well, and then Macmillan destroyed the plates and let it go out of print just at the time it was beginning to catch on, when readers were beginning to discover it. It was a terrible blow. I cried a good deal during those years. I tried to get work as a screenwriter, and it should have been possible, because *Night of January 16th* had had a good run on Broadway, I had published a novel, and I was becoming known — but my agent could get me nothing, and the word coming back from Hollywood was that no one wanted to get involved with someone so outspoken about Soviet Russia. I was blacklisted. And yet, there's an ironic postscript to all of this, that shows the power of romanticism, of writing in essentials and in terms of universal values. During World War II, the Italian government expropriated the literary properties of foreign authors — and a pirated film was made of *We the Living,* with Alida Valli playing Kira and Rossano Brazzi playing Leo. Both of them magnificent; in fact, the entire film was excellent. The goddamn fools allowed it because the story was anticommunist. It was an instant success: people flocked to see it in numbers that shocked everyone. Some official finally figured out that the story was fully as antifascist as it was anticommunist — that it was *antistatist.* I suspect the people making the film knew this from the beginning, but I don't know. The Italian people understood before their government did. In fact, *We the Living* is an indictment of *all* dictatorships. The film was withdrawn. In Nazi Germany, someone was a little smarter: the film was never allowed into the country."

As I listened I tried to make real to myself what it would have been like to live through the early years of Ayn's struggles, when she could not have known how it was all going to end. I wondered if I could have matched her perseverance. Any obstacle I had ever had to deal with seemed embarrassingly trivial by comparison. I felt privileged to be a witness to what I regarded as a heroic journey.

I wanted to offer some kind of comfort or protection but did not know what to say. Frisco watched us attentively, almost as if he were following the conversation. Reaching for a note of lightness, I said, "Do you realize that Frisco can't understand any of this? Can't conceive of it?"

She smiled. "Yes, and that's what I love about him. I said that about Wynand's cat in *The Fountainhead* — the purity of a consciousness incapable of grasping human irrationality or evil."

We began talking about *Anthem*. I expressed dismay that she had been unable, prior to 1946, to find an American publisher for this marvelous work — so much more lyrical than any of her other writings, by far the most abstract in its method of stylization. It had been written in the summer of 1937, while Ayn was still struggling with the plot of *The Fountainhead*: she had not yet devised the climax that would pull all the elements of the story together. She was exhausted by her efforts and stopped long enough to "rest" and write *Anthem*.

"When I found that novelette in the Toronto Public Library," I told her, "I learned it was out of print and not available for purchase anywhere — so I stole the library copy." Many years later, addressing a conference of librarians, I gave myself the pleasure of making a public confession. I sent the library a new copy of the book. Now I chuckled and asked Ayn, "What philosophical stand do you want to take about my stealing your book because I absolutely had to own it?" She waved her cigarette holder and said gaily, "I give you a special papal dispensation." Of course in this instance we were joking; but she was arrogating to herself just this kind of authority, which I did not challenge.

"But you know," she went on, "the struggle with *The Fountainhead* really sums everything else up. Twelve publishers rejected it as too intellectual, too noncommercial. Later I learned that some of the editors who rejected it thought it was a great book. Can you understand what it means to be rejected not because you're not good enough but because *you're too good*? That's the worst horror. Bobbs-Merrill was the thirteenth house to whom the novel was submitted." The novel was recommended there by Ayn's boss at Paramount, the story editor, Richard Mealand; he was enthusiastic about the project and offered to help. Archie Ogden was a new editor at Bobbs-Merrill, and when Ayn first met him she didn't expect him to like the book. "He seemed like an overly friendly Peter Keating." Archie Ogden loved the book. "His admiration for it — and his understanding of what I was doing literarily — were everything a writer could dream of asking for." He recommended that Bobbs-Merrill acquire the book, but his superiors turned him down. "At that time Archie was new at that firm; but he staked his job on his independent judgment and I will always be grateful for that. He wired his boss: 'If this is not the book for you, then I am not the editor for you.' Can you imagine such a thing? He got a return wire saying, 'Far be it from me to dampen such enthusiasm. Sign the contract. But the book better be good.' Now, do you want to hear something funny? On a previous job he had turned down Dale Carnegie's *How to Win Friends and Influence People*. How's that for a logical universe? Archie would smile and say that he was proud of his judgment both times. Thanks to the enthusiasm and integrity of Richard Mealand and Archie Ogden, *The Fountainhead* got its chance.

"Of course, the battle was not over. Bobbs-Merrill ran a couple of fairly meaningless ads that did not state what the book was about, and sales began very slowly. I was terrified it was going to be *We the Living* all over again. Bobbs-Merrill was very passive about the book, I was desperate, and there was nothing I could do." The book was made entirely by word of mouth. The first three months were slow, then sales began to rise, and then they exploded. It stayed on the best-seller list for a long time and went back on when the movie came out. "But, you know, the people at Bobbs-Merrill then were really dreadful. It was wartime and there was a paper shortage and they kept letting the book go out of print, in spite of incredible sales. It was a nightmare. Finally, they subcontracted to another company that had a large stock of paper and after that the book stayed in print. But nothing, absolutely nothing, came easily."

Ayn talked about all the hostile reviews and the failure of even the sympathetic ones to communicate the novel's view of individualism. One exception was Lorine Pruette, in the New York *Times Book Review*. She identified individualism as the novel's theme and wrote, "Ayn Rand is a writer of great power. She has a subtle and ingenious mind and the capacity of writing brilliantly, beautifully, bitterly. . . . Good novels of ideas are rare at any time. This is the only novel of ideas written by an American woman that I can recall. . . . You will not be able to read this masterful work without thinking through some of the basic concepts of our times." Ayn remarked, "Coming when it did, in the midst of all the attacks, the review really lifted my spirits, gave me the sense of a human world out there."

A rift between Ayn and Isabel Paterson, who she had once liked more than any other woman she had met (notwithstanding the fact that they disagreed about religion), deepened over the issue of the book's review. Paterson's chapter in *The God of the Machine*, entitled "The Humanitarian with the Guillotine," was pure Ayn Rand, but she did not acknowledge her indebtedness to Ayn's ideas. Strangely, Ayn did not seem resentful; she was very mild on the subject. She was less mild about the fact that Paterson, who professed love and admiration for Ayn, declined an opportunity to review *The Fountainhead* for the *Herald Tribune* when Irita van Doren, head of the book section, proposed it. In the early months of the novel's struggle, a favorable review by Isabel Paterson could have helped enormously. Ayn learned of the refusal some time later. Paterson explained her reluctance to air in print certain of their differences. "Our differences," Ayn said to me, "involved religion and, though we didn't discuss this, sense of life. The romantic spirit of the writing would have antagonized her. And she would not have liked my treatment of sex. She would see it as un-Christian." Ayn added, "Still, at the time we were friends, she expressed devotion to my work, and she knew the kind of battle I was fighting and what I was up against." Ayn waved her hand in a characteristic gesture of dismissal. "But that was not why our relationship ended. I was disgusted with her but I had promised to introduce her to some conservative friends when she visited California. Pat's own life had not gone well and she was becoming increasingly belligerent toward everyone. She spoke as if no one was really fighting for capitalism except her. Everyone else was a coward or a hypocrite, she was saying, not really willing to commit themselves uncompromisingly. She insulted some of the best supporters of capitalism I knew. In California, she became totally irrational. She could be brilliant, as you can see from her book, but that was the end between us. And she was the one woman with a mind I respected."

We returned to the subject of the book's reception, the distortions of her ideas in the press, the strange phenomenon of being world famous, widely read, and simultaneously grossly misrepresented and misperceived. We spoke of other innovators who had similar experiences.

Wishing to address the happier side of her, I said, "In the end, you won."

"Yes and no. Professionally, I did; I don't have to worry about money anymore or about finding a publisher for my next novel. But personally? My biggest disappointment was and is people. I thought somewhere in the world there were giants — my kind of men — and when *The Fountainhead* was published everything would change: I would find them. That's not what happened. But I'll never give up believing it's possible."

"And yet, look at the amount of fan mail you get, even after all these years."

"Bobbs-Merrill says it's unprecedented, in its experience, for a novelist to receive the huge amount of mail that comes in for *The Fountainhead*. But still . . ." She began to soften only at this point. "Shall I tell you what I regard as my greatest personal reward for *The Fountainhead*? You. You are the kind of reader I always dreamed of finding. You're the proof that what I write about is possible."

When I heard these words, a part of me felt a twist of pain. The thought in my mind was: life should have had more to offer her, as a reward, than a young man who had not yet accomplished anything. She deserved a contemporary, an equal in achievement and experience. And part of me felt elated, buoyant, powerful beyond imagination. I had never gotten used to the compliments she consistently paid me, and it was impossible not be affected by them.

Lying flat on my back on the floor, holding Frisco above my head, I felt swept free of everything but a confidently untroubled serenity. It was great to be alive.

"Well, Frisco," I said, "I guess it's up to you and me."

The first year of my marriage to Barbara was, from my perspective, the best in our entire relationship. Her loyalty now seemed absolute. We were going to school, planning the future, building a life together. "I really am happy," she said to me with glowing eyes, and I believed her. We shared our classroom experiences, critiqued each other's school papers, laughed about the intellectual fights we would get into with fellow students, talked endlessly about Galt, Rearden, Francisco, and Dagny, held hands in the darkness of movie theaters, visited Ayn and Frank and read the latest pages of the novel and felt bonded by our participation in a special world.

"I really am proud of you," she would sometimes say, after a visit with Ayn and Frank or after reading some paper I had written for a course in psychology or philosophy. "I really do love you," she would say. "You're so good-looking. Ayn is right. You're still not able to appreciate yourself fully." "I love you," I would answer.

She was now relatively free of anxiety. I observed that she chose to continue her policy of meticulous truth-telling about the smallest details of her actions, in spite of my assurances that it wasn't necessary.

But our sexual problems remained unsolved and threatened to keep the past alive and virulent. Often I was aware of being accommodated. I fought not to let it matter too much and told myself that everything else was getting better and that a day would come when Barbara's desires would match mine. But sometimes I would erupt over her passivity in bed and her periods of moody withdrawal.

There were occasions when Barbara made love with seemingly unreserved enthusiasm. Then I would feel that the breakthrough had finally happened. But it did not last. I might come home on an afternoon when there had been wonderful lovemaking the day before, and would find Barbara in the kitchen or operating the carpet sweeper; I would put my arms around her and she would fling them off, snapping impatiently, "How many times do I have to tell you? Not when I'm doing housework."

We asked Ayn for advice and she supported Barbara. "You don't understand," she explained, "how distasteful many women, myself included, find housework. One wants to get it over with. One doesn't want to be fully feeling and human in that moment — so your reaching out feels like an intrusion. My advice is, wait till she's finished." Walking home, resting her head for a moment on my shoulder, Barbara whispered, addressing my unspoken thoughts, "I know. Be patient with me. I love you. Everything will work out."

Sometimes we had strange clashes neither of us quite understood. I found her excessively sentimental, even maudlin at times; her feelings could be hurt over what I regarded as trivia; her quality of wistful sadness could be irritating and frustrating and I might lose control and say so. She sometimes found me abrupt, impatient, insensitive, arrogant. In my own eyes my impatience was my worst trait. "You can be so kind when you want to be," she would say to me. "Why are you sometimes so unfeeling?"

I desperately wanted to understand her. If I could understand her better, I could draw us closer together.

The desire to make sense out of my human encounters — the same drive that had led me into psychology — led me to write papers on two personality types; Barbara was one of them.

My frame of reference for understanding people was where they stood relative to respect for reason, respect for reality, and degree of personal autonomy or independence. These were the criteria by which I assessed healthy psychological development. The first paper I wrote, chiefly inspired by my efforts to understand Barbara and Frank, was entitled "The Emotionalist Metaphysics."

[T]he key here . . . is the role of feeling or emotion in their mental processes. Emotions are their ultimate guides. . . . their ultimate standard for deciding what is true or false, right or wrong, desirable or undesirable. *Feelings are the ultimate reality.* That is why I call this "the emotionalist *metaphysics.*" The ultimate "stuff" of their universe is feeling. . . .

Since, in fact and in reality, feelings or emotions reflect premises, ideas, value judgments, which may or may not be conscious, emotionalists are at the mercy of internal processes they themselves do not understand. . . . The fact that sometimes their feelings may be quite right, may lead them in good directions, is irrelevant — because without a rational, critical faculty to supervise and assess, feelings can lead us to destruction if followed blindly. . . .

> Still, rational individuals can be drawn to this type of person, if and when the feelings of the person are compatible with the feelings of the more reasoning individual. . . . because, after all, the emotionalist type does think some of the time, does observe reality, and sometimes draws valid conclusions which later show up as emotions.

These last lines were written, in effect, to explain how Ayn and I could love Frank and Barbara. I was aware of, but untroubled by, the motive of self-justification. I recognized, even then, that what I was writing was far from complete.

When I showed my paper to Ayn she became very enthusiastic and began elaborating on it almost immediately. Within a few months she wrote a paper of her own in which she distinguished between "good" emotionalists (Frank and Barbara) and "bad" emotionalists (almost everyone else of this category). The latter were those who had adopted emotion as their preferred manner of functioning virtually from the beginning, as an evasion of the responsibility of thought. But the good variety became emotionalists later in life, in consequence of confusions and errors of knowledge brought on by emotional repression and by trauma at the irrationality of the world.

In later years I did not find the idea of an emotionalist metaphysics useful; it had the power neither to explain nor predict; it never appeared in any of my published writing. Its significance lies in what it discloses about my approach, my desire to relate personal problems to the ultimate fundamentals of existence, to integrate psychology and philosophy.

Far more consequential for my own thinking and for many people's lives was the second of the papers I wrote, "Social Metaphysics." The observations that led to the formulation of this concept were rather more complex than in the case of the emotionalist.

First, there was the fact that in my philosophical and political discussions with people I was struck again and again by how difficult it was for many of them to grasp, let alone accept, unfamiliar ideas that went against the mainstream of "received wisdom" — how little impact reason, logic, factual demonstration seemed to have when the ideas I presented collided with more conventional belief systems. The world as perceived by others seemed to many persons to be the only world that mattered, the only world that was real. I could understand disagreement with my viewpoint based on clear-cut premises, but the opposition I encountered was of a very different kind, often consisting of statements like, "But this is not the way people think!" "But *everybody knows* that self-interest is not a moral motive!" "Who else thinks of reason the way you and Ayn Rand do?" "If what you're saying is true, it would be taught in universities." "How can you be sure you're right if others don't agree?" There was nothing to fight, nothing to engage — only someone's fantasies about the ideas inside someone else's mind. To such persons, thinking about a new idea meant bouncing it against the opinions of "significant others." "Where is their sense of reality?" I would ask Ayn. "Where is their concern with objective truth?"

Two people who had entered our lives in New York helped me focus this issue further. Both were to become members of our intimate circle.

One was a childhood friend of Barbara's, Joan Mitchell, an aspiring painter and a student of art history. She was twenty-three years old, blonde, petite, nervously arrogant one moment, shyly reticent the next. Joan struck me as affected, mannered, overly concerned with her image. I wanted to like her not only because Barbara did but because she did seem enthusiastic about *The Fountainhead* and wanted to learn about Ayn's philosophy. I wanted to expand our circle and wanted to believe she was a promising convert. Moreover, I believed I did sense in her that one important trait: a deep dissatisfaction with "things as they were," a longing, however inarticulate, for something "more," perhaps for ecstasy. "Joan," Barbara said to me, "is a much better person than she has ever let herself be — or perhaps than she herself knows." I did grow fonder of Joan as she embraced our philosophy, but I remained concerned with the fact that a woman could simultaneously see herself as an advocate of reason, individualism, and independence, and yet have a morbid preoccupation with favorably impressing other people.

Leonard Peikoff represented a far greater challenge to my understanding because I considered his a better mind. He had visited us in New York a number of times and in September 1953 he moved there with the intention of studying philosophy for a year, after which he would decide whether he wished to return to his pre-med studies in Winnipeg or remain in New York and pursue a career in philosophy. He was now twenty years old, of medium height, a somewhat frail build, and a coltish way of walking. When he spoke, his voice often had a nervous, almost hysterical quality. Leonard cared for nothing but philosophy — and for this, I warmed to him. But I could see almost immediately that in his consciousness there was no "objective reality," no sense of reality *as such,* apart from what anyone thought or believed; there were only Ayn's ideas and the ideas of his professors, and when Ayn was talking he couldn't retain the viewpoint of his professors, and when his professors were talking he couldn't retain the perspective he had learned from Ayn. I watched him, observed his struggles, tried to help him — and tried to understand how someone so intelligent could be so lacking in autonomy. Sometimes my frustration was greater than my compassion. I would say to him, "Leonard, never mind what so-and-so thinks — never mind what Ayn or I think — what do *you* think?"

In an interview he gave in June 1982, in *The Intellectual Activist,* he acknowledged this problem in his own understated way:

> "The problem [arose] when I went on for a Ph.D. and got bombarded with pragmatism and logical positivism and all the rest of modern philosophy. [His memory fails here; the problem merely became more pronounced at this time.] My method of approach became modern despite myself, because of the influence of graduate school. Then [Ayn] and I would have long talks, and I sometimes couldn't grasp her point because I was looking at it from the perspective of modern philosophy. I could name you many issues that took me years to clarify in my own mind. But they are all technical philosophic issues — the arch example being the analytic-synthetic dichotomy, which I finally published an essay on once I got it clear. It took years before I could understand that question. Another example was her theory of concepts — it took me many years to be convinced of that. . . . I had the problem both ways. Her philosophy made it harder for me to grasp what I was taught at NYU, and vice versa. I was in the position of trying to retain what I knew of her ideas so as not be brainwashed at school.

The ease with which Leonard could be "brainwashed" was bewildering and disturbing to Ayn, Barbara, and me. I said to Ayn, "He has the rationality and independence to select your ideas, even if they keep slipping between his fingers. I mean, if it isn't rationality and independence, what is it? But then why is he so easily overwhelmed, where is his judgment, why can't he retain anything from one conversation to the next?"

I was struggling with the phenomenon of people who seemed to have very little independent contact with reality, apart from what others thought, felt, or believed — until, late in the year, I believed I found the beginning of an explanation. This was the concept of social metaphysics. In my first paper on the subject, I wrote:

> As with the emotionalist, the question is: what does this person think, feel, believe "reality" is — and my answer is: other people. The ultimate reality here, the ultimate frame of reference — this is why I call it a "metaphysics" — is the consciousness, beliefs, values, perceptions of various other people.
>
> This person believes in *the primacy of consciousness* — not his own, but everyone else's. This is why it can be so hard to talk to him.

If you speak of reason, he wants to know "Whose reason?" If you speak of facts, he wants to know "Who determines what is a fact?" If you try to tell him that each of us bears that responsibility, *he literally does not know what this means.* Reality, to him, is reality-as-perceived-by-others.

Over the next decade I developed and amplified the idea of social metaphysics; I conceived of a variety of social metaphysical types with significant psychological differences; I explained how this orientation could coexist in some individuals with isolated areas of high independence, as in the case of great scientists who were able to challenge the assumptions of their colleagues about the nature of the universe yet were frightened to challenge the values of the folks next door. Years after my original paper was written I said in *The Psychology of Self-Esteem*:

> A man of self-esteem and sovereign consciousness deals with reality, with nature, with an objective universe of facts; he holds his mind as his tool of survival and develops his ability to think. But the man who has abandoned his mind lives, not in a universe of facts, but in a *universe of people*; people, not facts, are *his* reality; people, not reason, are *his* tool of survival. It is with *them* that he has to deal, it is on *them* that his consciousness must focus, it is they whom he must understand or please or placate or deceive or maneuver or manipulate or obey.
>
> It is his success at this task that becomes his gauge of his fitness to exist — of his competence to live. . . . To the man I am describing, reality is *people*: in his mind, in his thinking, in the automatic connections of his consciousness, *people* occupy the place which, in the mind of a rational man, is occupied by *reality*.

I explained that social metaphysics represents a *principle* that can be more or less present in a given individual's psychology. Then I proceeded to sketch some of the basic social metaphysical types I had identified, some of which were more sympathetic than others. I understood social metaphysics ultimately as a rebellion against the responsibility of consciousness and independence.

In rereading my treatment of this subject in *The Psychology of Self-Esteem*, I regret the subtle and inappropriate note of moralism underlying my entire discussion, which distracts rather than illuminates; unfortunately, it was typical of my thinking of the period. I also regret that I did not approach the problem from a more developmental perspective. My approach is badly oversimplified. I wish I had said more about how the problem is to be solved.

When I made my first notes on social metaphysics I did not foresee that Ayn would leap upon the idea with almost savage eagerness — as if I had offered her not a means of better understanding human behavior but a sword to be brandished in the battle against irrationality. People who did not think for themselves or did not uphold independent convictions or who accepted unthinkingly ideas and values that Ayn regarded as evil, were "social metaphysicians." Since many people do not think for themselves, it was not difficult to find evidence of the syndrome everywhere. A high level of autonomy, especially in moral issues, is the exception, not the norm.

"You've gone far deeper than my idea of the second-hander in *The Fountainhead*," Ayn exclaimed. "You've really gone into the root of human rottenness." Turning to Barbara, she said, "Now you see why I say Nathan is a genius! Now he is no longer simply my student. Now I am his student as well." Soon, I too was brandishing the concept as an intellectual weapon.

Ayn and I caused a great deal of guilt and suffering. We did not hesitate to use the label "social metaphysics" whenever and wherever we found it. In later years, friends and students would come to dread our verdict as if it were a diagnosis of cancer. So enamored were Ayn and I of the concept that we were irresponsibly oblivious to the anguish we caused.

One of the most interesting people to join our circle was a man to whom Ayn initially took a strong dislike.

He was an economic analyst, employed by the National Industrial Conference Board. For nine months he was married to Joan Mitchell, which was how we got to know him. He was tall and solidly built, with black hair, dark horn-rim glasses, and a propensity for dark, funereal suits. He was somberness incarnate, looking chronically weary, resigned, and unhappy. He was twenty-six years old. Barbara, Ayn, Frank, and I once encountered him, with Joan, coming out of an elevator. "He looks like an undertaker," Ayn commented. The man's name was Alan Greenspan.

At that time he was not a free enterpriser but a Keynesian, at least in some respects, believing that the economy could be managed constructively by governmental manipulations of the money supply. He was also a logical positivist, which meant that he was adamant about his inability to know anything with certainty. He announced that logic was empty, the senses were untrustworthy, and that degrees of probability are all that is possible. "I *think* I exist," he stated, "but I can't be certain. In fact, I can't be certain that anything exists."

Surprisingly, he admired *The Fountainhead* and displayed a strong interest in our ideas. I astonished Ayn by announcing that I enjoyed talking to him. I sensed the presence of a romantic buried deep in his psyche. I was convinced that he had a first-class brain, his philosophy notwithstanding. He seemed almost ashamed of that hidden side that drew me to him. He confessed once that when he responded emotionally to something heroic in a movie, he reproached himself for his impracticality.

"How can you stand talking to him?" Ayn demanded. I answered, "I'm going to bring him around intellectually." This was one of the rare occasions when I thoroughly enjoyed disagreeing with Ayn; in matters of psychological judgment, I deferred to no one. "Never!" she declared. "A logical positivist and a Keynesian? I'm not even certain it's moral to deal with him at all." I smiled. "Wait and see."

Barbara, not I, accomplished one of the most hilarious aspects of Alan's conversion. The four of us were in Winnipeg together, Barbara visiting her family and Joan visiting hers. At a party there, I spied Barbara and Alan talking intently in a corner, their heads close together. A long time later they emerged, and Barbara pulled me aside to declare gleefully, "Guess what? I got him to admit that banks should be operated entirely privately, that there should be no government-chartered banks." I laughed incredulously. "How?" I asked. "How did you do it? I didn't know you even knew what a chartered bank is." She grinned triumphantly. "I didn't. But somehow we got talking about them. So I led him into explaining what they were and why they were considered to be necessary — as if I were checking on *his* understanding. Then I persuaded him that government shouldn't be involved, that a free market in banking is preferable. I sold him on the merits of a completely unregulated banking system. *Just by arguing on the basis of the information he provided.*" I shook my head in admiration. We had acquired a grasp of economic and political issues that did not make this kind of "conversion" entirely unusual; we knew the fundamentals — and we knew how to reason from them, even when we lacked specific knowledge. We had been expertly trained. Back in New York I loved telling the story of Barbara's victory over chartered banks.

Persuading Alan on economic matters was relatively easy. It was apparent that he had an extraordinarily lucid understanding of how markets functioned — a fact that, years later, would be almost universally acknowledged by his colleagues; he would become economic adviser to two presidents and then chairman of the Federal Reserve Board. Persuading Alan on philosophical issues was much harder. His attachment to uncertainty was tenacious. "How's the undertaker?" Ayn would ask. "Has he decided he exists yet?"

"Probability is all that is possible," he would say to me, not only about economic forecasting but about everything, and I would answer, "Without something of which you're certain, how can you judge probability?" "Can you prove you exist?" he would ask, and I would respond, "Shall I send you my answer from nonexistence?" "Validate the laws of logic," he would insist, and I would reply, " 'Validate' is a concept that presupposes your acceptance of logic; otherwise, what does it mean?"

This went on for some months, while Ayn watched from the sidelines, mildly disapproving, but disarmed by my optimism. One evening I grinned and asked her, "Guess who exists?" "What?" she exclaimed. "You've done it? The undertaker has decided he exists?" I nodded triumphantly. "You'll have to stop calling Alan the undertaker now. He's really an unusual person. I think you're going to like him."

His enthusiasm over *The Fountainhead* was duly noted by Ayn. When, after a number of meetings with her, he was invited to read *Atlas Shrugged* as it was being written, he came alive with an excitement no one had ever seen in him before. Shyly and reluctantly he began to yield to the romantic side of his nature; he fell in love with Ayn's portrayal of business and industry. Ayn compared him to a "sleeping giant" who was slowly waking up. She grew progressively more fond of him. In fact, he became a particular favorite. "You were right," she said to me. "He has a first-rate mind."

I visited my family in Toronto, and my cousin Allan Blumenthal and I continued our talks. One of the main issues we discussed was his coming to New York to study music at Juilliard.

One day I was at his home and we were telling his mother about his dislike of medicine. She protested that her son was losing his mind because medicine offered such a respectable way to earn a living. "But he's unhappy in medicine!" I interjected, when I saw Allan's expression of forlorn helplessness. His mother looked at me as if I had said something totally irrelevant. She shrugged her shoulders. "So who's happy?" she answered heavily.

When we left the house I said to Allan, "Do you understand what your mother said and what it means? Allan, in any sane world, it matters whether or not you're happy. This is the time to fight for your life."

We talked at great length. I had become a crusader for human happiness, self-actualization, the realization of one's potential. I was determined to ignite Allan with my passion. Soon, Allan Blumenthal entered the New York circle — "the class of '43," as Ayn began to call us, because that was the year *The Fountainhead* was published.

To my aunt and uncle, I was the villain who had led their son astray.

He had become a licensed physician but was disinclined to pursue a career in medicine, in part as a result of my malevolent influence. They were completely unimpressed by the fact that, since he began studying at Juilliard, he seemed more cheerful and alive than he ever had before.

My sister Elayne moved to New York and became an enthusiastic member of our group. She required no urging. Although we had shared an apartment in California, it was only now that I began to experience her as a friend. Our relationship had become philosophical. Non-philosophical relationships had no serious status in my mind. I did not believe in the kinship of blood, only of ideas.

For me, *choice* was a concept standing at the center of my view of existence. One did not *choose* one's siblings, just as one did not *choose* one's parents; these ties were biological, not volitional. As such, I felt that they did not count for very much; perhaps they were not totally insignificant but neither were they very important. And yet the truth was that I *wanted* to love my sisters and to feel "justified" in that love. If Elayne became an enthusiast of Ayn's philosophy, I had a connection with her that had validity in my own eyes. We were philosophical kin.

The core group of Ayn's admirers, the inner circle of the Ayn Rand world that formed prior to the publication of *Atlas* in 1957, eventually included Barbara and me; Leonard Peikoff; Joan Mitchell; Allan Blumenthal; Alan Greenspan; Elayne; Harry Kalberman; and Mary Ann Rukavina, an art historian introduced to us by Joan. As she saw the group growing Ayn said to me, "You're creating our own society."

We met at Ayn's every Saturday evening, to read and reread the new novel, to talk philosophy, psychology, political economy, literature, art, and to have our own experience of family and community.

At some point it amused Ayn to call our group, in private, the Collective — presumably because such a name suggested our exact opposite, since we saw ourselves as highly evolved individualists. We all thought the name was funny and quickly adopted it. The joke was on us because in fact we were a collective in ways none of us was yet able to appreciate. "The class of '43" became the name Ayn used when talking about us to outsiders.

Slowly the pieces were assembling on the chessboard. Slowly they began moving toward the positions they would hold at the time of the final explosion.

"Our own society," said Ayn.

"Atlantis," Frank said, smiling gently, only half-ironically.

·   ·   ·

Frank had lost his healthy-looking ranch tan, and his movements were fractionally slower. The inactivity of his first year in New York had aged him. He would sit through long silent hours while Ayn worked — or while Ayn, Barbara, and I talked — and no one knew the contents of his inner life. Nor did we inquire. He projected a diffuse good will that was like a protective barrier around himself.

In the spring of 1953 he found work making arrangements for a Park Avenue florist, and in some cases selling his arrangements to buildings for their lobbies. He did not make a great deal of money, but the work gave him a purpose and the income gave him some small sense of financial independence.

I was taken by the self-assertive imaginativeness of his arrangements; they disclosed a powerful artistic force. "Is this what's inside you?" I asked him once. As if it were the most obvious thing in the world, he answered naturally, "Oh yes." I wanted to say, How come you don't express it in some more serious way? — but I knew that would be condescending, pompous, totally inappropriate; so I said, "There's more to you than meets the eye," oblivious to the fact that this too was condescending and pompous. He answered, with his special quality of gentle humor, "There's more to everyone than meets the eye, Nathan."

I gathered from Ayn that they had not talked about intellectual matters for years; not since the beginning of their relationship. Now they talked less than ever. Ayn's intellectual needs were now being met by Barbara and me and by the Collective. During our evening sessions Frank's role became more and more ornamental.

And yet even when he was sitting silently there was often something subtly life-affirming in his demeanor. He projected the most extraordinary benevolence. The whole group was very fond of him and I think he sensed that. Barbara felt especially close to him; she identified with him and I think he sensed that too.

When my sister Florence, curious about our life in New York, asked, "But what exactly does Frank *do*?" I knew that most people were puzzled by Ayn and Frank's relationship, and I could not blame them. Yet at some level I loved him.

At Ayn and Frank's apartment we again met Henry and Frances Hazlitt, and I regretted that Ayn did not see more of them because I would like to have known them better; it did not occur to me to seek them out on my own because they were so much older.

Progressively, Ayn was withdrawing from former friends — from anyone who did not intimately share the world she was writing about. "After working on the book all day," she said, "it's agony to switch my consciousness to the outside world. Discussions with the Collective are almost the only form of social life I can bear — because it's the same universe as the book."

Notwithstanding Ayn's withdrawal, we did meet Professor Ludwig von Mises and his wife, Margit. This was very exciting for me because, having studied many of his books, I thought Dr. von Mises one of the outstanding minds of the century. He was then in his seventies — witty, brilliant, almost impishly charming.

Ayn's attitude toward Von Mises was puzzling. I never saw her be anything but friendly, respectful, admiring — although I had heard stories about them clashing once, rather heatedly, over questions of ethics. Ayn was almost girlish in the way she complimented him on his momentous achievements, and he seemed to find her delightful and stimulating. I was therefore shocked when, looking through her copy of Von Mises's *Human Action*, I saw margin notes that condemned, in frank language, many of Von Mises's statements. Ayn was particularly offended where he attempted to defend capitalism without reference of moral principles, or when he seemed to support Kantian epistemology (which to Ayn was a disaster). The margins were filled with abusive comments. It was not her disagreement that disturbed me but the savagery of her attacks. The only way I could rationalize it was by reference to Ayn's own passion for ideas, which sometimes allowed normal human considerations to fall by the wayside.

"Do you really think of him as a 'bastard'?" I asked Ayn. "I can't really believe that." She looked thoughtful for a moment, then answered, "As a total person, no, I suppose I don't. But if I focus on that aspect of him, where he goes irrational, yes, I do." What I interpreted this statement to mean was: Von Mises is brilliant, his contribution is enormous, he is wonderful, but still, he is "of the world"; he is not one of us. I recognized some of Ayn's psychology in myself.

I was troubled by the disparity between Ayn's behavior toward Von Mises and her comments in the margins of his books. To accuse Ayn of hypocrisy would not have occurred to me. But I recall discussing my confusion with Barbara, who shared my reaction. We let the matter go, assuming that one day we would understand — and that *of course* Ayn would have perfectly good reasons for her behavior. Today I recognize that it is of such attitudes that cults are made.

Several years later, when he read *Atlas Shrugged*, Dr. von Mises was profoundly enthusiastic and complimentary, although I had the impression that ethics as an intellectual discipline did not particularly interest him and he did not see its urgent relevance to his own work.

He paid Ayn one compliment she treasured, related to her by Henry

Hazlitt. Hazlitt told her, "Lu Mises called you 'the most courageous man in America.' " "Did he say *man?*" Ayn asked, and Hazlitt replied yes. Recounting the incident to Barbara and me, she said, "Isn't that *wonderful?*"

Ayn thought more highly of Hazlitt and Von Mises than any other conservatives whom she knew. Von Mises was clearly a giant, their disagreements about epistemology or anything else notwithstanding. She was aware that Hazlitt was sympathetic to altruism and pragmatism, but she thought him a brilliant economic writer and, like Von Mises, an uncompromising advocate of freedom. Nonetheless, she was withdrawing from conservatives in general, not only because of her preoccupation with the novel, but also because she saw herself as having less and less in common with them.

"I am not *primarily* an advocate of capitalism," she would write in *The Objectivist,* in September 1971, "but of egoism; and I am not primarily an advocate of egoism, but of reason." In the 1950s, many of the conservatives were more anticommunist than they were pro–free enterprise. "Anticommunism by itself is almost meaningless," Ayn would say. "That's one of the things wrong with McCarthy. You can't fight communism effectively unless you're for something better. A lot of those people don't know what in hell they're for." Some of these conservatives favored certain forms of censorship, to protect "public morality"; many favored military conscription. "They're not defenders of individual rights," Ayn would say scornfully. Many attempted to justify capitalism by appeals to religion, "which amounts," Ayn would say, "to conceding reason and science to the enemy." Many of them were hopelessly nonintellectual; when Ayn attempted to explain that the battle was ultimately philosophical, their eyes glazed over.

For a long time I had been arguing that we had to find some other name for ourselves, politically. "We're not conservatives," I said. "There's no tradition left for us to conserve. Government intervention in the economy has been the status quo since the nineteenth century. What we stand for is actually radical."

I did not have Ayn's sense of history or her factual knowledge of the past, and while yesterday's traditions meant very little to her, they meant even less to me. *She* was the only tradition that interested me and it lay in the future, not the past.

Ayn detested Eisenhower, who was then president; she had been a supporter of Taft, with reservations. Eisenhower represented to her the epitome of the compromising, unprincipled conservative. I recall her indignation, several years later, when she showed me a *Time* magazine article, dated July 29, 1957. "*Here*," she said, "is proof of everything I ever said about Eisenhower — and why I hate the typical conservative mentality."

Recalling his tortuous postwar discussions with Zhukov — a "confirmed Communist" but an "honest man" — Dwight Eisenhower went on: "One evening we had a three-hour conversation. We tried to explain to the other just what our systems meant . . . to the individual, and I was very hard put to it when he insisted that their system appealed to the idealistic and we completely to the materialistic, and I had a very tough time defending our position because he said: 'You tell a person he can do as he pleases, he can act as he pleases, he can do anything. Everything that is selfish in man you appeal to him, and we tell him that he must sacrifice for the state. . . .' "

Asked by the New York *Times*'s James Reston if he meant to imply that democracy was more difficult to defend than Communism, the President patiently explained: "Look, Mr. Reston, I think you could run into people you have a hard time convincing that the sun is hot and the earth is round. . . . Against that kind of belief you run against arguments that almost leave you breathless. You don't know how to meet them."

When I looked up from the article, Ayn exclaimed, "Is that a sickening evasion or isn't it? That abysmal bastard *could not answer Zhukov.* A representative of the bloodiest dictatorship in history is boasting of his country's moral superiority — and the president of the United States, the greatest, noblest, freest country in the history of the world, *does not know what to say.* That's the intellectual paralysis produced by altruism. That's why, without a morality of rational self-interest, capitalism can't be defended."

By the time this article appeared we had long since ceased calling ourselves conservatives. Early in 1954, Ayn said to me, "You're right. We're not conservatives. We're radicals for capitalism."

We had discarded the label of conservative and chosen a new designation for ourselves. In a more personal area, I made another such change.

I had disliked my name for a long time. Nathan Blumenthal did not feel like me and I wanted a name that did, especially because I was going to be a writer. This was typical of how I thought, in that I had strong preferences about everything: books, movies, automobiles, clothes, even colors — everything was "me" or "not me." Moreover, I wanted a name that I had chosen myself — not one that had been decided for me by someone else. As in so many other issues, *choice* was supremely important to me. I was not yet aware that in many spiritual traditions it is quite common for an individual to adopt a new name following a major personal transformation.

"Why should I be stuck with someone else's choice of name?" I said to Ayn and Barbara. "A name is a very personal thing." They agreed, and wanted to know what names I had considered. I hadn't thought of any as yet, except that I wanted to keep my initials. Ayn chuckled and said, "All writers and criminals do that when they change their name. I did."

A few weeks later I announced, "The first name is easy. It's Nathaniel. It's the last name I'm stuck on. I'll try looking through the B's in the phone book; maybe something will strike me."

In the spring of 1954, I said to Ayn, Frank, and Barbara, "How do you like 'Nathaniel Branden'?" They liked it immediately. Barbara said, " 'Barbara Branden' — it has a nice sound — *let's do it.*"

Many years later a journalist, Nora Ephron, insisted that it was significant that the name "Branden" contained "rand" (a fact I had never thought about until I read her article), and that a translation from Hebrew, based on a rearrangement of the letters ("ben rand"), disclosed the hidden meaning, "son of Rand." I think this was intended to support her charge of cultism. Given my absolute ignorance of Hebrew, I found her suggestion amusing, not to say plain silly. However, I disliked the implication that I wished to conceal the fact of being Jewish, since I had always been outspoken about it. Ephron appeared eager to attack Ayn Rand and was reaching for any ammunition that was handy. Later, some other writer carried Ephron's speculations one step further: could it be "mere coincidence," he wondered, that *Atlas Shrugged* was published by *Rand*om House?

I became Nathaniel Branden legally in September of that year — a few days before all our lives were to change forever.

It began with the way I greeted Ayn when I arrived in her apartment and the way I said good-bye when I left. When I embraced her, either on arriving or on departing, I began to hold the moment longer than necessary for a casual greeting or farewell; and then longer still. When we kissed, the earlier sense of family affection had vanished, to be replaced by the faintest suggestion of sensuality. Nothing was said. I was aware of this change on both our parts and I knew that she was aware. I did not think about what this meant or where it might be leading. I did not suppose it was leading anywhere.

With each passing month we became closer. At some imperceptible point in our relationship, the awareness of being male and female had shifted into sharper focus. An invisible energy charged the atmosphere.

In her presence I experienced an enhanced sense of masculine power — and I knew that she felt a heightened awareness of herself as a woman. I liked knowing that I was the cause of what she was feeling.

There was an element of danger, and I liked that too. I felt almost reckless about it. Safety lay in the fact that I was married and that she was married; and in the fact that I was twenty-four and she was forty-nine. An affair was unthinkable.

On an afternoon in late June I visited Ayn alone. Frank was out and Barbara was working on an assignment for school. I felt restless, bored with my studies, and delighted that Ayn was willing to abandon her writing for a daytime meeting. There was an odd lack of direction to our conversation, as if I had infected Ayn with my restlessness. It was as if we were both waiting, neither of us knowing how to proceed.

Finally, Ayn asked, "How are you and Barbara doing?"

Barbara and I had been married for a year and a half. Our marriage seemed more or less harmonious. Most of the time my spirits were high. Many years in the future, long after our divorce, Barbara would inform me irritably that during this period she had been miserable much of the time. If this was true, I was not aware of it. But I knew that something was lacking in my life and I tried to convey this to Ayn.

"It's not easy to answer you. Barbara and I are okay, I guess. We have our frictions, naturally, and sex still isn't right, but there's something more basic that's frustrating and not what I had hoped for. I can't imagine life without Barbara, I feel we're connected in some very profound way, something deeper than I can explain even to myself. All of us have a sense of our own emotional capacity . . . a sense of what we're capable of feeling . . . and . . . there's a part of me that's not in the marriage at all, a part that wants . . . I don't know . . . something I've never felt, something more, something incredible . . . do you have any idea of what I'm talking about? . . . something inside me that hasn't been touched yet, a capacity, a passion totally outside the universe I share with Barbara."

If I had begun my answer in a state of innocence, I was not innocent now: I knew precisely what Ayn would hear in my words and how she would be affected. An answer begun in pain became an act of seduction. Not a seduction aimed at Ayn's body — there was no thought of anything that tangible — but at her mind. Everything I was saying was true; what made it an act of seduction was the knowledge that I was speaking for both of us, that she could have described her own marriage in similar terms.

"Do you remember the scene in the novel," I went on, "when Dagny is working in that old office building across the street from Taggart Transcontinental, and she's thinking about her life and about how the world she finds as an adult is not the world she expected and hoped for . . . it's so much less . . . and she thinks of Francisco and Hank Rearden, and is aware of some emotional capacity beyond what she feels for either man . . . something greater . . . and of course that's what she'll feel one day for John Galt, but she doesn't know that yet . . . so there's just this longing?"

Ayn's head had dropped, her eyes were closed, her hands were covering her face. She sat at the edge of the sofa and I sat a few feet away, by the window, watching her. She was wearing a green short-sleeved blouse, and I looked at her bare arms, suddenly aware of her vulnerability.

What are you doing? a voice within demanded angrily, and another voice responded, *It's all right. This is only a dream. In a few minutes you'll both go back to reality. But you can at least permit yourself this.*

Lifting her head Ayn answered, her voice weighted with emotion, "I understand you fully. I understand you better than I care to say."

We looked at each other through a long, tortured moment of silence. Neither of us was willing to venture further. I imagined what might be taking place in her mind and she imagined what might be taking place in mine. For the moment, we had reached the limit of acceptable self-disclosure.

A few minutes later Frank returned home and Ayn rushed to embrace him.

"Hello, Fluff," he said gaily, using his pet name for her.

"Hello, Cubbyhole," she whispered, using her favorite term of endearment for him.

When she turned back to the room, I imagined I saw something in her eyes I had never seen before: the faintest suggestion of guilt.

During the summer, Barbara and I visited my family in Toronto. I was almost uncontrollably impatient; I could think of nothing but returning to New York; I was tense, short with people, distracted. I wondered why this separation from Ayn felt so difficult. I wondered what was the matter with me. I caught my mother looking at me strangely. Barbara, in contrast, seemed to find my behavior quite normal; I assumed she shared my restlessness in Toronto.

When I insisted on cutting our visit short, my mother announced that she would accompany us back to New York for a visit. This would give her an opportunity to spend time with Elayne. I agreed readily; this was a matter of complete indifference to me. When I next visited Ayn's apartment, Barbara and my mother were with me. Mother was keenly curious about the woman who had become some kind of obsession in her son's life.

Later, she said to me, "I will always remember the look on your face when we were riding up the elevator in Ayn's building. You looked happier than I had ever seen you. Nathan, what is it? Was I such a terrible mother? Did you want a second one? Is that what Ayn is to you?"

In September, Allan Blumenthal was to give a piano recital in Toronto. He had engaged an auditorium for the occasion and had sent out invitations. Barbara and I and several members of our group were planning to fly to Toronto for the event. Ayn and Frank were planning to drive; incongruously, Ayn was fearful of flying, although later in life she did occasionally travel by air. This trip to Canada would be the first time she had left the United States since her arrival. We were all cheerfully excited, as if the recital represented some kind of triumph for all of us and for our vision of life.

Allan was radiant, as if the very best of him had at last risen to the surface. It seemed to me that he moved with a new dignity and pride. Watching him I thought: this is the power of psychology and philosophy combined, this is what we are able to do, to release human ability, to liberate human energy. I felt drunk with a sense of efficacy.

Sitting in the darkness of the auditorium, seeing Allan in white tie and tails at the piano, listening to his music rising through space past all the walls of his life, I felt proud of having contributed to this moment. I experienced enormous affection for Allan and the most precious feeling of all: admiration.

I looked at Barbara and saw that she knew what was taking place within me. This is part of the bond between us, I thought — that in moments such as this, she will always know. She pressed my hand and whispered, "What the recital must mean to you."

I cannot offer an objective assessment of Allan's playing that night. I thought he had talent but could not judge the degree. But to me, his performance sounded magnificent. Afterward, Ayn and the others were very enthusiastic about his playing.

Later, when Allan and I were alone for a moment, he said solemnly, "You gave me tonight. Whatever happens in the future, whether or not I make it, I will have had this. Thank you."

It was impossible to believe that he and I had ever been anything but friends. Whatever that past foolishness had been about, it was irrelevant now. It was a benevolent universe.

Next afternoon, in the home of Florence and Hans, Ayn and I sat facing a group of people who had wanted to meet the author of *The Fountainhead* and to ask questions about her philosophy. Ayn had insisted that I join her for the question-and-answer session. We fielded

questions almost playfully — moving effortlessly from ethics to political economy to aesthetics to epistemology to current events — sometimes elaborating on each other's answers, sometimes beginning the
same sentence in the same instant, sometimes inserting parenthetical
comments within the other's response, laughing openly in the pleasure
of our intellectual comradeship, and experiencing a level of fusion that
was intoxicating.

The sense of intoxication remained, next day, when we drove back
to New York — Ayn, Frank, Barbara, Elayne, and I. In the first part
of the trip Barbara and Elayne sat in the back seat and Frank, Ayn,
and I sat in the front. Frank drove.

Ayn was on a talking jag and could not seem to contain herself.
"Weren't the past few days wonderful? This is the way life should be.
Allan is talented. I can see why you wanted to encourage him, Nathan.
That question-and-answer session yesterday afternoon — we were
like Siamese twins; our minds work exactly the same way. Your answers were models of precision. I didn't even have to be there: you
could have represented me flawlessly. I couldn't have imagined quite
such integration with another person. Frank, just think — Nathan is
twenty-four and look what he's accomplished already . . . his psychological theories . . . his triumph with Allan . . . his work with the
others. . . . Elayne, did you know you had such a remarkable
brother?"

"Well, Ayn," Elayne began, amused, "that's a long story."

I laughed and protested, "Ayn, I'm becoming shy. Please stop. And
besides, you never ask a sister what she thinks about her kid brother."

"I guess you're all right," said Elayne in her flat, good-natured way.

"Well, I know Barbara agrees with me," Ayn said brightly.

"I do," Barbara announced cheerfully from the back seat.

For the next several hours, Ayn would not stop. With occasional
excursions into other subjects, she kept bringing the subject back to
me, insisting that I was a genius, a great psychologist, a man of destiny.
At some point I began answering in kind, praising her writing, speaking of what she given me intellectually and inspirationally, predicting
her future impact on Western civilization.

Then it was evening, Ayn and I were now sitting in the back seat,
her head was resting on my shoulder, and she was saying, "I really
don't know how to identify our relationship. It's not exactly friendship, as I've ever thought about friendship; it's much more than that.
I certainly don't feel maternal; I have never thought of you as my son.
You're way beyond being a student, you're much more than a fellow
fighter. You're just . . . Nathan. That's the only way I can think of you:
you're just Nathan."

"That's how I feel about you," I said softly, my arm around her, "You're just . . . Ayn." I began speaking of my appreciation of her more intimately and more personally than I had ever permitted myself before. "I can no longer imagine what life would have been, if we hadn't met."

I heard the huskiness in her voice and in my own. I was not ready to know what it meant. I listened as she went on talking, as my words mingled with hers, and I was vaguely aware of feeling irresponsible, unaccountable, but indifferent to the fact, indifferent to the awareness that the meaning of what we were saying would eventually catch up with us. I felt that Ayn was taking the initiative in leading us where we were going, but that her conscious mind was a few steps behind mine in grasping the implications. In retrospect I would say I was naive in that assumption.

In the front seat, Frank, Elayne, and Barbara were silent. It did not occur to me to wonder what they were thinking. They were somewhere far away.

"Just . . . Nathan," Ayn was saying and then her eyes widened as if awareness had finally come. She looked at me almost for reassurance, as if she were uncertain of the reality of what was happening. Recklessly oblivious to what we were setting in motion, I smiled arrogantly, intimately, tenderly.

We stopped for the night at a motel. When we went to our separate rooms, and I was alone with Barbara, I felt oddly suspended, fragmented, disoriented.

While I was familiar with the concept of dissociation, a psychological state in which the thoughts and feelings of the moment do not connect to one's wider context, do not connect to reality, I did not identify my own condition as dissociation. I merely experienced myself as moving through a void, with no assessment of what that signified.

Reality came back, demanding integration, when I faced Barbara and saw the pain and rage on her face, and heard her say to me, "*Do you know what it's like to be trapped in a car for several hours and have to listen to your husband make love to another woman?*"

I froze. Cut off from my own knowledge, suspended in a kind of emotional vacuum, I wondered: what was Barbara talking about? was she talking about Ayn and me? I had had no time to grasp, let alone assimilate, the significance of what happened in the car. I did not yet know whether anything of enduring consequence had really taken place. I did not want to know — not yet, not until I had some opportunity to meditate and reflect. I tried to answer Barbara, not too articulately, struggling for a mental focus that eluded me.

"You two are in love with each other!" she shouted. "My God, *don't you know?*"

I could not force my mind to work. I had left the context I shared with Ayn and was struggling to re-enter the one I shared with Barbara. I felt suspended between the two. I needed time to be alone, to think, to digest what had happened, but there was no time; my wife was standing in front of me, demanding answers to which she was entitled — and I had no answers.

One thing was urgent and immediate: I saw Barbara's pain and I wanted desperately to heal it, to put her mind at rest. I muttered something meant to be reassuring.

"Don't try to tell me I wasn't hearing what I was hearing!" Barbara cried. "I know what I know!"

Drawing on every resource I could summon, fighting for calm, I said, "Barbara, come on now. Ayn is twenty-five years older than I am."

"What has that got to do with what you two were saying to each other? Obviously the age barrier is not a barrier!"

"But . . . but, you know how Ayn and I are, how we've always been. We're a mutual admiration society. We even joke about it. Perhaps in the car we got carried away, but can you tell me you heard anything new, in principle, that you haven't heard us say before?"

Later I learned that Elayne had perceived the conversation precisely as I was now explaining it.

This perspective seemed to quiet Barbara a bit. "No," she conceded thoughtfully, "but still . . ."

I had no sense of lying to Barbara. What she was suggesting, in the cold, clear light of ordinary reality, truly struck me as unthinkable. My mind had now slammed tightly shut against it; all I desired was a return to the "normality" of yesterday What had happened in the car now felt like a hallucination. Whatever it had been, I knew beyond any doubt that I had no desire to leave Barbara for Ayn. I told her that.

"That may be true," she said, "but that's not the issue."

We agreed to try to sleep. It was a confused and anguished night for both of us.

The next morning, we all met for breakfast, and while Frank and Elayne appeared relaxed, Ayn, Barbara, and I were strained and quiet. Early that afternoon we arrived back in Manhattan. Our good-byes were muted.

Barbara and I did not pursue the subject further. We moved through the rest of the day almost with resignation, as if we knew that another shoe was yet to drop — this would happen with my next visit to Ayn — and that until then, conversation was useless.

Next day, I walked from our apartment on Thirty-fifth Street to Ayn's on Thirty-sixth, thinking that we might have a long, intimate conversation about what had happened in the car or that we might not speak of it at all. I could not have said which I hoped for.

Frank was working at the florist shop, and Ayn was alone in the apartment when I arrived. At first she seemed at ease and relaxed, and I thought: everything is going to be all right; we're not going to talk about what happened; we have simply reached a deeper level of intimacy, and now life can continue as before — only better.

Many times in the years ahead I would wish passionately that I had been right.

For an hour we talked about everything except our feelings for each other. I did not realize, but should have, that Ayn was waiting for me to speak first. Finally she said, in a note of gentle urgency, "Now, then, we really must talk about what happened in the car. You know what I mean, of course?"

In such moments one does not hesitate; one does not falter. I felt the spotlight fall on me, and the moves had to be impeccable. When we were alone together and connected in our special way, we created a universe that was uniquely ours; I would not fail it — or her.

"Of course I know what you mean," I smiled in a manner of total and absolute assurance.

"Well," Ayn went on, "don't you want to say something?"

With the sense of moving across a minefield I answered, "I wasn't certain if I should . . . or whether it was better just to leave the situation . . . to our understanding . . ."

She looked at me as if what I had just said was incomprehensible.

"In the car," she persisted, "what we said to each other . . . what you said to me . . . it sounded like love." She pronounced this last word in a hushed voice. "Or have I misunderstood everything?"

I was very faintly aware of feeling pressured, pulled at a speed not of my choosing. I knew her well enough to recognize the meaning of her intensity; her dark, luminous eyes searched my face for possible signs of betrayal. I could almost read the question in her mind: will Nathan be another Leo? If she were merely inquiring about *my* feelings, if she were not struggling with her own feelings of love, she would have been much lighter in her approach. The quiet urgency of her questioning said everything. I looked at the woman who had been my idol since I was fourteen years old — I looked at the author of *The Fountainhead* and *Atlas Shrugged* — and saw her struggling to contain emotions she could not express until and unless I released her to do so.

Suddenly I had the sense that everything I had ever done, every choice I ever made, had led me to this moment. Part of me wanted to escape, to fly back to life as it had been before. But the more dominant part made my voice steady, my manner indestructibly serene.

I said, as if I were the one who would now lead the way, "Ayn, you misunderstood nothing. *Of course* I am in love with you."

PART
TWO

EIGHT

"OF COURSE I am in love with you."

In the moment of saying these words I knew that my life had changed irrevocably and that there could be no turning back. I did not yet know what precisely I was committing myself to, but I knew I was making a commitment of enormous consequence, and I thought: whatever is to happen now, I can deal with it, I am ready. I felt expectant and energized as we looked at each other through a moment of exquisitely charged silence.

Then her expression changed and she stared at me almost as if her intention were to intimidate. "Do you understand what you are saying?" she whispered challengingly. "This is not an impulse? You are not being capricious?"

I shook my head as if to say, you know better than that.

Her words were like steps taken across a tightrope high in space: "If I love . . . if I give myself emotionally . . . it's such an exception for me . . . the man has to understand . . . what he's undertaking . . . ."

Rising within me was a euphoria that clashed with the tense solemnity of her manner, and I had to fight a desire to laugh exuberantly. I could see the cautious older woman struggling for control over the young girl within her who wanted only to surrender to the moment. Her expression shifted from eagerness to caution and back again. The ferocity of her struggle unnerved me a little, but even my apprehension contributed to my buoyancy. This was life as it was meant to be lived, filled with danger and ecstasy and unimagined possibilities. I felt as if I had broken free of a whole network of constraints, had shattered the ordinary framework of existence, and that I, Nathaniel Branden, had taken Nathan Blumenthal by the hand and led him into a context uniquely his own, where he could be fully himself. "Do you really understand," she was saying, almost ominously, "what you would be undertaking?"

"I love you," I said, feeling it with the power of absolute certainty, and implying that nothing else needed to be said.

She went on questioning me: was I prepared to make the emotional commitment implied by my declaration? I was not entirely clear what this meant; nonetheless I nodded confidently. It occurred to me that she was seeking to draw me out while she had as yet made no declaration of her own; she wanted the initial risks to be mine. I thought, a little impatiently, that she needed always to be in control, the master of any encounter; but I did not mind too much because her feelings were so transparent: it was obvious that she wanted to stop talking and to embrace and that she would not permit herself to do so. She did not look formidable; she looked uncertain and vulnerable.

She said, with a touching quality of almost youthful honesty, "I know . . . in a novel . . . it wouldn't happen quite this way . . . the woman wouldn't be interrogating the man . . . but, please understand and . . ."

Disarmed by her words and manner, feeling intensely how precious she was to me, I assured her that I understood completely.

"*What* do you understand?" she asked.

"I understand that, in some sense, you see yourself as putting your emotional life in my hands." The thought lifted me to a great, dizzying height.

"Exactly. That doesn't frighten you?"

"No."

"If this is a mistake," she said, "I have more to lose than you do, if only because I'm older."

I accepted her statement uncritically, without pointing out that the risks for me were hardly negligible, even though she seemed oblivious to them.

"I don't know what we're going to do," I said, "but this is not a mistake."

"This changes nothing about how I feel about Frank or how you feel about Barbara," she said, confident of her right to speak for both of us.

I found her statement only slightly doubtful; I did not yet know what the truth was. I told myself: Ayn surely knows; she seems so certain. "It changes nothing," I affirmed.

"I do love you," she confided, almost shyly. "There, I've said it." Then, with more certainty, she said it again: "I love you."

Wanting to put us both at greater ease, I answered, in a tone of light mockery, "I was wondering when you were going to get around to it."

"Please don't joke. Not now."

I apologized, while knowing that my deeper motive for teasing her had been to shift her off her center, to challenge her sense of control. I felt an expansive sense of power.

She lifted her face to mine, and we kissed and held each other in a way that was new for both of us, and it felt natural and normal and inevitable. She kissed as she did everything, with absolute and total commitment, which I thought wonderful. For me the moment was exquisitely erotic. We trembled with excitement. I knew that in this arena her deepest desire was not to control but to drop any semblance of control, to melt and yield and respond, and I welcomed what she now expected from me.

Ayn whispered self-chastisingly, her eyes sparkling with humor, "What's the matter with me? This is what should have happened the moment you walked in the door today."

"This is the difference between art and life," I said chuckling.

She laughed in agreement. We were both still a little nervous and that too was enjoyable, as if sharing nervousness was itself an act of deepening intimacy.

Any thought or feeling, any confusion or uncertainty, that might have clashed with the happiness of the moment seemed unimportant. I identified the impulse that drew me into this new relationship with Ayn as the voice of reason, the voice of my highest self, to which any other internal voice would have to give way. I was dimly aware that in some compartment of my consciousness there was agitation and protest — an alarm signal too faint to have an impact. I had committed myself. I felt love, excitement, dismay, disorientation: I felt alive.

"We must do nothing to hurt Frank or Barbara," Ayn uttered suddenly and firmly.

I did not know how we could avoid it, but I agreed that we would do everything we could to protect our respective marriages. The thought occurred to me that we were already contradicting that agreement by the very nature of our discussion, but was there any other sane way to proceed?

"We won't have an actual affair," she said. "The romance will be nonsexual, in the ultimate sense."

Part of me felt relieved by this statement; another part, more dominant, felt disappointed.

"You mean it will be sexual in everything but fact," I answered.
She nodded.

"We must do nothing to cause them discomfort publicly," I declared.

Again she nodded and said that we would do our best to respect their feelings in every way we reasonably could. We discussed this for a long while and then she declared, "We will ask them if they object to us meeting alone once or twice a week, just to talk."

"We meet by ourselves occasionally anyway."

"But now it will be a regular and integral part of our lives."

"That would be wonderful."

"I'm sure they'll agree to that," Ayn said. "We have a right to something."

There was an edge of anger in her voice, directed against Frank and Barbara. Intuitively I felt I knew the source of that anger: in this moment and context, they were impediments. Whatever the reasons, we felt that they did not match us in energy, initiative, strength, ambition, or passion, although we did not explicitly acknowledge this. These were matters we talked around, rather than addressed head-on. Now, in Ayn's voice, the unexpressed had risen to the surface for the briefest flash of an instant. It was not named but it was felt, and it was in our eyes as we looked at each other in silent understanding: we would not be stopped.

Then the conversation switched back to our importance to each other and how each made the other feel uniquely understood, and as we talked Ayn continued to shift between two different aspects of her personality — one moment, happy and vulnerable and open, the next, guarded, detached, stern.

"I've never given anyone but Frank this kind of power," she said, almost as a warning.

I wondered about the nature of Frank's "power" and what it meant practically. From the way she looked at me I believed that she was continuing to question: Am I seeing him objectively? Is this encounter really what it seems? Can I trust him? I thought that, given the extraordinary and unexpected nature of what was occurring, her response was entirely understandable; did she not have every right to her concerns? Only in retrospect am I fully aware of the annoyance I felt at Ayn's suspiciousness, which in fact I experienced as onerous.

I was aware of an adjustment taking place deep within me. If, in the past, I had often felt with Ayn that I had to be older than my chronological age and that the younger parts of me had no place in our relationship, that feeling had now risen to an unprecedented degree. I felt that I had to be the man she had never had in her life but urgently needed and deserved — a contemporary who could match her strength and give her the kind of support she said she had never experienced. I now required of myself that I be fifty years old.

In the excitement of facing this challenge I was aware of something powerful emerging within me, a force indomitable and inexhaustible.

I was less aware that something else, more delicate, was dying: the joy of being twenty-four. If there were cries of protest from that disowned self, I chose not to hear them.

I was Nathaniel Branden and I could do anything.

If ever a decision had multiple motivations, it was the decision to become romantically involved with Ayn. I loved her, but there was also the matter of ego. The challenge was exhilarating. She was a stupendous mind and an electrifying personality — and when I looked into her eyes the image I saw reflected was that of a god. It was inevitable. Too great an electric charge had built up between us. She was a passionate woman, I was a passionate young man. It was drama, it was theater, it was an adventure, it was idealism, it was vanity, it was madness.

Barbara knew I needed to see Ayn alone this afternoon, but I had asked her to come by later, at four o'clock. Nonetheless, when the doorbell rang I was unprepared. I did not think to ask Ayn to wait until I could discuss the situation with Barbara by myself. However, Ayn projected an urgency that conveyed that Barbara must be informed of the facts at once. In retrospect, the way we proceeded strikes me as barbaric.

Almost immediately Ayn said, in a compassionately gentle voice, "Well, Barbara, it must have been very difficult for you since the car ride, and you've probably been wondering what Nathan and I have been saying to each other today."

Barbara nodded her head numbly. Her face disclosed no discernible emotion beyond a tinge of apprehension. It was as if she already knew everything, and no transitions, no explanations, were really needed — as if, in her own mind, she had heard everything Ayn and I had said to each other that day, and what she was hearing now was only a confirmation.

I stood by silently, disconnected from all emotion, as Ayn proceeded to explain that the shift in our relationship had been coming for a long time and probably should have been obvious to us all: it was logical and normal and quite unastonishing, if one thought about it, that she and I would love each other not just as friends but as man and woman.

"We're not Platonists," Ayn said. "We don't hold our values in some other realm, unrelated to the realm in which we live our lives. If Nathan and I are who we are, if we see what we see in each other, if we mean the values we profess — how can we not be in love?"

As I listened, the image of Ayn as matron of honor at Barbara's and my wedding came flashing through my mind and for one instant I felt horror; then the image and the horror were gone, like a fading fragment of a dream. Ayn went on talking for a very long time, amplifying her argument in such a way that the validity of what she was saying seemed more and more self-evident. She was a sorceress of reason.

Barbara kept nodding her head, like someone in a trance. I felt a sudden surge of agonized protectiveness, but stood frozen and did not move toward her.

"This does not mean that Nathan does not love you," Ayn went on, "just as I love Frank. You must understand that."

Why is Ayn choosing to speak for me? I thought, a bit irritably.

"I know Nathan loves me," Barbara said, with a dignity I found immensely attractive. I walked over and took her hand.

"Barbara," I said softly, "what's happened between Ayn and me had to happen. It changes nothing about how I feel about you." I meant it.

"You have nothing to fear," Ayn said. Even in that moment, I knew that statement was preposterous, notwithstanding what I had said to Barbara. Ayn went on, "He's your husband and nothing will change that. Look at the age difference between Nathan and me. We have no future, except as friends. I'm not going to make myself ludicrous with a younger man. All we would like is time to be alone together, one afternoon and one evening a week . . . ." While Barbara sat in a visibly dazed state, Frank returned home. It was clear from their exchange in the first moments of his arrival that he and Ayn had already had some preliminary discussion. He looked as if the entire situation were already known to him, as if he too had been present in the room all afternoon. The skin of his face seemed paler than usual and more drawn. I thought I saw a hint of anger in his eyes, but not when he looked at me, only when he looked at Ayn.

In a manner as persistent as a drill cutting through granite, Ayn proceeded to repeat what she had said to Barbara, now going into many more details about her feelings, about her intellectual loneliness, about what I had given her and how she saw me, about the uniqueness of our relationship. "Frank, you yourself have spoken of how much you love Nathan, of what he's brought to our lives. You've seen the whole struggle of my career, so you know what it means to have found a mind and a character like his. He gives me a kind of understanding I thought impossible. He's my future, he's the one who will carry the work forward, only he exists now, he's here in our lives now. Frank, in a way you saw what was coming before I did: it was you who said Nathan was the reason I came back from California when I did. It's a rational universe: this *had to happen*."

When Barbara, and then Frank, flared up in angry protest, conveying that they found the whole situation intolerable, Ayn became warmer, gentler, more implacable still — acknowledging their feelings, conveying compassion for their pain, and moving toward the goal of their eventual acceptance of the situation with the single-mindedness of a military commander who, looking neither to the right nor to the left, moves relentlessly forward. "I can't stand this!" Barbara cried, then slowly melted in surrender to the sounds of Ayn's hypnotic voice. "I won't put up with this, it's outrageous!" Frank shouted, then relapsed into passivity and impotence even before Ayn could complete her response.

I was silent. I was fascinated by the artistry of her persuasiveness, I felt more like a spectator than a protagonist in the drama. I did eventually say to Barbara and Frank, "This is something apart from our normal, everyday lives. But it's not really all that new, if we're honest about it — Ayn and I have always had a special connection. Both of you have known that. And I never felt that either one of you resented it or was jealous."

"It's not as if we were proposing a sexual relationship," Ayn added.

For the first time I found myself wondering why we were not proposing an affair and whether Barbara would really care: I could not imagine her feeling sexual jealousy where I was concerned. Now, I nodded in support of Ayn's statement.

Ayn asked Frank and Barbara, rhetorically, "Do you want to leave us because of Nathan's and my feelings for each other?"

The answer was instantly no. They acknowledged that they understood and in fact respected those feelings.

Ayn persisted, "Then do you want us to go on as before, pretending that our feelings do not exist?"

That did not seem reasonable either, Frank and Barbara conceded, looking more and more defeated. They were not fighters. They had no chance.

"Faking reality does not work," Ayn declared. "What realistic alternative is there to what we're proposing?"

Some part of me was carried along by sheer excitement, some by Ayn's certainty, and some by an accumulation of pain and rage at Barbara that now made me indifferent to her suffering.

"There isn't an alternative," Frank said in response to Ayn's question; he did not say it happily. Barbara's expression had an unself-pitying austerity when she nodded her head in acquiescence.

Ayn's manipulative dishonesty, and my own complicity in it — so obvious to me in retrospect — seemed in this moment like "rationality" and "realism."

When Barbara and I said good-bye to Ayn and Frank, we all hugged one another. We were attempting to create a spirit of love, a spirit of transcendence and of triumph over unworthy fears. I felt pain at any suffering I might be causing and at the same time I felt exultation, as if we had all reached a height none of us had conceived before.

Later that night, back in our own apartment, Barbara said to me, "I love Ayn so much. And it's no mystery to me why she's in love with you. You're the kind of man she should have. I want to see her happy." There were tears in her eyes, and I held her close, stroking her hair, not knowing what to think, say, or do. She whispered, "I want to see you happy. I know what I've never given you. Both of you deserve more than you've ever had. I want you to have it. I mean this selfishly. This is not self-sacrifice."

We made love that night — Barbara, for once, taking the lead — with more feeling than she had brought to our bed for a long time.

Ayn's and my affair began — sexually — five months later, in January 1955.

I was clearly the initiator, much more so than I had been previously. In my private afternoon and evening meetings with Ayn, I became aware of my impact as a man in a way I had not experienced before. When Ayn looked at me I saw what I had always longed to see on a woman's face: appreciation that combined the sexual and the spiritual. Her admiration did not remain abstract, or divorced from her body; it was immediately translated into physical terms. Her mind and her sexuality were integrated. This was the kind of woman I could understand.

Ayn frightened most people who were in awe of her authority and intellect. What she wanted was a man whose esteem would reduce her to a sex object. This seemed so simple and natural to me that all I could think was that in this arena I was at last free to be uninhibitedly myself — to release an energy that had very little outlet in my marriage.

"I don't want a platonic relationship," I announced to Ayn, "not in any sense whatsoever. With you, I want to experience everything."

I felt a new and deeper level of confidence, certainty, and knowledge of female sexuality that seemed to have materialized out of nowhere. I discovered that whereas I could falter in the emotional realm, I felt as secure in the arena of sex as I did in the arena of intellect.

"I'm afraid of what's happening," Ayn confided. "This could change our lives in a far more radical way than we had thought. Are you sure — are you absolutely sure — you want to proceed?"

"Absolutely."

I had lost all sense of restraints or barriers: there was only what I wanted. I did not think how either Ayn's marriage or mine would be affected. I still wondered if Barbara really cared; if she did suffer somewhat, part of me was comfortable with that — the part that felt wounded and unforgiving.

And if I could shatter the equilibrium of my idol, if her progressive loss of control in our encounters disclosed the depths of her surrender, then this was sexual love as I understood it, this was what I wanted and felt fulfilled by. She was too powerful a being to desire gentleness or restraint; on the contrary. In her novels she had announced loudly and clearly what she wanted — and our desires were perfectly matched. The impossible, the unattainable, the ultimately challenging was what I wanted to conquer — not woman weak and uncertain, but woman strong and supremely confident.

Ayn had spoken more than once of her admiration for the tale of Siegfried and Brunhild — Brunhild, who could defeat any suitor in combat and who surrenders only when Siegfried, passing through one obstacle after another, passing finally through a ring of fire, conquers her with his sword: she falls worshipfully at his feet. "That is my metaphor," Ayn had said, "for my favorite image of ideal love — or at least the beginning, the 'courtship.' "

She *wanted* to be a little frightened of taking the final step, and she *wanted* me to persevere, to overcome her fears and blast through her objections. She wanted to care about Frank's feelings, and she wanted me not to care at all. As to Barbara's feelings, I doubt if Ayn seriously considered them. She wanted me to override two marriages, the age difference, every kind of conventional objection — and I did so, not tensely but laughingly, feeling supremely at home. The optimism and arrogance of youth fueled my self-assertiveness.

I was sometimes astonished by the degree of my ease and comfort in getting what I wanted, the sense of operating in a context where mastery was effortless. Looking back, more than three decades later, I am still somewhat astonished and unable to explain my certainty in an area where my previous experience had been so limited.

When we discussed our desires with Barbara and Frank, it was clear that they had expected such a development.

Ayn asserted, as she had asserted five months earlier, that nothing need change; that we loved our respective spouses as much as we ever had; that we were an indestructible foursome.

Her primary focus, however, was on her own emotional needs. "You both know how little I've had in my life, by way of personal reward." I shuddered when I heard this: could Ayn be unaware that she had slapped Frank's face? But Frank displayed no visible reaction. "And you two understand, as perhaps no one else could, what Nathan is to me . . . the realization of everything I write about . . . and what it means to have him in reality, on earth, not just in my writing or in my mind." I felt uncomfortable, but took my reaction as a sign of immaturity. "If the four of us were of lesser stature, this would not have happened, and if it somehow had, you would not accept it. But it is the logic of who we are that led us to this. It's completely rational that Nathan and I should feel as we do toward each other. It's totally rational, given our premises, that our feelings would include the sexual." I relaxed; this perspective sounded valid. "If he and I were the same age, the problem would be entirely different, but we're not the same age. So what we're talking about, at most, is a year or two. Can either of you see me as an older woman, a few years from now, pursuing a younger man? It would be contemptible. This is the very last period in my life when I can think about or permit myself this — I'm a realist about age. What we're asking for is temporary . . . just to have had it . . . for a little while. . . . I think we are all great enough to handle this without tragedy for anyone."

This conversation took place in November 1954. By December, after several more discussions, we all knew that some time soon the affair would begin. At no point in our talks did I entertain any doubts.

Ayn's and my cruelty did not lie in falling in love nor even, primarily, in pursuing an affair. The cruelty lay in how we dealt with the matter: our lack of genuine empathy or compassion for Frank and Barbara's predicament; our lack of contact with them at the level of genuine human feeling, as contrasted with the rarefied atmosphere of philosophical abstraction; our failure to relate on a simple husband-and-wife plane, rather than as storybook characters. Ayn and I prided ourselves on our rationality and realism, and yet these were precisely the traits that we failed to offer Frank and Barbara, or to bring to our emotional life.

Just the same, during this period Barbara and I grew, oddly, closer. There was a special kind of affection and caring between us, not sufficient for the intensity of romantic love but real and valuable nonetheless. "I want you both to be happy," Barbara said often, with desperate, even heartbreaking, earnestness.

It was obvious that some part of her motivation in agreeing to the affair was expiation for not loving me more. "I want you to have everything you deserve," she said. "And Frank has said in so many words that you are the kind of man Ayn deserves." When I heard the pain in her voice, I felt tormented, torn, confused. She said, "If I had the power to push a button so that none of this would have happened, I would not push it. I don't want to live in a world in which you and Ayn could never find each other as man and woman. I can't wish that for either one of you. I want a world in which such things can and do happen, because it's right, it's what I want to see in life . . . even if, in this case, it's hard for me. . . . I know you're concerned for me, you don't want to hurt me, I can see what this is costing you. It will be all right; it will really be all right." Whatever it was that held Barbara and me together, and made it so hard for us to let go of each other, was made stronger by such moments.

In her words I heard loneliness, longing, even despair. I also heard her struggle to be brave, to say and do what she believed the situation required, to fulfill her own vision of a heroine. I understood her effort to make herself a full participant rather than an outsider. She is a giant, I told myself, wanting to believe it, needing to believe it. Never mind the things we sometimes fight about. She is an incredible human being; her values really matter to her.

At no time did Barbara ever hint at leaving me. In fact, she would say, with childlike solemnity, "When it comes to marriage, we're like Catholics, right? We don't believe in divorce?" And I would answer, no less seriously, "When it comes to marriage, we're like Catholics." Since both of us knew the other approved of divorce in principle, this was our way of stressing that, whatever our problems, our commitment was for life. This was very important to both of us. It was almost as if we knew that worse storms lay ahead and that we would need each other.

"A year or two," Barbara said, "and then you and Ayn can be just friends again, and by then I'll be fully ready to be your wife." She spoke as if one day our sexual difficulties, and any other conflict we might have, would be resolved, would be behind us, and our love would fulfill what it had once promised to be when we walked through the snow in Winnipeg, on fire with the discovery of each other. How this was to happen, neither of us knew.

Some months after the affair had begun, I asked Ayn how Frank was taking it, and she smiled enigmatically and answered, "Sometimes he finds it a sexual inspiration. He looks at it as a wonderful adventure of which he's a part."

"Barbara also enjoys the situation sometimes, maybe just a little, as if our relationship makes her own life more glamorous, more exciting."

Ayn smiled. "You see? We'll have our year or two together — and there will be no victims, no tragedy."

Since Ayn and I had become increasingly intimate prior to the start of the affair, the intensity of our embraces building for months, "the first

time" did not entirely feel like "the first time" but rather like the cul-
mination of many sexual encounters, beginning with our return from
Toronto.

It was as if we had been engaged in foreplay for four years — since
the evening in March 1950 when we first met. Later Ayn told me that
was exactly how she felt.

In this realm I knew her as thoroughly as someone I had been intimately involved with for years. Having been engaged in the act of penetrating her consciousness in every way I possibly could, since first
reading *The Fountainhead,* the actual act of sex felt almost like a continuation of the same endeavor. The desire to "know" her in every
conceivable sense, including the biblical, was central to my interactions with her.

I was conscious of two different responses to our first experience.
My body, so to speak, was completely unastonished, completely serene, as if what was now happening was the most natural thing in the
world. My mind, in contrast, had flashes of amazement and disorientation at the thought, "I am now *sleeping with Ayn.*" The two perspectives were like musical themes running in counterpoint to each
other, yielding a result more thrilling than either could produce by itself: a high level of excitement devoid of any trace of tension or anxiety. In Ayn I believed I did see a touch of apprehension but of a kind
one welcomes because it makes one feel more alive, makes the moment
more momentous.

She made love with the same single-track concentration that she did
everything else; nothing existed but the moment, our bodies, this sensation, then the next. What was electrifying was that in her gentlest,
most sensual touch I could feel the full force of her personality, as if
the voltage of her mind and the voltage of her flesh were one.

Watching her eyes watching me was aphrodisiacal. I knew that what
she wanted most was not my tenderness but my aggressiveness, my
willingness to do anything I felt like doing, without asking and without
. hesitation — a master, to use her language, exercising his rights over
his property. This and this alone allowed the female in her fully to
emerge. Since I had no unusual sexual predilections and no interest in
giving or receiving pain and every interest in giving and receiving pleasure, our lovemaking was simple, uncomplicated happiness.

At one point I lay still, leaving all action and initiative to her, then
suddenly rolled over and immobilized her, reversing the flow of energy, moving in a way that answered the greed in each of us — knowing that this was precisely what she wanted. I was in exquisite alignment with her and with the deepest meaning of sex as I perceived it.

That I could bring such joy to a woman twenty-five years my senior, who I admired so passionately, nourished my sexual self-esteem. That she could evoke a response of such intensity in a man so many years younger, who she perceived as the incarnation of her values, nourished hers.

A year or two: that is how I thought about it in the beginning. Safe, time-limited, not a way of life. And the first few months of the affair brought me a joy that nothing that happened subsequently could extinguish.

Whatever Ayn's insecurities, in the bedroom there was no split between the novelist and the woman. She was sensual, passionate, uninhibited, aggressive, submissive, strong, helpless, magnificently greedy. She made it abundantly clear that her most ardent desire was to be reduced to a state of total surrender, and that meant I was free to release my own aggressive energy. We were like two prisoners let loose.

Nothing we could say or do could frighten or overwhelm the other. Nothing was too much. Whatever one gave, the other welcomed. Whatever one wanted, the other responded. We embraced sex as a person underwater too long embraces oxygen.

"What's happening to me?" Ayn would say. "You're turning me into an animal." And I would grin mockingly and answer, "Really? What were you before?" "A mind," she would say. And I would reply, "Really? Do you have a mind? Who ever told you that?"

Sometimes I would arrive in the afternoon and say, "Hi. How's the writing going?" And she would answer wryly, "What writing? I've been sitting at my desk for the past three hours, unable to concentrate on anything except . . . I don't know myself anymore; I can't believe this is me. Have you been sent by the enemy to prevent me from finishing this book?"

She was in the midst of writing the most difficult part of the novel: Galt's radio speech to the world in which he explains the reasons for the strike, exposes the philosophical ideas that have brought the world to destruction, and expounds the new moral vision needed to redeem civilization. The challenge in the writing was to present the essence of a new philosophical system and to do so in the dramatic style appropriate not to a treatise but to a novel. We spent many hours discussing the smallest details of her formulations — exhilarating hours for me, often tense and stressful for Ayn. I was in awe of her achievement. The sixty-page speech took her two years to write, the two most painfully difficult years of her career. But it was not merely the difficulty of the project that made the writing take that long; it was the fact that her mind and time were divided between the novel and our relationship.

"I'm proud of the fact," she said to me, "that I'm willing to set aside the most important project of my life — so that I can spend time on us, either with you or else alone, thinking about you. I'm proud of the fact that love matters to me this much. I'm almost ashamed to admit that what I'm experiencing now, I have never experienced before. I have never permitted Frank to be a distraction from my work. I feel disloyal even telling you this."

I replied that, given the greatness of the novel and what I knew it meant to her, I found it incomprehensible that she was so often willing to set it aside — for anyone or for anything.

She smiled. "Then you don't really understand what you are to me."

I did not want to think that I loved less than she did. Yet I was concerned that if she was willing to set aside everything for our relationship, I would be expected to do the same. I reproached myself for this reaction and told myself that I had failed to understand her: Was she not the high priestess of creative work? Had she not spoken more than once of her scorn for novels that centered on love, as contrasted with novels in which love was integrated with the character's pursuit of other goals?

I asked her, "You don't mean that love — as a way of life — comes ahead of work?" And she replied, "No, of course not. The two are equal in importance. But for me, now, this relationship will be given everything it needs. Don't you feel the same way?" I answered yes — what else could I say? — and felt somewhat relieved. But a sense of obligation that would not yet come into focus remained. I knew that love versus work was not really the issue; the issue had more to do with what precisely was involved in loving Ayn. Was there an implicit commitment to make every other value and interest in my life, including my marriage, subordinate to her needs? Ayn had actually given me clear signals to this effect. I suddenly felt myself plunged into agitation and chaos, which must have been apparent to Ayn, who asked, a little sharply, "What's the matter? Where have you gone to? You've disappeared."

She loved to talk, for hours, about the emotional meaning of our relationship. Intellectualizing made feelings acceptable. I felt awkward in these discussions. Whereas the age difference did not seem important in intellectual or sexual contexts, it became confusingly important to me in contexts where the primary focus was on emotion. Philosophical discussions were by their nature abstract; and sex too was abstract in our case, existing in a private world of its own, cut off from the normal flow of daily living. In the world of philosophy and of sex, we were not so much persons as *forces* achieving union in a unique dimension created anew at each meeting. But in the domain of daily emotion I confronted the fact that I was twenty-five and she was fifty and both of us were married and we were at very different developmental stages. Since I was constantly striving to adjust to Ayn's level rather than she to mine, she saw no problem in any of this. And I did not know how to explain it, neither to myself nor to her. "I know that the average woman finds it easier than the average man to talk about love, relationships, and emotions," she said to me, "but you're not the average man. What's the matter with you? Are you repressed?"

In fact, self-liberation and self-alienation were proceeding simultaneously along different tracks of my personality — so that while I was becoming emotionally freer in important areas, I was becoming more emotionally repressed in others. Emotional repression is a defense, a survival strategy; but I did not yet recognize what I was defending or why.

I did believe that I was more troubled than Ayn over the pain we were causing Barbara and Frank. When I raised the issue, her manner often became subtly impatient, as if to say, "Why talk about it? It can't be helped." I faulted my inability to match her ruthlessness; I had flattered myself in imagining a toughness I now seemed to lack. I thought she was more realistic than I was.

When I told her I felt awkward, embarrassed, and miserable about forcing Frank out of his own apartment twice a week, she suggested the idea of renting a small apartment in the same building that would be exclusively ours; I was enthusiastic and implored her to do so, since I could not have afforded to. But she kept putting it off, saying, "Suppose someone found out what it was for?" She was obsessed with keeping our affair a secret. "Can you project how our relationship could be twisted and used against me by malicious gossipmongers? I am proud of everything I have done in my life and I am certainly proud of what we are to each other, but you know how it would be interpreted by conventional standards — and why should I have to justify myself or explain anything to anyone?" All four of us had agreed that no one else was ever to know. This meant the relationship was to be kept secret not only from the world but from our closest friends. Ayn had begun to lay the foundation for a life of lies and deception. Earlier there had been the lie to Barbara and Frank that "nothing will change" — and now the lies to everyone in our circle.

Often, Frank would be leaving as I arrived; we would shake hands, Ayn would kiss him good-bye, and he would depart. She could not understand why this sometimes left me strained and on edge for the next hour or two. "What's the matter with you today?" she would ask, and when I would explain, she would say, "Well, I don't like it either, but reality is reality."

What neither of us suspected, and what I would not learn until many years later, was that Frank's usual destination when he left the apartment was a nearby bar — and that he was becoming an alcoholic.

Ayn was oblivious to the enormity of his suffering, just as she was oblivious to the tension she sometimes brought to our meetings — the tension of wrestling with the challenges of Galt's speech, along with her own nervous irritability. If I tried to describe its impact on me, she would apologize — and then wonder why her apology didn't instantly put me at my ease.

The magnitude of these problems became evident only much later. In the first few months, when our sexual relationship was at its peak, no small frictions, no strains or tensions or periods when I seemed to pull back, were assigned any importance: there was too much to be happy about. I told myself that whatever wasn't yet quite right merely pertained to the early stages of a new relationship. Nonetheless, Ayn began to ask me more and more often: "*What's the matter with you?*" That was the first crack in the structure of our serenity, a crack that eventually would become an abyss. All my life I had been supremely unconcerned with the opinions of others; but I could not be unconcerned with the judgment of my idol; her rebukes were very painful to me.

Skirmishes aside, and we did typically resolve them quickly, Ayn continued to compare me to her heroes and to wonder aloud how she could survive without me. And when Frank and Barbara were present to hear such statements they smiled in acquiescence.

"I felt that Ayn *couldn't* live without you, for all practical purposes," Barbara said to me many years later. "But if I had dared to suggest that that was a trap not only for Frank and me but also for you — you would have been outraged and indignant."

I sighed and answered, "True."

"In a sense you were as much a victim as Frank and I."

I did not agree. "No," I said. "There were no victims. I don't believe in victims in situations of that kind. There was ignorance, confusion, misguided idealism if you like, but there were also payoffs, there were very real benefits for each one of us, and until we can be honest about that, we can never come to grips with what happened."

A few months after the affair began, Barbara awakened one night, in a state of terror. Concerned that she might be having a heart attack, we summoned Allan Blumenthal. It was not her heart but her mind and emotions that had been stricken: she was having an anxiety attack — far worse than anything she had experienced at the time of her "confessions."

"What's happening to me?" Barbara cried in bewilderment. The essence of an anxiety disorder is that one feels assailed by feelings of dread that do not connect to any concrete, tangible threat. Barbara's whole system was flung into emergency alert — except that there was no discernible emergency.

I was familiar with the phenomenon of anxiety disorders, but I proceeded to read everything I could find on the subject and question my professors at NYU. Nothing I learned seemed useful: I had no idea what I could do that would help. Someone suggested that perhaps Barbara should enter psychoanalysis, which, after several years of treatment, might alleviate her suffering; I thought this suggestion absurd. No one proposed medication and I was not yet aware of the early tranquilizers that existed. I felt it was my duty to produce a solution and I did not know what to do.

Barbara's anxiety began to flow into different spheres of her life in the form of phobias. Suddenly, flying terrified her, then heights, then elevators — and I watched with agony and with admiration her desperate battle not to surrender. She forced herself to do everything she was afraid of doing — she rode an elevator to the top of the Empire State Building — as if by sheer dint of will and courage she could defeat her demons. For about eighteen months, her terror was relentless. Then, mysteriously, it began to fade away.

Eager for an explanation, Ayn drew on my theory of "emotionalist metaphysics" and began to speculate that Barbara's anxiety was a consequence of her overreliance on feeling as a guide to action. She wrote a psychological paper on this subject. Desperately sharing Ayn's curiosity, I asked myself: if we live by emotion rather than reason, is it not inevitable that we will feel increasingly out of control, and increasingly apprehensive that disaster, or retribution, is imminent? My point seemed valid, but it added to, rather than diminished, Barbara's guilt. It was provocative theoretically but in no way immediately helpful therapeutically. Also, it did not address the question of why the attack should come *now* — at a time when Barbara was living more "rationally" than she ever had before. Neither Barbara nor Ayn nor I raised the possibility that there might be some connection to Ayn's and my affair. None of us was willing to deal with that.

Sometimes when I arrived at Ayn's apartment I was clearly agitated over Barbara's condition — the truth was, I felt I should be at home by Barbara's side — and if I did not become cheerful and loving within a few minutes, Ayn would reproach me for my sentimentality, my lack of concern for *her* feelings, and my failure to appreciate that, whatever was wrong, Barbara had almost certainly brought it on herself.

"Why should *I* be victimized," Ayn demanded, "for Barbara's problems?" The fact that Barbara was my wife lost all reality for her; confused and horrified, I had to keep reminding her. I thought of the contrast between Ayn's attitude now that her own interests were involved, and her compassion when Barbara had begun to disclose her infidelities several years earlier.

The more Ayn rebuked Barbara, the more protective of Barbara I became. Once Ayn said, her voice hushed and trembling with intensity, "Do you think there's some other man in Barbara's life *now?* Could that be the cause of her anxiety?" I was stunned by the violence of my anger, and I answered, my words flat and toneless, "Absolutely not." I was certain of my judgment then and never had grounds to doubt it later.

During one of our private meetings Barbara telephoned Ayn — something she normally would never do when I was there — explaining tearfully that her panic was reaching new and unbearable heights, and pleaded for permission to come over so she could talk to us. I listened in horror as Ayn began to reproach her in a loud voice, saying things like, "How *dare* you invade my time with Nathan?" and "Are you indifferent to *my* context?" and "No one ever helped *me* when I needed it! You'll always be unhappy until you learn to stand on your own feet!" Ayn came back into the living room, raving against Barbara and then against me when she saw the stricken expression on my face, and for the next hour I listened to harangues on my "irrationalism." She cried, "Is this what your love for me means? Why do you allow Barbara to manipulate you? *What happens to your mind and values?*"

There is something worse than feeling trapped in a nightmare: forbidding oneself to *know* that one feels trapped in a nightmare. I tried to persuade myself that all that was involved was Ayn's unbearable tension over her difficulties with Galt's speech, the great pressure she was under, and her fear that what we had together would somehow be taken away. I would not permit myself the thought that Ayn's behavior was sick or evil. I tried to feel compassion for the distress she had to be experiencing. Sensing this attitude in me, she gradually became calmer, even mellow; I made love to her — somehow; and afterward, she began speaking of Barbara with care and concern.

The next time I saw Ayn and Barbara together, they were both warm, affectionate, relaxed, as if the blowup had never happened. Ayn conveyed that she wanted to do everything in her power to help Barbara. They had many long discussions in which Ayn was totally supportive. But the anxiety raged on, unabated. And Ayn's bouts of suspicious disapproval returned, alternating with times of benevolence. Watching this, I fought feelings of anger and despair, and told myself it would all pass and we would be happy again.

I was now in graduate school and had officially begun the practice of psychotherapy. For some years past I had been a psychological consultant to some of our friends, who had mentioned their experiences to other friends and acquaintances. Soon people were telephoning to request appointments. The fact that I was not yet a professional psychotherapist did not deter them; I felt flattered and more than a little excited. At first, I did not charge for my time, welcoming the opportunity to try out my ideas and to learn. But by the spring of 1955, as the requests for therapy continued, I decided to make my work official, and I announced a ten-dollar fee for a two-hour session. Still, a question taunted me: if I was able to be effective with other people, why could I not help my own wife? Another question that I should have asked myself was: if I was able to bring sanity into the lives of other people, why could I not bring it into my own?

I had begun to appreciate how widespread the problem of anxiety was, and I was evolving a theory about it. I was impressed by Freud's contention that virtually all neurotic problems could be understood as direct expressions of anxiety or of the defenses erected by its sufferers. But in his account of the causes of anxiety, I thought he was making an unwarranted generalization. Freud had decided, in the final version of his theory, that anxiety is triggered by forbidden sexual desires that break through the barrier of repression and cause the ego to feel threatened and overwhelmed. Decades later Karen Horney countered with the declaration that this may have been true in the Victorian age, but in our day the source of anxiety is the emergence of *hostile* impulses. I could not see why Freud and Horney confined the problem to one particular impulse: *any* feeling that was experienced as overwhelming and threatening to ego control had the potential of activating anxiety. And then I pondered: Is it only *impulses* that the ego experiences as dangerous? And what about. . .? I began to make notes.

I learned about the work of Kurt Goldstein, who studied the anxiety suffered by brain-injured veterans. These men were comfortable only in rigidly organized environments; if, for instance, a nurse moved a hairbrush a few inches from where the patient had placed it, the patient panicked. The mind, I reasoned, is our basic means of survival; these men are impaired at the cognitive level; they are impaired in their ability to cope with the environment — impaired in their fitness for survival. How logical that they would suffer anxiety.

When the ego feels in danger of being overwhelmed, rendered unable to function appropriately — by the emergence of unacceptable feelings or impulses, for instance — might this not be a parallel problem to that of Goldstein's veterans? *Any* threat to a person's ego, I decided, anything that he or she experiences as a threat to the mind's efficacy and control, is a potential source of pathological anxiety.

The concept of anxiety I evolved over time is presented in *The Psychology of Self-Esteem* and then again, much more briefly but without moralizing and with certain refinements, in *Honoring the Self*. In the former book, I wrote:

> The experience of pathological anxiety [later I would call this self-esteem anxiety] always involves and reflects conflict . . . and the acute anxiety attack is occasioned by the ego's confrontation with that conflict. . . .
>
> In every instance . . . there is a conflict in some such form as: "I must (or should have)" — and "I cannot (or did not)"; or "I must not" — and "I do (or did or will)." There is always a conflict between some value-imperative that is tied, in a crucial and profound way, to the person's self-appraisal and inner equilibrium — and some failure or inadequacy or action or emotion or desire [or fantasy] that the person regards as a breach of that imperative, a breach the person believes expresses or reflects a basic and unalterable fact of his "nature."

In other words: I must know what to do — and I don't; I must be able to understand this — and I can't; I mustn't feel this — and I do; I must not have such thoughts — and I have them; I must not have done such and such — and I did; I must not do such and such — and I will.

What I did not identify until years later was that my relationship with Ayn was shot through with these conflicts — and that if they had erupted into acute attacks of anxiety, it might have have been far better for me: my consciousness might have been raised much sooner.

When I had developed the first general sketch of my theory of anxiety, I took it to my adviser at NYU, a professor I particularly liked, Dr. John Tietz, as the subject of my master's thesis. He said it was much too ambitious for an M.A. project, but that I should go ahead and do it anyway; he would protect me from anyone's objections. As I was quite outspoken in class, and often challenged my instructors, he knew I might need a defender. He and I had hit it off from the moment when he announced, in mockery of the behaviorists, "Ladies and gentlemen, I shall conduct this class on the assumption that you are all conscious." I had burst out laughing in appreciation, and he and I had grinned at each other. Now he said to me, "I think you're on to something very important."

But the early versions of my theory were so abstract, more philosophical than psychological, that I could not make my ideas useful to

Barbara. I did not yet know how to translate my ideas into therapeutic tools.

Later, reflecting on this period of her life, Barbara suggested that conflict between "I must" and "I can't" was: "I *must* accept my husband's love affair with Ayn, since it's right and rational — and I *can't*." I would cast the core conflict that triggered the anxiety somewhat differently although our interpretations are not far apart. Barbara must have felt appallingly stifled by Ayn and me and would almost certainly have felt enormous rage against us both. But her own guilt, coupled with her surrender of all moral authority to us, forbade her to express this rage or even to experience it. Indeed, to experience it was to risk expressing it. If she expressed it, she would risk being damned and risk losing us. *Barbara wanted the life she had with us, whatever the cost.* Our moral approval was supremely important to her; her involvement with us had become profoundly significant for her sense of identity and for her self-esteem. While her rage, in fact, reflected the healthy side of her, the side fighting for her life, she experienced it in the exact opposite way: as a threat to her self-esteem and therefore to her survival. Her fury was not to be allowed or even acknowledged. At the first hint of its emergence, the organism was flung into a "catastrophic reaction" — the alarm signal of anxiety began to sound, and then went on sounding louder and louder, to block out the screams that dared not be heard. So, my formulation of the core conflict would be: "I must not feel rage against Ayn or Nathan — and I do!" I never offered this interpretation to Barbara, but I would be surprised if she would dispute it. (Although I did not suffer anxiety attacks, there is obviously a great deal in this paragraph that I can relate to myself.)

During the eighteen months that Barbara's anxiety lasted in its extreme form, she saw my deep concern, and this became a new bond between us. Ayn continued to vacillate between support and suspiciousness. In her view of reality, *neurotic* was a term of moral opprobrium, and Barbara's anxiety clearly established her as neurotic. So far as the rest of the world went, and this included Ayn, Barbara was "my woman" — I could find fault with her, but I became agitated when Ayn made disparaging remarks about her "irrationality" and "emotionalism." No one was permitted to find fault with Barbara except me. The effect of Ayn's negative comments was not to alienate me from Barbara but to push me closer to her. Barbara and I did not discuss this explicitly, but there was a silent understanding between us that whatever our private differences, against the world we were an alliance.

When I defended Barbara, stressing her virtues, such as her intelligence and idealism, Ayn sometimes relented. At other times she would turn her anger against me: "Why are you so out of focus? All Barbara cares about is her feelings. She's a whim-worshiper." Later she would modify such statements or pretend she had never made them, but they were a poison fed into our relationship.

I was trying to honor my feelings for both Ayn and Barbara and to respect their legitimate claims, and that might have been easier if one of them had meant less to me than she did.

Both relationships seemed to demand the total of what I had to give, which is the practical problem with loving two people at once. Whatever I felt for Ayn, my desire to remain married had not changed and I began to fear that she — who had once seemed incapable of unfairness — looked for opportunities to criticize Barbara in order to justify her own feelings and demands.

Ayn once said to me, "If, by your own statement, I am the highest, most consistent embodiment of your values, then I expect your first consideration always to be given to me. I expect not just you but the whole Collective to make me their highest loyalty, so far as any other people are concerned, if it ever comes to a conflict. Otherwise, what you do you imagine the principle of loyalty to one's values means?"

In the abstract, and in the light of my then highly simplified view of life, this did not strike me as unreasonable. Today it strikes me as irrational and depraved in its disregard for the actual conditions of sane human reality. Even then, however, I knew I was unwilling to sacrifice my feeling for Barbara. My job therefore became to see that no serious conflict developed between the two women or my two allegiances.

That my own feelings for Barbara contained so many conflicting elements did not make this assignment easy. My feelings fluctuated wildly. I did not acknowledge to Ayn that Barbara's anxiety seemed to intensify just those traits that most provoked my own impatience: her tendency to regress to a very young level of consciousness, her ruminations about having been rejected by her mother and disappointed by her father, her predilection for dreamy wistfulness, her waiflike dependence, her belief that nature intended husbands to wait on wives and to spare them the slightest physical effort.

I had not begun to grasp how essential Barbara's relationship with her parents, her mother in particular, was to my understanding. "How can it still matter what happened when you were a child?" I would ask her, perplexed. In my view, only the present counted; I had not yet learned to think developmentally, except in fairly superficial terms. When I worked with therapy clients I focused on how attitudes held *today* could sabotage their happiness. I was a pure present-tense cognitive therapist.

Barbara spoke of wanting to sit on her mother's lap when she was a little girl, and of her mother pushing her away, saying "You'll wrinkle my dress." Or she talked about lying in bed, gasping for breath with asthma, wanting desperately for her mother to come upstairs and comfort her; but her mother was in the living room playing bridge and would not leave the table. "My mother was so beautiful," Barbara would tell me wistfully. "She was so glamorous. I wanted so much for her to love me."

I did not think, at that time, that these are the kind of experiences through which a child can learn to associate love with pain. I did not appreciate the significance of the fact that Barbara never spoke of her mother with anger or indignation. She wanted to be loved by her mother. She wanted to be perceived as a good girl. That much was obvious to me. But it did not occur to me that now another mother was inflicting pain — and that this time Barbara was determined to prove herself. She would bear whatever was necessary. In childhood she had lost her battle to be loved; this time, with Ayn, she would win it. This time she would vanquish the rejecting mother and win her blessing. The drama of childhood would have a different ending.

But the sanest part of her — her rage against Ayn and me — could undermine her efforts, and her anxiety stood firmly on guard against it. Her anxiety was both her protector and her tormentor.

During this same period, I was on to an idea that would affect my entire professional future, influencing my work in psychology for the next three decades.

As clients came for consultations, I looked for a common denominator among their complaints and problems — for some underlying principle or principles that could illuminate the various forms of their unhappiness. All of my philosophical training with Ayn led me to look for fundamentals, for essences, not to see only concretes and particulars.

Before long I was struck by the thought that the underlying problem is faulty self-esteem — a flawed self-concept, intellectual self-doubt, a sense of unworthiness or guilt, an experience of inadequacy, a feeling that "Something is wrong with me" or "I am not enough."

I went to the university library to read the literature on self-esteem — and was astonished to learn that almost nothing had been written on the subject; not by that name, at any rate, and not as the concept was forming in my mind.

One day, alone in the apartment, I paced the floor, trying to find words for ideas that were still vague and unformed. On an impulse I telephoned Ayn, apologized for the interruption, and asked, "Can I think aloud with you for a few minutes?" I had evidently caught her at a fortunate moment because she answered cheerfully, "Sure."

"I have been thinking about something I've noticed in all the people I work with — something they have in common. And if I'm right, this issue is really at the root of everything, and what I'm after is terribly important — it will explain a lot. *I think the basic problem with people is poor self-esteem.*"

Ayn began to laugh.

"What's the matter?" I asked.

"Wait until you read what I'm writing in Galt's speech about self-esteem!" she announced, delighted at being able to surprise me.

"Oh! You're going to be writing about self-esteem?"

"Just a few sentences really, but it's very important. . . . Go ahead: tell me what you wanted to say." She sounded warm, receptive, a full participant in my process.

I was in a fever of excitement. "I can't stand this. Can I come over?"

When she opened the door to me a few minutes later, I noticed that she did not look strained but refreshed and relaxed. "How did you get here so fast?"

"I ran."

In those days I almost always ran when I was on the streets alone, a practice I continued into my thirties, even when dressed in a suit and tie; people would sometimes glance at me oddly as I raced by. I ran not for the purpose of exercise but as an outlet for my energy and excitement. Rarely did I move as fast as I had that day.

She settled down on the sofa, inserted a fresh cigarette into her holder, and said, her eyes bright with amusement, "You might as well speak first — because if I try to talk before you've told me whatever is on your mind, you'll interrupt and not let me finish, anyway."

I began to pace again, stopping to face her, then erratically moving on, waving my arms as if I were addressing a crowded classroom. "Now then, listen," I said. "Suppose we discover that just about every psychological problem can be traced to faulty self-esteem — that is, can be understood either as a direct expression of poor self-esteem or else as an expression of what people do to escape facing the problem, or to compensate for it, or to prove to themselves and others that no problem exists. Do you appreciate how much this would explain? Okay, so we have to know: what is self-esteem? I've looked and I can't find a decent definition anywhere." I could see that Ayn's eyes were looking at me with good-natured mockery and that she was forcing herself not to speak; I held up my hands as if to keep her at bay and rushed on: "What's tricky about self-esteem is that it contains two separate but intimately related ideas: *efficacy* and *worth*." Ayn leaned forward eagerly. Why was she grinning? "Either alone is not yet full self-esteem. If you feel efficacious but unworthy, you don't enjoy good self-esteem, and if you feel worthy but unefficacious, you don't enjoy good self-esteem." Ayn was now nodding and beaming, as if she were anticipating my next steps. "By *efficacious,* I mean intellectually self-confident and self-reliant — and by *worthy,* I mean entitled to assert your own interests and needs — something like that — and if this is what self-esteem is, then self-esteem has survival value, self-esteem is a powerful need, maybe our most basic need. And when, for whatever reason, the need is unmet and unfulfilled, *then the consequence is what we call neurosis!* Why are you looking at me as if you love me?"

"Because I do." She laughed happily. "Now then — may I speak?"

"Speak!" I shouted exuberantly. In the rigid, overintellectualized structure of our lives, there was not much room for playfulness — except in exchanges like this.

"In Galt's speech, you'll see that I describe self-esteem as one of the three cardinal values of my moral code. I define it as the conviction that you are competent to live and worthy of living."

"That's a brilliant way to say it."

"It's the same idea as what you're groping for — efficacy and worth. I'm not writing psychologically, I'm writing philosophically, about the importance of self-esteem for a rational life and about the danger of tying your self-esteem to the wrong values. Look how rational minds arrive at the same point. Are we or are we not brain mates?"

I was not to be distracted by talk of love. I told her about my efforts to find discussions of self-esteem in the psychological literature. "Would you believe," I said, "that you can go through book after book and not even find 'self-esteem' in the index? I can't understand it. *What do they think is important if not this?*"

"I'm amazed that you have the patience to read all those books."

I knew by now that Ayn read very little, which astonished me. During this period of her life, she occasionally read mysteries or thrillers, but very little else, except the *New York Times.*

"Freud doesn't write about self-esteem as such," I said, "but do you know what he says about the feeling of inferiority? He says its roots are a child's discovery that he — or she — can't have sex with the opposite gender parent! Hence the feeling that 'I can't do anything!' And Alfred Adler claims that the origin of feelings of inferiority are the infant's experience of being smaller and weaker than everyone else! Plus, he claims, everyone comes into this world with one kind or another of 'organ inferiority.' And the rest of our life can be understood as our struggle to compensate for our original deficiencies. Our tragedy, in other words, is that we're not born as fully empowered adults. And people take this seriously. . . . I can't wait to graduate. Most of the time school drives me nuts."

"Well, darling, your work in psychology is cut out for you. You're beginning from scratch."

"No, that's not true," I answered quickly, uneasy about her penchant for dismissing the work of thinkers whom she had not read. I began defending Freud and Adler, explaining the importance of some of their ideas. "Only, what I'm after is something else — something they're not talking about."

Ayn began to lecture me on my generosity to other writers — how could I claim to find anything valuable in Freud? — and she insisted that I was crediting them with insights of my own.

Whatever Ayn's intention, I did not feel complimented, I felt reduced. Ayn's praise somehow always took the form of reasserting her own authority. And at the moment I was not interested in the direction she was pursuing; I wanted to talk about self-esteem.

We did return to the subject of my interest, but the slightest edge of my happiness was gone until I succeeded in catching Ayn up in my enthusiasm again.

Perhaps I recall this encounter with particular clarity because of the importance the study of self-esteem was to have for me. Perhaps it has remained so vivid because of the pleasure I felt in sharing my discovery with Ayn. And perhaps because Ayn once recounted this incident, with great delight, in the question period following a lecture. But I think there is another reason, and this pertains to my thoughts while walking home, which in their own quiet way were ominous and terrifying.

I was grinning happily as I bounced along the street, until I heard an inner voice saying: *this* is what you want from Ayn — *this* is the kind of relationship with her that you find fulfilling.

I knew that my mind was light years away from any thought of sex or romance during this meeting, and that I far from welcomed Ayn's overtures. I was horrified by the sudden feeling that I did not want our relationship cluttered by such an intrusion. I loved the lightness and freedom of our intellectual comradeship. In this arena there were no rebukes, no emotional demands, no conflicts with any other loyalty.

Then, as I recalled the car ride from Toronto to New York, as I replayed the conversation in Ayn's apartment the day we declared our love for each other, as I contemplated the chain of events I had set in motion, changing all four of our lives forever, the voice began to pound louder and louder in my head: *What have you done? What have you done? What have you done?*

NINE

"THIS IS GENIUS," I said to Ayn. It was a Saturday evening in the spring of 1956. Galt's speech was finished and I was rereading it for the fifth or sixth time.

Scattered throughout the living room of Ayn's apartment were the various members of the Collective, each of them reading a different chapter of *Atlas Shrugged* — Barbara, Alan Greenspan, Leonard Peikoff, Allan Blumenthal, Joan Mitchell (who was to marry Allan), my sister Elayne and her new husband, Harry Kalberman, Mary Ann Rukavina. As usual, Frank was half-sitting, half-lying, sprawled out like a cat, neither reading nor speaking, but gazing around the room tranquilly and distantly.

Ayn's entire social existence was now confined — almost without exception — to the people in this room. The oldest person present, apart from Frank, was more than twenty years her junior. But we all had one attribute in common: absolute devotion to Ayn and her work. As she entered the final stages of writing *Atlas Shrugged,* she had almost no capacity for any other kind of relationship. The Collective was both her fortress and the fellow inhabitants of her fortress. Everyone she cared about was now in her apartment.

Ayn and I were sitting together at the dinner table, apart from the others. We kept our voices low so as not to disturb anyone. Indicating the pages of Galt's speech, I said, "I can hardly believe what you've managed to cover, to condense, and yet keep lucid and convey in an exciting and dramatic form."

"Galt doesn't sound like he's arguing or debating, does he?" She had asked this before. "His speech must never convey that, and yet I have to provide the reasons and proofs for all of his statements."

"You've succeeded."

"The publisher will tell me the speech is too long, of course. Not that that matters. It's the length it has to be."

"Yes, of course. To hell with that. It *is* the length it has to be." I turned the pages of the chapter. "Listen, I've been studying the section where you demonstrate why 'Man's Life' is the proper standard of morality — and the economy and clarity of your explanation, to say nothing of the central concept itself, is awesome. You've addressed one of the most challenging problems in philosophy, the derivation of an ethical standard, and you've provided the answer — *in a novel!*"

"Philosophers say you can't derive an 'ought' from an 'is' — you can't derive a code of ethics from the facts of reality — but Galt does just that."

"It's so funny to hear you talk about what 'Galt' does. *You* did it. You've given morality a nonmystical foundation. You've shown that a morality of reason is possible."

I felt unconflicted love and admiration. At such moments, it was impossible to believe that there could be any discord in our relationship. The terrible thought, *What have I done?*, and everything the question implied, now seemed infinitely distant. But it arose, unpredictably, in other contexts, then quickly receded again into the dimness of an almost-forgotten dream.

These shifts of perspective had become habitual. When one was dominant, the other was barely real. There were times with Ayn when I felt utterly and totally fulfilled — I was where I was meant to be — but there were other times when I felt only a numb detachment and the sense of being trapped in a role I did not wish to play. There were times when I could speak happily and passionately of my feelings for her — and times when I could hardly speak at all, and whatever I said sounded hopelessly stilted and awkward.

When I was caught in this latter state and could not free myself, Ayn would sometimes become angry. "I felt more as if I were a person to you, and not just a mind, before our affair began. Now, if I want us to talk intimately, you keep running away into philosophical abstractions. Instead of feeling more visible than before, I feel less visible." She said this at times when she wanted to talk love and I wanted to talk philosophy or psychology or *anything* that would remove me from the realm of the personal; out of a helplessness and estrangement that baffled me, I acted in ways that were detached, elusive, abrupt, inappropriate, and immature.

Looking back, I cannot help thinking that another woman, more experienced and less self-alienated than Ayn, would have grasped rather quickly the essence of the problem: that there was no way that a young man of my age, no matter how precocious, could maintain a romance with someone twenty-five years older, of Ayn's character and personality, without sooner or later displaying erratic behavior. Add to that the fact that we were both married — and that the affair was a secret from even our closest friends.

At the time, however, I shared Ayn's conviction that a romantic relationship between us *should* be possible, and that if it was not working the problem was some defect of mine. What sustained this conviction was the fact that at times I felt like a man in love and acted like a man in love, and then we were both ecstatic. I often paced the streets, struggling to think my way through this dilemma; but I rarely confronted the fact that I most enjoyed our relationship not in romantic moments, but in moments when our focus was more intellectual or literary: when we were sharing the world of *Atlas Shrugged*, discussing ideas, answering philosophical or psychological questions raised by members of our group. As an intellectual companion, Ayn was the fulfillment of more than I had ever dreamed; but for a romantic companion I wanted a woman of my own age. I could hear Ayn's voice asking what woman my age could conceivably compete with her in *any* department. And to this I had no answer.

As we sat facing each other across the dinner table, Ayn was radiating a happiness that I thought would be obvious to everyone in the room. I was often amazed that our friends were so oblivious to what Ayn's and my relationship had become. It was as if they had a particular picture of us and our relationship in their minds and they could not think beyond it or even notice conflicting evidence. At this moment the sexuality in her glance was as loud as a shout; how was it possible that no one in the room but me could hear it? Many years later, after the break, Barbara would tell me that the one person who had had suspicions was Joan. But tonight I dared to join Ayn's mood — and genuinely to experience love, desire, playfulness, romantic exhilaration. It felt exciting and a little dangerous to match her signal with my own glance, in defiance of everyone else present — simultaneously enjoying our secrecy and wanting to proclaim the truth to the room and to the world.

"So what were you saying about Galt's discussion of the foundation of ethics?" she asked playfully.

As usual she was smoking. Her long cigarette holder, a gift from Barbara and me, was sterling silver, engraved with the names Galt, Francisco, Rearden, and Dagny. She had abandoned her usual uniform of skirt and blouse in favor of a gray silk dress; I reached over to brush ashes off her sleeve, my fingertips pressing her arm for an instant.

Laughing silently, and trying to ignore the open eroticism of her manner, I struggled to organize my thoughts. "What I think is so im-

portant," I said, "is your approach to the whole subject of ethics. You
don't begin by taking the phenomenon of 'values' as a given. You don't
begin by merely observing that men pursue various values and by assuming that the first question of ethics is: what values ought man to
pursue? In Galt's speech, you go to a much deeper level, asking: *what
are values and why does man need them*? Your approach is not statis-
tical, sociological, or historical — it's metaphysical. Your starting
point is: what are the facts of reality — the facts of existence and of
man's nature — that necessitate and give rise to values? And this is
where a true science of ethics should begin — and, in the history of
philosophy, never has."

I should mention that in 1956 it would not have occurred to us to
question the use of the word *man* to denote both sexes — and unfortunately even today no one has proposed a satisfactory alternative.
Ayn, of course, would have been vigorously opposed to the search for
a better word.

We talked about her concept of *value* as that which one acts to gain
and/or to keep. A value was the object of an action. In Galt's speech
she had written, " 'Value' presupposes an answer to the question: of
value to whom and for what? 'Value' presupposes a standard, a purpose and the necessity of action in the face of an alternative. Where
there are no alternatives, no values are possible."

I understood this to mean that an entity who, by its nature, had no
purposes to achieve, no goals to reach, could have no values and no
need of values. There would be no "for what." And an entity incapable
of initiating action, or for whom the consequences would always be
the same, *regardless* of its actions — an entity not confronted with alternatives — could have no purposes, no goals, and hence no values.
Only the existence of alternatives could make purpose — and therefore values — possible and necessary.

Having established this progression of thought in Galt's speech, Ayn
went on to one of the most important philosophical statements in all
of her writing:

There is only one fundamental alternative in the universe: existence
or non-existence — and it pertains to a single class of entities: to living organisms. The existence of inanimate matter is unconditional,
the existence of life is not: it depends on a specific course of action.
Matter is indestructible, it changes its forms, but it cannot cease to
exist. It is only a living organism that faces a constant alternative: the
issue of life or death. Life is a process of self-sustaining and self-gen-
erated action. If an organism fails in that action, it dies; its chemical
elements remain, but its life goes out of existence. It is only the con-

Left: Nathaniel Branden, 1934, age four

Below: Nathaniel, 1948, age eighteen

Right: Ayn Rand and her husband, Frank O'Connor, Chatsworth, California, 1951

Below: Ayn and Nathaniel in the mid-1950s, at the height of their affair

Above: Barbara and Nathaniel's wedding, February 1953
Below: The newlyweds with Frank and Ayn

Above: Nathaniel and Barbara in 1957, the year *Atlas Shrugged* was published (Copyright © Star Newspaper Service, Toronto)
Below: Barbara Branden in the late 1960s

Above: Members of Ayn's inner circle, the so-called Collective, including the Brandens, Ayn Rand, Frank O'Connor, Patrecia and Larry Scott, and others

Below: The Collective at the wedding of Nathaniel's sister Elayne to Harry Kalberman. From left: Joan Mitchell, Alan Greenspan, Nathaniel, Barbara, Leonard Peikoff, Elayne Kalberman, Harry Kalberman, Ayn, Frank, and Allan Blumenthal (A. Levine)

Nathaniel lecturing at the Nathaniel Branden Institute, 1964

Patrecia in 1965, the year after she met Nathaniel

Above: Wedding of Patrecia and Larry Scott. From left: Ayn, Larry, Patrecia, Nathaniel, and Barbara (Bradford Bachrach)

Right: Patrecia, February 1977, six weeks before her death

Nathaniel and Devers Branden, 1983, ages 52 and 49. They have been married since 1978.

cept of 'Life' that makes the concept of 'Value' possible. It is only to a living entity that things can be good or evil.

Given the appropriate conditions, the appropriate physical environment, all living organisms — with one exception — are set by their nature to originate automatically the actions required to sustain their survival. The exception is man.

"Do you think people will understand this idea?" Ayn asked. I knew that she meant, not one idea, but the whole argument, including her derivation of the concept of "value" from the concept of "life."

"I doubt the average reader will think about it very deeply. Passages such as this will probably go over most people's head. To me the idea seems very simple, and I think your presentation is totally clear."

"That one paragraph would really need to be a whole chapter in a nonfiction treatise, but of course one can't do that in a novel. I kept condensing and condensing, boiling the argument down, to the briefest, clearest statement I could achieve. A good mind will know how to fill in what I've left out."

I nodded in agreement.

It was only a living entity that could have needs, goals, *values* — and it was only a living entity that could generate the actions necessary to achieve them. This was an idea of the most momentous consequences, and I thought that if philosophers understood it and its implications, it could radically benefit the field of ethics, demolishing religious and tribal notions of morality, and linking ethics to man's needs as a living organism.

Barbara and I had spent many hours retracing Ayn's argument in our own words, as if we were explaining it to a third party. I felt a warm sense of connection when I looked at her across the room; she was reading intently, and her face had an expression I loved: that of a fully focused consciousness enjoying its own function. I thought how fortunate I was to have two such women in my life.

Then, my mind returning to the steps of Ayn's progression, as to a pleasure from which I could not tear myself, I thought: Man, like a plant or an animal, must act in order to live, must gain the values his life requires. But man does not function solely by automatic chemical reactions or automatic sensory reactions; the method of survival possible to plants and animals is not possible to humans; there is no physical environment on earth in which man can survive by the guidance of nothing but involuntary sensations. And being born with no innate knowledge of what is true or false, he can have no innate knowledge of what is good or evil. For man, survival is a question — a problem to be solved. The perceptual level of his consciousness — the level of sensory awareness he shares with animals — is inadequate to solve it. To remain alive, man must think — which means he must exercise the faculty of forming abstractions, of *conceptualizing*. The *conceptual* level of consciousness is the human level. It is upon his ability to think that man's life depends. But to think, Ayn had written in Galt's speech, *is an act of choice*. In contrast to the functioning of stomach, lungs, or heart, which is automatic, the functioning of mind is not: *man is a being of volitional consciousness*.

"The implications of this idea for psychology are enormous," I said to Ayn. "Nothing is more important for understanding the behavior of an organism than understanding its unique and distinctive means of survival."

"I don't envy you the job of explaining that to your colleagues," Ayn answered. I did not know whether she was referring to the difficulty of the issues or the presumed resistance of psychologists to her approach.

The undertone of erotic playfulness had faded as we became caught up in the intensity of the issues we were discussing. As we went on talking I felt as if we were alone. It was an exalted feeling.

Like watching a movie being played in my mind, I found myself irresistibly continuing the line of Ayn's thought, to satisfy and resatisfy myself that I had mastered it. I wondered idly why no one else in the room, with the exception of Barbara, seemed to share my pleasure in this pursuit. Why wasn't the process as exciting to the others as it was to me? Sometimes I would ask myself: if all of Ayn's writings disappeared, and if Ayn and I were dead, was there anyone in our circle who could reliably reconstruct and re-create all her philosophical work? I doubted that even Barbara could do that. This thought evoked a faint sadness in me.

Ayn belonged in the company of giants, I told myself. The best minds in the country should be sitting in this living room — philosophers, scientists, writers — not this group of young people who were all devoted to her and her work, true enough, but who had yet to accomplish anything significant of their own.

Shrugging off the wave of sadness that was now more pronounced, I flung myself back to the progression of Ayn's thought in Galt's speech. A being of volitional consciousness, a being without innate ideas, must discover, by a process of reasoning, the goals, the actions, the values on which his life and well-being depend. He must discover what will further his true interests and what will subvert them. If he acts against the facts of reality, he will fail, suffer, and perish. If he is to sustain his existence successfully, he must discover the principles of action required to guide him in dealing with nature and with other human beings. His need of these principles is his need of a code of values. Galt states, "A code of values accepted by choice is a code of morality."

The reason, then, of man's *need* for morality determines the *purpose* of morality as well as the *standard* by which he selects moral values. Man needs a moral code in order to live; that is the purpose of morality — for every person as an individual. And different species achieve their survival in different ways. The course of action proper to the survival of a fish or an animal would not be appropriate to the survival of man. Man must choose his values by the standard of that which is required for the life of a human being — which means he must hold *Man's Life* (man's survival qua man, that is, qua rational being) as his standard of value. In summary of this point, Galt states, "All that which is proper to the life of a rational being is the good; all that which destroys it is the evil."

Later in the speech he says:

> To live, man must hold three things as the supreme and ruling values of his life: Reason — Purpose — Self-esteem. Reason, as his only tool of knowledge — Purpose, as his choice of the happiness which that tool must proceed to achieve — Self-esteem, as his inviolate certainty that his mind is competent to think and his person is worthy of happiness, which means: is worthy of living.

This is what I wanted to fight for. I recalled a discussion with Florence, when I was sixteen, about a crusade that would mean something, a battle that would be worthwhile. What I had been struggling for then, I told myself, was this vision of the good. . . . *I want to be the champion of man's self-esteem. I want to tell people: Your life matters. Your life is important.*

I did not recognize that in the lesson I wanted to teach others there were vital elements I still needed to learn myself. I was not honoring my own life as I needed to, I had submerged too much of it in Ayn. I was not sufficiently loyal to my own perception of reality; I had allowed it to be confused by my admiration for Ayn and my desire for her esteem. But I was not thinking about myself that night; I was thinking about Ayn and the brilliance of Galt's speech and the intellectual progression I wanted to continue following.

I reflected: traditional religionists and mystics declared that if God did not exist, morality would be unnecessary — everything would be "permissible." More socially oriented neomystics (as we called them) declared that if *society* did not exist, morality would be unnecessary; any course of action would be as valid as any other. *Would it?* Ayn asked. Morality, she demonstrated, is a practical, *selfish* necessity —

this was the idea I found so inspiring. Alone on a desert island, man would face constant alternatives requiring moral choice: to think — or not to think; to perceive reality, identify facts, and act accordingly — or to sulk and pray; to work and produce — or to demand a miracle that would spare him the effort; to act on the judgment of his mind — or to surrender to terror; and his life would hang in the balance.

Living in society, when men attempt to survive not by thought and productive work but by parasitism and force, by theft, appropriation, and violence, they still count on the faculty of reason: the reason that some moral persons had to exercise in order to create the goods that the parasites propose to loot or expropriate. When men attempt to exist by means other than reason, it becomes a matter of little more than chance who lasts a decade and who lasts a year, who is wiped out by whom, and who is able to consume some part of his gains before the club descends on *him*. Man's life depends on thinking, not blind action; on achievement, not destruction; nothing can change that fact. Mindlessness, passivity, and parasitism are not and cannot be principles of survival; they are merely the policy of those who do not wish to face the issue of survival.

The entire novel, I realized, could be read as a dramatized amplification of what "life as the standard" means, as applied to every major sphere of human endeavor, to work, love, sex, human relationships, art, and politics.

It was not within my view of the universe that night to imagine that the most violent attacks hurled against Ayn's moral philosophy would not even mention its intellectual foundation, or acknowledge what I regarded as one of her most extraordinary achievements, her justification of Man's Life as the standard of value and the basis of ethics.

That was only a small part of the shock in store for me. I saw in her work such respect for human beings, such true concern for human happiness, such a celebration of the human potential, such reverence for life on earth, that I could not have conceived what lay ahead.

The group went on reading, and Ayn and I went on talking. "For some reason I cannot understand," she whispered, "Leonard cannot seem to hold the argument for 'life as the standard'; he keeps losing it and asking me to re-explain it."

"Funny. Barbara is like me — she finds it simple and can present it beautifully."

"Oh, I think Barbara has a better philosophical mind than Leonard — much faster, much clearer."

"Sure, but Leonard is very intelligent."

"Yes, he is. That's why I can't understand why he doesn't seem able to hang on to his own knowledge."

I wondered how Leonard could manage to look nervous even while sitting perfectly still reading a manuscript. He had a quality of fragility about him, combined with a high level of excitability and a boundless enthusiasm for the enterprise of philosophy, which often tended to evoke in me feelings of protectiveness; others in our group responded similarly. He was wildly enthusiastic about Ayn's work as well as about Ayn personally. One felt certain that he would happily die for her — he had that air about him. Toward me also he projected a feverish kind of hero-worship. "You're what he would like to become," Ayn once said to me, approvingly.

As if sensing our attention, Leonard lifted his head, looked at me, and proclaimed loudly, "Ayn makes reading any other philosopher unbearable." I did not doubt that he meant it, and I regretted my sense that part of his motive in saying it was to elicit our approval.

Of our entire group, he was the only one who planned to make philosophy his profession. Relative to Ayn's work, he saw his role as especially important, a viewpoint Ayn and I shared. Some of his problems at school were particularly embarrassing to him, and mystifying to the rest of us. If, for example, he was studying the philosophy of John Dewey, he could very easily fall into Dewey's perspective without noticing it, accept the premises of Dewey that he in fact knew to be mistaken, and then proceed to panic. This might happen with any philosopher, from Plato to Wittgenstein. Leonard would sense that he had been had, but not know how to think his way out, and he would come to Ayn or me in a state of intellectual chaos, desperate for an answer to Dewey or Bertrand Russell or A. J. Ayer.

It was difficult not to become impatient with Leonard, and sometimes Ayn became so angry that Leonard would pale with terror. "What's the matter with you?" she would thunder. "Can't you hold any context whatsoever? Can't you see that you've been conned by a lousy equivocation, plus a whole series of unjustified assumptions? I thought we cleared all this up months ago!" Seeing the expression of misery and desperately conscientious attentiveness on Leonard's face, I could feel only sympathy for him. Poor Leonard, I thought, and tried to inject a calming note into the discussion. I could understand Ayn's frustration better than her rage, which seemed vaguely anxious, as if she was afraid she would lose Leonard to "the irrational."

Later, alone with me, Ayn would say, "Without the concept of social metaphysics, I would be totally at a loss to make sense of Leonard's behavior. Still, I don't understand psychology, not really. I hate your profession. How can you stand it?" By now, "social metaphysics" had become a brand of near-infamy; everyone feared the diagnosis, although in our immediate group only Joan and Leonard had been labeled. On some other occasion, Ayn would say, "You must ask Leonard to show you the paper he wrote for Sidney Hook's class. The paper is brilliant — Leonard at his best! What intelligence he has, when he doesn't allow himself to become confused! . . . Thank God you're a psychologist. Without you, how would I understand anyone? In this area, you've taught me everything I know."

Such compliments were flattering and at times irresistibly seductive, yet I could not escape the sense that Ayn *took pride* in her ignorance, and this thought led me down a dark corridor of my psyche, labeled: "Not understood — to be considered some day in the future."

Everyone was optimistic about the impact of *Atlas Shrugged* (still called *The Strike*) on our culture, but Leonard's projections were so extravagantly wild that they bordered on hysteria. He spoke of the conversion of the country to laissez-faire capitalism and the ideals of individualism "within a year of the publication of the novel." More than once Ayn and I had to remind him that the transmission of ideas through a culture was extremely complex. He was dismayed when Ayn told him, "I can't be sure that I'll begin to see the real impact of the book during my lifetime." I pointed out how radical Ayn's ideas were and how challenging. "Just the same," I assured him, "if the novel sells fifty thousand copies, this culture will never be the same again." We all expected the book to sell in the millions, and it did.

If we sometimes smiled at Leonard's flights of unrealistic exuberance, we nonetheless felt great affection for him. Today I would say that he represented the excited child in us all. And the ambivalence he could evoke may have been a reflection of the ambivalence evoked by the child in each of us. "I feel sympathy for Leonard," Ayn once said to me, "because there's a part of me that *wants* life to be as simple as Leonard thinks it is."

My glance swung across the room from Leonard to Alan Greenspan — or "A.G.," as we called him, to distinguish him from "A.B.," Allan Blumenthal.

A.G. and Leonard were Ayn's favorites, and she kept changing her mind about which one she liked most. One month Leonard was in, and A.G. had the number-two spot, but a month later their positions would be reversed. What she enjoyed in Leonard was his loyalty, his passion for philosophy, and what she regarded as his idealism. What she enjoyed in A.G. was his greater sense of practical reality, his passion for the world of business and industry, his appreciation of Ayn's portrayal of this world in her novel, and his greater maturity. During times when Leonard was number one and A.G. was in second place, she would say, "Not counting you and Barbara, of course, Leonard is the most idealistic member of the Collective, and the most philosophical. Alan Greenspan is too 'worldly,' too impressed by success. The trouble with Alan is, he thinks Henry Luce is important." When she changed her preference, she would say, "What I like about A.G. is that basically he has his feet on the ground. I love his love for life on earth. He really is a passionate person in his own quiet way. Leonard is too hysterical, too scattered and disorganized." Once I teased her about her proclivity for switching favorites. "Can't you just accept that you really like both of them and that both have traits that sometimes annoy you?" She shook her head. "You know me. I've got to have favorites. I always think hierarchically. In the Collective, first there's you — you stand alone on your own level. Next, there's Barbara. Then, on still another level down, there's Leonard and A.G. Then, all the rest. I exempt Frank from this, of course, because he's in a unique category of his own. These are the terms in which I think. And observe — everyone knows it and accepts it. It's rational, isn't it?"

Now, looking at Alan Greenspan, I wondered to what extent he was aware of Ayn's opinions. He rarely voiced his feelings about anything of a personal nature, and his language tended to be detached and passive. Complimenting Ayn on some passage in the novel, he might say, "On reading this . . . one tends to feel . . . exhilaration." Or, "The reader is really inspired here." But occasionally he would break down and exclaim, "Ayn, this is *incredible*. No one has ever dramatized what industrial achievement actually means as you have. What you've written is a hymn to human intelligence. *This is fantastic*." Because he was not given to such outbursts, when they erupted they especially endeared him to Ayn — and to me.

The first love of A.G.'s life had been music. When he was nineteen years old he played the saxophone in a swing band — a picture I absolutely could not integrate with the somber figure I knew, with his passion for classical music and the study of economy. Sometimes, when we had lunch together, I would kid him about his "nonphilosophical past." I also asked him many questions about economic theory and about how an economy actually functioned, and I enjoyed learning from him.

A number of our talks centered on the role of the Federal Reserve Board in influencing the economy by manipulating the money supply. We talked about the Fed's destructive contribution to the Great Depression. He spoke with vigor and intensity about a totally free banking system. It was an odd sensation to recall those discussions when Alan was appointed chairman of the Federal Reserve Board, in 1987.

Alan had left the National Industrial Conference Board, where he had worked when I met him, to accept an invitation from bond trader William Townsend to form a business consulting firm — Townsend-Greenspan & Company. We had spent many hours discussing the pros and cons of Townsend's offer, because Alan feared the loss of security associated with the change. "I don't know if I have the talent to make this thing work," he said to me. I answered, "You're still in your twenties. How can you be worried about security now? Take the leap. You can do it. And if it doesn't work out, for any reason — so what? You'll do something else. Anyway, this is nonsense, because you're not going to fail — not with your brains. You just don't appreciate how good you are."

Alan had taken the leap — and was succeeding spectacularly. He was acquiring a reputation as an outstanding economic analyst who could find significances in figures that no one else could.

In 1958, Townsend died. The company, 99 percent Alan's, climbed to higher and higher levels of success, making Alan a wealthy man. "You believed in me," he said, shaking his head wonderingly. "How could you be sure? I would never be sure of such a thing." I said, "What difference does it make? You've done it." He laughed. "Nathan, I'll never forget what you've given me."

This last statement I had heard, or would hear, from almost everyone in the Collective. "I'll never forget what you've given me, I'll never forget what you've done for me." The sentiment's painful irony was to become apparent only many years in the future.

None of us found it strange that Alan Greenspan, Joan, and Allan Blumenthal should be friends. The fact that for nine months Joan and A.G. had been married now seemed irrelevant. The relationships that counted in this room, we said, were philosophical. In the outside world, we had all seen ourselves as loners, even aliens. Here, we were family. We were an intellectual community. We had intimate access to truths not yet revealed to the world.

While he admired Allan Blumenthal's playing, A.G. had difficulty understanding A.B.'s pursuit of a musical career. "The odds are too much against it," was A.G.'s comment. Moreover, it was clear that A.B. lacked the aggressiveness he needed. He knew little about how to fight for what he wanted, and none of us knew how to advise him. Watching A.B.'s struggle, I decided that I would never make a career choice that put me so much at the mercy of other people; the musical world appeared to be a very small one with depressingly limited opportunities for a concert pianist. "So much seems to hang on who you know," A.B. complained. He began to discuss with me the possibility of practicing psychiatry. I volunteered to assist him in any way I could.

The happiest part of Allan's life was his relationship with Joan. I had the sense that with her he felt validated as man. "She believes in me," he said.

Because of his somewhat prissy manner, Ayn sometimes joked when she and I were alone: "How do you suppose Allan would react to our affair?"

I shook my head. "I really have no idea."

"Oh," she said, "I think he would be shocked. But not as shocked as Leonard would be."

"That's because Leonard knows for a certainty that you are a virgin."

Looking around the room at everyone, I realized that the magnitude of my secret made close friendship with any of them impossible. I was aware of the strain between us, but I shrugged it off. What difference did it make? I was most comfortable with intellectual friendships, anyway. I did not own my feelings of isolation and loneliness.

I did not have a single relationship in which I felt fully free to share my thoughts and feelings in a spirit of true intimacy and trust. That was painful, if I allowed myself to think about it.

On the sofa, three members of our group were reading; two days earlier Ayn and I had lain there, embracing. I looked at Ayn and enjoyed thinking, in this moment, in this setting, that I knew every detail of the body underneath her dress.

In one corner Joan and Frank were whispering and laughing. "Joan," Ayn said, "has justified her existence by introducing Frank to drawing and painting. I mean it. He's become a new man. It's magnificent to see what's happening to him."

It had begun one evening when the Collective was discussing painting, and Barbara had said that she was so lacking in the premises and orientation of a visual artist that she could not possibly learn to draw. Other members of our group made similar remarks about themselves. Joan insisted that any intelligent person, properly taught, could learn to draw competently, and offered to conduct a class to prove her point. Frank was among those who agreed to try.

It was as if a new world had suddenly opened to him. All his life his primary orientation had been visual, and now he had an outlet. From his first sketch he shot ahead of everyone else in the class. He began to draw constantly. Then he began working in pastels. His sense of drama and composition were there from the beginning. We were all stunned by the sensuality and theatricality of his work and by its imaginativeness. Soon he was enrolled in the Art Students League on Fifty-seventh Street. At the age of fifty-eight he was a man on fire, alive as none of us had ever seen him alive before, totally dedicated to the work that would consume him until, years later, his declining faculties made work impossible.

Among Frank's teachers at the Art Students League was Robert Brackman, a member of the National Academy of Design and a highly respected painter. From the beginning he decided that Frank was an unusual talent and supported him enthusiastically. With everything Frank had to learn, Brackman said, he brought to painting an individuality and expressiveness that many artists try for all their life.

Unfortunately, Frank had two weaknesses that he never resolved: perspective or anatomy. He lacked the patience and discipline to study them as consistently and thoroughly as he needed to. Or perhaps he was rebelling against Ayn's invasions of his most precious territory. When she attempted to reach him on this subject, he sometimes growled back with the irritability of a teenager at a domineering mother; she might speak very gently, not to antagonize him, and sometimes he professed to agree with her, but the conversations never led to a fundamental change of his attitude.

In the spring of 1956, when Frank's new work was just beginning, none of us foresaw that he would carry his limitations as a painter unchallenged until the end. We saw only his electrifying talent.

My private impression was that he had now become almost indifferent to my relationship with Ayn, except, perhaps, for feeling a sense of relief that I had lifted a burden from his shoulders; Ayn seemed to be placing fewer emotional demands on him. I did not yet know about his drinking.

The person in our group I knew least well was Mary Ann Rukavina. She was a student of art history, as Joan had been. Quiet, a little pedantic, a little mischievous, she had an impish smile that lent a note of charm to her formal, somewhat stilted, yet almost regal, manner. She seemed to enjoy seeing herself as crusader — as we all did. She was tall, slender, remote in a way that suggested someone on her way to becoming a middle-aged spinster, although she was then in her twenties and not unattractive. Some years later she married one of Ayn's admirers, a lawyer named Charles Sures. She was a member of our inner circle, and our relations were always friendly, but I never really felt I knew her; I never had a sense of her core; perhaps I was not curious enough to find out. But I would have said I liked her.

I felt a special kind of affection for Elayne and Harry. Harry Kalberman had left Nazi Germany with his family at the age of thirteen. Like Ayn, he had a European's enthusiasm for America. Although Harry and Elayne were liked by everyone in our circle, they were not "intellectuals" or "in the arts" — Harry was in business and Elayne was an operating room nurse. So there was always a subtle distance between them and the others, although not one of us would have acknowledged our implicit snobbism. Ayn spoke of them as being "of very good character," whereas she spoke of Alan Greenspan as "a sleeping giant," of Leonard as "an idealist," of Allan Blumenthal as "very intelligent," of Joan as "talented and struggling."

Although I did not have a great deal in common with him, I felt affection for Harry, in part because I perceived him as more manly than the other men in our circle; he had a quality of street toughness I liked. He and Elayne seemed unusually well matched. When their daughter was born, they named her Kira, after the heroine of *We the Living*. Harry became a vice president at Merrill Lynch.

Growing up, Elayne and I had not been close. Now she showed a fondness and even a deference that was new to our relationship. We had come from a family in which affection was almost never expressed, and while we were able to show it in our own private spheres, we remained a little stiff with each other. Our warmth almost always came packaged in humor. But Elayne was absolutely committed to the value and importance of Ayn's work — she was as inspired by *Atlas* as any of us — and to have that connection with a *sister* was very important to me. It contributed to my sense of having found roots.

Except for Ayn and Frank, who were in their fifties, none of us at that time was older than thirty. Not yet twenty-six, I was next to the youngest in our group. I remember telling Ayn, "I'm not yet in full control of my life. I've still got too many jagged edges to me. I think by thirty I'll come properly into my own."

I was eager to complete graduate school and to earn my own living. I wanted to continue practicing psychotherapy, to learn more about the human mind and the process of change and growth, and to write books — that was to be my future. However, the idea for yet another career activity was already germinating.

It was sparked by the enormous amount of fan mail Ayn was still receiving from readers of *The Fountainhead*. Men and women wrote glowingly of the ways the book had changed their life, given them courage, shown them a new perspective, projected new possibilities. Ayn read me letters written by soldiers in World War II about how the novel had given them a vision worth fighting for — and had inspired their determination to survive the war, come home, and work toward that vision in their own lives. The letters came in the thousands. Many of the writers asked philosophical questions about ethics, politics, art, epistemology. "If this is the kind of interest *The Fountainhead* stimulates," I had said to Ayn a few weeks earlier, "can you imagine the response the new novel — which is so much more philosophical — is going to evoke? You're going to be bombarded. We ought to have a school of some kind." "A school?" Ayn had said. "What kind of school?"

Now, sitting at the dinner table, I broached the subject again. "A school is too grand, too ambitious. I have something simpler in mind. Suppose I create a course of lectures — say, twenty lectures — that would distill the essence of your philosophy — epistemology, metaphysics, ethics, political economy, literary aesthetics, and perhaps some of my work in psychology — and suppose I offer this to people?"

"Offer it? Offer it how? To whom?"

"Well, I haven't thought this out clearly yet but, let's say, I offer it to people within commuting distance of New York who have written you fan letters, and we can see what happens."

Ayn looked faintly uncertain. "I don't know." I decided to reflect on the idea further before raising it again.

One by one, the members of the group finished their reading for the evening and began talking among themselves. Ayn and I returned to the living room, where she sat beaming with pleasure as everyone spoke with high-spirited appreciation. It was as if her novel had brought out whatever was most alive and vibrant in each one of them, and I thought about the unique power of art to evoke such responses.

Someone said to Ayn, "There is so much passion in your writing, so much deep, intense feeling — how can people say we're anti-emotion?"

"Because we're pro-reason," someone else responded.

"They assume a dichotomy," said a third voice.

"Exactly," said Ayn. "They assume that if one is an advocate of reason, and has no tolerance for the irrational, this means one is against feelings and emotions — because they equate feelings and emotions with mindlessness."

"Speaking for themselves," I said, "they might even be right."

"Yes, exactly," said Ayn.

All of us had encountered the accusation that we were "antifeeling." All of us felt misperceived and misunderstood — and we looked with scorn on people who could not grasp the relationship between reason and emotion as we conceived it. Reason and emotion — thinking and feeling — were not two contradictory or mutually inimical faculties, we insisted, but their functions were not interchangeable. *Emotions were not tools of cognition.* What one *feels* in regard to any fact or issue was irrelevant to the question of whether one's judgment of it was true or false, right or wrong. It was not by means of one's feelings that one perceived reality.

Like a chairperson addressing her board of directors, Ayn declared, "If a person tells you that he regards reason and emotion as antagonists, he is telling you that *his* emotions are irrational, that he feels things reason cannot support, and that he wants to get away with something dishonest."

This was a statement that all of us would echo many times across the years, no one more often than I.

We had grown accustomed to hearing Ayn not merely dispute an idea she regarded as mistaken, but provide a psychological interpretation of her opponent's motivation. Most of her future nonfiction writings reflected her penchant for this kind of psychologizing (in spite of her repeated insistence that she knew nothing about psychology). It was second nature to her and became second nature to us.

I listened peacefully while Ayn went on talking about reason as the foundation of healthy passion, rather than its enemy, and I thought how simple and logical it sounded, and what order she had brought to my understanding of life.

To Ayn, nothing was more important about her than her conviction that reason must be the supreme arbiter in all matters. "If any part of your uncertainty," John Galt tells Dagny Taggart, when she must make an agonizing choice between joining his strike and returning to her railroad, "is a conflict between your heart and your mind — follow your mind." This was a message that Ayn conveyed to all of us: actions were to be ruled by the mind, not the heart.

This was a message I conveyed to myself, in moments when my heart seemed to be pulling me away from a romance with Ayn. It was a rule of life to which everyone in this room had pledged allegiance. We had also pledged allegiance to the belief that there were no hidden complexities in this rule that might need untangling.

As our group went on talking about reason and emotion, agreeing that one must be guided by the conscious mind in all matters, that one must not follow emotions blindly — who could dispute that to do so was anything but undesirable and dangerous? — no one suggested that to live by such a rule might not always be as simple as it sounded. No one pointed out that such counsel does not deal with the possibility that feelings or emotions might sometimes reflect a more accurate assessment of reality than consciousness beliefs ("reason"?). Or, to say the same thing differently, that the subconscious mind might be right while the conscious mind was mistaken.

And yet, ironically, Ayn was not unaware of this phenomenon, making it central to the evolution of Hank Rearden. He ruthlessly suppresses his feelings, always at his own expense, giving others the benefit of a doubt they do not deserve; he tragically reproaches himself for his passion for Dagny and his indifference toward his wife; his liberation is tied to appreciating finally the rightness of the very feelings he has been struggling to repudiate. The message was not lost on us, however, that Rearden's error is treated in heroic terms: *he does the right thing,* in his own conscientious, tortured way, within the limits of his knowledge; he is not like the villains who follow their emotions blindly. He makes errors of judgment but never of morality. Francisco d'Anconia, seeking to help Rearden, cautions him against being so quick to sacrifice his emotions, and advises him to "examine" them — but there Ayn stops. And I have no recollection of Ayn ever giving even this much pro-emotion advice to any of us.

What we are not shown in the novel is a character who knows how to listen to feelings, reflect on them, and perhaps gain new insights and modify conscious thinking accordingly, without following emotions blindly. Other than suppression or repression, encouraged by highly intellectualized kinds of "analysis," we had learned no real strategy for dealing with "reason versus emotion" conflicts; nor did we grasp the need for such a strategy.

What we call a clash between mind and emotion, or reason and feeling, is a clash between two assessments, two thoughts or judgments, one of which is conscious, the other of which might not be. It is not inevitable that the conscious judgment is superior to the subconscious one; that needs to be determined. We do not follow the voice of emotion unthinkingly; we try to understand what the voice may be trying to tell us. We do not simply suppress or repress; we try to resolve the conflict without assuming in advance that we know where the error lies. Sometimes our conscious mind is right and our feelings do reflect a mistake or confusion; sometimes the reverse is true.

What I did not understand that night — what none of us understood — is that we must be open to exploring, open to finding out, and in the meantime we treat *all* of our experiences with respect. We need to strive for balance, harmony, integration. Not simply slash away the pieces of ourselves that do not fit our official notion of the good or the right or the rational. It would be fifteen years before I understood this fully, and, in 1971, presented my own perspective in *The Disowned Self.* If we had understood and practiced what healthy self-acceptance truly means, if we had been willing to acknowledge and own all the disowned parts of ourselves, our whole world would have blown apart.

The conversation in the room shifted. Mary Ann Rukavina was talking about what a romantic and colorful character Francisco was. Harry raved about Francisco's speech on the meaning of money, given at Rearden's anniversary party. Barbara, whose comments tended to be the most specific and the most literary, discussed one of our favorite sections in the novel, the first train ride on the track of revolutionary

Rearden Metal, which is a true tour de force of physical description, particularly for capturing the sensory experience of motion. With an air of superiority Joan spoke of enjoying the names Ayn gave her villains, such as Wesley Mouch, Floyd Ferris, and Walton Scudder. In his typically flat, uninflected manner, Alan Greenspan spoke of his enthusiasm for the climax of Part I, when Ellis Wyatt goes on strike, setting fire to his oil fields and disappearing. Allan Blumenthal talked gently and almost dreamily of the inspiration he felt at the description of life in the hidden valley in Colorado, home of the men and women who have followed Galt and refused to give their talents to the world. Elayne spoke with a simple, sharp clarity of the musical quality of Ayn's writing. Leonard wondered what there was left for him to do in philosophy, since Ayn had "said everything."

"It's wonderful to be part of history!" Mary Ann said suddenly and enthusiastically, changing the subject abruptly; she stretched her arms wide. A few people smiled. No one asked what she meant. Everyone knew.

A year or two at most, Ayn had said. Then we would be just friends again, special friends, to be sure. Then my life would once more be my own. I clung to the memory of her words, and the possibility filled me with hope and relief.

"No one can fail to understand this book," Alan Greenspan declared solemnly. "Ayn, your celebration of intelligence, ability, and achievement is so clear, so powerful, so unanswerable . . . your demonstration of what human life depends on is so radiantly exact . . . so precise . . . that a person would have to do very strange things to his mind to blank it out."

"And people will," I interjected.

"I know that, but I can't believe it," said Barbara.

"No one will hate this book as much as the Catholic Church," Ayn announced. "Not even the communists."

"That's right," I agreed. "In its glorification of life on earth, its man-worship, the novel is antireligious in the most profound sense. It's pro-self and antiguilt. It's pro-happiness."

"It *spiritualizes* the secular," said Ayn. "That's what mystics and religionists won't forgive."

"All I know is, when the book comes out, it's going to be a lot of fun," I said cheerfully.

Someone asked Ayn about the evolution of her concept of the ideal man which animated and inspired all of her writing. This was a favorite subject of Ayn's, and her voice became bright and eager. "Philosophy," she said, "is only a means to an end. But man is the end. And for me, in fiction, the projection of the ideal man is the end. Everything else in my writing exists for the purpose of creating Galt, Rearden, Francisco — or earlier, Roark — all the philosophy and all the events."

Then Ayn began speaking of the first literary love of her life, a hero she had encountered long ago in a boy's adventure magazine. His name was Cyrus and his story, "The Mysterious Valley," dealt with a villainous rajah who kidnaped a group of British officers in a plot to overthrow British rule. Cyrus was the officer who defied his captors; laughed at threats of torture; led the escape; rescued the heroine, a beautiful, blonde English girl; and led everyone to safety. To Ayn he was a breath-stopping representation of the virtues of independence, audacity, and courage — the ultimate man of action. "Physically, Cyrus was the model for all my heroes: tall, slender, long legs, hair falling down over one eye. . . . I was only nine years old, but I was in love. I mean this seriously: I was in love then — and still am. What I felt for Cyrus, then, is the essence of what I feel for all my heroes, for *all* my values. . . ." Her glance stopped on me. "Do you think I should be telling this to everyone?" she asked.

"I think it's *wonderful,*" someone said.

"At nine years old, you were already a man-worshiper!" exclaimed someone else.

Typically, whenever Ayn chose to speak about her early life, or the process of her development, the group listened, entranced, as if whatever she said was magical. I watched the group's reaction with approval: I wanted Ayn to have this kind of audience and I was proud that I had provided it for her.

"Cyrus," Ayn was saying, "helped me to identify more clearly what I admired in a man, what I wanted to find. The abstraction, not the concretes, of that story, of course. The *essence* of the heroic. I thought: 'This is what I want.' After Cyrus, 'ordinary people' interested me much less. I thought I would find my kind of people when I grew up. And I would write about them."

When Ayn first told me about Cyrus, I felt vaguely uneasy. Now I could not shake off the idea of arrested emotional development. Were Frank and I characters in Ayn's storybook? Then I stopped myself abruptly: Was I insane? Where had that thought come from? What was the matter with me? I forced my mind back into the room as Ayn went on talking.

In 1914, the year Ayn discovered Cyrus, her family vacationed in Switzerland. Ayn described it as the happiest summer of her life, climbing mountain trails with a boy she had met and liked. But while she and her family were traveling to Paris, war broke out. They hurried on to London, in search of a ship that would carry them back to Russia.

"I could not know how much was going to end that summer, not only for me, but for the world. Not yet understanding what it all meant, I was happy. It was in London that I decided to become a writer. Of course I was already inventing stories, and I loved telling them to my sisters, but, you know, I had not yet grasped that writing stories could be a profession. I was walking with my governess through the streets of London, and we saw posters for some musical revue that showed attractive blonde women with bobbed hair — and when I got back to my hotel room I began inventing stories about these women — and then suddenly I realized that this was what writers do — writing was an occupation. Very seriously, very decisively, I told myself, 'I am going to be a writer.' I hated the sentimentality of Russian children's stories and the tragic sense of life. I wanted what 'The Mysterious Valley' stood for in my mind. Purposeful people fighting for important goals *and succeeding.*"

I watched Barbara watching Ayn, and the expression on her face was one of complete, undivided love. Barbara was about a month away from turning twenty-seven. Tonight, she showed no discernible trace of anxiety or pain. It was as if she was receiving some kind of spiritual transfusion from Ayn's words.

Yet the conflicts and frictions between them were real. Ayn's condemnations of Barbara's emotionalism, value confusions, and general un-Kira-like, un-Dagny-like, demeanor continued unabated — mixed, to be sure, with affection, support, even nurturing. Barbara's pain over Ayn's and my affair was also real, her idealistic acceptance notwithstanding.

And the same, bewilderingly, was true of me. My erotic love for Ayn was real and so was my desire for a nonromantic friendship. My love for Barbara was real and so was my estrangement. My desire to have an exclusive relationship with each of them was real and so was my awareness that each relationship helped make bearable the frustrations in the other. My sense of profound connection and affinity with each of them was real and so was my sense that neither of them was truly the woman I wanted. I could not find a single perspective that embraced harmoniously the conflicts and ambivalences with which I lived. I could only swing between one state of consciousness and another, and wait for the bad periods to pass — and be grateful for times such as tonight when all my values seemed to be in relatively benign balance.

Whatever I might be confused about, I knew that I admired Ayn more than anyone I had ever met. Why, then — this was the question that rose up at unpredictable moments to torture me — why, then, should the difference in age between us sometimes matter so much that it nullified all the values in our relationship? Should not a mind such as mine be able to transcend such a consideration? And then more difficult questions: Was I absolutely certain that age was the core problem? Could there be other yet unrecognized incompatibilities? And how was it possible that there were times when I felt so serenely and happily in love?

Many months ago, I had attempted to tell Ayn of my struggle over these issues. Instantly I saw her transformed into distant, icy rage. She became more than a stranger, she became an adversary. "Do you wish me to understand that this has all been a mistake?" She launched into an attack on my values as if we had no history and no context. I could not bear losing her, and assured her that I did not doubt my love for her. I told myself that this was a conflict I would have to work through alone — and that I must be the one not to fail her, not to cause her suffering.

There were other blows that wounded our relationship. Most of the time I told myself they were senseless and insignificant. If Ayn had fought with Frank; if she was bothered by some throwaway remark of mine; if she had spoken lovingly to me and I had been a little distant, or too light in my response, or had shifted to some unrelated philosophical issue — *and when she had telephoned I was out with Barbara* — Ayn's voice would convey the unmistakable message that I had failed her in some way the next time we spoke. Given the fact of my marriage, I would remind myself, was she not entitled to some feelings of insecurity? Confused and self-reproachful, I would be extra-attentive until she relented. But first, there would be a detailed, often hours-long, analysis of what had taken place — until she was satisfied that I understood why she was upset and did not think her unfair or irrational. It was intolerable to Ayn that someone important to her should ever think her irrational.

Sometimes our blowups were even more intense. Once I telephoned her from a restaurant, just to say hello, and she was troubled about something and wanted to talk. I found her demanding tone abrasive and unpleasant and explained that I needed to go to a class. When I hung up I felt so irritated that I took Barbara to a movie instead. Barbara later happened to mention to Ayn where we had gone. This led to an all-night session between Ayn and me in which, in a voice as quietly ominous as thunder, she proceeded to explore the possible significance of my lie. If I could deceive her about this, might I not deceive her about other things? My confused feelings made me particularly vulnerable to this line of attack, and I probably projected a guilt that served only to worsen her suspicions. She proceeded to remind me of every instance that she could recall of elusive or inappropriate behavior on my part, which made it harder for me to think clearly about the immediate issue. She wondered whether I might not be an admittedly brilliant but nonetheless diabolically manipulative person who was not at all that he represented himself to be. Her speculations grew worse and worse, and more removed from reality. I felt traumatized. And the rage that paralyzed me into silence made me a poor spokesman in my own defense. I told myself: you have no right to be angry; she's not entirely wrong, after all, even if she's grossly exaggerating; she senses that something is off — and, some of the time, she's right. I struggled to remain calm, to show compassion for her anguish, and to stay nondefensively open to whatever she wished to say. Eventually she would decide that she had overreacted, and by dawn she was arguing on my behalf against her own accusations. Not knowing what truth, honor, or sanity, meant anymore, I was simultaneously miserable and relieved.

At home, when she learned of these attacks, Barbara's typical response was protective indignation. "What does Ayn *expect* of you?" She observed more than once that if someone did something to displease Ayn, it was as if all history and all context vanished, and Ayn reacted as if she knew nothing about that person except the infraction. I reluctantly admitted that everyone in our group was always on trial with Ayn. She gave her unconditional acceptance to no one. At any time, in response to some dubious behavior — such as liking a movie or a piece of music Ayn disapproved of, or dropping a facetious, irreverent remark about her work, or being too pleasant to the "enemy" — she might begin to wonder aloud if that Collective member was basically "a Peter Keating" or "an Ellsworth Toohey," "a whim-worshiper" or "a mystic." I cannot recall a single instance when any of us questioned aloud Ayn's policy. Only Barbara and Frank knew how many hours I spent defending one of our friends against Ayn's speculations about his or her basic character or "sense of life."

However, for the past few months, riding on the euphoric energy of writing the concluding chapters of *Atlas*, Ayn seemed more easygoing, less inclined to criticize, and even to revel in having a "family" with which to share the most important creative experience of her life.

I looked around the living room at our family. Frank and Joan were once again locked in private conversation, about art, I assumed, and Ayn said to me, "I don't want to disturb Frank. Let's you and I get the coffee and pastry. Will you help me?" When we were alone in the kitchen, Ayn turned and whispered, "Isn't it wonderful, darling?" I knew that she meant all the elements of her life at present: our affair, Frank's discovery of painting, the Collective's response to the novel, the emotional vibrations of joy and excitement in the room tonight.

"Yes," I said, meaning it, "it's wonderful."

For a brief instant she stepped forward, pressing herself against me, smiling like a schoolgirl who was delighted by her own daring. I responded by holding her ferociously, moving my hand along her thigh. I felt desire — and a tenderness that was almost painful.

She began to tell me that the Collective was only an extension of me; that without me, it wouldn't exist; that none of them would have pursued her and begun a relationship with her on their own. "You were and are the prime mover."

I felt gratitude for this acknowledgment, but I began to tense, knowing that more was coming.

"Without you, none of them would mean to me what they do. If you admire *The Fountainhead*, if you admire the new novel — well, darling, you'll understand what I am telling you: you are my reward; you are my reward for everything — for my work, for my life."

I closed my eyes, allowing the boy of fourteen who read *The Fountainhead* to hear what Ayn Rand had just said to him; not thinking of it in those terms, but feeling an emotional equivalent, the sense of a reward, an answer, a vindication, a miracle extended back through time.

"Darling," she said, "there's something I think I was wrong about."

"Impossible," said the adult Nathaniel firmly, while fourteen-year-old Nathan struggled with intoxication. "What could you be wrong about?"

"About our future together. Why did I say the affair could only last a year or two? Can you think of any good reason why we can't go on this way forever?"

If my emotions could have shrieked out, passed the barrier of my conscious mind, I would have cried that it seemed suddenly that a gun was pointed at my temple. But I had no illusions, then or later, about who pulled the trigger.

"No," I said. "I can't."

T E N

ONE OF THE MOST important professional developments for Ayn in the period following the completion of Galt's speech was the selection of a publisher for *Atlas Shrugged*.

Ayn knew she would not allow *Atlas* to be published by Bobbs-Merrill, although her contract required that she submit the book there first. "Not after their rotten treatment of *The Fountainhead*," she declared. I asked, "But suppose Bobbs-Merrill wants the new book, as it almost certainly will?" She answered, "I'll set terms they'll never agree to."

Through her literary agent, Alan Collins, head of Curtis Brown, Ayn submitted the manuscript, exclusive of Galt's speech (she would show that only to the book's ultimate publisher) to Bobbs-Merrill; Ross Baker, the New York representative of that house, proposed to Ayn that she and Collins join him for dinner — to discuss the cuts and changes that *Atlas* would require. Ayn was adamant that the novel be published exactly as she had written it; Baker's insistence on cuts provided just the solution she wanted. When he declared that in its present form the book was unsalable and unpublishable, Ayn remained intransigent — and so freed herself of Bobbs-Merrill.

The word spread that Ayn was in the market for a publisher, and most of the major houses approached Alan Collins. "What is it you want in a publisher?" I asked Ayn, and she answered, "Not agreement with my ideas necessarily; that's not the issue. But I do want understanding of the ideas — and the courage to stand by the book, to fight for it, not to be cowed into silence and passivity by the antagonism of critics. And imagination in promoting it."

The four houses that Ayn and Alan Collins selected for serious consideration were Viking, where Archie Ogden now worked; Knopf; McGraw-Hill; and Random House. On her own Ayn would not have included Random House, since she thought its editorial policy left-wing; but Hiram Haydn, editor in chief at Random House, had been an editor at Bobbs-Merrill and had maintained contact with Ayn across the years, always inquiring about her new work. She thought Haydn was a reasonable person with whom she could work. Haydn told Ayn that Random House had changed politically — pointing to its publication of Whittaker Chambers's anticommunist *Witness* as evidence — and Ayn agreed that she and Collins would lunch with the owners, Bennett Cerf and Donald Klopfer, so she could judge for herself.

When I visited Ayn after this meeting, she was enthusiastic. She liked both men immediately, she said. She found them open, straightforward, fair-minded, intellectual. She was impressed by Bennett Cerf's proposal that she submit the book to all four publishers simultaneously, staging a kind of contest, not for the purpose of raising the price of the advance, but to discover whose approach to the book she liked most. This was the kind of unconventionality Ayn admired.

Although she did not tell Cerf then, his suggestion virtually won her over. Donald Klopfer impressed her in a different way, no less important. When Ayn outlined the general philosophical stance of the novel, and stated that it offered a *moral* defense of capitalism, Klopfer stunned and delighted her by replying, "If it is a *moral* defense of capitalism, wouldn't it have to clash with the entire tradition of Judeo-Christian ethics?" Ayn told me excitedly, "He *understood* the clash between religion and capitalism. And I think he's a liberal, politically. And most defenders of capitalism don't understand the issue." I asked, "Does he agree with you?" She replied, "I didn't ask him and I don't care. It's such a pleasure to talk to a publisher *who can think.*"

Ayn met with representatives of the other three firms, all of whom compared unfavorably, in different ways, with Random House; none was as intellectual in its approach and none thought much of Bennett Cerf's proposal, which persuaded Ayn that the idea had already accomplished its purpose. Random House was given the first, exclusive submission, and the manuscript was read by Cerf, Klopfer, and Haydn.

One day Ayn telephoned, her voice radiant. "I have a great story to tell you and Barbara. Can you come over?" When we arrived, Ayn looked exuberant. "Alan Collins and I went to Cerf's office. We weren't given any advance notice of anyone's reaction to the novel. Bennett stood at his desk, very formally, didn't even say hello, just opened the meeting by saying, 'It's a great book. Name your own terms.'" She spread her arms wide and announced, "*This is life as it might be and ought to be — and, for once, is.*"

In the weeks and months that followed, each time Ayn had a meeting with any of the three men she would tell us about it in detail. Although none of them professed to be a convert to her ideas, all spoke repeatedly of the impact her thinking had on them. Donald Klopfer spoke of becoming more comfortable with his success, more respectful of earned wealth. Bennett Cerf spoke of being forced to rethink his views of the role of government in human affairs, and, like Klopfer, of being less apologetic about success. Hiram Haydn, who was perhaps the most uncomfortable with Ayn's philosophy — and, in my judgment, the least independent of the three — spoke of feeling that everything he had ever thought or believed had somehow been turned upside down, leaving him more than a little shaken up. All three professed great admiration for Ayn as a person.

Later, when I met them, they would shake their head in wonder at Ayn's ability to make them doubt their most cherished beliefs, and would praise her brilliance, her courage, and her integrity. One of them said to me, "Whether you agree or disagree, nothing in the way you look at the world is ever quite the same after you've spent time with Ayn."

Bennett was the most effusive. "Ayn's ideas will be discussed and debated in Congress!" he announced. It was with Bennett that Ayn eventually formed the closest friendship. She found him witty, charming, optimistic. "Of course he's a social metaphysician," she said, "very concerned with being liked, but he's very intelligent, very fair — and honest. I can deal with him."

Mary Ann Rukavina nicknamed him "Benny the benevolent univ-erser."

For six years, since Barbara and I had met Ayn and Frank, the four of us had lived in an essentially private world, which had expanded to include the Collective. Now, with the completion of the novel in sight, it seemed that our period of social isolation was approaching an end. The Collective looked to publication day — and beyond — with euphoria. So did I, for the most part, although sometimes I was uneasy, in anticipation of dark happenings ahead, knowing how foreign Ayn's vision was to the culture in which we lived. But uneasiness was not my predominant feeling. Mostly I felt the solemnity and excitement of a warrior on the eve of a battle it is his dream and destiny to fight, combined with the eagerness of a child who believes he is about to see the world transformed into a place where battles are no longer necessary.

Not long after the signing of the Random House contract, Ayn and I were dining at the Russian Tea Room on one of our evenings alone together. Her writing was going well, our relationship was going well, and the results showed on her face. She was wearing a dark blue blouse with a huge bow; she looked foreign, exotic, intense. She had the look of a woman at home in the world. It gave me pleasure to see her this way.

She contemplated me with an expression of special tenderness and said, "I want to dedicate the new novel to you."

The restaurant was crowded and fairly noisy, but it was as if suddenly there was total stillness, all sound had vanished, and there was only the meaning of her statement. I reached across the table and crushed her hand in mine. I could not speak. I could only look at her. "Oh, Ayn," I finally whispered. I experienced pride, gratitude, euphoria, and solemnity.

"Thank you for your reaction, darling," she said.

"There are no words to say what this means to me. I feel as if I've been hit over the head — with something so wonderful I need time to absorb it."

"I've been thinking about it for a long time. I haven't wanted to say anything until I was certain. I want to dedicate the book to Frank as well; I can't leave him out of this. It will be 'To Frank O'Connor and Nathaniel Branden.' That is, if you accept?"

"If I accept?" I asked incredulously. "Are you joking? If I accept the greatest honor anyone could ever bestow on me?"

"Think about it," Ayn said to me. "Don't be so quick to say yes. It's going to be the most controversial book of this century. I'm going to be hated, vilified, lied about, smeared in every possible way. If your name is in the book, if I acknowledge you publicly, you'll be a marked man. The attacks on me will also be directed at you. You have your own future and your own career to think about. Do you wish to be saddled with such an impediment?"

"Impediment?" I repeated, still astonished. "Please don't talk nonsense. Impediment? It's a badge of honor."

Once again she thanked me for my reaction, her face glowing with earnestness and happiness.

As if reading the page, I said, "*Atlas Shrugged* — to Frank O'Connor and Nathaniel Branden." I wondered about Frank's reaction to the dedication but Ayn did not speak of that and I did not ask.

"The title sounds right, doesn't it?" Ayn asked.

"Atlas Shrugged" had been the title of the chapter in which Hank Rearden finally goes on strike. One day Frank had suggested — to Ayn's enthusiastic agreement — that it would work ideally for the novel as a whole.

"I think the title is perfect," I said.

As she returned, with her usual dogged persistence, to the subject of the attacks, my joy and exhilaration made it almost impossible to concentrate on her words. Why was she asking me to think about the world or about what the world thought about anything? As if that had ever mattered to me. I wondered if she felt the need to test me, even now.

Seeing my reaction she chuckled with satisfaction, her eyes bright. "All right. I give up." Contemplating the intensity of my happiness, she asked, almost mockingly, "Are you pleased?"

"The idea of the greatest literary masterpiece I've ever read being dedicated to me is almost more than I can hold in my brain. I'm thrilled, I'm honored, I'm overwhelmed. I feel like I'm in the midst of the most marvelous dream. I'm speechless. I don't know what to say."

"You've said it," she answered. She looked at me appraisingly. "Oh, I think we both have tears in our eyes. Not quite, but almost. Out of character for both of us, but perfectly in character for this occasion, perfectly proper." Then she added, "Sometimes you're a disappearing professor. You go off — inside your mind, or somewhere — and I can't reach you; but when it really counts, you come through."

"Oh, I hope so!"

Her statement had lifted me still higher. I thought, if only I could always feel with Ayn as I do this evening. If only I could always be worthy of what she has given me. I want that more than I want anything else in this world.

"*Tonight,* darling," said Ayn, as if reading my thoughts, "is reality. Not the things I sometimes get upset with you about. Right now, none of that seems real, does it?"

She was as happy as I had ever seen her: one moment childlike and cheerful; the next moment adult, sensual, seductive; the next moment rubbing her foot against my leg under the table while looking around the room with an impish grin on her face. "Do you ever wonder what people think when they look at us?" she asked. I answered, "No, I don't have to. I know what they think, they think you're my daughter." She laughed. On another occasion she might have been annoyed.

But I could not help being aware of the psychological significance of my remark — a reversal of the obvious problem in our relationship. We rarely discussed the significance of our age difference, and when we did it was exclusively from the aspect of its meaning for Ayn. She took it as axiomatic that all the disadvantages were hers. It was she who had to be worried about the physical aspect of aging. It was she who would be scorned were our relationship made public, and it was she who had a reputation to protect; given the radical unconventionality of her philosophy, she was surprisingly undaring in this respect. At no time did she acknowledge that I might have difficulties of my own — not in terms of anyone's reaction, which I did not care about, but simply in terms of adapting romantically to someone who was then twice my age. "Age doesn't matter," Ayn said often. "*Values* matter. Our souls are ageless." I repeated her words to myself many times. Tonight I felt them.

Walking along Fifty-seventh Street toward Park Avenue, her arm through mine, Ayn declared that were we not having an affair, had we remained only friends, she would not have chosen to dedicate *Atlas* to me.

"A dedication in *this* book could only be for a supreme value of mine, not just a 'friend.' I wonder if anyone will be smart enough to figure that out."

"I love you," I said, "and right now I do not give a good goddamn what anyone knows or thinks or figures out about anything."

My name was to appear on the dedication page of *Atlas Shrugged*. How could I be expected to give space in my consciousness to anything else? I stopped in the middle of the street, puts my hands on her shoulders, and looked at her.

"Well, Mr. Nathan Blumenthal of Brampton, Ontario?" she said, looking up at me smilingly.

Brampton, Ontario — a small town not far from Toronto, where I had been born and had spent the first six years of my life. I thought of the road from that beginning to this night. I felt the presence in my body of some force that had no name but that had driven every step I had taken. I wondered why it sometimes felt that that force, whatever it was, separated me from other people, from everyone I had ever met except Ayn. And how could something be both a source of loneliness and a source of joy?

Now, suddenly, I wanted to talk, I wanted Ayn to understand something, I wanted to understand it myself, and perhaps her input would help. We continued walking.

"Funny you should mention Brampton. Strange the memories that pop up at odd moments, like now. I was about five years old. I was wearing a yellow sunsuit and riding my tricycle up the street. It had been raining and the ground was wet. I saw three boys my age playing in the mud, making mud castles, and they waved to me, but I just kept riding my tricycle up and down the street. I remember the feelings I had but not the words; I can't quite imagine what the words would have been for someone that age. I looked at the boys, I looked up at the sky, I had some sense of the immensity of things that evoked in me an odd, painful kind of longing, I looked back at the boys, then up at the sky again — and if I could have expressed what I was experiencing, the words would have been: there's something more; more than playing in the mud; more than what they're seeing; more than anyone sees; more than this life around me; and something inside of me is reaching for it. This memory has haunted and intrigued me all my life."

We walked and Ayn listened attentively, without speaking, knowing there was more that I wanted to say. "As to my parents and the other adults I encountered, I was already feeling — again, without these words, obviously — that I had been born into a lunatic asylum. Everyone seemed out of control. No one really knew why they did anything. I had the most overwhelming sense of human irrationality. Grown-ups said one thing and did another; claimed to be feeling one emotion but plainly were feeling something different; changed the rules and expectations every other hour; lied to us children and to one another all the time; were generous and kind one day and mean the next. As if they were possessed by demons. And everyone looked unhappy. And I could not understand *why*. I told myself I must not be afraid, must learn to understand all this, and never, ever be like these people."

"That's what saved you," Ayn said.

What was I struggling to say — or not to say? I experienced a kind of static in my brain, like a radio signal that could not break through.

"To me," I said, "and I think to all of us in the Collective, you represent everything we did not have when we were young: sanity."

She answered, "That's what I want to be. To you above all. There's no higher compliment you can pay me. I love you."

I looked at the sky and at the great buildings around us, metaphors in stone for the full spectrum of human aspiration and achievement. "You shoot your gracious tension to the stars," Ayn had written long ago in *The Fountainhead*, "out of the slack, the tired, the accidental." This was a line I had always loved. But I was too shy to tell even Ayn the sentence that suddenly flashed through my mind: *I am one of you now.*

Next morning over breakfast I told Barbara about the dedication. I expected her to be stunned. Instead, it was I who was stunned by the wise smile that greeted my announcement.

"I thought Ayn would do that. It's wonderful. I'm proud for you."

We wondered what Frank would feel, and we both immediately agreed that he would find the dedication entirely natural and appropriate, just as Barbara did. There was an easygoing sense of relaxed harmony between us, as there usually was when we weren't focused on our relationship.

Barbara was my first friend as well as my first lover. She gave me my first important experience of psychological visibility, even if it was incomplete. In spite of our conflicts, she still had the power to inspire a sense of connectedness between us untouched by her pain or mine.

I had never before let another person in so deeply; having done so, I now felt incapable of letting go.

We had moved from our studio apartment into a one-bedroom apartment on East Thirty-fifth Street. Our bed folded up into a sofa, and the bedroom became my office where I studied, wrote, and saw clients. My practice was growing steadily. Our dining room table folded into a desk for Barbara. She had earned her master's degree in philosophy, and had written her thesis on free will at this table, where we were now drinking our morning coffee.

Barbara was working as a receptionist at *Woman's Day* magazine — her first job after graduating. Soon she would land a job teaching philosophy, only to discover that she preferred publishing to academia. The job she would enjoy the most, and where she would remain the longest, was in the editorial department of St. Martin's Press.

After breakfast she hurried off to *Woman's Day,* and I to New York University for an appointment with my faculty adviser, Dr. John Tietz. When I arrived at his office, he informed me that he was retiring. This was unexpected, and I wondered if he was ill but did not think it appropriate to ask. I had begun to work with him on my master's thesis, which was to present my theory of anxiety. Now he repeated his opinion that my subject was too ambitious, even for a doctoral dissertation.

"Without me here to stand by you and defend you," he said pleasantly yet matter-of-factly, "you'll never get what you're trying to do through the committee. You'll be fighting them for the next three years. If you want my advice, you need to get out into the world and on your own; that's where you'll learn the things you want to learn; not in this school or any other. So here's what I propose — and I can take care of this before I go, so there'll be no question of your graduating. Instead of writing a thesis, *any* thesis, you'll take extra coursework, which will be a thesis equivalent; I can arrange that. It'll be neat, clean, uncomplicated — and you'll be on your way. What do you think?"

I was delighted and instantly agreed.

"Now then," he went on, "were you planning to continue on for a doctorate?"

I said I had not yet decided, but that I did not think so; not for the time being.

"Well, it's your decision. For some people, a Ph.D. would be important. But again, if you want my opinion, not for you. You're going to be an outsider no matter what credentials you acquire. I want you to know that I absolutely believe in you and in what you can accomplish."

I thought that one day I would return to school for my doctorate — which I did, years later in Los Angeles — but for now the thought of being out of school, free to learn, study, and grow on my own, and to earn my own living, sent me sailing out of the building and across the street to a pay phone. I wanted to tell Barbara the news.

Knowing my impatience with school, she was pleased that I could graduate without stress or complications; but she said, a little regretfully, "It would have been a good thesis."

I assured her that I had every intention of writing it, not as a thesis but as a work to be published. "This will be my first book," I announced confidently.

It seemed entirely appropriate to burst into my profession with an original treatment of a problem as central as anxiety. If it truely held the key to understanding most psychological ailments, then what better subject with which to begin my writing career?

Walking toward home from Washington Square, in a state of eager excitement, I wondered when Barbara would begin to write a book of her own. She continued to speak of her ambition to write fiction, and I could not understand what was standing in the way. As I saw it, she had the greatest teacher — and model — in the world; she had support and encouragement, and still, all she seemed to do was yearn. She *talked* about writing. Once, when I asked her about her procrastination, she said, "I'm not happy enough to write."

To me, this response was incomprehensible. "Not happy enough? I would think that one of the ways we *make* ourselves happy is by writing."

She sighed. "Perhaps for some people; not for me. When I'm not happy — this is the only way I can explain it — I don't feel worthy enough to write."

Still mystified, I persevered. "Do you mean that you don't feel *confident* enough to write?" I thought perhaps fear of Ayn's criticism might be inhibiting her, or that Barbara's own expectations were too high.

She shook her head. "No, I'm just not happy enough."

I asked her if her unhappiness centered on my relationship with Ayn.

She answered emphatically that that was not the problem. "It's all within me," she said sadly and a little helplessly.

"Your tragic sense of life?" I suggested.

"I don't know. Maybe you can call it that."

I desperately wanted the look of sadness to vanish from Barbara's face; I wanted her to be happy; I wanted her to be fulfilled — and she said constantly that her life would be unfulfilled until she was writing fiction. Thinking that it was only two or so years since she had graduated, and not wishing to create undesirable pressure, I asked, as gently as I could, "Do you have any gut feeling of when you're likely to begin a novel." "Certainly before I'm thirty," she said firmly. She was then twenty-seven.

I knew Barbara was not entirely comfortable with Ayn's insistence on the importance of plot. Ayn had defined plot as "a purposeful progression of logically connected events leading to the resolution of a climax." In 1968, in an article entitled "Basic Principles of Literature," reprinted in her book on the aesthetics of literature, *The Romantic Manifesto,* she wrote:

> Since a novel is a re-creation of reality, its theme has to be dramatized, i.e., presented in terms of action. . . . A story in which nothing happens is not a story. A story whose events are haphazard and accidental is either an inept conglomeration or, at best, a chronicle, a memoir, a reportorial recording, *not* a novel. . . . Contrary to the prevalent literary doctrines of today, it is *realism* that demands a plot structure in a novel. All human actions are goal-directed, consciously or subconsciously; purposelessness is contrary to man's nature. . . . Therefore, if one is to present man *as he is* . . . one has to present him in goal-directed action.

Barbara explored ideas such as these endlessly, and she clearly loved Ayn's discussions of writing and found her analyses of different novels and styles illuminating and inspiring. But her intellectual agreement with the importance of plot was greater than her emotional acceptance. "My mind just doesn't seem to work that way," she complained. Today I can appreciate that it would have been extraordinarily difficult, if not impossible, for Barbara or any of us to write fiction in so repressive an atmosphere.

By the fall of 1956 her anxiety had largely subsided. The worst storm of her life — in terms of immediate emotional anguish — appeared to have passed. Whatever internal struggles she was having relative to Ayn and me, she did not choose to talk about, and I do not know how receptive I would have been. We communicated well about everything except the things that mattered most.

She frequently rejected my sexual advances, but that was true even before the affair with Ayn; whatever was wrong between us had been so almost from the beginning. Unfortunately for me, my desire for Barbara had not abated. Any night I could go to sleep without reaching out to touch her, I regarded as a victory of self-discipline and I congratulated myself.

Paradoxically and bewilderingly, more than ever before Barbara professed to love me. She often spoke as if she shared Ayn's view of me. Riding down the elevator of our building on one of our evenings out, she would look up at me tenderly, even erotically, and say, "You're so good-looking." This made the mystery — and the agony — worse. I did not know what to say when she would declare, just when I was about to explode with exasperation, "One day everything will be as we both want it to be. You'll see."

Strangely, I was inclined to believe her. My confidence seemed to stem from two elements. One was some indestructible optimism that rendered me incapable of believing that my life could be tragic. The other was a deep sense that it was natural for Barbara to desire me as I desired her, that one day she would reciprocate my feelings, and that whatever was wrong now was a senseless mistake that would be resolved at any moment. Had my problems with Barbara been more real to me, I might have seen my life more clearly, acted more decisively, and spared both of us a good deal of suffering. As it was, I left too much unsaid and unchallenged too long.

But perhaps the status quo suited me. While I would never have permitted myself this thought at the time, in retrospect it seems obvious that Barbara was my protection against Ayn, just as Ayn was my protection against Barbara. My relationship with each woman imposed restrictions and limitations on the demands that could be made by the other. And then there was the matter of ego-gratification: I was the emotional center of two women's worlds. I suffered from the delusion that two incomplete loves could make one whole one.

Barbara, of course, had her own agenda, her own reasons for ignoring the pain. Although there was a subtle note of tension in her relationship with Ayn, their friendship in many ways was becoming more affectionate. Her enthusiasm for Ayn's work was boundless and the intelligence and sensitivity she brought to the novel, in her understanding of what Ayn was doing, inspired Ayn to speak of her as a soul mate. Barbara was the only person in our group besides me who could give Ayn the highly detailed literary feedback that she treasured. I do not doubt that what I often saw in their eyes when they were talking together was love.

But Barbara's support did not prevent Ayn from making overly critical remarks from time to time. "Barbara is not purposeful enough in her own life. Didn't you tell me she likes to bask for days on the beach? That's why the importance of purposefulness in writing — purpose-

fulness in the sense of plot and in the sense of goal-directed characters — isn't fully real to her." I myself had made statements very much
like that; but I did not like hearing them from Ayn.

I could not arrive at a balanced perspective on Ayn and Barbara's
relationship, just as I could not reach a balanced perspective on any of
our relationships. Incongruity and ambivalence were the norm. Yet I
lived in a world in which incongruity and ambivalence were presumed
hardly to exist — in our behavior or among ourselves. Were we not
all apostles of reason? Did we not live in the kingdom of sanity?

The night Ayn and I had walked from the Russian Tea Room, along
Fifty-seventh Street — what had I been trying to say? On a subconscious level, I was looking for a link between the world of my childhood and the world we all shared in New York. And if there was a
connection, wasn't it only that the world I had found with Ayn was
the exact opposite of the world I had come from? That, as an adult, I
might be cooperating in a nightmare worse than that of my childhood
was inconceivable.

Now, striding up Lexington Avenue toward home, I thought: *I
don't care about any of this.* I was happy, I was excited, I was riding
a current of inexhaustible energy, I was an unconquerable force.
Whatever was wrong, solutions would be found. In less than a year I
would graduate, in less than a year *Atlas* would be finished and on its
way to publication — and in scarcely more than a year I would be
ready to begin writing my first book: a critique of major existing theories of pathological anxiety, those of Freud, Adler, Horney, Fromm,
and Sullivan, and an exposition of my own theory. *To hell with everything else,* I thought joyfully, without specifying what I meant by
"everything else."

Soon I was not merely running up Lexington Avenue, I was taking
occasional leaps. As usual, people looked at me strangely.

One of the safest and most interesting topics of discussion between
Barbara and me was our admiration for Ayn, and exploring this issue
intensified our bond. We agreed that Ayn was extraordinarily independent. She appeared to be absolutely firsthand in her approach to
everything. It was as if she were the first person born on earth, who
had no choice but to look at life through her own eyes. This was the
very trait that had so impressed me in Howard Roark. Today I would
say that she had attained a superlatively high level of individuation.

"The difference between me and other people," Ayn liked to say,
"is that I am more honest." She was speaking of *intellectual* honesty.
I would laugh and ask her if she thought anyone else we knew, if completely honest, could have produced *Atlas Shrugged.* She resisted the

idea that her powerful intelligence was at least as important as her honesty. In retrospect it seems clear that not only did she lack insight about her faults, she often lacked it about her strengths.

And yet, if one understood what she meant by "honesty," she was not entirely wrong, either. With the exception of certain personal areas where she could be appallingly unconscious, she had the most profound and passionate respect for facts. For her, such respect was the essence of morality, the foundation of all the other virtues. In reading *Atlas*, I was impressed by the virtuosity with which she developed this idea, taking what could be cold and abstract and making it living drama. She projected that same attitude in her person and to some extent she inspired it in our whole group. "What you're teaching," I once said to her, "is that respect for reality is the ultimate virtue." "Well, of course," she answered, as if I were stating the self-evident. She conveyed to us that this attitude was intimately bound up with the heroic. She made it basic to the characterization of John Galt.

Ayn was convinced that ideas ruled the world and, consciously or subconsciously, ruled the life of every individual. Barbara and I absorbed this viewpoint completely. When meeting a new person, Ayn would sometimes say, "Tell me your premises" — which, to most people, is a puzzling and disorienting question. Ideas *mattered* to her. No one could understand her who did not understand her conviction concerning the supreme importance of philosophy. If, for example, she heard a statement to the effect that man has no right to exist for his own sake, but exists only to serve society, or the state, or the race, or the planet — or if she heard a statement to the effect that reason is impotent to know reality, or that all value judgments are ultimately arbitrary, or that notions of good and evil are merely expressions of subjective emotion — she saw, concretely and specifically, the oceans of human blood that were spilled as a consequence of such beliefs — she saw Nazi Germany and Soviet Russia — and she reacted accordingly.

This conviction concerning the importance of ideas could lend her enormous patience in intellectual discussions. If anyone in our group was confused about some issue, Ayn would sit down with him for eight or nine hours, if that was how long it took, until he was intellectually satisfied. She conveyed that what we thought — about the most abstract issues in philosophy, or about today's headline, or about a movie we had seen — was of the highest order of importance. Ayn took us seriously in an unprecedented, profoundly nurturing, way.

I witnessed this nurturing process even with people who disagreed with Ayn violently. I sat in on many conversations with men and women who shared almost none of her principles yet who would say,

"Why do I feel so inspired talking to you?" "Why do I feel like a better person — or more alive — or as if my life matters more — when I'm with you?"

Ayn thought in terms of principles. This was evident almost immediately to anyone who spoke with her. It was one of her most striking characteristics. When she asked me, at our first meeting, if I accepted the principle that man has a right to exist, she expected me to understand that this meant that his life did not belong to others, that the government had no right to set the price at which he would offer his goods or services, and that his fellow citizens had no moral entitlement to vote his freedom away. "If you understand a man's right to his own life," she said to me, "you understand the moral base of capitalism."

In discussions with adversaries, she always challenged them to "name your principles" — by which she meant to name the underlying premises implicit in their utterances. "If you believe in military conscription, you believe that man's life belongs to the tribe." "If you believe that man's mind cannot know existence 'as it really is,' then you support irrationalism — since we have to act on the basis of *some* ideas or beliefs, and you have ruled out reason." "If you believe that certain sexual practices between consenting adults should be forbidden by law, you believe that some persons have a moral right to impose on others, at the point of a gun, their notions of appropriate sexual behavior." *By what right?* she would demand. *By what standard? Name your principles.*

Since most people do not care to name the implicit principles behind the positions they take — or do not even know how — her request often evoked considerable discomfort and hostility.

"I never had to teach Barbara or you the importance of principles," she said to me more than once. "You both understand their *practical* necessity. That's one of the things I love about both of you." In the Collective, a standard joke was about the mentality of the person who, having been convinced that the government should not nationalize the steel industry, then asks, "But what about the coal industry?"

Ayn also had a great talent for establishing intellectual rapport with "ordinary people" — a cleaning woman, a taxi driver, a telephone installer. She was very proud of the fact that in conversation she could make her ideas clear to almost anyone — "except," we would sometimes joke, "a professional intellectual."

In reflecting on the traits that made Ayn so exhilarating to talk to and be with, and that I myself wanted to master, I was often impressed by her ability to reduce any issue to its essentials, not to get waylaid by details and not to accept uncritically someone else's definition. For example, she would say, "Don't be tricked into believing the choice is between sacrificing yourself to others or others to yourself. That's the trap you're intended to fall for — by those preaching altruism. The choice is between recognizing that a human being is an end in himself, not a means to the ends of others — and practicing human sacrifices. This is what I meant in *The Fountainhead* when Roark said the choice is between independence and dependence. You wouldn't accept it if someone told you your only choice was between sadism and masochism, would you? The same principle applies here." Or, when a young physicist named Russell Targ protested our conviction that governments should not coerce taxpayers into financing scientific research, and demanded, "What do you want us to do? Go to private citizens, businesses, or institutions for our money, *hat in hand?*" Ayn replied, "Yes, I do. That's morally preferable to going *gun in hand.*"

In epistemology she rejected the notion that "rationalism" and "empiricism" were one's only choices, on the grounds that both doctrines were flawed and that they offered a false alternative. On similar grounds she rejected both "idealism" and "materialism" in metaphysics. In ethics she rejected notions of "intrinsic good" and "subjective preference" as equally irrational. "In an intellectual debate," she would say, "don't be misled into accepting your opponent's definition of the problem. Go for the essential, go to the root of the issue, which may be completely outside his premises and frame of reference."

Apart from Barbara, the person with whom I was most likely to discuss Ayn was Leonard. I enjoyed thinking aloud with him on the subject of her most interesting and admirable traits, even though he was still at a stage where he was frozen in awe of her and did not perceive her as fully human. "That's bad for Ayn and bad for you," I would tell him. "Bad for Ayn because she won't feel completely visible with you if you can't see her as a real, living person. Bad for you because you won't understand that what you admire in her, you can emulate, you can learn to make part of yourself." To which Leonard would typically answer, worshipfully, "Ayn is so lucky to have you in her life. How lonely she would be otherwise!" And I typically would be left suspended between appreciation and frustration.

There were aspects of Ayn's psychology that I did not discuss with anyone. They had to do with her attitudes as a woman. "I never wanted to be a general," she would say, "let alone a commander in chief. My dream has always been to be the ideal lieutenant — to my kind of man." When I heard this, I thought, I wish I were Ayn's age. It was almost as if, in being so much younger and therefore unable to give her the experience she wanted, I had somehow failed her.

At the same time, I wondered: her need for control was so powerful — could she really surrender it in any context other than sex? And even in sex I sometimes found the ideas of "control" and "surrender" far from transparent. Once, laughing, I said to her, "Your sexual slave will now proceed to dominate you." She smiled but did not find this as amusing as I did. She was profoundly invested in the concept of male domination.

And yet she was scornful of those who, based on a reading of the love scenes in her novels, wondered if her psychology was touched by sadomasochistic impulses. I never read her this way or found this attitude present in her personal behavior, not to the smallest extent. Her heroines were no more passive "clinging vines" than she was. A good many self-confident women seem to find the metaphor or fantasy of male dominance and female submission appealing (in certain carefully limited contexts); so do a good many nonchauvinistic men. Regarding the "rape scene" in *The Fountainhead*, Ayn would say, "If that was rape, it was by engraved invitation. Literal rape would be contemptible and disgusting and unthinkable to any hero of mine."

Barbara and I believed we understood Ayn better than anyone else did, and I believed I understood Ayn better than Barbara did, not only because I saw us as more similar in outlook, but also because of our physical intimacy.

"Barbara," I said to her one day, "it's worth it — isn't it?"

"Of course," she answered.

Ayn and I met privately twice a week, once in the afternoon and once in the evening, a pattern that we established at the start of the affair.

This afternoon, walking from my apartment to hers, I hoped Frank would be gone by the time I got there. I found it painful, awkward, and embarrassing when he greeted me at the door or when I stood in his living room, trying to look normal, while he smiled and kissed Ayn good-bye and left, a husband exiled by his wife's lover. It was not jealousy; it was discomfort at Frank's position — and my own.

I was glad Barbara was at work; I had not had to face leaving her at home, both of us struggling to be affectionate and easygoing. Ayn and I met from one to five o'clock, and I liked to be home before Barbara arrived from work, although often I failed to do so. "One word led to another," I would say, sometimes cheerfully, sometimes sheepishly, sometimes brusquely.

I had reluctantly accepted the fact that Ayn and I would not have an apartment of our own. A resistance I did not understand prevented her from leasing an "office" in the same building where she lived, which would have been very simple for her to do and where my presence would arouse no questions. I had given up pressing her on this issue, but I knew that displacing Frank from his own home was barbaric.

My positive spirits vanished, my perspective on our handling of the affair shifted, as happened from time to time, and it seemed to me that Ayn and I were cold, uncaring persons, blind to the devastation we were causing, even though neither Frank nor Barbara complained. But I told myself: you're not thinking clearly; you've slipped into conventionality. *I* was capable of cruelty, I thought, knowing that at times I could be single-tracked, insensitive, self-absorbed — but not Ayn. She loved Frank; if what we were doing was wrong, surely she would know and would propose a better course of action. I fought down my own agitation, and called my doing so "being rational." It did not occur to me that I might be committing the very mistake we fiercely inveighed against, that of placing someone else's moral judgment above my own.

But I had begun this day feeling buoyant, and that mood returned in full force, sweeping everything else aside. It was easy to forget my reluctance, easy to shake off my sense of doing something unconscionable. I felt energized, optimistic, sexual — insulated by the ruthlessness that happiness sometimes inspires.

I recalled the day last winter when, returning to Ayn's apartment after lunch, I had made love to her in the living room, both of us dressed, Ayn still in her fur coat. I heard myself saying, "I've always wanted to make love to a woman in a fur coat," and her answering, "Next time, without the dress, just the coat." I replayed the images and sensations of our mouths on each other's bodies — and I felt my sense of eagerness and excitement expanding in anticipation of the afternoon. In this relationship I was making love not only to a woman but to a world — as if, through the act of penetration, I was making contact anew with all of my most precious values. Sex was a bridge to another level of consciousness, to another kind of reality.

Once, when I wondered aloud if we had chosen the right course in having an affair, Ayn said, "This relationship is sexual or it's nothing. If we are not a man and woman to each other, in the full sense — if we are merely disembodied minds — our philosophy is meaningless."

My memory of specific acts of intimacy was vivid and immediate. Images of things we did together, of our eager search for more extravagant forms of closeness, became vibrations moving through my muscles and nervous system as I walked, making me walk faster.

"Hi, Nathan!" Frank said brightly and warmly, opening the apartment door and gesturing me into the living room.

"We're having a quarrel," Ayn announced, her voice sharp, and I quickly gathered that Frank's greeting was relief at the interruption.

My arrival did not bring their discussion to an end. Instead, Ayn chose to involve me, as she had done several times before to my acute discomfort. I felt my mood melting into numbness.

Ayn wanted to know why Frank did not take her shopping and advise her on what to wear, as I did. I could not afford to buy her clothes, but I did like to take her to stores and offer suggestions. Left to her own devices, she was more or less unconcerned with what she wore — because her writing, she said, "leaves no space in my brain for such things." But a young man of twenty-six, she told Frank, had the initiative to ignore her protests, drag her out of the apartment, and force her to buy new outfits — *his attitude inspiring her to want to do so* — so why was her husband, more than twice Nathan's age, *so passive, so unwilling to put more into their marriage?*

I could not understand how Ayn could subject Frank to this. I could not understand how she could subject me to it. Did she not realize how inappropriate it was to compare us? Why did she do such things? There was so much rage in her today, as if a lifetime of frustration was erupting over the issue of clothes, this issue becoming the focus and symbol of everything she wanted and did not get from a husband. It was painful to see Frank so pathetic: helpless, guilty, angry and afraid to show it, empathic toward Ayn — and simultaneously detached, almost dissociated.

I thought of how little I really understood their marriage. Ayn spoke of Frank as her hero. She always seemed loving and affectionate with him. She complimented him constantly. She insisted on cooking him dinner no matter how exhausted she was. "A wife's job," she said. "And if I don't force him, he never eats enough." Her attitude about cooking Frank's dinner was a prime example of what puzzled me. Sometimes she did not stop writing and begin cooking until eleven or twelve o'clock at night, and she asked him to wait for her — she professed to feel guilty when he prepared his own dinner. By the time dinner was ready, Frank was often too tired to touch his food, which precipitated a lecture on his poor eating habits. Ayn's motive was clearly *her* self-image, not *his* welfare. More than once I tried to cajole her, humorously, into grasping the impracticality of her behavior, and she kept promising to serve dinner earlier, but the problem remained unchanged. She had a highly valued picture in her mind — she would cook dinner, then she and Frank would eat together — which had to be preserved, regardless of what this meant in terms of actual reality. The *form* of romantic love had to be maintained, for herself and for others; but it seemed to be imposed on a set of facts that did not match it.

Standing awkwardly in their living room I now wondered what Ayn could want me to do or say to Frank. Couldn't she see how many advantages I had, how much easier my role was than Frank's? If he was passive to begin with, could he be anything but more passive in the present circumstances? I felt cast, ludicrously, in the role of umpire or marriage counselor. Yet I was not an outsider, I was one of the participants. The image of being five years old and sitting at the kitchen table, listening to my mother complain to me about my father flashed through my brain.

One does not have to introduce an oedipal interpretation to appreciate that patterns learned in childhood often surface again in later years. Both in Ayn's home as a child, and in Frank's, the mother was the dominant force and the father relatively more passive. Precisely the same was true in Barbara's home and mine. In this sense, we had all grown up with similar role models. No doubt this prepared us for perceiving Ayn and Frank's relationship as "normal."

Now, when Frank looked at me, he projected no sign of resentment; on the contrary, he had the man-to-man look of an ally, who counted on me to understand everything that could not be said and as if he saw me, too, as needing a defender. There were times when my father had looked at me the same way.

All I could think of saying to Frank, gently and almost diffidently, was that this conflict demonstrated how important he was to Ayn and that whatever Ayn had needed from him, she still needed — which meant, I have not replaced you. I sounded stupid to myself as I spoke. Yet my statement served its purpose; it seemed to have a tranquilizing effect on them both, and when Frank got up to leave, they were very affectionate, the quarrel already fading into unreality.

Ayn complimented me on my "brilliant sensitivity." How had I known exactly the right thing to say? I tried to communicate the difficulty of Frank's position, and she quickly agreed, pleased that I was sticking up for him.

She walked toward me and we embraced. But the mood in which I had arrived was gone again. "Shall we get something to eat?" I said.

Over lunch at a neighborhood restaurant she spoke enthusiastically about the progress of her writing. She was nearing the end of the novel and felt an almost feverish need to talk about it. "The philosophical part is now done. From here to the end of the story, it's pure action. The final big event is Galt's rescue from the torture chamber, by Dagny, Rearden, Francisco, and Ragnar. Now I'm free to enjoy myself; no more explaining to do; just an exciting rescue scene. That's what I'd like to write next: a novel that would be pure action and drama, with no new philosophical ideas. A novel about a man who has mastered the enjoyment of life — perhaps an adventurer of some kind — something in the spirit of Francisco d'Anconia — but *no philosophical speeches*. What a relief that would be!"

I sensed some residual tension in her, which I related to the incident with Frank, and I asked her if she wanted to talk about it. She answered, her voice like iron, that we had only a few hours together and they were not to be wasted. "Priorities, darling," she said sternly. "Priorities."

She went on to talk with excitement about how *Atlas Shrugged* would end. She now seemed genuinely cheerful. She was saying, "All the key strikers are now in the valley and the battle is essentially finished. The government has collapsed. It is night, and Galt and Dagny are walking in the mountains, high above the valley's lights. Looking out over the world, Galt says, 'The road is cleared. We are going back to the world.' And then here is the last line of the book: 'He raised his hand and over the desolate earth he traced in space the sign of the dollar.' The dollar sign is the symbol of the free mind and of free trade. Of course I'll be denounced for that — for the deliberately religious implication. They'll blank out what Galt's gesture means in the context of the story."

I thought the ending magnificent and told her so. I added, "Not just the ending but the whole treatment of Galt in the story has an almost religious feeling — perhaps I should say 'spiritual.' Anyone who senses that won't be mistaken. I think that will be a source of the book's inspirational power."

Our discussion of *Atlas* had drawn us into our own world, as it always did. As we walked back to the apartment, I told Ayn I was impatient to make love. Looking around as if committing a daring act, she pulled my arms around her body. Once, inside, we went directly to the bedroom.

That we made love in Ayn and Frank's bedroom was sometimes hard to bear. And yet it remained the symbol of our relationship at its most harmonious. I cannot recall a single conflict in that setting. It stood in my mind as a place of unique safety, almost a sanctuary.

Entering it now, I was aware of the special quality of earnestness that Ayn always brought to the act of sex. She was intense as a human being and never more so than in this realm. She was everything I could wish, except playful. When she looked at me, it was with the eyes of a priestess contemplating the object of her worship. When she touched me, it was with solemnity, even reverence. Nothing was casual or frivolous. When she attempted lightness, the seriousness of her attempt made me smile. I liked it more when she was her naturally earnest self. She could abandon herself, she could surrender fully to the experience, yet I was always aware of the powerful presence of her searchlight consciousness — of those eyes that missed nothing. When I mentioned this last to her once, she told me that I projected the same quality. "We are not people who sex makes unconscious," she said.

It was always important to me that she feel desirable, sexual, physically fulfilled. I wanted to give her that — selfishly. I believed that if two people truly cared for each other, not only did they desire the other's sexual satisfaction, they also wished to strengthen and reinforce the other's sexual self-esteem, the other's sense of self as a woman or a man. Earlier in our relationship, if I devoted a long period of time to Ayn's pleasure, she might ask, "You're not being altruistic, are you?" She meant it; she had a horror of the man doing anything in bed that was "unselfish." I would laugh and assure her of the selfishness of my motives. By now, such questions were long behind us.

Even in surrendering, Ayn manifested her unique kind of power. She had a quality of the most extraordinary presence, her eyes, her voice, her gestures, all asserting existence, all asserting confidence, in every expression. It is said that many women find power in a man an aphrodisiac; I found Ayn's personal power no less erotic. I enjoyed thinking that she was a cosmic force I was able to tame — if only for a moment.

Whatever this relationship is ultimately about, I told myself, wherever we're headed, this is what one lives for.

Sex was an act of self-celebration. It was the integration of body and spirit. It was union of a kind that melted any barrier between man and woman. It fused the elements of self-assertion and self-surrender and transmuted them into ecstasy.

There are rituals in sex, not only physical ones but also verbal ones — things couples take pleasure in saying again and again. "With you," she said, "I am totally and absolutely a woman. You've accomplished that."

"And with you," I answered, "I feel totally and absolutely fulfilled as a man. I feel as if . . . the kind of man I am . . . is what you want. That's what you've given me. We've always had an incredible intellectual relationship — we're so intimately connected, at times it feels supernatural. We've always had an incredible spiritual relationship. We truly are soul mates — we think and feel about so many things in the identical way. Just being with you is the most exhilarating adventure of my life — and then to become involved sexually and to see how you respond, to me, to what I do, to everything . . . not to have to explain or discuss or defend or hold back . . . after what I've experienced before —"

"Forgive me for saying this, but in some respects Barbara is a fool."

"Let's not get into that. I just want you to know —"

"I do know. And what I want you to know is that what I give you is only what any woman in her right mind would give you. My kind of woman, anyway."

"I love you," I said to her.

She raised one naked foot high in the air. "Don't you think I have good legs?"

"Yes, I do."

"We would have made a good team," she said reflectively, "if we had met at the same age."

"We make a good team now."

"Yes, but that would have truly been an explosion — in the good sense. Can you just imagine what it would have been like?"

I had imagined it many times and told her so. I thought of it now, both of us in our twenties, learning and growing together.

"It would have been ideal," I said, meaning it. If I had been with her since her twenties, I flattered myself, the traits in her personality I sometimes found difficult would not exist. She would be more serene, free of anger, suspicion, and bitterness, lighter. She had had to carry too much alone.

We talked about the fact that our relationship felt like a marriage — "a spiritual marriage" — occupying a separate universe of its own. "With no disloyalty to Frank or Barbara," Ayn often hastened to add.

We lay in bed for a long while without speaking, holding each other. The clock on the bureau across the room assured me that Frank would not be home for at least two more hours. Suddenly Ayn was smiling impishly.

" 'Woman is clay, longing to become mire,' " she said, quoting a line she knew I would recognize from Hugo's *L'Homme qui rit*.

"What made you think of that?"

"Guess."

"Well, have you satisfied your longing to become mire?"

"The line is right if one knows how to understand it. Poor Hugo. The pagan and the Christian fought within him constantly. He gave his best line about sex to a woman we're supposed to think of as immoral — but as one writer reading the psychology of another, I can tell you his heart was with her."

She was using dialogue from Hugo to achieve a deeply personal act of self-disclosure, the intellectuality of her form intended to mute the intimacy of her content. I could not help feeling some satisfaction in noticing that she, too, was capable of "turning philosophical" at questionable moments.

In spite of myself, I began to reflect on Hugo's line. Spoken by a woman of high self-esteem, it conveys one kind of message, a very erotic one. Spoken by a woman of low self-esteem, seeking *actual* degradation, it has an opposite meaning, a tragic one. Spoken by Ayn, I believed it was intended to stress her desire to surrender to masculine strength, to give up all authority, to be treated as an instrument of the man's pleasure — provided, of course, it was *her* man. I found her superabundant self-confidence inspiring and challenging.

"Oh-oh, where have you gone?" she asked. "Are you off somewhere thinking? It serves me right for bringing up Hugo in bed."

"I was just thinking that right now life is exactly as it should be."

We held each other, feeling happy, contented, fulfilled. I was very sure of myself — and of the future.

I marveled at the fact that, in spite of my periodic attacks of misgivings about the affair, my sometime longing to return to the original form of our relationship, afternoons such as today were still possible — times when I felt that I was exactly where I wanted to be, doing exactly what I wanted to do. The unresolved problems in my relationship with Barbara were not unreal to me; they were merely filed in an entirely separate category of my consciousness, and I experienced them as totally unrelated to my relationship with Ayn. It was the unresolved problems in my relationship with Ayn that were now unreal.

One day, this afternoon would stand in my mind as a time of sunlit brilliance — among the last of my unclouded memories in the history of our relationship.

In the winter of 1956, I felt as if all of us in the New York circle were on an express train that was roaring toward the completion of *Atlas Shrugged*. Exhilaration and anticipation were the dominant themes. We were profoundly convinced that Ayn was bringing an inestimable value to the world — intellectually, literarily, socially — and that it would be virtually impossible for people not to recognize this fact. It was very difficult not to feel that we might actually see the beginning, in our own lifetime, of a philosophical and cultural renaissance. And that we would be part of it.

That winter, I graduated from New York University, began writing my book on anxiety, and established a fairly busy practice in psychotherapy. My sense of mission regarding Ayn's philosophy was growing more urgent and powerful. Whatever my other goals, one part of my destiny was to transmit her message to the world. I had decided to give a public course of lectures on Objectivism some time soon after the publication of *Atlas*. My intention was to elucidate our key positions in epistemology, metaphysics, ethics, political economy, literary aesthetics — and to introduce some of my ideas regarding self-esteem, social metaphysics, anxiety, and the foundations of a benevolent sense of life. I saw myself as a crusader with a sacred cause.

Ayn was not especially enthusiastic about the lecture project — she had misgivings about whether it could be successful financially, and she feared that I would martyr myself — but she did not oppose it. She asked me again, "Do you understand that you will be making yourself a public target?" The Collective in general was more enthusiastic and always wanted to hear my latest plans, which were still in the early stages. I felt encouraged by their interest and support.

One issue with which Ayn and I had been grappling for some time was what name to give to our philosophy. Finally Ayn proposed "Objectivism." The name was applicable to her theory of existence, of knowledge, and of values. In metaphysics, she held that reality is objective and absolute, existing independently of anyone's consciousness, perceptions, beliefs, wishes, hopes, or fears — that that which is, is what it is; that "existence is identity"; that A is A. In epistemology, she held that man's mind is competent to achieve objectively valid knowledge of that which exists. And in ethics, she held that values appropriate to human beings are objectively demonstrable — in other words, that a rational code of morality is possible.

Ayn's opposition to contemporary epistemological theory was no less intense than her opposition to contemporary ethical and political theory, as Barbara and I had discovered during our early discussions with her in California. As Ayn saw it, the same rejection of reason which in politics was expressed in the resurgence of the rule of brute force throughout the world, was expressed in philosophy in the cult of uncertainty and epistemological agnosticism. She insisted that modern political barbarism was a product and consequence of philosophical nihilism. At a time when the need for answers to crucial questions was a matter of life and death, Ayn declared, modern philosophy had nothing to offer people but a choice of irrationalisms (or, in her language, "mysticisms"): the "neomysticism" of pragmatism, positivism and linguistic analysis, which taught that it is meaningless to speak of "facts of reality" and/or futile to imagine that man can know any facts — and the old-fashioned mysticism of existentialism, which taught that man *can* know reality, but not by means of reason, only through his "blood and bowels" (to quote my NYU professor William Barrett, who championed "blood and bowels" above mind). To me, Ayn's analysis of this resurgence of irrationalism, which had been growing since the time of Kant and was usually parading as the voice of science, constituted one of the most brilliant, challenging, and illuminating aspects of Galt's speech.

Objectivism, I agreed, was the ideal name for our philosophical approach. Objectivism was the banner under which our crusade would be waged.

On a Saturday evening in March 1957, while the Collective sat in the living room waiting for her to emerge from her study, Ayn was writing the final pages of the novel.

Wondering if we should all depart and leave her undisturbed, someone tiptoed to the door of her study to get some sense of what to do. Ayn, her back to the door, heard the tentative step, muttered "I'll kill you," and went on writing.

An hour or so later, thirteen years after she had begun the novel, Ayn rushed out to show Frank the words "The End."

I recall nothing of that evening except an overwhelming sense of solemnity and joy — and a vague, distant hint of sadness, coming from the knowledge that a precious part of my life had now come to a close.

I would have said, then, that for all these years Ayn had been obliged to immerse herself in a kind of alternate reality — the world of *Atlas Shrugged* — and that now, her task accomplished, she was bringing her creation back to the world in which we lived. But I was wrong. The truth, which I would need some time to discover, was that Ayn had disappeared into that alternate reality and was not coming back. She was like the strikers in her own novel who, having seen John Galt's vision, give up everything and disappear, because the life they have lived is no longer acceptable to them.

The completed manuscript was now at Random House. Ayn had been open and receptive to Archie Ogden's editorial suggestions in *The Fountainhead,* and had nothing but praise for his skill. She was not, however, receptive to editorial suggestions from Hiram Haydn. She now regarded herself as a master of her craft who did not need the services of an editor. And, in contrast to Ogden, who had always been keenly sensitive to her literary intentions and had helped her to realize them more effectively, Haydn displayed no comparable grasp of Ayn's work, her literary premises, or her goals. She found most of his suggestions dissonant if not offensive.

When Hiram could not prevail on her to shorten Galt's speech, Cerf promised to try. But when Ayn countered Cerf's request for cuts with the question, "Would you cut the Bible?" he knew enough to give up. Some time later he said to me, "Ayn can be maddening, but I think that's part of what I love about her. She stands up for what she thinks is right." I grinned at Bennett and answered, "Besides, the speech is barely long enough."

I was joking, and at the same time I meant it. The speech *was* too long. But it fit the scale of the book. To me, it was a marvel of economy. Even today, I would argue that the speech, like the book, needs to be seen and understood in its own context, in its own terms, and not judged by an outside standard that may be thoroughly inappropriate.

Publication day was scheduled for October of that year. Barbara and I thought of giving Ayn a surprise party hosted by the entire Collective for all the key people involved with her professional life — the Cerfs, the Klopfers, the Haydns, the Collinses, the Ogdens. We held the event at the Plaza hotel in a private dining room. Frank did the floral decorations.

The invitations informed the guests that Ayn was not to be told about the party. Ayn assumed that Frank was taking her to an elegant restaurant for a private celebration.

When Frank led her into the suite where all the guests had assembled, Ayn froze. Then she declared in a chilly voice, glancing reproachfully at Barbara and me, "I do *not* like surprises." My spirits crashed. Then I told myself that I should have expected it: Ayn could not bear to be out of control — least of all in any matter pertaining to her career. She had anticipated a different kind of evening. Now she had to adapt her expectations, and adaptations of this kind did not come easily to her.

Everyone struggled to cheer her up, and the man who succeeded best was Bennett. She was delighted by the cigarettes he had had especially made; they were stamped with a bright gold dollar sign (the strikers in *Atlas* smoked such cigarettes), and each package bore the Random House trademark and the words, "Who is John Galt? They know at Random House." She seemed genuinely pleased when the guests toasted her and talked about the importance of her work and their devotion to her as a person. Only I, and possibly Barbara, could know how many times in the months and years ahead Ayn would refer to this evening chastisingly, with an appalling lack of benevolence or grace, for our daring to take any action involving her without her say-so.

Although the evening became progressively more festive as Ayn brightened up, I have no happy memories of the occasion; what I recall chiefly are Ayn's later scoldings. "The Collective," she said, "might not have known better. But Barbara and you should have — and you, above all."

On a happier side, I loved being consulted by Ayn on the jacket material for *Atlas*, which she herself wrote and which I thought superb. Phyllis Cerf, Bennett's wife, took the photograph that was to be appear on the back of the cover. Ayn gave Barbara and me a copy of this picture, in which she adapts a line from Galt's speech and, in parenthetical comment, calls us her "fellow winners."

In Barbara's copy of *The Fountainhead* Ayn wryly compliments her for all their shared "values." With a smile of irresistible charm, Ayn asked us, "Do I have to explain what I mean by '*all*' in that sentence?" In that moment, amused, I felt less like the master of the situation than like an object of their joint possession. With a smile of equally irresistible love, Barbara responded, "No, Ayn, you don't."

In my copy Ayn noted dates of importance, such as the day we met and the day of the car ride from Toronto to New York.

I recall an incident, not long after the novel's publication, when a journalist who was interviewing Ayn in her apartment turned and said to me, "You're a young man. Do you feel entirely worthy of the things Miss Rand says about you?" I answered, without arrogance and with total honesty, "Yes, I feel worthy." It all felt entirely natural; entirely right. The journalist asked Ayn, "What exactly do you mean by 'intellectual heir?'" Ayn replied, "It means Mr. Branden is the most consistent embodiment of what I write about, that he understands my philosophy better than anyone, and that he represents the next generation who will carry my work further." I felt myself standing in the spotlight of history.

Ayn was not pleased with the Random House ads — she had already had her first quarrel with Bennett because of them — and she asked me to accompany her to a meeting with him. She liked my idea of using the magnificent portrait of Frank I had admired on the night of our first meeting, with the caption: "This is John Galt — who said he would stop the motor of the world — *and did*. Meet him in *Atlas Shrugged*." The stylization of the painting projected a strength that would work perfectly. The final wording of this caption was both Ayn's and mine — and Bennett loved the whole concept.

Riding home in a taxi, Ayn exclaimed, "I wish I had your good-natured relaxation at these meetings. I went there prepared for a fight. You were so benevolent, so confident, so easygoing — I admire that — and you have no past experience with publishing, and I do."

"That means I have no bad experiences in publishing either, nothing to sour me, no memories of disappointment or betrayal."

"But didn't you have any self-consciousness about giving advice to one of the most famous publishers in the world?"

"No," I said, "I didn't."

One evening in early fall, Ayn, Frank, Barbara, and I went for a drive in the country to dine at a favorite restaurant. Ayn was in especially high spirits. In her mood of optimism about the future, she almost reminded me of Leonard. In contrast, my own mood was one of uneasiness. I was preoccupied with my perception of the culture at that time and my sense that *Atlas* was so profoundly radical in its basic vision, so contrary to the dominant beliefs of our age, that inevitably it was going to meet with terrible hostility — more terrible than even Ayn was projecting.

Slowly, tentatively, not knowing how much to say or how to say it, I voiced some of my concern aloud, not too clearly. Ayn startled me by her anger and impatience — not at me, exactly, but at my line of thought. "I don't want to hear about 'premonitions,' " she said. "If you can't articulate your ideas more concretely, you'd better be silent. Because if I don't break through this time — if the book doesn't get the understanding it deserves *from someone* — I mean, from some serious *minds,* not just 'fans' — then I'm finished; finished with this society and this century. I'll go totally on strike. You've got very good 'instincts' about the culture; you know how to read it. Is that what you're forecasting I'm going to have to do?" I assured her that I was only trying to consider every possibility. A few minutes later, she was euphoric and lighthearted again. I was not.

The Random House offices were then on Madison Avenue and Fifty-first Street. They occupied one wing of a large brownstone palazzo, the rest of which was occupied by the headquarters of the Archdiocese of New York. Important new books were usually featured in the Madison Avenue window. I was eager for the day when I might see *Atlas Shrugged* there, and one evening, a week before the publication date of October 10, 1957, Ayn, Frank, Barbara, and I drove to the publishing house, to see if the novel was on display. It was: a single copy, brightly illuminated, no other author's books around it. We stood there, grinning happily. Then Barbara burst out with a statement that would long endear her to Ayn: "That's us!"

Ayn laughed, the gay, carefree laugh of a young girl, a laugh of simple delight. I would never hear that laugh from her again.

ELEVEN

A FEW MONTHS before the publication of *Atlas,* Bennett Cerf invited Ayn to speak at a Random House sales conference. Everyone's expectations for the book were high and the room was alive with excitement. A salesman asked her, jokingly, if she could summarize her philosophy while standing on one foot. This was the kind of challenge to which Ayn responded with glee. She lifted one foot in the air, and answered, "Metaphysics — objective reality; Epistemology — reason; Ethics — self-interest; Politics — capitalism." She was proud of the instant rapport she could establish in such situations. The salesmen applauded her.

When Ayn recounted the incident, I recall thinking how exciting it was that something as explosive as *Atlas Shrugged* should be involved with a sales conference and all the other routine business of publishing; I enjoyed the sense of connection to "ordinary reality."

I did not think it strange that Ayn should choose to present to the world a new philosophical vision by means of a novel. She had said to me, "All of the world's major religions have, in effect, their own mythology — tales, parables, stories of various kinds, that are intended to dramatize and illustrate abstract values and precepts. Although that is not how the novel started out in my mind, that is what it developed into: a mythology that concretizes, by means of the actions of its characters, the meaning of my philosophy."

To Barbara and me she said, "I know I am challenging the cultural tradition of two and a half thousand years." She said it to the whole Collective and to Bennett Cerf and Donald Klopfer. She warned them that they should not expect — should not count on — any favorable reviews. I did not think they fully believed her; I do not think she fully believed it herself.

The *New York Times* assigned *Atlas Shrugged* to Granville Hicks,

an ex-member of the Communist party and an ex-apologist for Stalin-
ism — the same editor who, years earlier at Macmillan, had opposed
the publication of *We the Living*.

The article appeared in the October 13 issue of the Sunday *Book
Review*. When I saw Hicks's name I was shocked; I did not yet know
how typical this was of the *Times*; I thought that such a choice was
the depth of irrationality and injustice. Few reviewers feel morally
obliged to communicate clearly what a book is about before proceeding to their evaluation. I did not know that at the time, either.

"This Gargantuan book," wrote Hicks, "comes among us as a dem-
onstrative rather than as a literary work. . . . Not in any literary sense
a serious novel . . . this book is written out of hate." The review attacked the novel on every possible level. I recall, as clearly as if it were
ten minutes ago, my stunned inability to grasp how anyone, even a
Granville Hicks, could permit himself such dishonesty and lack of intellectual scruples.

Ayn appeared almost indifferent to the review. I had the impression
she barely read it. When she saw shock and anguish in Barbara's eyes,
she said, gently, "Darling, what would you expect from a collectivist?
You mustn't let such things hurt you. Worse is ahead."

She was right in her prediction. "Galt is really arguing for a dictatorship," declared Robert R. Kirsch in the *Los Angeles Times*. "The
destruction of the weak to the advantage of the strong is applauded,"
wrote Patricia Donegan in *The Commonweal*. The philosophy advocated in *Atlas Shrugged,* said a reviewer in another New York newspaper, "makes well-poisoning seem like one of the kindlier arts." A
few writers thought this line especially clever, because it began appearing, without acknowledgment, in other reviews.

Although Ayn read very few of these pieces, I made myself read
every one of them, telling myself: this is the world in which you are
living; learn to understand it; face fully the nature of the battle you
have to fight. "Execrable claptrap," I read in one review. "Crack-
brained ratiocination," I read in another. "Terrible writing," I read in
a third.

"Of course political liberals and left-wing intellectuals will hate the
book," Ayn told us many times, "but wait. The worst attacks will
come from the religionists." Again she was right. Of all the hostile
reviews I saw, none quite matched the ferocity of Whittaker Chambers's in William Buckley's conservative magazine, *National Review*.

Ayn had met Buckley some time earlier; he had invited her to tea.
With characteristic bluntness she had asked this practicing Catholic,
"Tell me, how can an intelligent young man like you believe in God?"
Later, when she reported to Barbara and me on this meeting, she

summed Buckley up as follows: "Clever, but an intellectual light-
weight. An opportunist. Very 'social'; not genuinely interested in
ideas. And potentially dangerous, if he acquires an influence — because he tells people that the foundation of capitalism is religious faith,
which implies that reason and science are on the side of the collectiv-
ists."

Whittaker Chambers was a former confessed communist spy turned
religionist. To expect him to review with integrity a book whose values
were the antithesis of his own in every essential respect was like asking
him to step outside of his own soul — like asking Satan to review the
Bible. He accused the novel of advocating crude materialism and dictatorship; he implicitly equated its ideas with Nazism. "The Dollar
Sign," he wrote, "is not merely provocative . . . it is meant to seal the
fact that mankind is ready to submit abjectly to an elite of techno-
crats. . . . From almost any page of *Atlas Shrugged,* a voice can be
heard, from painful necessity, commanding: 'To a gas chamber —
go!' "

I do not know if Ayn ever read the review in its entirety; she said
she did not. Her voice was like ice when she told the Collective: "If
Buckley's goal is to establish himself publicly as the champion of capitalism — God help the country! — then I am the one person he and
his gang have to try to discredit and destroy."

Ayn remained typically indifferent to Chambers. It was Buckley
who she condemned, because his public persona was that of a champion of capitalism and freedom. She knew he was not, pointing out
that he merely favored different political controls from his liberal adversaries — censorship, for one, to protect "public morality"; military
conscription, for another. "He's a champion of property but not of
human life," she said with disgust. Soon her disdain for him became
widely known; she would not sit on any platform with him and would
not remain seated at any meeting where he stood up to speak.

I recall visiting Ayn, a year or two after the publication of Chambers's review, and seeing a postcard Buckley had written her from a
New York restaurant, wanting to know why they could not be friends.
Ayn speculated that he must have been drunk when when he wrote it.
On another occasion I was present when he telephoned her, teasing
her about her animosity and suggesting that they "make up." Again
she commented, "He sounded as if he'd been drinking."

There were many enthusiastic reviews for *Atlas Shrugged,* but most
of these appeared in publications outside New York City. However,
there were two exceptions. In the *Mirror,* Ruth Alexander wrote,
"Ayn Rand is destined to rank in history as the outstanding novelist
and profound philosopher of the twentieth century." In the *Herald*

Tribune, John Chamberlain wrote a long and passionately complimentary review in which he praised *Atlas* as an artistic masterpiece
with a magnificently uplifting vision; only in the concluding paragraph
did he express dissatisfaction that Ayn had chosen to "re-write" the
Sermon on the Mount, that is, to challenge Christian morality. While
she appreciated the practical value of his review, in terms of selling
books, his remark about the Sermon on the Mount effectively destroyed any personal meaning his praise could have for her. Also, she
was angry that Chamberlain referred to the novel as an allegory. "My
characters are *not* symbols," she declared. Her reaction puzzled me,
because even though her characters are not, literarily, symbols, neither
can they be taken as fully realistic; in retrospect I am convinced that
the book can best be appreciated as a unique blend of the romantic,
the realistic, and the allegorical, and that Chamberlain was more right
than wrong in this respect.

Reviews that came in from around the country often hailed the
book's literary quality in enthusiastic terms. Ayn was praised as a great
stylist, a master of plot construction, an expert at orchestrating ideas,
action, and suspense. The book's themes were described as "challenging," "daring," "exciting," "provocative," "stimulating," "revolutionary."

However, the attacks significantly outnumbered the raves. The
negative reviews echoed the same kind of ferocious animosity I had
seen in the New York publications, sometimes using the same language. It was as if there was an invisible network, and every wire was
transmitting the same message: *Stop Ayn Rand. Say whatever is necessary to discredit her.*

I had foreseen disagreement; I had not foreseen the violence of the
hostility, the quality of enraged hysteria. I especially had not foreseen
the widespread misrepresentation of Ayn's ideas. To me, her opponents were debating with straw men. They equated her philosophy
with that of Spencer or Nietzsche or Spinoza or Hobbes, thereby exposing themselves to the charge of philosophic illiteracy. What they
did not do was identify accurately and then challenge the ideas for
which Ayn in fact stood. No one wrote, "Ayn Rand holds that man
must choose his values and actions by reason; that the individual has
a right to exist for his own sake, neither sacrificing self to others nor
others to self; that no one has the right to seek values from others by
physical force, or impose ideas on others by physical force — and I
consider such ideas wrong, evil, socially dangerous."

I was prepared to hear them say, "In advocating freedom and individual rights, Ayn Rand goes too far." Nothing could have prepared
me for the accusation that she was advocating dictatorship — nothing

I had previously read or seen, nothing Ayn had warned me of, nothing in my darkest prepublication premonitions.

Now is not the time to feel, I told myself, fighting a sense of being engulfed in madness. Now is the time to try to understand.

Ayn acted equally indifferent to praise and criticism. The gaiety had largely disappeared from her manner, and she conveyed the stony calm of someone in a fortress who is settling in for a long siege. "It's earlier than you think," she said to all of us. "Historically speaking, even earlier than I had imagined. It's not the attacks that are depressing — I expected that. It's the absence of any good mind with a significant reputation who has come forward to say publicly what *Atlas* actually is. Someone with the power to make himself heard. I had counted on *some* kind of better understanding."

The advance sales for the book had been high. Then, presumably in response to the negative reviews, sales began to drop. But as more and more readers began to share their own reactions, sales began to climb and went on climbing; the novel stayed near the top of the *New York Times* Best Sellers list for a very long time. Later, when it was obvious that the book was on its way to becoming a classic and that nothing and no one was going to stop it, Bennett Cerf remarked, "In all my years of publishing, I've never seen anything like it. To break through against such enormous opposition!"

Nonetheless, I saw a change in Bennett's attitude. It was obvious that he himself had been affected by the countless denunciations — not only in books and articles, but also at dinner and cocktail parties, in literary circles, in every corner of the world in which he moved. He faced rebukes from friends and associates for having published *Atlas*. He spoke less and less of being personally influenced by the book's ideas; he went out of his way to stress his disagreements.

I was not surprised. I remembered a conversation he and I had, in which he said to me, "I think Ayn is right about a lot of things. Her respect for personal achievement, for one. Her opposition to the welfare state, or much of it, for another. But one mustn't say that. You have to throw welfare programs at people — like throwing meat to a pack of wolves — even if the programs don't accomplish their alleged purpose and even if they're morally wrong." "Why?" I asked. Bennett leaned forward and whispered in the manner of sharing a confidence, "Because otherwise they'll kill you. The masses. They hate intelligence. They're envious of ability. They resent wealth. You've got to throw them something, so they'll let us live." I answered, "It looks like we respect human beings more than you do." This was not a man, I knew in that moment, who was likely to weather the storm that was coming.

We had all thought that the success of *The Fountainhead* had sufficiently established Ayn so that *Atlas Shrugged* would be recognized and appreciated more readily, in spite of the inevitable attacks. "We were wrong," said Ayn. "It's *The Fountainhead* all over again. *Atlas* will have to make its way by word of mouth, against every kind of public opposition. Only I'm more well known now, so it may happen faster."

Today, both books have sold in the many millions of copies, and continue to sell actively both in hardcover and softcover. Combined sales of all her titles have topped twenty million.

Not long after publication, Ayn appeared on Mike Wallace's television show, "Night Beat." Wallace asked her how she felt about the torrent of attacks against her. She answered by citing her favorite poem, Rudyard Kipling's *If.* " '. . . if you can bear to hear the truth you've spoken twisted by knaves to make a trap for fools . . .' " Then she said, "I can bear it. It's not fools that I seek to address." The station received a great number of wildly enthusiastic calls and letters, as would always happen when she appeared on television.

She and Mike Wallace became friends. Like Bennett Cerf, Mike Wallace seemed to be liberal; nonetheless, Ayn found him both intelligent and courageous; she offered him as a prime example of why she often found liberals easier to talk to than conservatives. "One can *reason* with Mike," she said. Because of his fascination with her ideas, notwithstanding many disagreements, she labeled him, jokingly, "an Objectivist fellow traveler." I liked Mike, as I liked Bennett, but I was a bit more cautious than Ayn, feeling fiercely protective of her; I knew that neither of these men, in the ultimate sense, was an ally — and in a war, I thought, that is the standard by which one judges people.

What Ayn wanted most of all was to find *minds* — men and women of the kind she wrote about. She had imagined, when she sent the beacon of *Atlas Shrugged* out into the world, that she would find them. In a twist on George Washington's famous statement, she said, "I have raised a standard, but the wise and honest have not repaired to it." She appreciated, in a perfunctory sort of way, the praise *Atlas* received, and was happy about the book's sales, but on a deeper level she was bitterly disappointed. She was, in the main, unimpressed by the intellectual caliber of those who wrote about her favorably. She had expected to receive from someone in the culture — someone who was a public figure and had an influence — a more profound kind of understanding.

We in the Collective were, in effect, "family," insiders, brought up by her; what she longed for now was an outsider, someone she had not educated, a contemporary with eyes that could see and a voice that could speak. No such person appeared.

"How is Ayn taking the reception of *Atlas*?" the various Collective members would ask me, and I would answer, "It's tough. Very tough." I would try to convey Ayn's point of view to them. "Isn't she happy about the sales?" they would say, and I would respond, "Sure. But more is involved than sales. She wants something more personal." They talked about their own disappointment and bewilderment only with one another. With Ayn they felt obliged to put on an air of detachment and confidence, not to pass to her the burden of whatever hurt they might be experiencing.

"How is the Collective taking the reception of *Atlas*?" Ayn would ask me. I would shrug and say, "Well, you know. Pretty stunned, I guess." She would smile sadly and say, "I can't help them; not this time; not with this. Can I leave it to you to teach them the proper philosophical perspective?" I assured her that she could. On many occasions she did lecture them on the state of the culture, in an effort to lift their spirits and, no doubt, her own.

Only with Barbara could I be fully open about my own pain, as she could be about hers. "What kind of world is this?" I would say. And with her mouth pulled tight in her own quiet anguish, she would nod her head knowingly, and sometimes we would embrace each other in mutual support and comfort. "It's our turn now," I said to her. "Ayn has done enough. She's entitled to rest. It's we who have to carry the work forward." We stood in the midst of a battlefield, bonded together more powerfully than ever before, by virtue of a shared cause, a shared vision, and a shared suffering. I thought that Barbara and I might yet create a true marriage — a marriage of fellow warriors. Some dreams take a long time to die.

In January 1958, a few months after the publication of *Atlas Shrugged*, I initiated a lecture course entitled "Basic Principles of Objectivism," which was a systematic presentation of Ayn's philosophy, including aspects she had not covered in her writings and material from my work in psychology. "I admire what you're trying to accomplish," Ayn said to me. "I hope you won't be hurt."

An example of the kind of summary I offered concerning the essence of the philosophy I would be teaching:

> that reality is what it is, that things are what they are, independent of anyone's beliefs, feelings, wishes, judgments or opinions — that that which is, is — that existence exists — that A is A;
>
> that reason, the rules of logic applied to the evidence of the senses, is fully competent, in principle, to understand the facts of reality and to assess all claims to truth;

that any form of irrationalism, supernaturalism, revelation or mysticism, any claim to a nonsensory, nonrational form of knowledge, is to be rejected;

that a rational code of ethics is possible and is derivable from an appropriate identification of the nature of human beings as well as the nature of reality;

that the standard of the good is not God or the alleged needs of society but rather "Man's Life," that which is objectively required for man's/woman's life, survival, and well-being;

that a human being is an end in him or herself, not a means to the ends of others — that each one of us has the right to exist for our own sake, neither sacrificing others to self nor self to others;

that the principles of justice and respect for individuality, autonomy, and personal rights must replace the principle of sacrifice in human relationships;

that productive achievement is our noblest activity, and happiness our highest purpose;

that no individual — and no group — has the moral right to initiate the use of force against others;

that force is permissible only in retaliation, and only against those who have initiated its use;

that the organizing principle of a moral society is respect for individual rights, and that, the sole appropriate function of government is to act as guardian and protector of individual rights.

I knew nothing about the business of offering public lectures and had asked Ayn if she could put me in contact with someone who might have practical advice to offer. Ayn spoke to a few people, but when they heard that a young, unknown psychologist without a university affiliation was proposing to offer lectures on philosophy in a hotel meeting room, the consensus was that the venture was inherently impractical and they had no counsel to provide. Ayn's own skepticism and lack of enthusiasm grew as well, especially during her dark moods, which were occurring more and more frequently, in spite of the sales of *Atlas*.

I did not not know whether I would succeed or fail; I knew only that I had to try — not simply because Ayn's philosophy was so important to me and I wished to disseminate it, but because I felt a need to *do something* in the face of the animosity surrounding us, and the lecture course gave me an action outlet, so I did not have to feel passive and helpless. My motive was selfish: it was *my* battle for *my* ideas. I had made Ayn's vision an intimate and integral part of me.

I asked her to let me borrow all the "intelligent" letters from fans within a hundred-mile radius of New York, in order to prepare a mailing list. Barbara did the typing, and I sent a letter to each of these people inviting them to take the course — twenty lectures, given once a week — at a tuition of seventy dollars. I rented a room in the Sheraton-Russell hotel on Park Avenue and Thirty-seventh Street, two blocks from where I lived. My initial capital outlay was for stationery, stamps, and the rent on the meeting room. Ayn had no financial participation in the venture then or later; it was entirely my own project. However, she agreed to join me for the question period at the conclusion of each lecture, and her presence was enormously helpful.

In the winter and spring of 1958, when the course was first given, I had twenty-eight students. When I offered it again that fall, forty-five students attended. When I offered it a third time in February 1959, the number of students jumped to sixty-five — and thereafter went on climbing, eventually leveling off at about one hundred sixty per class. The course was given twice a year and growth was stimulated by the word-of-mouth enthusiasm of students and by the small announcements I began running in New York newspapers, chiefly the *Times*.

I originated the project under the name Nathaniel Branden Lectures; later, I incorporated as Nathaniel Branden Institute. The reason for this choice of name, rather than, say, the Objectivist Institute, was to establish a certain distance between Ayn and myself, publicly — to communicate that as a business I was operating entirely on my own, although with Ayn's intellectual approval.

One of the most inspiring aspects of the project was the high intellectual caliber of many of the students — from a sixty-year-old professor of physics to a twenty-seven-year-old Ph.D. in economics to a precocious sixteen-year-old high school girl. Students came from every sort of background and profession: businessmen, housewives, lawyers, secretaries, college students, physicians, scientists, stock brokers, nurses, teachers, psychiatrists, engineers. A significant number of the men and women instrumental in founding the Libertarian party, which today is the country's third largest political party, took one or more courses at Nathaniel Branden Institute.

Students soon demanded additional programs, and I next created a course entitled "A Critical Analysis of Contemporary Psychology." I invited the other members of our group to join me in offering lectures. Barbara gave a course entitled "Principles of Efficient Thinking"; Leonard offered "A Critical History of Philosophy"; Mary Ann gave "The Aesthetics of the Visual Arts"; Alan Greenspan lectured on "The Economics of a Free Society." In later years, still other courses were added, including ones in which I presented my evolving psychological theories.

In the beginning, all I was aware of doing was offering a structured,

nonfictional presentation of Ayn's ideas, into which I had incorporated some of my own. I did not know that I was in the process of
launching a philosophical movement. Later, when Ayn pointed out
what I had accomplished, I protested, saying that it was her novels that
had launched the movement. "No," she answered. "My novels created
readers. Nathaniel Branden Institute created the movement. Until
NBI, there was no public focus for my ideas — no place where people
could study my philosophy systematically, meet one another, form
groups, coordinate efforts to spread the ideas further. All that began
with your lectures. You made the name 'Objectivism' famous."

By the fall of 1958 it was apparent that Ayn was sinking into a deep
and tenacious depression. Neither the sales of her novel, nor the torrent of enthusiastic fan mail, nor any of the more interesting people
we were meeting, seemed to cheer her for more than a few hours or
evoke in her any desire to write again. The thought of another
project — *any* other project — exhausted her. Every day she sat long
hours at her desk playing solitaire, the game becoming a metaphor for
her sense of her position in the world. She did not read; she left her
correspondence largely unanswered; her body ached with numerous
tension pains. She had written a novel about a man who stops the motor of the world; now it was as if her motor had stopped.

She saw herself as trapped in a swamp of mediocrity, malice, and
cowardice. She had found admirers but no champions. She saw herself
lied about, misrepresented, dismissed, or trivialized, while thinkers
and writers she regarded as third-raters were hailed as "serious," "significant," "profound." She gave interviews to journalists who came
earnestly, respectfully, benevolently, or so it seemed, then went off to
write a hash that twisted and distorted every thought she had tried to
convey. She heard herself labeled a "fascist" by totalitarian utopians
and authoritarian liberals, because of her ferocious opposition to collectivism. She heard herself praised by enthusiasts whose understanding of her work was often superficial, off-center, even frivolous. She
felt, she complained, like an adult sentenced to live in a world of children, some of whom might be very "nice" but children nonetheless.

I did not at first grasp the severity of her state. I thought she was
experiencing a delayed letdown after eleven years of high emotional
intensity while writing *Atlas* full-time. Ordinary living could hardly
compete. In many of our discussions, from the summer of 1958 and
into the next two years, she would begin to cry while describing her
perception of the world and of her own place in it, and she confided
that she cried almost every day. This hit me as shockingly out of char-

acter, and I realized that I had underestimated the depth of Ayn's struggle.

We had long conversations on the telephone every day. I visited her two or three evenings a week, sometimes alone, sometimes with Barbara, for the purpose of discussing how we might better interpret the events that were such blows to Ayn's ambition, energy, and enthusiasm. These sessions typically lasted until five or six in the morning.

Her suffering was devastating to watch. I knew that what I needed to project most, in her presence, was calm, serenity, and my own belief that answers could and would be found. It was hard at times to fight down my own feelings of despair. My tendency to emotional repression grew much worse during this period. I cannot recall a single occasion on which Ayn invited me to explore my own feelings about our battle — my thoughts, yes, but not my feelings.

The Collective was hit badly. "How is it possible," they would ask on Saturday evenings, "that we can be accused of advocating the complete opposite, politically, of what we stand for?"

"It's an aberration that will pass," I would say, simultaneously trying to bring sanity to my friends and to pump Ayn with a transfusion of hope. "Look at our historical and social context. This country was born in rebellion against European aristocracy, so there's a tradition of animosity toward anything that even remotely sounds like elitism. Yet Jefferson himself spoke of America as a home for a 'natural aristocracy' — not the aristocracy of inherited privilege but an aristocracy of ability — and of course *Atlas* supports that idea. After all, some individuals achieve more, create more, contribute more than others; all men are equal before the law, or should be, but all men are *not* equal in intelligence, talent, and productiveness. But we're living in a century when this fact is not supposed to be acknowledged. We're living in the midst of a tidal wave of egalitarianism, and God help anyone who says, for instance, that Thomas Edison is in any sense superior to the village idiot. *Atlas* says the distinction between the earned and the unearned, and between the competent and the incompetent, is a difference worth respecting, and the enemy says, 'How cruel, how undemocratic, how antisocial!' And then, finally, don't forget how hard the left has worked to sell the idea that anyone opposed to socialism or communism must be a fascist — an idea which the liberals have bought totally, adapting it to read, 'Anyone opposed to the welfare state is a fascist.' "

"But Ayn," someone in the Collective would protest, "is the most ferocious opponent of fascism — and every other kind of statism — in history. *Can't people read?*"

"Never mind that," Ayn would interject. "The left doesn't care to know what I have said; they're consciously dishonest. The question is, what of the people I am defending, the men of ability? Where are they? Why don't they come forward? Why don't they speak up?"

I would shrug and grow silent — because to these questions I had no answer.

I began to hear a statement from Ayn that I would hear again and again over the years. "You are my lifeline to reality. Without you, I would not know how to exist in this world." It did not occur to me in the beginning that this statement could become a burden of steadily increasing weight; hearing it, I felt only pride and pain — pride that I was able to give so much to Ayn, and pain that it should be needed.

Sometimes I would say to Ayn, "Everything negative you say about the world is true. And yet, to be honest with you, there are times when I think: You wrote *Atlas Shrugged* — and in the face of that fact, how can anything else be important? How can any pain get to you? How can it matter?" And Ayn would smile sadly and answer, "Sometimes I tell myself that, too. I tell myself that's the way I should feel. That's how I imagine Galt would feel. If I am making a mistake, if there is something I'm not seeing, I don't know what it is. That's why I drive you crazy, night after night, looking for answers. I'm not passive; I'm not just resigning myself like the sort of people I despise; I don't stop thinking. Thinking is all I do."

She complained that she had lost all sense of who she was addressing when she wrote — "The state of the culture is far worse than I imagined." She said that she could not fight lice, could not fight when all she felt for the adversary was contempt — "So what is the sense of continuing to write? For whom?" She said that she was not an altruist, she did not work merely to serve others, and that she had no interest in monuments erected to her honor after she was dead. "I want some meaningful reward for my work *now.*" I always felt something was missing from any description she offered of what would constitute an appropriate reward.

When I asked if the writing itself was not a reward, she smiled bitterly and replied, "It used to be. When I was younger. But with *Atlas Shrugged* I've said what I wanted to say and needed to say. There's no reason to say or do more. Not without something coming back to me that I didn't generate."

On one occasion I said, "Look, I loved *The Fountainhead,* but it never would have occurred to me that you needed anything from me, that I would have anything to offer you. Right now there are good people reading *Atlas* who lead private lives of their own, wouldn't think of trying to contact you, wouldn't think there's anything they ought to be doing except reading you, appreciating you, talking about your work in their own circle — which they're obviously doing because it's got to be word of mouth that is responsible for the terrific sales of the book." And Ayn would answer, "True. Those people are not the problem. I appreciate them. The problem is that not one first-class brain has stood up for me in public to defend me — to give me some sense that there's a human race out there and the struggle is worth it."

That was part of the truth but not all of it. The darker, and now dominant, side of her emotional life, had been present long before the publication of *Atlas*. Certainly she had always felt profoundly alone. Perhaps it was the penalty of genius, I told myself, thinking of all the great minds in history who had been tortured by bouts of depression. Perhaps the real root of her anguish is the simple fact that one gets tired of being able to see clearer and farther than anyone else. Genius means isolation, I thought. But if this was true, what could I possibly say that would be helpful?

The bitterness that had always been part of her make-up was becoming progressively more pronounced. She was impatient, irritable, angry, quick to condemn — Frank, me, Barbara, Leonard, anyone in the Collective who said or did anything even slightly ambiguous or questionable. If some of Joan's paintings were dark or grim, Ayn would wonder aloud about Joan's "malevolent sense of life." If Allan Blumenthal expressed enjoyment in listening to Beethoven or Mozart, both of whom Ayn disliked, she would say, (although not to him directly, since musical standards could not yet be "proven") "That's why there will always be a wall between us. Our souls are essentially different." If Alan Greenspan mentioned a social event he had attended, Ayn would speculate about his fundamental seriousness or lack of it: "Do you think Alan might basically be a social climber?" If Leonard was too friendly to one of his professors, or insufficiently outspoken on Ayn's behalf, he more than once had to face Ayn's accusation of treason: "If I can't count on Leonard to recognize the enemy, who can I count on?" Sometimes I defended them against Ayn, sometimes I joined her. I shared some of the uneasiness she expressed about our circle but not necessarily for her reasons; I saw them (most of the time) as good in their own way, but not very exciting — loyal and dedicated, but not very heroic. I would have said I liked them but I did not see them as "giants." Later I would learn that they sensed this and were badly hurt by it. Ayn vacillated constantly; she could be withdrawn and unfriendly toward one or another of them at one meeting, then warm and affectionate at the next. Thoroughly caught up in Ayn's emotional world, I often manifested the same vacillation, as my feeling of isolation went on deepening.

During this period, Frank had never seemed so helpless; he looked on in mute despair, participating in Ayn's suffering, the gaunt planes of his face occasionally broken by flashes of angry indignation on her behalf; much of the time he disappeared into the private world of his painting, where not even Ayn could reach him. Once, when I asked him how he felt about the reception of *Atlas*, he answered bitterly, "People are swine." "Frank," I said urgently, "you mustn't abandon Ayn now." "Thank God she has you," he answered.

I struggled to keep my balance, not grasping what was happening — feeling only that the comparative paradise of our prepublication years had vanished irretrievably.

I blamed the world — for being irrational; I blamed myself — for not knowing how to bring Ayn back to life; I blamed the Collective — for not supporting Ayn's work more creatively and aggressively, and for not being more than they were. The one person I did not blame was Ayn. If her reactions were excessive at times, if she could even be cruel — didn't she deserve our understanding and compassion? I did not want to hear that anyone's feelings had been hurt by Ayn; as I saw it then, no one else's feelings, including my own, mattered now — only hers.

I communicated this viewpoint to our friends. I was Ayn's bodyguard. I was her protector and defender. When necessary, I made myself as ruthlessly implacable as she. I had always sought to participate in her inner world, to join with her intellectually and spiritually; now I chose to enter into the dark perspective that was swallowing her — *I would follow her anywhere to maintain our connection* — and I too became impatient, irritable, harsh in my judgments, leaving more and more of my humanity behind, while telling myself that this was what it meant to live one's idealism in the world. To some extent, Barbara did the same. I saw this — and approved.

Ayn's depression persisted — relentlessly. "I'm ashamed of myself for crying so much," Ayn said one evening. "The Collective would be shocked if they knew. You don't tell them, do you?" I told her I did not. "Galt would handle all this differently. Somehow he would be more untouched by it. More realistic. But I don't know how or in what way. I would hate for him to see me like this. I would feel unworthy, as if I had let him down." I was used to hearing her discuss Galt as if he were a real person; all of us did that. I said, "I look at it differently. If I were knocked down, hurt badly by something that had happened to me, so that I was crying a lot or devastated or whatever, I think I would say, 'All right, look at me. I'm in a bad way? So what? In a little while I'll pick myself up again. Meanwhile, this is reality. Why pretend it isn't?' " She chuckled unhappily. "You're quoting my own philosophy back to me. Only — for once — I can't seem to apply it."

I did not know what to think. Ayn despised self-pity and when she asked me if I thought she was guilty of it, I answered truthfully that I didn't. And yet I could not shake the thought that in her place I would not react as she did. I reproached myself for not understanding — look how much easier life was for me than it had been for her. I thought: it's too easy to tell myself that I would be more resilient; I have not been tested as she has. In addition, Ayn had the gift of making her own perspective utterly convincing, so that all my efforts to find an answer took place entirely within her frame of reference.

Meanwhile, the response to the lecture courses was growing. We were now receiving inquiries from all over the country, as well as from Canada, Europe, India, and Australia. An enormous demand was mounting for our courses and for more information about Objectivism.

"This is the one bright spot in my life," Ayn said, "so far as my view of the culture is concerned. I could not have imagined this. Ideas *do* matter to some people. I see it in your students. From week to week they're changing. Because of your lectures, all of them are becoming better human beings."

She could extravagantly praise my students one moment, then be furiously impatient with them the next. In the question periods following my lectures, she often became angry with any question she felt should not have been asked, perhaps because it had been answered in *Atlas Shrugged,* or perhaps because she believed that any honest person would figure it out for himself. Most of our students seemed to love her; but sometimes she could be terrifying.

I recall an incident in which a man with a thick Hungarian accent began his question, "In his speech, Galt contends that —" He never got any further because Ayn exploded. "Galt does not *contend,*" she shouted. "If you have read *Atlas Shrugged,* if you profess to be an admirer of mine, then you should know that Galt does not 'strive,' 'debate,' 'argue,' or 'contend.' " The man looked stricken. He pleaded, "But Miss Rand, all I meant was —" Ayn thundered back at him, "If you wish to speak to me, first learn to remember to whom and about what you are speaking!" Ayn was obsessed with clarity and precision in speaking and writing; it was a passion I generally shared — certainly we trained the Collective to high standards in this regard — but I did not feel sympathy for the passion in this instance; I thought it totally misapplied. The man sunk back into his chair, embarrassed and defeated. I felt concerned for him, appalled by Ayn, and annoyed with myself for not speaking up on the spot. Later, when we were alone, I pointed out that the man had a foreign accent and probably was not aware of the nuances of meaning contained in the word *contend*. "I never thought of that," Ayn replied, with a look of astonished, child-like innocence. I noticed, sadly, that the man never came back. I can still see the expression of hurt and shock on his face.

There were, of course, question-and-answer sessions when Ayn was warm, friendly, benevolent, charming. Once, when a student apologized for the naiveté of some question, she told him encouragingly, "There are no stupid questions, only stupid answers." Yet the rage was always there, lingering in the background of her consciousness, and it could be activated any time she felt that a student had brought the perspective of "the world" into the lecture room by asking a question that hinted too loudly at alien influences. Sometimes, Ayn would apologize for her outbursts, later, to me. "I'm not promising it won't happen again," she always added.

In the main, the students idolized her. They were thrilled by the opportunity to have such direct access to her. If she occasionally lost her temper, most of them seemed to feel, what of it? As one former NBI student put it, when I interviewed him two decades later, "Look how much she had to offer! Look at how much I was learning! If she got a little berserk now and again, *so what?*" They were participants in a marvelous intellectual adventure. For one evening a week, they were in a world of unlimited possibilities. They were acutely conscious of what she gave them.

She offered them a comprehensive and intelligible view of human existence. She offered them a frame of reference by means of which they could understand the society around them. She was not only a superb dramatist who created vivid and inspiring heroes and heroines, she was a philosophical system-builder — during a century when system-builders were out of fashion and almost impossible to find. She provided them with a vision of what life on this planet is essentially about. She offered a unique vision of human nature and of human relationships. And today, reflecting back on those years, it is clear to me that what matters is not whether her vision was correct in all respects — I know now that it wasn't — but that she *had* a vision, a highly developed one, that promised comprehensiveness, intelligibility, and clarity; one that provided answers to some of the most burningly important questions of life. And human beings long for that; I did and our students did.

We need to feel we understand the world in which we live. We need to make sense out of our experience. We need some persuasive portrait of who we are as human beings and what our lives are or should be about. In short, we need a philosophical vision of reality. I knew that twentieth-century philosophy had almost totally abandoned the responsibility of offering such a vision, or addressing itself to the kind of questions men and women struggle with in the course of their existence. Twentieth-century philosophers typically scorn system-builders. The problems to which they address themselves grow smaller and smaller, and more and more remote from human experience. In their journals and at their conventions they explicitly acknowledge that they have nothing of *practical* value to offer anyone. And during the past few centuries, orthodox religion has lost more and more of its hold over people's minds and lives. It has been perceived as of diminishing relevance. Its demise as a culture force began with the Renaissance and it has been waning ever since.

Yet the need for answers has not vanished. The need for values by which to guide our lives, I knew, was as urgent as it ever was. The world around us seemed to be growing more and more confusing — and threatening. The need to comprehend cried out in anguish. This was the need to which Ayn — and I as her representative — was speaking.

We had an extraordinary vision to offer, a radiantly rational one, I believed then. Today I am convinced there are errors in that vision, elements that need to be changed, eliminated, modified, added, or amplified, but I am still convinced there is much in that vision that will stand.

We did not tell our students that the mind is impotent. We did not tell them that they were rotten or powerless. We did not tell them that life is futile, or that they were doomed, or that existence is meaningless. We told them just the opposite. We told them that their main problem was that they had not learned to understand the nature of their power — therefore, of their own possibilities. We told them that their mind was and could be efficacious, that they *were* competent to understand, that genuine knowledge was attainable, that achievement and happiness were possible. We told them that life was not about dread, defeat, and anguish but about struggle, triumph, and exaltation.

This message ran counter not only to the dominant religious and philosophical teachings most of them were exposed to, but, no less important, it ran counter to the teachings of most of their parents. Their parents, who said, "So who's happy?" "Pride goeth before a fall" "Adventure is for the comic strips; who do you think you are, Buck Rogers?" "Real life is learning to make your peace with boredom" "Life is not about exaltation, life is about duty."

And then along came Ayn Rand who said, "Oh, really?" and proceeded to create characters who did not live in the Middle Ages or in outer space, but who were of our time and of this earth — characters who work, struggle, pursue difficult career goals, fall in love, participate in intensely emotional relationships, and for whom life is a great adventure *because they have made it so.* Characters who face opposition, endure hardships, suffer, struggle, persevere — and who, predominately, *win.*

This was a major reason why her books were having such an impact on young people, on those still fighting to protect themselves, to protect their own souls, against the world of adults, against the cynicism and despair of their elders — fighting to hang on to the conviction that they can do better, can rise higher, can make more of their lives than those who had gone before them.

As someone who was closer to most of them in age, I knew that I was often perceived as concrete proof that what Ayn wrote and I taught was realizable. This was a perception that Ayn actively encouraged and that I accepted. In later years many former students would tell me, "Miss Rand was someone far away, an abstraction, almost a person living on another planet; but you were our contemporary, you were just starting out yourself, and look at what you had done, look at what you were. It was inspirational."

As Ayn's impact became more visible, as she saw what happened at the lectures, her spirits began to lift. It happened slowly. For two years she lived a good deal of the time in hell, and I lived there with her.

Barbara remained the only person to whom I could speak with candor about what this period was like for me. "I'm proud of the lectures and what we're accomplishing, but some part of me feels very much as Ayn does. I feel as if, in some very profound way, this world has died for me — the world has become an essentially boring place in which to live — because, with all the good things that are happening, the new people we're meeting, all of it, I feel worse alienation than I did as a teenager. If this is what happens to Ayn at the triumph of her career, what's the point?"

Every Sunday morning I had a ritual: I forced myself read the *New York Times Book Review* from cover to cover. This section had become the symbol of everything I loathed. Reading what was praised and taken seriously was torture; I felt blinding rage and indignation. I thought of the treatment accorded *Atlas Shrugged,* and I saw the kind of fiction that was saluted as great literature, and at times my pain was unbearable. I told myself that I would read the *Book Review* every Sunday, no matter how long it took, until I could do so indifferently, until "the culture" no longer had the power to hurt me. It was almost a form of meditation, to look into the darkest face of social reality as I perceived it then, and to await the arrival of equanimity. It was a spiritual rite of passage that took nearly two years. In part, I regarded this training as preparation for my own future.

Now and again Ayn would say to me, "Sometimes my point of view changes, and then I wonder why I'm feeling so sorry for myself. I detest viewing myself as a martyr. And besides, who ever heard of a martyr on the best-seller list? Maybe I need to get back to work and stop thinking about the culture so much." I would try to encourage this. For a few days her spirits would brighten, and I would think the worst was over; but these moods would not last; one day she would awaken and the despair would be back.

I was always in search of new hypotheses to account for her depression. I thought that for all the years of writing the novel, Ayn had lived with Dagny, Rearden, Francisco, and Galt as her daily companions; they were more real to her than almost anyone she knew. When the book was finished, they remained in her mind as the "friends" with whom any new person she met would be compared, and what actual human being could compare favorably? "Are you accusing me of being that unrealistic?" Ayn asked angrily, when I told her my idea. But an hour later, with one of her typical mood switches, she said, "I think you're right." Then, a while later: "*Of course* you're right." I knew that my idea was almost as applicable to me as to Ayn, and that it would continue to create frustration for me in my social relationships. But neither of us pursued the subject; it remained a dead end beyond which we could not travel.

As 1959 approached, I found myself entertaining yet a different hypothesis about Ayn's depression. "Do you know what I think a major part of the problem really is?" I said to her. "I think that you are one of those people who, in effect, had a mission in life — and that was to write *Atlas Shrugged*. I think everything that happened earlier was just preparing you for that assignment. By a 'mission,' I mean a task logically and psychologically entailed by your deepest essence, by who you are at your core, so that its actualization leaves you thinking, 'This is what I was born for. This is what I came on earth to do.' "

Ayn nodded her head eagerly. "That's exactly how I feel about *Atlas*," she said.

"The problem is," I continued, "what do you do now? The mission has been accomplished and you're only in your fifties and in good health. You've got to find a new challenge. That might be tough, I suspect, no matter how people responded to *Atlas*."

Ayn was now happily excited. "Absolutely true," she declared.

"Well, if it is, then talking about the state of the world, even if everything we say about it is right, is on another level, beside the point — irrelevant — because we're not addressing the real issue."

Ayn threw her arms around me and announced, "I have not felt this hopeful since *Atlas* was published! This is the right track, darling, this is the right track!" Thereafter she referred to this idea as the "mission theory." It did not end her depression but it helped.

When Barbara and I were visiting one evening, she said to Barbara, almost as if I were not present, "It's Nathan who's saving my life. Because of my conversations with him and his sense of the culture, his understanding of how to fight this battle. The success of his lectures gave me hope and a new sense of what's possible. Seeing Nathan start on a shoestring, with the whole intellectual atmosphere against him, standing totally alone and establishing an institution — that was an enormously crucial, concrete example of what can be done."

To me alone, she said, "Whatever I have given you, you have given an equivalent back to me. Consider us even."

In the two years following the publication of *Atlas Shrugged,* Ayn and I made love less than a dozen times. The joy and excitement between us had vanished. Our meetings predominantly were spent discussing the issue and events I have described. Our affair died, not by conscious decision, but by default, as a casualty of Ayn's depression.

"I have nothing to bring to the realm of sex," Ayn said sadly. "Perhaps, one day in the future, when I'm alive again, but now all we can be is friends."

I did not argue. I was relieved. I did not want the burden of a "romance" for which I no longer had genuine enthusiasm. I needed all of my resources to continue functioning. I had a private practice and was developing the lecture series. In addition, I was pursuing my studies in psychology and philosophy, evolving my ideas about self-esteem, social metaphysics, and motivation in general, writing the book on anxiety, operating as Ayn's emotional support system, thinking constantly about how to advance Objectivism in the culture — and trying to find some joy in a marriage that had become more and more cerebral.

Barbara and I accused each other of coldness; we were both right. And yet there continued to be times of warmth and affection. We were not passionate as husband and wife; but we were often passionate friends. We supported each other emotionally.

I was grateful for the fact that at last my sexual interest in her had begun to decline. There had been too many nights of lying in bed fighting my desire, too many rejections, alternating with occasional lovemaking sessions that were mechanical and soulless. She was becoming a fantasy figure, an abstraction called "my wife," for whom I felt a sadly detached kind of love; but it was a love that remained important. She was a friend as no one else in my world was a friend. I did not think of divorcing her. She was my wife and she would remain my wife, and I told myself that someday, somehow, we would find a way to be happy together. I would not, or could not, concede defeat; I would not, or could not, acknowledge failure.

Barbara was as emotionally unfulfilled as I; but she, too, never spoke of divorce. She, too, did not want to fail. When she referred to our future, it was with optimism. "We have been through so much together," she said tenderly. "The worst is behind us. We'll be together for life." I drew a kind of nourishment from hearing her say this. It was as if she had said, "Not *everything* is falling apart. There are some things you will always be able to count on. I am one of them." Later she would tell me that at this time she had felt unbearably lonely and I would tell her the same about myself.

Part of her liked my male energy; another part seemed uncomfortable with it. I once complained that sometimes with her I felt like a bull in a china shop, and she answered, "That's because you're not fully civilized." Inevitably, I contrasted her with Ayn — who was far more intellectual, and simultaneously far more visceral, organic. Yet Barbara enjoyed one chief advantage: she was my own age. That was important to me because of my desire for a life-companion with whom I could share the normal stages of development.

I never thought of seeking this companionship with another woman. I did not flirt, did not look around for attractive females, did not respond when other women attempted to flirt with me. In fact, I rarely noticed, unless Barbara pointed it out, as she did from time to time.

My affair with Ayn notwithstanding, I regarded myself as a man committed to sexual exclusivity and to monogamy. Ayn was a once-in-a-lifetime exception; I did not see our affair beginning a pattern of acceptable behavior. Barbara expressed the judgment that I was fundamentally a puritan; once, she had said this as a criticism; now, she said it with affection.

I was sitting on the edge of a volcano. All of us were. But no one was more oblivious than I.

TWELVE

"ACCEPT THE FACT that in the realm of morality nothing less than perfection will do," Ayn had written in Galt's speech. By "perfection" she meant an "unbreached rationality" — that is, a commitment to use one's mind to the fullest of one's ability, a respect for facts, reality, and logic, and a refusal to indulge *wishes* by evading knowledge or evidence.

As a psychologist I knew that at least on some occasions a denial or avoidance of some aspect of reality was inevitable — fear, pain, and desire virtually guaranteed it — and that in any event the notion of flawless consistency in this sphere was a fantasy. Philosophically, I was committed to the idea that "unbreached rationality" was not merely a powerful guiding principle, a commitment to do one's best to live honestly, congruently, and responsibly, but a practice within *anyone's* power to attain *all of the time.* That Ayn had herself achieved such a state was a not-to-be-questioned axiom.

In our world, psychology was implicitly viewed as the handmaiden of philosophy. As a result, the psychologist in me almost always yielded to the philosopher. I upheld the absolutism of "unbreached rationality" as a moral imperative at my lectures — and in my own circle of friends.

Ayn and I did not say, "Live consciously. Try to be as rational as you can be. Don't make allegations you can't support. Be on the lookout for contradictions and work to resolve them. Do your best to face the things that need to be faced. When you act, make every effort to know what you are doing and what the consequences are likely to be. Live responsibly. Accept that sometimes you will fail; don't collapse into guilt, because that serves no useful purpose; pick yourself up, acknowledge your error, and try to do better in the future." That would have been genuinely rational advice. What we said, in effect, was, "Be rational twenty-four hours a day and in every issue; there's no excuse not to be. The root of all evil is evasion. Value your own moral perfection above all things." These are very different communications with predictably different consequences.

Among us nothing was worse than to be accused of "evasion" — deliberate unconsciousness, the willful suspension of sight, the choice of an action known to be wrong. The prospect evoked considerable anxiety. In Galt's speech Ayn had stated, "Make every allowance for errors of knowledge; do not forgive or accept any breach of morality." One member of our group confided to me, "Every night before going to bed I review the day to see if I have done anything immoral, if I have evaded anything, refused to properly consider some relevant facts." When I said that I found this appalling, I was greeted with hurt astonishment.

Of all the accusations raised against our philosophy by hostile critics, none is more ludicrous than that we advocated hedonism. If there was anything Ayn did not teach, it was the idea that a person should do whatever he or she pleases. It would be closer to the truth to say that she viewed life as a moral tightrope and that it was easy to lose one's balance and fall into immorality. Certainly this was the perspective that profoundly affected all of us in the Collective. We despised "whim-worshipers" and looked with suspicion at anyone who seemed too interested in emotions or who said, "I feel," rather than "I think." We demanded reasons for everything.

If reason was our supreme and ruling value, it was a value to be respected scrupulously in the daily conduct of life. That ideals were to be lived, not merely espoused, was a dominant theme of Ayn's. She was moved by passions, true enough; she would hardly deny that; but she was fanatical in justifying them within the context of her vision of the rational and of her code of values. What is obvious to me today but was not obvious to me then, was that if Ayn was a genius at reasoning, she was no less a genius at rationalizing.

Once she had a desire — almost any desire — she could generate a chain of reasoning to justify it. No, she did not advocate doing what one pleases — not as a general rule and not for other people — but if one considers her dealings with Frank in the context of her affair with me, if one considers her blithe obliviousness to the devastation being wrought, and not only upon Frank — one sees a recklessness and irresponsibility completely at variance with a life of reason. This is not a statement about the validity of Ayn's philosophy; it is a statement about her own psychology. This contradiction in values may help explain why she became so agitated if anyone dared to suggest that she was being irrational in any respect whatsoever.

Since our ideals were presumably all grounded in reason, there was no important difference, to our way of thinking, between "living by our ideals" and "living by reason." *Reason* was a word we used a great deal. It was a code word, or shorthand, that stood for much more than the faculty and process of integrating, without contradiction, the data provided by the senses. It stood for a set of ideas — indeed, for the entire Objectivist philosophy: from the laws of logic or the validity of sensory perception, to our esteem for productive work, to our advocacy of Romanticism in art, to our convictions concerning individual rights and the proper separation of state and economics.

Our commitment to the life of reason generated many positive consequences. We thought philosophically and in terms of principles. We strived for lucidity. We were keenly concerned with precision in our thought and speech. There was a clarity and focus in our behavior. We were not blamers; we took responsibility for our actions. There was a dignity in our dealings with one another. We cared deeply about being fair and just. That which we liked or admired, we praised unstintingly and enthusiastically; we believed in supporting our values. Such was the orientation of our group at its best.

At the same time there was a rigidity, a fear of falling into error — and, for the others, a fear of incurring Ayn's or my displeasure and critical judgment. "In the Collective," Harry Kalberman remarked to me, many years later, "there was always that dread of moral condemnation from on high. I don't know if you ever really understood how bad our anxiety was." To a lesser extent I shared the apprehension of being judged morally delinquent by Ayn; I was protected only by a higher level of self-confidence and moral certainty. But, for all of us, there was terrible violence done to our emotional life — the repression or suppression of any feeling that clashed with what an ideal Objectivist was supposed to experience, be it a sexual impulse, an artistic preference, a longing for greater spontaneity, irritation or anger with me for my sometimes abrupt and impatient manner, or hurt at Ayn's coldness when she found some act to disapprove of.

"I've never had an emotion I couldn't account for," Ayn liked to announce. She could turn out explanations of her emotional life with dazzling virtuosity, and it did not occur to us that her explanations could be spurious. Ayn made many self-congratulatory statements that we accepted at face value; or if any of us didn't, we remained silent about it, suppressing our misgivings.

When we had difficulty accounting for some emotion of our own, we told ourselves we had to learn to be "better introspecters." "Introspection," at that time, meant a fairly cerebral and analytic unmasking of the "premises" generating our feelings. It had very little to do with the art of self-awareness as I would describe it years later in *The Disowned Self.*

Not that we were insensitive to the problem of emotional repression. We discussed it often. I talked about it as an issue to be concerned about in my lectures on Objectivism. Nonetheless its encouragement was always subtly and insidiously present.

For some years Ayn had contemplated writing a book the theme of which would be "the mind versus the heart," her thesis being the superiority of the mind and the evil of placing the heart above it. She decided against writing the book because she felt she had covered the issue adequately in *Atlas Shrugged.* The intensity of her concern with this issue, manifested countless times in discussions, became a profound if unacknowledged message to distrust emotions, and was experienced by our group as such. This message *never,* of course, applied to Ayn's emotions, which were uncritically interpreted as manifestations of irreproachable rationality.

Our official position was that emotions are not tools of cognition, which they are not. But to disparage feelings was a favorite activity of virtually everyone in our circle, as if that were a means of establishing one's rationality. All we achieved was to drive our own feelings underground.

Along with the opposite message, the tendency to encourage emotional repression was present in *The Fountainhead* and *Atlas Shrugged,* although I came to see this only after my break with Ayn. Here is an example from *The Fountainhead* — a passage that inspired me at fourteen. Howard Roark is at the low point of his struggle to succeed as an architect; he is working in a granite quarry, doing grinding, mindless, exhausting labor.

Sometimes, not often, he sat up and did not move for a long time; then he smiled, the slow smile of an executioner watching a victim. He thought of his days going by, of the buildings he could have been doing, should have been doing and, perhaps, would never be doing again. He watched the pain's unsummoned appearance with a cold, detached curiosity; he said to himself: Well, here it is again. He waited to see how long it would last. It gave him a strange, hard pleasure to watch his fight against it, and he forgot that it was his own suffering; he could smile in contempt, not realizing that he smiled at his own agony. Such moments were rare. But when they came, he felt as he did in the quarry: that he had to drill through granite, that he had to drive a wedge and blast the thing within him which persisted in calling to his pity.

How my adolescent self longed to be capable of that! Unfortunately, by my late twenties, I had become a master at it. And I believed that everyone else in our group should do likewise. Having little patience or compassion for my own suffering, I had little for theirs. I could be supportive, affectionate, and playful, true enough; but I could also be arrogant, impatient, demanding, and capable of projecting arctic remoteness. With my staff I could be a holy terror of high expectations and zero empathy.

In *Atlas* there is a scene in which Hank Rearden comes to Dagny's apartment on a night when he feels assailed by revulsion at the deterioration of his world, at the injustice he sees everywhere, and at the seeming helplessness of the good to combat it. He tells himself that he must not convey any of his suffering to the woman he loves.

> He grasped a feeling that he had always experienced, but never identified because it had always been absolute and immediate: a feeling that forbade him ever to face her in pain. It was much more than the pride of wishing to conceal his suffering: it was the feeling that suffering must not be granted recognition in her presence, that no form of claim between them should ever be motivated by pain and aimed at pity. It was not pity that he brought here or came here to find.

What is the implication? That if ever we are honest with the person we love about our suffering, our goal is to evoke pity. Certainly this was not Ayn's actual belief, but it is what the passage conveys. And this passage is far from being the only one of its kind in the book.

I recall how concerned Ayn was, when she did speak of her own suffering, that she receive appropriate understanding and sympathy from the listener; and how miffed she could be if this response was not forthcoming. So perhaps this passage is psychologically revealing in a way she did not intend.

Later in the story, when Dagny quits Taggart Transcontinental in protest against outrageous government regulations, she goes to a cabin in the country to recover emotionally — to learn how to live without the work that had been her lifelong passion. She finds the suffering of her loss to be almost beyond endurance.

> She had come here with three assignments given, as orders, to herself: rest — learn how to live without the railroad — get the pain out of the way. Get it out of the way, were the words she used. She felt as if she were tied to some wounded stranger who could be stricken at any moment by an attack that would drown her in his screams. She felt no pity for the stranger, only a contemptuous impatience; she had to fight him and destroy him.

Here again we are offered a heroic vision of emotional repression. This passage is more than a dramatized counsel against feeling sorry for oneself; it upholds an adversarial relationship to one's emotional life as *admirable.*

All of us were consciously or subconsciously influenced by this "ideal." It would take me another decade fully to understand that the denial or disowning of our suffering is a major source of psychological tragedy.

In passage after passage of *Atlas* — even though passion is celebrated — repression, denial of feeling, the sweeping aside of emotion, are dramatized as strength and virtue; concern with feeling is indulgent and irrational, indicative of weakness and immorality. Psychologists tell parents, "Your children will be influenced far more by the example you set than by your verbal pronouncements." The examples set by the behavior of Ayn's characters have an impact on the reader far more powerful than any explicit philosophical statement about the legitimate place of emotion in human life. I cannot think of any other book in which there are so many passages in which emotion is treated in a negative way — paradoxically, in a novel exploding with passion on almost every page. The temptation to apply Freud's concept of reaction formation is irresistible. Certainly in the end it was Ayn's emotions that proved her undoing — or, more accurately, her failure to deal with them appropriately. As is always the case, the beast she feared most lay within.

Suspicion, if not hostility, toward emotion was the message that we in the Collective absorbed from Ayn's novels and from Ayn herself. The subtle encouragement of emotional repression, and therefore the encouragement of self-alienation, was a powerful component of our world — side by side with exhortations toward greater emotional honesty and authenticity. (Ironically, Ayn's own violent emotional explosions served only to make repression seem more desirable.)

Absorbing this dangerous message made it easier to absorb others, equally dangerous.

There were implicit premises in our world to which everyone in our circle subscribed, and which we transmitted to our students at NBI.

- Ayn Rand is the greatest human being who has ever lived.
- *Atlas Shrugged* is the greatest human achievement in the history of the world.
- Ayn Rand, by virtue of her philosophical genius, is the supreme arbiter in any issue pertaining to what is rational, moral, or appropriate to man's life on earth.

- Once one is acquainted with Ayn Rand and/or her work, the measure of one's virtue is intrinsically tied to the position one takes regarding her and/or it.
- No one can be a good Objectivist who does not admire what Ayn Rand admires and condemn what Ayn Rand condemns.
- No one can be a fully consistent individualist who disagrees with Ayn Rand on any fundamental issue.
- Since Ayn Rand has designated Nathaniel Branden as her "intellectual heir," and has repeatedly proclaimed him to be an ideal exponent of her philosophy, he is to be accorded only marginally less reverence than Ayn Rand herself.
- But it is best not to say most of these things explicitly (excepting, perhaps, the first two items). One must always maintain that one arrives at one's beliefs solely by reason.

We were not a cult in the literal, dictionary sense of the word, but certainly there was a cultish aspect to our world (in the same way that one might speak, in the early years of psychoanalysis, of "the cult of Sigmund Freud," or "the cult of Wilhelm Reich"). We were a group organized around a charismatic leader, whose members judged one another's character chiefly by loyalty to that leader and to her ideas.

Ayn did not create this atmosphere on her own. We all actively contributed. In every respect I was a full and willing partner, for whom the rightness of what we were doing felt very close to self-evident. Our entire group fed Ayn's exalted view of herself, and no one did so more fervently than I. In fact, I often argued that she underestimated her own greatness. I was absolutely convinced of it. It pleased me to believe that I was providing her with an experience of greatly enhanced self-appreciation. And Ayn performed the identical function for me.

It troubled me sometimes that I could not find any area, philosophically, where I thought Ayn might be wrong. Looking at the history of human thought I knew that the greatest of geniuses made mistakes and that Ayn must be making them too. But what were they? What was I blind to? I knew that as a human being Ayn was not without flaws. But in terms of her abstract principles I found nothing to object to — only ideas that might need more amplification and development, or better, more detailed grounding.

I once asked Ayn if the possibility of error ever troubled her. "No," she replied, "not because I think I'm incapable of error, but because if reason and observation lead me to certain conclusions, what can I do except hold them as true — until and unless someone can prove I've made a mistake? What can any person do, except go by his best rational judgment and remain open to conflicting evidence when and if someone is able to present any? In the meantime I'm not going to say 'it seems to me' about matters where I am convinced reason is on my side."

Riding on the success of *Atlas*, Random House decided to publish a new edition of *We the Living*. In December 1958, Ayn received her advance copies. She showed me the new introduction, in which she stressed that the theme is abstract: the evil of dictatorship — *any* dictatorship and *all* dictatorships — not the evil of Soviet Russia in the mid-1920s. "Its basic theme," she wrote, "is the sanctity of human life."

In its depiction of a young woman growing up in Soviet Russia, *We the Living* is more autobiographical than anything else Ayn had written — not in terms of its literal events but in terms of background, environment, and philosophical development — and for that reason it had always been of particular interest to me.

The plot-theme of *We the Living* is the struggle of three young and talented people to achieve life and happiness in Soviet Russia and about the manner in which the system destroys all three of them, not in spite of, but because of, their virtues. In order to obtain money to send Leo Kovalensky, the man she loves, to a tuberculosis sanitarium, Kira Argounova becomes the mistress of Andrei Taganov, an idealistic communist. Neither man knows of Kira's relationship with the other; and their hate is mutual. Leo is an aristocrat, Andrei, a member of the Soviet secret police. The idea of a woman forced to sleep with a man she does not love in order to save the life of the man she does love is not new; that is the situation in *Tosca*, for instance, and in many other stories. The originality of Ayn's treatment of the subject is the way in which it intensifies the conflict and makes it more complex. In *Tosca* and stories like it, the man to whom the woman sells herself is a villain whom the woman despises; he *knows* that she is selling herself. But in *We the Living* Andrei is not a villain; he genuinely loves Kira and believes that she is in love with him; he does not know of her love for Leo. And Kira does not despise him; increasingly she comes to respect him. At the start of the affair she acts in desperation, knowing that it is her only chance to save Leo, and knowing that Andrei has helped to establish the system that forced this action upon her. As their relationship progresses, as Andrei finds the first happiness he has ever known, he begins to understand the importance of an individual life — and begins to doubt the ideals for which he has fought. And now the two relationships are on a collision course.

In my copy of the book, Ayn quotes a line describing Kira which I had once remarked on. I said that it conveyed something essential to what I admired in a woman: a combination of powerful innocence and a sense of purposefulness. I also said that I saw just those attributes in her. Reading Ayn's inscription, I felt a muted, distant pleasure, the kind of pleasure that goes with the thought, This would have meant a great deal to me, once.

In the period following the publication of *Atlas,* many new people entered our world, and people we had known before entered it in a new way.

One such person quickly became a member of our inner circle. Edith Efron then worked for Mike Wallace; later she would go on to a successful career in journalism, and later still would write several books, her most important, *The Apocalyptics,* a groundbreaking study of the politics of cancer.

What made her fascinating to me, apart from her unusual intelligence and entertaining sense of humor, was that when Ayn met her she was a committed "New York liberal" whose views on most issues were diametrically opposed to ours, especially in politics. She had been profoundly affected by *Atlas Shrugged,* and Ayn fascinated her; she had never before heard the kind of arguments and explanations Ayn offered. When, at Ayn's suggestion, she read some of the economic writings of Ludwig von Mises, as well as other members of the free-market Austrian school, she decided that she had been mistaken about most of the things she "knew" about politics and economics — she became a more conscientious student of this subject than most members of the Collective — and she became a supporter of laissez-faire capitalism. She was the only one in our group who read as much and as widely as Barbara and I. A superb communicator, she proceeded to convert a number of her friends.

"I feel as if all this time I've been living under some kind of censorship," she told Ayn and me. "I'm a college graduate who discovers that she's a complete illiterate in a major area. Every book I've ever heard recommended in college or out of it has been slanted to the left. Why don't more people know about these books you're showing me? Why have I not heard of these thinkers?"

At a dinner party, Mike Wallace chuckled at her conversion. "It's not just Edith," he said. "Ayn appears to have seduced my entire staff."

My sisters Reva and Florence, and their husbands Sholey and Hans, read *Atlas* and were enthusiastic. We continued to grow closer — intellectually, not personally, because personally I was now close to no one; I was carrying too much in my private life that I could not discuss. When they visited New York they saw Ayn and Frank and participated in Saturday night meetings. They became part of a widening group of people who were not part of the inner circle but who were keenly interested in and supportive of our ideas and with whom we maintained warm relations.

The real surprise to me was my father: he fell in love with *Atlas*, and this silent, reticent man became as talkative on the subject of Ayn's book as I had never heard him on any other. "What's happened to Daddy?" my mother wanted to know. I had the impression he identified with Hank Rearden and saw my mother as Rearden's wife, Lillian — one of Ayn's least appealing characters. I was no longer a disappointment who had turned his back on business to pursue some incomprehensible career in New York: I was an intellectual, doing important work the world badly needed. *Atlas* had opened his eyes to that. I was treated with new affection and respect. When my father talked with Ayn during a visit to New York, he found her to be the essence of clear thinking and common sense. "You see?" he said to me, as if it were his own discovery. "A woman can be highly intelligent. And a highly intelligent woman is a fine thing."

During this same period, the year following *Atlas's* publication, Ayn began to receive extraordinary quantities of fan mail. One letter was from a student of Professor von Mises, a young economist named Murray Rothbard, who would one day become prominent in the Libertarian movement. The letter was movingly and beautifully written, profoundly insightful concerning what Ayn had accomplished in *Atlas,* and full of what seemed like the most genuine appreciation and admiration. It was almost a model of an ideal fan letter, at the highest intellectual level.

Murray lived in New York and Ayn invited him to a meeting. While he clearly had striking intellectual gifts, I felt a stab of disappointment almost from the first moment. Fear and malice seemed to leap from his face. Murray told us that he differed from us on one important intellectual issue: he was an anarchist; he was convinced that government by its nature was oppressive and evil and that our idea of a constitutionally limited government in which the rights of citizens would be protected was hopelessly unachievable. Without a government, we asked, how did he propose to assure individual rights? We thought his answer ludicrous: "Private, competing defense agencies." Ayn quickly responded, "You mean — as in civil war?"

Years later Ayn would write on her own view of government, criticizing the anarchist position, in an article entitled "The Nature of Government." It first appeared in *The Objectivist Newsletter,* and was reprinted in two collections of her essays, *The Virtue of Selfishness* and *Capitalism: The Unknown Ideal.*

We had a few debates with Murray about government and its necessity, which were initially calm and good-natured. One evening he brought with him his own circle of friends — young students of economics, history, and the like — all of whom were anarchists and all of whom, at least in my perception, had something of Murray's manner about them, something fearful and given to sarcasm and hints of unidentified superiority. In appearance and style they were indistinguishable from any of the young socialists I had ever encountered. All conveyed admiration for *Atlas*. Murray and some of the others took my course on "Basic Principles of Objectivism." An uneasy truce was declared.

When the explosion with Murray finally came, it happened not over anarchism but over Murray's refusal to acknowledge Ayn as his source for some of the ideas, having to do with the concept of causality, in a paper he was publishing. Murray insisted to me that he got the ideas from a scholar in the Middle Ages, an Aristotelian who indeed had anticipated some of Ayn's arguments. Since I remembered Murray's and my discussions and knew specifically how Murray had been introduced to the ideas he was using — even if they had been anticipated earlier — I challenged his assertion, on the telephone, and asked him to come over so we could discuss the situation in person. He refused angrily in a way which signaled that this matter was far more serious than I had supposed. An associate of his confided that Murray had dug up this medieval scholar as his source because Murray felt it would reflect on his scholarship if he credited a *novelist* in his writing. "Academic respectability is very important to Murray."

Following our phone call, Murray went on the attack — speaking violently against Ayn, me, and all the others in our circle, effectively saying the opposite of everything he had said in his original letter to Ayn. I did not know how to interpret his reversal except as the expression of a guilty conscience. Most of Murray's friends remained loyal to him, although some of them subsequently became disenchanted with him for reasons of their own. In later years he authored many books championing "anarcho-capitalism," and for a while attracted a following.

This following would have an unfortunate impact, in the 1970s and 1980s, on the emerging Libertarian party. While the majority of those in the Libertarian party favored limited constitutional government, a minority — where Murray had his influence — favored anarchism, and this split significantly impeded the progress of the movement, costing it some loss of credibility. As a number of surveys established, far more persons were influenced toward libertarianism by the writings of Ayn Rand than by that of any other figure; but Murray and his friends contrived to create the illusion that *he* was "Mr. Libertarianism," a task made easier by the fact that Ayn repudiated and disassociated herself from this political movement, in part because of its tolerance of the anarchist wing.

Our experience with Murray Rothbard brought to light an element of Ayn's psychology I had not seen before. Prior to our break with him, both Ayn and I regarded Murray as highly intelligent; after the break, I still thought so; it was my view of his *character* that had changed. Ayn responded differently; she challenged not only his morals but his mind; it seemed to me that each time she spoke of him she thought him less intelligent than before, as if no virtue could be credited to him after his betrayal. This struck me as a rewriting of history, and when I suggested this to Ayn she became angry and demanded, "What good are his brains if this is how he acts?" I saw that further argument was futile. I was left with another residue of uneasiness, not about Murray but about Ayn; like other such uneasinesses, it was swallowed up — by the enormous esteem in which I continued to hold her.

We met a number of professed enthusiasts who thought our advocacy of self-interest meant license for the smallest, pettiest kind of range-of-the-moment indulgence. Ayn called them "Nietzschean whim-worshipers." She said, "They're the people who give 'selfishness' a bad name and make our battle harder. I go to such lengths in my writing to make clear in what sense I use the word 'selfishness.' I use it in the context of reason. Those people ignore my context — and pretend to agree with me. I wish they would stay away from us. For once I feel sympathy for Marx. He said somewhere that he was not a Marxist. God protect me from Randians."

I enjoyed it when, through Ayn, I had the opportunity to meet non-Randians, such as the composer Deems Taylor, whose daughter, Joan Kennedy Taylor, was a student at NBI. I recall an especially absorbing evening at Ayn's when, sitting with me in a corner, he helped me to understand some of the things Rachmaninoff was doing musically that I had felt but could not articulate. He also told fascinating stories about personages such as Vladimir Horowitz and Leonard Bernstein. He invited Ayn to his home to listen to recordings of his own compositions, and she spoke of her visits with pleasure. Frank, too, seemed to enjoy these encounters. Because of Deems Taylor's age, perhaps — he was some years older than Ayn — she seemed able to enjoy him on his own terms without requiring that he be a convert.

Another, more surprising friendship was the one that formed between Ayn and Mickey Spillane. I had discovered his early Mike Hammer stories, which I liked, and recommended them to Ayn, knowing she enjoyed detective novels. Ayn admired the "black-and-white moral absolutism" of Spillane's writing and also felt he was underappreciated as a stylist. "Granted his writing is uneven," she said, "and some passages are crude, but his descriptions at their best are excellent. Compare his descriptions of New York City in *One Lonely Night* with Thomas Wolfe's descriptions — and you'll appreciate the difference between a writer who knows how to make you *see* and one who just throws adjectives at you." I agreed with her, at least to some extent, but I was uneasy about the degree of praise she heaped on him publicly, as if she enjoyed shocking everyone — or as if she wanted to do for him what no one had done for her. At that time liberal reviewers went literally berserk on the subject of Mickey Spillane; I would not have imagined that a writer of thrillers could push so many hostile buttons.

Ayn learned that Spillane admired *Atlas Shrugged*. When they met, Ayn tried to get him to think more philosophically about his work and about life, but he only shook his head. We had the impression that he had been very badly hurt by the savagery of the attacks on him, but when Ayn offered him sympathy he insisted on playing tough indifference. "They sure hate us, don't they?" he said wonderingly — and then he grinned. He could be very amusing. He told us about a dinner party where "some literary guy" came up to him and declared, "I think it's disgraceful that of the ten best-selling novels of all time, seven were written by you." Spillane responded, "You're lucky I've only written seven books." But he stopped writing for several years, after *Kiss Me, Deadly,* and when he came back he was never as good; the energy and fire were gone. "They got to him," Ayn said. "He will never admit it, but they got to him. He won't give his best because he doesn't want to be hurt anymore."

Some years later, when they were no longer in touch, Spillane unexpectedly sent her a postcard saying, "When is *Atlas* going to start shrugging again?" — by which he meant, when are you going to begin a new novel?

That was the question we all wondered about. Ayn had no answer but "Perhaps — some day."

The day never came. I knew, very early after the publication of *Atlas*, that it never would.

In the spring of 1959 I turned twenty-nine. I was not a lover to Ayn or a husband to Barbara. I had very little time or inclination for recreation or leisure. *Play* was an empty word to me. We had parties and they were sometimes pleasant and yet essentially devoid of gaiety. I wrote, I thought, I studied, I lectured — I harassed my friends to read more, learn more, become more effective communicators — and I fought not to be overwhelmed by frustration and by bouts of unhappiness.

My writing was proceeding slowly; the task of spreading Objectivism had replaced psychology as my central concern. Unexpectedly, the one person who tried to speak to me about this was my mother. "What is all this lecturing and talking about Ayn Rand doing for *you*?" she wanted to know. I tried to explain that I was not fighting for Ayn Rand, I was fighting for my own convictions. She was not impressed.

The signals I got from Ayn gave me the sense of being on a perpetual roller coaster ride. One day I was a hero, taking on the entire culture, making a success of a venture that even she had not believed in; I was her champion, the one man able and willing to proclaim to the world who and what she was. On another day I was a bewildering disappointment, insufficiently supportive of her suffering, uninterested in her romantically, concerned only with her mind. One day the fact that I seemed to know how to be "in the world but not of it" was admirable, the proof of a high level of development; in this area, Ayn would say, she could learn from me. On another day the fact that I could be relaxed and easygoing with people, and rarely become angry — with students or interviewers, for instance, or with some of the intellectuals who visited her — she viewed with suspicion, as manifesting a possible lack of seriousness and integrity.

If I ever showed the slightest sign of impatience when she made the same complaint about "the world" for the two thousandth time, we would be up all night discussing what was wrong with my psychology. Usually I walked on ice expertly but once I made the mistake of referring casually to the "hospital atmosphere" of her home; this was late in 1959 and the air of tragedy and crisis was present almost constantly, especially when we were alone. *"Don't you understand my context?"* Ayn thundered at me and did not stop reproaching me for the rest of the night, comparing me, morally, to the worst of her enemies. When Frank tried to intervene in my defense she shrieked at him and he relapsed into withdrawn silence. I felt sorry for her and at the same time I felt rage. The youngest part of me, which had once felt so safe in this world, now felt flung back into the nightmare of childhood, where all grown-ups are crazy and not to be trusted. In the end I almost always made excuses for her, but the distance between us had begun to grow, like the early fissures that will one day split apart a mountain.

Even though she did not suggest a resumption of our physical relationship — she was still too troubled for that — in every other respect she clearly wanted the continuation of our romance, and this I found difficult. I survived much of the time by disconnecting from my feelings. The realm of emotion was dangerous to my equilibrium. I made myself increasingly cerebral as a means of preserving some kind of harmony with Ayn and of suppressing awareness of how frustrating my life had become. I could give Ayn intellectual companionship; I could give her compassion, empathy, support in her battle with the world — but I could not give her romantic passion; and I felt guilty about it. I agonized over the thought that I was doing to Ayn what Barbara was doing to me, and found it intolerable that I could be the cause of that kind of suffering. I contemplated the indifference of my body and searched my soul for the flaw that would explain it. I saw myself as failing my "highest value" — even if another part of me felt angry rebellion against the burden of a duty that gave me no right to my own life.

I looked for alternative ways to reassure Ayn of my devotion. I became her "enforcer." If someone in our group did something to offend Ayn or "the cause," or was not behaving as a "good Objectivist," I would invite that person to lunch and in a quiet but deadly voice I would inform him or her of the nature of the transgression. If the offense was big enough — say, being friendly with someone who had been critical of Ayn, or gossiping about another Collective member — our whole group convened to hear the charges, and almost always it was I who took the role of prosecutor. I am appalled at remembering my ruthless behavior on such occasions.

I recall an evening, for example, when the person facing charges was not a member of our circle but a girlfriend of Leonard's, a young, aspiring actress, who professed to be a passionate admirer of Objectivism and who had somehow wronged Leonard. No doubt associating her behavior, subconsciously, with past behaviors of Barbara, I became an avenging angel, laying before her the wrong she had done, with the cold, quiet earnestness of an inquisitor out of the Middle Ages — while Frank listened passively, Leonard looked righteous and wounded, Barbara watched the frightened girl with gentle sternness through circles of smoke rising from her cigarette holder, and Ayn listened eagerly, clapping her hands in appreciation of my theatrically lucid formulations. "This is one of the aspects of you I love most," Ayn told me afterward, "the purity of your moral ruthlessness." My feelings of pride collided with feelings of revulsion.

One of the worst things I had done to myself over the past several years — which became a crime against others as well — was to disown my compassionate impulses. I came to view my capacity for empathy, sympathy, and simple kindness as a potential weakness, except when directed to Ayn. At times, the more human side of me would break through and I would defend someone against Ayn's condemnation, but my defense would be highly intellectualized — I knew that this was the only way to reach Ayn — because any talk of ordinary kindness would most likely be interpreted as lack of appropriate realism, or a flawed sense of justice, or "treason against the good." In Galt's speech Ayn had stated, "Justice is the recognition . . . that to withhold your contempt from men's vices is an act of moral counterfeiting, and to withhold your admiration from their virtues is an act of moral embezzlement." Ayn was firmly convinced not only of the importance of giving support and admiration to virtue, but also of projecting contempt for moral flaws (and we did not think to ask whether the communication of contempt was likely to inspire improvement in anyone's behavior). Once or twice Barbara feebly (since she was caught up in the same madness as I, and sometimes played the role of Lord High Executioner herself) tried to speak to me of the benevolence and generosity that had once been so intrinsically a part of me; her tone of urgent wistfulness reached me, past the barrier of my defenses, but I did not know how to respond. To have admitted how well I understood her would have threatened every key pillar of the life I had erected. This was my first and only sense of "home." I was not prepared to give it up.

There were rewards for my moral ruthlessness. One was Ayn's esteem. Another was the counterbalance for my own feelings of having failed her. Another was the implication of my own moral irreproachability. Yet another was having an outlet for my rage, the rage whose actual object was Ayn — which was not to be admitted, and so was redirected at more acceptable targets. And last but not least, there was the simple fact that most of the time I was convinced I was doing right.

My marriage to Barbara continued as before, somewhat happier since the termination of my affair with Ayn, but essentially unchanged. We had a love for each other, we frustrated each other, we felt simultaneously understood by and misperceived by each other. If Barbara thought about other men, I did not know it. I did not think about other women. I tried not to suffer over the issue of sex. I repressed or channeled into work a good deal of my sexual energy. I remained committed to the idea that our marriage was forever.

If any other man did exist in Barbara's mind during this period, it was almost certainly Wilfred Schwartz. During her periodic visits to Winnipeg over the years to spend time with her family she had contacted him, reported to him on her activities, and was delighted that he had become enthralled with *Atlas Shrugged*. It gave them a new connection. He was now married and had children; nonetheless, it seemed obvious to me that he was still preoccupied with Barbara. Her stock had risen in his eyes due to her sustained relationship with Ayn;

he evidently took this as a sign of her seriousness. I listened to Barbara's summaries of her activities in Winnipeg and felt only a detached, untroubled support for her desire to enlist Wilfred in our cause. She seemed to be succeeding and I encouraged her.

I believed that if only Barbara would begin writing she would be in better spirits and more confident, and our relationship would benefit. She was now working at St. Martin's Press. She was no closer to beginning a writing project than she had been years earlier. "I'm not happy enough," she continued to say by way of explanation.

That we worked together in developing Nathaniel Branden Institute (or Nathaniel Branden Lectures, as it was still called) contributed to the closeness we did feel much of the time. We saw ourselves as comrades-in-battle.

Barbara drove to Philadelphia once a week to offer "Basic Principles of Objectivism." Sometimes Ayn, I, or someone else in the Collective drove down with her to deliver a guest lecture. We were besieged by requests to offer our courses in other cities.

We received a letter from Peter and Jan Crosby in Los Angeles, a young couple who admired Ayn's work and proposed that we tape-record our lectures and offer them via tape transcription. Why not do it everywhere? Barbara proposed. We would find a suitable representative in a given city, work with that representative to develop a student population, then make our courses available at a central location where everyone would gather to hear our programs on tape. This was the concept that caused the explosive growth of NBI.

Barbara left her job at St. Martin's to work for our organization full time; I appointed her executive director. She would be the administrator; I would be the master strategist, the one responsible for creating or supervising the creation of new projects. I largely withdrew from the practice of psychotherapy. My working life was divided between lecturing and writing. In a short time our courses were being given on a continuing basis in Los Angeles, San Francisco, Seattle, Chicago, Boston, Philadelphia, and Toronto (where my sister Florence was our representative). First, we were in ten cities, then twenty, then thirty; through the 1960s, the number went on climbing.

The process of our expansion was always basically the same. People would write us, asking that we offer our lectures in their city, and offering to help. If they seemed appropriate to represent us, we began running newspaper ads in that city — "To Readers and Admirers of *The Fountainhead* and *Atlas Shrugged*" — announcing "Basic Principles of Objectivism."

As a result of this strategy, Ayn's name and the titles of her two most important books, and my own name, appeared in newspapers around the country on a regular basis. Since the ads spoke of "the philosophy of Ayn Rand," they contributed to the change in the public perception of who Ayn Rand was — from Ayn Rand, novelist, to Ayn Rand, novelist-*philosopher*. In newspaper articles and on radio and television interviews — where both Ayn and I were being featured more and more frequently — this shift of perception was amplified. People began speaking of the "Ayn Rand philosophy" and the "Ayn Rand movement." They began speaking of "Ayn Rand and Nathaniel Branden." "You're beginning to be famous," Ayn said. "How do you like it?" I answered truthfully, "I like it very much."

With the growing success of NBI, Ayn's spirits continued to lift. "You've brought me back to life," she said more than once. She lost the more obvious signs of depression, but her sense of gloom never vanished completely; her irritability and dispiritedness were there much of the time, brightened by occasional flashes when she seemed like her old prepublication self. Although these flashes never lasted, she was happier than before.

Her enthusiasm for philosophical discussion seemed to have lessened, which I regretted, and when I mentioned this to her once she denied my observation and became angry at me for daring to suggest such a thing. Her interest in discussing the worst trends of the culture — artistically, politically, sociologically — struck me as obsessive; I made myself participate in her endless analyses, but I found her relentlessness exhausting. In her presence there was less and less air to breathe.

To the Collective she praised me constantly, sometimes to my embarrassment. I was a demigod. Occasionally, if I tried to joke about it, she would chastise me gently as if I were a child, informing me that I should not laugh at my own "greatness." I was the standard against which everyone else was judged. I was the ideal man. Her private outbursts, when I failed to be appropriately responsive to her needs and expectations, did not cease, but they were never shared with our friends; as far as I could tell, no one but Barbara and Frank knew of them. At times I resented the Collective's ignorance of the price I paid for my privileged status.

I valued the appreciation I received from them for my accomplishments with NBI. Its growth raised everyone's spirits, not just Ayn's. It became the focus of our hope for the future and our conviction that an impact on the culture was possible.

Having curtailed my practice, I referred many patients to Allan Blumenthal. He by now had abandoned his musical ambitions and was exercising his rights as a licensed physician to offer his services to the public as a psychiatrist. We assumed that his knowledge of Objectivism, plus the training and supervision he received from me, qualified him for this profession. He continued to play the piano for his own pleasure and that of his friends. If part of him was sad over the loss of music as his central focus, another part seemed relieved. "Being a psychiatrist is so much more practical," he said to me. Soon he was earning an excellent living, which favorably impressed his family.

While everyone's life in our circle seemed to be progressing in one respect or another, in the years following the publication of *Atlas,* the Collective seemed to have lost its focus. In the past we had been bound together by the excitement of reading the novel as it was being written and of learning Objectivism; now all purpose appeared to have vanished and our Saturday-night meetings often struck me as perfunctory and lacking in energy.

Increasingly, the energy we did muster depended on stimulation from the outside — provided by the continuing stream of visitors to Ayn's apartment: professors, writers, scientists, businesspeople who, if not always converts, were nonetheless profoundly impacted by *Atlas.* I swelled with admiration for Ayn when I saw how she functioned with visitors whose occupational specialties were remote from her own. She would question her guest about his work, draw out the information she needed, then proceed to make connections between her guest's particular field and her philosophy, which would astound whoever was present. She would argue about physics, mathematics, evolution, biochemistry, or Einstein's theory of relativity with consummate skill, using her visitor's own statements to support her points. She had the gift of making her guests feel that they and their work were uniquely understood and appreciated. After one encounter, I said to her, "I felt such love, watching and listening to you tonight. You bring out the best in people. You are so brilliant." Almost shyly, Ayn asked, "Is it still romantic love?" My heart suddenly felt like lead. I nodded.

My pleasure in this stream of visitors notwithstanding, the odd inertness of the Collective continued to frustrate me. To a lesser extent Barbara seemed to share my feelings. For a long time I said nothing. Then, in the late spring of 1960, shortly after my thirtieth birthday, I visited Ayn one afternoon and began almost involuntarily to ventilate my concerns.

"I feel very frustrated with the Collective. There's a certain kind of passivity in them — intellectually. We're all supposed to be committed to the spread of Objectivism, right? To me that means constantly perfecting my grasp of the issues, constantly studying and reading in philosophy, history, economics, literature. It doesn't mean just saying, 'I think Ayn Rand and *Atlas Shrugged* are wonderful.' Why isn't Leonard thinking about how to evoke interest in Objectivism at meetings of the American Philosophical Association? Why isn't Allan Blumenthal attending meetings of the American Psychiatric Association and seeing what he might accomplish there? I have to hound Allan even to read books in his own field! What the hell does Alan Greenspan do, other than praise you on Saturday nights among people who already agree? I feel as if everything rests on Barbara and me; we do everything — and the others eagerly inquire about our progress and praise us but don't do anything on their own, don't work at grasping how this world works and what it would take to change it, don't develop their skill at presenting our philosophy more effectively, *don't carry their own weight.* Joan thinks that if she acts snooty and superior to people who don't agree with Objectivism, that's her contribution to the cause. What's the matter with everyone? Maybe I'm overlooking something; I know I don't want to feel what I'm feeling. Am I being unreasonable? What do you think?"

When Ayn attached particular importance to a subject, she had a special, weighted way of speaking that lent enormous significance to every word, as if it were a projectile shot from a cannon; that was how she spoke now. "The Collective are not giants. You and I know that. They will never be you, darling, and you must accept that."

I answered that I did not think I was asking anyone to be me, I was only asking that they take more responsibility for advancing a cause they claimed to be devoted to.

"You have a passion for understanding," Ayn said, "greater than theirs will ever be. And also, a sense of responsibility — you're like Rearden in that respect. But still, I think you're right: they could do more than they're doing." Then she proceeded to talk for almost an hour on her own view of the group's passivity, amplifying what I had said and reinforcing it with almost ominous gravity.

I had begun the discussion wanting clarity in my own mind more than anything else; after that, I wanted ideas about what might be done to improve the group's attitude. What our conversation had deteriorated into was simply an analysis of the shortcomings of our friends, which was typical of Ayn, and I became restless and irritable.

Finally, to get Ayn off this track, I laughed in exasperation. "What will we call this? The 'understanding premise'?" We had a habit of labeling certain basic attitudes as "premises," like "the benevolent universe premise" or the "pro-Man premise."

"Exactly," Ayn answered. " 'The understanding premise.' The premise of seeking to understand down to the root whatever bears on your interests, purposes, and goals. I think you should have a talk with the whole Collective about this idea. It's very important."

Not long thereafter, when our group was together, I laid before them the concept Ayn and I had identified. Many years later, reflecting on this period, Elayne said to me, "That was the beginning of really enormous guilt for everyone in the Collective. There was some guilt before that, of course, about not being a 'good enough Objectivist,' but now it was much worse. We told ourselves you were right, and yet we really did not have the drive or motivation to live the kind of life you and Ayn seemed to expect. I suppose most of us were not really crusaders in your sense. But we reproached ourselves and — though no one would have admitted it at the time — we felt resentment against you. You, after all, were the immediate source of the guilt. The understanding premise was devastating to our self-esteem. We all made resolutions to do better, which of course we did not carry out. So we accused ourselves and buried our negative feelings toward you."

No doubt I should have seen that what I hoped for from my friends was totally unrealistic. They were not warriors or crusaders — they were merely people who loved Ayn and *Atlas Shrugged* and wanted the world to feel likewise. Through the accident of knowing or being related to Barbara or me, they were brought into a world they would never have found on their own. Still, when they arrived in this world, it engaged their souls. Objectivism was my whole life; it was not theirs, with the exception of Leonard; the others had careers and spaces in their lives not comparably interwoven with "the cause."

I did not see that a great explosive rage was building within each one of them — safely held in abeyance until the day when I would light the fuse.

When I think back to this period of my life and what was most important to me, I do not think of the growing tensions within the Collective, or the dramatic expansion of NBI, or my relationship with Ayn or Barbara, or our struggles with the world. I think of my pursuit of a deeper understanding of romantic love — just at the time when that aspect of my personal life was at its emptiest emotionally.

If I believed in fate I would want to say that fate had a sense of humor. Perhaps a more serious statement would be that sometimes the subconscious mind manifests a wisdom several steps or even years ahead of the conscious mind, and has its own ways of leading us toward our destiny.

"Why is love so important to human beings? Why do we need the experience of love?" I asked Barbara, Ayn, and Frank, during one of our drives into the country for dinner. Frank smiled and remained silent. "Well, why *wouldn't* it be important?" asked Barbara. Ayn responded, "It's in our nature, metaphysically, to want to admire, to find values we can esteem."

I replied, "In the first place, while admiration is essential to healthy love between adults, admiration and love are not synonymous. There are people we admire whom we don't love. Love is something more. And in the second place, why and in what sense is the longing to admire in our nature 'metaphysically?' How would one prove that?"

I had made considerable progress, these past several years, in developing my ideas about self-esteem and autonomy. Now I wanted to deepen my understanding of romantic love. That we longed for that passionate experience seemed self-evident. What was it about us as human beings that could explain this longing? What were its roots in human nature?

When I explained myself more clearly, Ayn shook her head in appreciation. "I'm fascinated by the questions you think of asking. I have to admit that in the sense I now understand you to mean, the question would not have occurred to me." When I said that I wanted to provide a psychological foundation for the vision of romantic love we all shared and upheld to the world, Ayn remarked, "This is one of the few issues in life that I have no wish to argue about or even to explain. I know that the value of romantic love is not axiomatic, but that's almost how I want to treat it."

In seeking to understand romantic love, I wanted to identify the particular psychological needs that romantic love fulfills, and I wanted to grasp the roots of those needs.

I decided that after *The Psychology of Self-Esteem,* writing about the psychology of romantic love would be my next major project. "The two great issues," Ayn remarked.

For some time, as part of my reflections on love, I had been thinking about our desire for human companionship, for people we can respect, admire, and value. We could explain this desire in part by the fact that living and dealing with other people in a social context, trading goods and services and the like, afforded us a manner of survival immeasurably superior to that which we could obtain by ourselves on a desert island. We obviously found it preferable to deal with men and women whose values and character were like our own, and normally we developed feelings of benevolence or affection toward people who shared our values and who acted in ways beneficial to our existence. When in the course of a discussion Ayn raised these points, I remarked that practical, existential considerations such as these did not address the basic question or provide an adequate answer.

The desire for companionship and love rises out of more intimate considerations, reflecting at their root motives that are more psychological than existential. Almost everyone was aware of the desire for companionship, for someone to talk to, to be with, to feel understood by, to share experiences with — the desire for emotional closeness and intimacy with another human being — although there are differences in the intensity with which people experience this desire.

I was impressed by some research reported in Magda Arnold's *Emotion and Personality,* which suggested that an infant's need to love was as powerful as its need to be loved. We have a need to value, to find things in the world which we can care about, can feel excited and inspired by. It is our values that tie us to the world and that motivate us to go on living. If a person were to grow from infancy utterly incapable of finding anything nourishing, beneficial, or pleasurable in the environment, what would inspire such a person to persevere in the struggle for existence?

I reflected that as adults many of us have known the pain of a capacity for love that did not have an outlet. We wish to experience admiration; we long for the sight of human beings and achievements we can truly enjoy and respect. Very well then: one of the values of passionate love was that it allowed us to exercise our capacity to love; it provided a channel for our energy; it was a source of inspiration, a blessing on existence, a confirmation of the value of life. The desire to love, as well as the desire to be loved, contained other elements. What were they? Why is consciousness attracted to consciousness? Why is the experience of affinity and attraction greatest when the consciousness of the other most resembles our own, in values, cognitive style, and sense of life (the meaning of "soul mates")?

Through romantic love, I announced to Ayn, Barbara, and Frank, we experience *psychological visibility* — a powerful need. I had been working toward this idea for more than a year. "We perceive and experience ourselves in a unique way, through the responses of our partner."

I went on to elaborate: Consider the fact that we normally experience ourselves, in effect, as a *process* — in that consciousness itself is a process, an activity, and the contents of our mind are a shifting flow of perceptions, images, organic sensations, fantasies, thoughts, and emotions. Our mind is not an unmoving entity that we can contemplate objectively — that is, contemplate as a direct object of experience — as we contemplate objects in the external world. We normally have, of course, a sense of ourselves, of our own identity, but it is experienced more as a feeling than a thought — a feeling which is very diffuse, which is interwoven with all our other feelings, and which is very hard, if not impossible, to isolate and consider by itself. Our self-concept is not a single concept but a cluster of images and abstract perspectives on our various (real or imagined) traits and characteristics, the sum total of which can never be held in focal awareness at any one time; the sum is experienced but it is not *perceived* as such. In the course of our life, our values, goals, and our missions are first conceived in our mind; they exist as data of consciousness and — to the extent that our life is successful — they are translated into action and objective reality. They became part of the "out there," of the world that we perceive. They achieve expression and reality in material form. This is the proper and necessary pattern of human existence. *To live successfully is to put ourselves into the world, to give objective expression to our thoughts, values, and goals.* Our life is unlived precisely to the extent that this process fails to occur. Yet our most important value — our character, soul, psychological self, spiritual being — whatever name one wishes to give it — can never follow this pattern in a literal sense, can never exist apart from our own consciousness. It can never be perceived by us as a part of the "out there." But we *desire* a form of objective self-awareness and in fact *need* this experience. *Since we are the motor of our own actions, since our concept of who we are, of the person we have evolved, is central to all our motivation, we desire and need the fullest possible experience of the reality and objectivity of that person, of our self.*

When we stand before a mirror, we are able to perceive our own face as an object in reality, and we normally find pleasure in doing so, in contemplating the physical entity that is ourself. There is a value in being able to look and think, That's me. The value lies in the experience of objectivity.

I said to Barbara, Ayn, and Frank, "Is there a mirror in which we can perceive our *psychological* self? In which we can perceive our own soul? Yes. The mirror is another consciousness." When we were alone, Ayn said, "Now you know why the car ride had to happen."

Week by week I kept adding details and refinements to my theory and eagerly presented it first to the Collective and then to our students at NBI. Lecturing on romantic love, I declared:

"When we encounter a person who thinks as we do, who notices what we notice, who values the things we value, who tends to respond to different situations as we do, not only do we experience a strong sense of affinity with such a person but also we can experience our self through our perception of that person. We perceive our self through our lover's reaction. We perceive our person through its consequences in the consciousness — and, as a result, in the *behavior* of our partner. Here, then, we can discern one of the main roots of the human desire for companionship, for friendship, and for romantic love: *the desire to perceive our self as an entity in reality, to experience the perspective of objectivity through and by means of the reactions and responses of other human beings."*

When we had first met, Barbara had given me an experience of visibility greater than any I had experienced before; that made what happened later so excruciatingly painful. With Ayn, I was lifted to a still higher level of visibility; her understanding and appreciation of me, particularly in our early years, had been inspiring and empowering. And each woman had said I made her feel uniquely visible. Everything we said to one another on this subject was true — but it was not the whole truth. It did not address what was missing. We did not confront the areas of *in*visibility we all felt.

Yet the abstract theory I was formulating was driving me closer to that confrontation.

Yes. The subconscious part of our mind can be many steps ahead of the conscious. While we are consciously concerned with the immediate business of our life, the subconscious can be preparing us for our future.

She sat in the third row, near the center aisle, and at first I did not notice her.

It was February 1961. I stood on the podium of the lecture room, preparing to welcome the new class of students to "Basic Principles of Objectivism." There were approximately one hundred eighty people in the room. I looked out at them, feeling relaxed, buoyant, at home in this room and in the world.

"Good evening, ladies and gentleman," I said. "My name is Nathaniel Branden." Barbara stood at the back of the room, leaning against a wall, smiling at me. This was *our* setting — the space she and I had created together. Moved by the pleasure that thought evoked, I did something out of character for me in its informality and in what today would be called male chauvinism. Pointing to Barbara, I added, "And that blonde at the back of the room is my wife — Barbara Branden."

This is the man, thought the young woman in the third row, although it would be years before she would tell me. *He is the man I have wanted and waited for since I was twelve years old. But he is married. And he looks like a man in love. So — he cannot be for me; he will have to remain an abstraction.*

"Most of you," I said to the class, "and most of mankind, believe that philosophy is some vague, abstract, esoteric science, which has nothing to do with your actual life. I shall begin by stating that every one of you — and every living human being — possesses philosophical convictions; that these convictions rule every action and every moment of your life; that without these convictions you would not be able to exist — you would not be able to cross the street, let alone cook a meal, hold a job, or get married. You have no choice about the fact that you do hold a philosophy of life. The only choice you have is whether you know it or not, whether you chose your philosophy consciously or subconsciously, whether your philosophy is true or false."

He is the one. And I will never have him. But now I know he exists.

After a while I became aware of her watching me. A young woman in the third row. Her head raised to me. It was the intensity of her glance that arrested me, and the quality of life in her eyes. Blue eyes, very conscious, set wide apart; high cheekbones; an exquisitely sculptured face; light hair.

I heard myself saying, "The concept of existence and the concept of identity cannot be divorced: to be aware of one, is to be aware of the other. They can only enter the mind together. They are indivisible, in reality and in consciousness. To know *anything*, is to know that that which is, is what it is."

How odd: there is such an expression of exaltation in her glance. Why is she looking at me like that?

PART
THREE

THIRTEEN

IN THE BEGINNING I did not think about the young woman who always sat in the third row — or not very much.

Her glance projected such an intensity of eagerness and joy that I could not help smiling at her when our eyes met. She always smiled back. That was all. I did not approach her, did not speak to her, did not ask anyone her name. She was simply a beautiful point of focus for me sometimes when I was lecturing.

If in one sense I did not quite have a wife, in another sense I had two. There was no space in my consciousness for a third woman. And she looked so young. The very idea was inconceivable — enough so to produce a short circuit in the brain.

Usually I saw her arrive a few minutes before my lecture was to begin. She was tall and slender, and her gaze had a kind of open fearlessness — almost, I thought, like that of a young boy. In contrast to most attractive woman I had observed, she did not seem preoccupied with her appearance; it was as if her looks were just a fact. I liked the way she moved, with the relaxed energy of a person thoroughly at home in her own body. There was something profoundly physical about her and at the same time something profoundly spiritual; her posture and movements suggested the first, the expression in her eyes, the second. She evoked in me a sense of lightness.

I noticed that sometimes, when talking with a group of fellow students, she would display a touch of coltish awkwardness. I liked that; it stressed her vulnerability. Perhaps I saw a touch of my own unacknowledged shyness reflected in her.

When I began lecturing she would sit motionless, looking up at me, almost always with the gaze of someone contemplating a private vision that wiped out everything else. The expression on her face was rapture. There was nothing expectant in her glance; it was as if she were alone with what with she was seeing and what she felt about it.

In some airtight compartment of my mind, I knew that I liked her presence at my lectures. Just that — I liked her being there. The thought hung in a vacuum, connecting to nothing and not to be pursued further.

I lived in a rarefied atmosphere where the passion of pure intellect — so I chose to believe — reigned supreme. My life was organized around that conviction. I had no friendships outside our inner circle and even within the circle the cerebral dominated. For the most part, I had little time for concerns unconnected to Objectivism. I looked at what most people filled their time with and I believed I existed on another plane entirely. Ayn had declared me the apotheosis of her philosophy and this concept became the means of making my isolation tolerable.

I was shocked at my reaction one Monday evening when the young woman did not appear at my lecture: I became tense and irritable. I tried to delay beginning, until my staff looked at me curiously.

The following Monday, when she entered the room, I walked over to her and said, with unexpected sharpness in my voice, "Where were you last week?"

She answered brightly, and as if my question were entirely normal, "I had to work late."

I heard the hard impersonality in my voice and felt powerless to control it. "What kind of work do you do?"

"I'm a fashion model."

"What's your name?"

"Patrecia Gullison."

"How old are you?"

"Twenty-one."

"Young," I announced, and wondered what was the matter with me.

"How old are you?" she asked gaily, with none of the formality and deference I was used to seeing in my students.

"Thirty-one."

Suddenly I felt awkward and foolish. I was behaving like a pompous teenager. A little less stiffly, I said, "Hello, Patrecia."

She grinned as if there was absolutely nothing strange in my manner. "Hello, Nathaniel. Or do people call you Nathan?"

And yet, even after that, for many months I did not think about her — not very much — even though, each week, we now said "Hello" and "Good night."

·   ·   ·

"Time to bring out a new book by Ayn Rand," Bennett Cerf had been declaring for the past two years — and in March 1961 Random House published *For the New Intellectual,* a collection of all the philosophical passages from Ayn's four novels, plus the long title essay that Ayn wrote specifically for this volume. It was all she could bring herself to do. She was not ready for a more ambitious project.

The essay grew out of a series of philosophical discussions in which we talked about the historical steps by which the dominant intellectual and cultural trends of the twentieth century developed. One of my contributions was the suggestion of two metaphors or archetypes: Attila and the Witch Doctor, which represented two philosophical orientations, two psychological symbols, and two historical forces that alternately fought each other and conspired together for control over men's minds and bodies. Ayn liked the symbols and made them the centerpiece of her essay. She wrote:

> The essential characteristics of these two remain the same in all ages: *Attila,* the man who rules by brute force, acts on the range of the moment, is concerned with nothing but the physical reality immediately before him, respects nothing but man's muscles, and regards a fist, a club or a gun as the only answer to any problem [for example, Hitler] — and *the Witch Doctor,* the man who dreads physical reality, dreads the necessity of practical action, and escapes into his emotions, into visions of some mystic realm where his wishes enjoy a supernatural power unlimited by the absolute of nature [for example, Hegel, and all the irrationalist philosophers and religionists who paved the way for Hitler or supported him].

I saw her essay as a dazzling tour de force, exciting in its historical sweep, lucid in its arguments and integrations, dramatic in its imagery, moving and inspiring in its conclusions. It called upon the "new intellectual" to take up the banner of reason and to repudiate the initiation of force as a means of achieving social goals.

Later, some professors of philosophy who admired her work told me that while they agreed with her conclusions in the main, they saw her treatment of historical figures such as Hume, Spencer, and Kant as oversimplified, in some respects erroneous, and gratuitously hostile in ways that did not serve the valid points she wished to make. When they first conveyed this to me, I was unreceptive, since I believed Ayn wrote at a level of broad essentials they did not appreciate; later I came to think they were right. If Ayn disagreed with someone, she rarely confined herself to stating her reasons; in a biting mixture of moralizing and psychologizing, she typically impugned her opponents' motives, often casting them as villains in an almost theatrical sense. Moreover, she was not a conscientious scholar of the history of philosophy; far from it; in the eighteen years of our relationship I cannot recall a single book on philosophy that she read from cover to cover. She skimmed; she read summaries and distillations; and she depended on the reports of her associates, such as Leonard, Barbara, and myself; progressively, Leonard became her primary resource. "What is awesome," one professor remarked to me, "is how often she is right. She hears or reads two paragraphs — and goes right to the heart of the issue. Her intuitions are staggeringly on target, even if the word 'intuition' would probably make her angry."

Sidney Hook attacked *For the New Intellectual* at length in the *New York Times Book Review,* declaring that Ayn was wrong to identify intellectual freedom with economic freedom and to insist that a free mind and a free market are corollaries, since Socrates had a free mind in a society that did not have a free market. In view of how and why Socrates died — he was sentenced to death for teaching ideas of which his fellow citizens did not approve — I found this an astounding argument, especially from a professor of philosophy; I wondered what Hook thought "a free mind" meant. I was determined to write, and publish, a detailed rebuttal of Hook's piece. I knew it would be too long for the *Times* "Letters to the Editor" column. So I raised money from Ayn's friends and admirers and took a full-page *Times* ad. It gave me considerable pride and satisfaction to see my answer in print.

This was the occasion of my discovering anew that I found the atmosphere of intellectual combat exhilarating. Seeing this, Ayn briefly became more cheerful. "It was almost worth Hook's review," she said exuberantly, "to see you in action. You're a born crusader." I agreed happily.

At the age of thirty-one, I was clear in my convictions, knowledgeable in my fields of interest, an effective communicator, and generally enjoyed a high level of equanimity. If I lived with considerable tension, part of me found this a value, as if tension were my natural and desirable state. Whatever the frustrations in my personal life, I enjoyed the work I was doing and the subculture in which I moved. I had created my own world socially and at NBI, and I felt proud of what I had done. Growing up, I had lacked any sense of structure; now I had created for myself the structure I wanted and needed. My life at last had roots.

I was beginning to be asked to lecture at various colleges and universities. I found that I especially liked addressing audiences where there was some hostility toward my ideas, not only because I was surrounded by so much agreement and wanted the excitement of a different experience, but also because I was stimulated by the challenge of turning adversaries around. In retrospect, I see myself at those lectures as combining an incongruous mixture of arrogance and good humor, impatience and benevolence, that sometimes antagonized and sometimes impressed favorably. Whatever my assets or liabilities, I had a good time.

Among my other activities, I was giving a series of radio talks (invited by Pacifica station WBAI-FM) on "the moral revolution in *Atlas Shrugged*." Bennett Cerf was present one evening at Ayn's as we sat listening to a recorded broadcast. Afterward, when Bennett complimented me, I wondered aloud if there might be a worthwhile book in these talks, and Bennett enthusiastically said yes. Soon we were discussing the book I would write — *Who Is Ayn Rand?* The title was inspired by "Who is John Galt?" in *Atlas*. My initial intention was to do three essays, one on Ayn's philosophy, one on her contribution to psychology, and one on her literary accomplishments; that was to be the entire book. But when Bennett suggested that I include a biographical essay on Ayn, I saw a way to launch Barbara as a writer; I suggested that *she* write the biographical essay. Bennett, Ayn, and Barbara were all enthusiastic. It was in preparation for this essay that Barbara and I taped many hours of Ayn talking about her life and development.

The opportunity to convey in print my perception of Ayn's achievements struck me as the most thrilling way to begin my writing career. I did not hesitate to set aside the book I had been writing on anxiety; I was already growing dissatisfied with that project, anyway; I wanted to present my theory of anxiety not by itself but rather in the context of my theory of self-esteem, which I was continuing to develop — and I had begun to wonder if I should begin again, from scratch, with self-esteem as my central subject. For the time being, all that was put on hold, in favor of *Who Is Ayn Rand?*

In the lead essay, "The Moral Revolution in *Atlas Shrugged*," I undertook my own distillation of Ayn's philosophy, principally the ethical and political ideas, to indicate how the novel dramatized these ideas, to place the work in historical context, and to sketch the new type of man Ayn was upholding as a moral ideal.

He is the man passionately in love with existence, and passionately in love with his own consciousness — the man of intransigent rationality and inviolate self-esteem. . . . He is the man who holds nothing above the rational judgment of his mind — neither wishes nor whims nor the unproved assertions of others. He is not the man without desires; he is the man who has no desires held in defiance of reason. He is not the man without emotions; he is the man who does not substitute his emotions for his mind. . . .

Ayn Rand is not the first writer to project a hero who is a genius; nor is she the first writer to project a hero who fights courageously to achieve his chosen goals. But she is the first to project a hero who is a hero *all of the time* — that is, a hero who does not go out to fight a great battle and then come home to marry a hausfrau and to live his *private* life by a less demanding code of values.

This was an important theme of Ayn's and mine: that a true hero wants a heroine — a spiritual equal. I struggled painfully with the implications of this view for my own life, since I knew I did not truly regard Barbara as a heroine. When, not long after writing this passage, I voiced my concern to Ayn, she replied firmly, "Barbara has potential. One day she will fulfill it."

It occurred to me, as a thought leading nowhere, that Ayn seemed keenly interested in seeing my marriage to Barbara preserved, in spite of the negative observations Ayn made from time to time. It did not enter my mind that she would see Barbara as safe, as no conceivable threat to her, whereas a more happily passionate relationship would change Ayn's place in my life. Only years after the break did this become obvious. For me to have a wife like Barbara was convenient for Ayn.

Since Ayn had been compelled in *Atlas* to present her metaethics (her derivation of "man's life as the standard of value") in its barest essentials, I welcomed the opportunity to write a more detailed presentation. In later years, she praised it as being clearer than not only the version in the novel, but also clearer than in her own nonfiction essays such as "The Objectivist Ethics" (*The Virtue of Selfishness*). During a question-and-answer period at NBI, Ayn announced to our students that once I understood an idea I could almost always explain it better than the person who had taught it to me. "Whatever Mr. Branden tells you about my philosophy, you may be sure it is being presented correctly."

I concluded my essay by declaring:

In an age when their ideals have turned most of the earth into a slaughterhouse, the worn-out, fifty-year-old, collectivist intellectuals, posturing as daring, idealistic, adolescent rebels, have become grotesque. They are the representatives of an exhausted, cynical, bloodstained *status quo*. Today, Objectivism is the new radicalism.

Some of those who read *Atlas Shrugged* will recognize that they are being offered that which had never existed before: a rational morality proper to man's nature and to his life on earth. Some of those who read *Atlas Shrugged* will cry . . . 'Nobody's ever said it before! We don't have to believe it!' No, they don't have to believe it. They are free to think or not to think. They are free to hold life — or death — as their standard of value.

But the moral revolution in *Atlas Shrugged* is not to be stopped. The mystics' monopoly on morality has been broken. Man the rational being has found his spokesman and defender, and has been released from his moral underground. That is the imperishable achievement of Ayn Rand.

In my essay on "Objectivism and Psychology," I wrote about the importance of value theory to psychotherapy, about what one could learn about motivation from the characters in Ayn's novels, and the importance of her ideas concerning volition. This essay was by far the briefest, since I did not regard psychology as Ayn's strong point, and my compliments felt a bit stretched to me even then.

I turned with great enthusiasm to "The Literary Method of Ayn Rand," because I was eager to offer an analysis of what I so greatly admired in her as a novelist. I discussed her four books from the standpoint of theme, plot, characterization, and style, stressing her extraordinary talent for integration. I especially enjoyed analyzing details of her style, pointing out how she achieved some of her effects and what extraordinary technique was involved. In regard to *Atlas*, I wanted to communicate the importance of appreciating it as a unique kind of literary event.

Atlas Shrugged — the greatest of her novels — is an action story on a grand scale, but it is a consciously philosophical action story, just as its heroes are consciously philosophical men of action. To those who subscribe to the soul-body dichotomy in literature, *Atlas Shrugged* is a mystifying anomaly that defies classification by conventional standards. It moves effortlessly and ingeniously from economics to epistemology to morality to metaphysics to psychology to the theory of sex, on the one hand — and, on the other, it has a chapter that ends with the heroine hurtling toward the earth in an airplane with a dead motor, it has a playboy crusader who blows up a multibillion dollar industry, a philosopher-turned-pirate who attacks government relief ships, and a climax that involves the rescue of the hero from a torture chamber. Notwithstanding the austere solemnity of its abstract theme, her novel — as a work of art — projects the laughing, extravagantly imaginative virtuosity of a mind who has never heard that "one is not supposed" to combine such elements as these in a single book. To those who believe that "one is not supposed to," Ayn Rand would answer: "Check your premises."

As a consequence of my writing *Who Is Ayn Rand?*, Ayn and I shifted to a deeper level of harmony. Her reproaches almost entirely disappeared. She could hardly complain that I was neglecting her when her rival was this book. Our times together had a warmth and affection that allowed me to imagine, for brief moments, that our problems were behind us.

Once, when I expressed appreciation for something she had done, she replied, with the faintest edge to her voice, "That's me the mind. What of me the woman?" I felt a stab of alarm and pain. Something must have shown on my face; she touched my arm and said softly, "No, that's not right. Sorry, darling. Haven't you shown me enough? Forget I said that." But we both knew that she had said exactly what she meant; only now, because I was writing *Who Is Ayn Rand?*, she did not feel entitled to reproach me. "You're my lifeline to reality," she said. "Without you, how would I exist in this world?"

If Ayn and I grew closer during this period, Barbara and I once again began drifting apart. This pattern had been operative from the beginning: when one relationship was better, the other was worse. The three of us were part of one continually shifting system. None of the problems between Barbara and me had been resolved. The moments when I felt connected to her never lasted.

The world saw her as cool, aloof, perhaps glamorous. I saw her as overly sentimental, waiflike, low in kinetic energy. I had hoped that writing the biographical essay would make her happier. It did, but not much. The theme of gently muted sadness — the forlorn child betrayed by life — remained central to her.

Barbara's insistence that she loved me was as fervent as ever. I was confused and paralyzed when, in the midst of an argument, she would project that I was cruel to be so impatient with her in light of how much I meant to her; I was often left feeling speechless and guilty. *Did* she love me? Then why couldn't she show it in ways more recognizable and meaningful to me? She was now conveying the unmistakable message that she could not live without me; this was new. After a quarrel about her penchant for gloominess and self-pity, or about the relative sexlessness of our marriage, she would tell me, with tears streaming down her face, "I would *die* without you in my life." I would feel grateful, irritated, remorseful. But the question persisted to haunt and mystify me: if I was so important to her, of what did the importance consist?

After such episodes, I would plunge back into writing, into lecturing, into studying, into urging my friends to do more, fight harder, lift themselves higher, for Objectivism and for Ayn — recapturing the single-track focus that allowed me to feel that I was a force nothing could stop.

It was Ayn who sensed the danger and tried to warn me. "You're in love with struggle," she said to me. "In some ways you romanticize it. Is that the legacy of *Jean-Christophe*? Short range, that can be a source of strength. Long range, it can hurt you — it can blind you to issues you need to resolve. You have to be willing to struggle when it's necessary. But remember, the goal is to be serene — like Galt — and to be happy."

I laughed, and answered, "Lots of time to be serene when I'm older." I knew this was not a viewpoint I could defend intellectually, but it was how I felt.

Ayn shook her head, nonreproachfully. "Right now you're in love with your own energy. You're drunk on Nathaniel Branden. I understand that, it's good, but it's not the whole story. Life is more than a battle and being a fighter." In her eyes I could see that she was thinking not of Barbara and me but of herself and me — and that she still hoped for the day when we would be together again in the full sense.

.

"I hate bitterness," Ayn said to me. "That would be the real victory of pain that I don't want to allow — to turn bitter. I've got to keep my sense of the benevolent universe."

She made some version of this statement every few months. She was obsessed with not being affected by pain in any fundamental way, and I always did my best to reassure her that her spirit remained untouched.

"When I sit at my desk alone, I'm happy," she went on. "I reread *Atlas* and nothing else matters. It's when I come out of my office, above all when I have to deal with the world, that I droop. If only I didn't feel such loathing. If only there was someone to respect and admire." She continued to speak as if she were in a vacuum, as if nothing that *Atlas* and NBI were accomplishing in the culture really reached her.

About a year earlier, in 1960, she had given her first university lecture, at Yale Law School. Ayn, Frank, Barbara, and I had driven to Yale together, and Ayn finished writing her talk in the car, fighting motion sickness. That she had left the preparation of her talk to the very end revealed the strength of her resistance to public speaking; this was not the last time I would see her carsick while endeavoring to finish a speech en route. Her subject had been "Faith and Force: The Destroyers of the Modern World." Although there had been no special advance publicity, the large auditorium was filled to overflowing, and additional students listened to the lecture via loudspeakers in another room and in still other speakers outside the building.

Now she was accepting more such invitations. During the early

1960s she spoke at Harvard, Johns Hopkins, the University of Wisconsin, Hunter College, Columbia, Brooklyn College, Purdue, Massachusetts Institute of Technology, Sarah Lawrence, Brown, and the University of Michigan, among others. Invariably she attracted enormous crowds, so much so that typically Barbara or I would call the university in advance, inquire as to the size of the room they had scheduled and then suggest they get a larger one. Students came to applaud her and a few came to hiss, but they came in enormous numbers, electrified by her clarity, unconventionality, and intransigence. One could see hostile students laughing in appreciation at some of her answers, in spite of themselves. She was provocative, challenging, sui generis — she stood before them, often wearing a black cape and a gold dollar-sign pin given to her by Frank — and they responded with an answering passion of their own.

"She," I heard one student remark to another, "is what a teacher *should* be. She *cares* about ideas."

Ayn liked the question periods the most. She did not enjoy lecturing as such, regarding it as a duty, to be done "for the sake of *Atlas*." On this subject Barbara has quoted her as saying, "I didn't, and don't, want to do it. . . . I know why they need to see me in person, that seeing me gives them the reality of Objectivist ideas existing here and now, not merely in a book. If this helps to spread Objectivism, and helps the sale of my books, then it's publicity for which I'm being paid, and I'm willing to do it. I don't like the personal adulation or any of the 'fan' atmosphere. It's not on my terms. I appreciate the intention in an impersonal, professional way, but it means nothing to me personally. When anyone compliments me, my first question is: What's my estimate of the source of the compliments? Is it a mind I respect? When it's a mind that understands what I've done, then it's an enormous pleasure. Anything less than that — no. I don't really want anything but the response of top minds. . . . How I would love to meet a really first-class mind, a first-class person."

I understood this perspective but did not always sympathize. I was not convinced that meeting one or two "first-class minds" would really change anything; they would still be competing with her fictional creations. And if Ayn saw herself as a great innovator, if she believed that she saw certain issues more clearly than anyone else, I felt that there was not much sense in complaining that the world needed time to catch up with her.

In her own writings she ferociously attacked the intellectual establishment, the literary-artistic establishment, the educational establishment, the religious establishment — just about every establishment I could think of. And Newton had taught us that for every action there is an equal and opposite reaction, so it could be argued that the enormity of the establishment's hysterical animosity toward her had its own logic. She knew how to reach people — above all the young — and it seemed to me that if one thought and planned long-range, one should forget about her contemporaries and realize that her most important converts were now in the universities. I continued to wish that she would complain less about this lack of "top minds" and reach out more to the young people eager to learn from her. Her public demeanor remained far too remote, far too moralistic, suspicious, critical, and lacking in simple human warmth. That was her way of staying in control — and of reinforcing her alienation.

Yet I was guilty of the same error, the same manner of inaccessible remoteness, less only, perhaps, in degree — in emulation of this woman who stood at the center of all my values.

In June of 1961, I gave the last lecture in "Basic Principles of Objectivism." It was entitled "Why Human Beings Repress and Drive Underground Not the Worst Within Them but the Best." I wanted my students to honor their own idealism, their hunger for a life superior to the life they saw around them — to have the courage of their own deepest longings and highest aspirations. In some respects this was my favorite lecture in the course and I took great pleasure in giving it.

Tonight there was an unexpected pang at the thought that I would not be seeing Patrecia Gullison again until — I did not know when. I had come to look forward to the sight of her face each week. For the space of an evening my consciousness split in two, part of it giving the lecture and answering students' questions, with Ayn beside me on the platform, while another part disappeared with Patrecia into some special realm where there were feelings but no words. In that dream I was free to experience the unique sense of connection between us without having to reflect on its meaning. The thought of losing the experience felt suddenly, shockingly, painful.

"Have you had a good time here this spring?" I asked her at the end of the evening, when people all around us were saying good-bye to one another. She had waited until I had said good-bye to everyone else.

"I've had a *wonderful* time," she answered radiantly. "Do you know, when I first heard about these lectures, I pictured everyone as being much older and I imagined you as a man in your sixties. I thought I would be the only young person here." She looked at me with a kind of stunning directness, as if there were nothing between us, neither space nor air, and I thought her face went beyond any concept of purity I had ever imagined. I must have frozen, because she asked, abruptly and good-humoredly, as if there was no reason why she shouldn't ask it, "What's happened to your breathing?"

"*Nothing* has happened to my breathing," I insisted, feeling shy and excited at once. "Did you find my lectures clear? Do you find me easy to understand?"

"You?" she said brightly. "Oh, you're *very* easy to understand. I guess that's a compliment to both of us, isn't it?"

"Yes, it is," I answered, happy now to be on safer ground. "I wonder if you'll be taking any more of our lectures."

"I'll be back to take this course again in the fall. And if you give any other course, I'll take that too. I want to learn."

"Why?" I asked challengingly.

"Nothing is as important as learning," she said earnestly.

She went on to tell me that she planned to go to college; her family had not been able to send her and she was now saving every dollar she could from her modeling to finance her education. I commented on a book she had with her, and she said that wherever she went, on any job, she always carried a book. She communicated this in one long rush, as if she wanted me to know everything about her in a single moment and, simultaneously, as if speaking were a distraction.

"What do you want to study in college?" I asked.

"I don't know. Everything. I like history. I want to understand the world and people."

Neither of us wanted to end the conversation, but when I saw Ayn and Barbara looking at me, pleasantly and patiently, I held out my hand and said, "See you in the fall, Patrecia."

She shook my hand with the faintest touch of exaggerated formality, and I was amused at the thought that she was mocking me a little, impishly. I liked the touch of her skin.

"Who was the girl you were talking to?" Ayn asked, as we walked out of the hotel.

"She's a model. Her name is Patrecia Gullison."

"Good appearance," she said with easy, matter-of-fact good will. Ayn was very aware of people's looks and was typically complimentary about any appearance she admired. Not once did I ever sense in her the slightest jealousy about anyone's attractiveness.

"She's very excited about the lectures," I said.

"She has the type of looks I like — you know, long legs, very slender, high cheekbones, light eyes. She's the physical type of my heroines."

And yet, over the summer, I still did not think about Patrecia; not very much.

That August I proposed to Ayn that together we create an intellectual newsletter, an outlet for articles we would write on a variety of subjects and also a means of maintaining contact with students and admirers of her work.

My intention was that Ayn and I would be the chief writers for the newsletter, and the other members of the Collective would also contribute. Ayn liked the idea and all our friends seemed eager to participate. We worked on developing the concept all through the fall, and the first issue of *The Objectivist Newsletter* was planned for January 1962. Ayn became progressively more enthusiastic about the undertaking as the months passed.

Ayn's attorney, Paul Gitlin, drew up the papers of incorporation for the project. Ayn and I were to be equal partners with equal rights and authority in all matters pertaining to the newsletter. "What happens if you two have a falling out?" asked Paul Gitlin. "What happens if there are differences you can't resolve?" Ayn smiled and answered, "Hardly likely. Still, you're right; we must cover that. First, let's agree that nothing is published that the other opposes; each of us will have absolute veto power. Second, if our differences are basic and can't be resolved, we will terminate publication, so that neither of us will be able to profit from the work and contribution of the other."

Ayn and I were listed as publishers and editors; Barbara, as managing editor; Elayne, as circulation manager.

In early fall Barbara went home to visit her family in Winnipeg and came back with more reports of Wilfred's growing interest in Objectivism and his desire to involve himself somehow in our work. The thought occurred to me that perhaps some romantic interest in Wilfred had reawakened, but the idea felt remote and not fully serious.

Barbara and I gave parties at regular intervals and almost always the pattern was the same: I would look forward to the event in advance, begin the evening with high enthusiasm, and an hour or two later be bored, restless, and remote. "It's like clockwork," Barbara chided me more than once. "Two hours into the party, your eyes begin to glaze over. You're no longer there. I don't know why you keep suggesting we give parties."

I knew what she was saying was true and I searched my mind for an explanation. I felt that I started out really *wanting* the party.

"Of course you do," Barbara said, "because you're frustrated for some form of pleasure and some form of social life. Then you get bored because deep down you don't like our friends very much."

I protested, "What are you talking about? What do you mean, I don't like them? Of course I like them."

"I don't mean you *dis*like them. I mean, they're not really your kind of people. Think about it. Leonard? I know you're fond of him, but look how often he gets on your nerves; he is so dependent. Allan Blumenthal? Much too weak for you. Joan? You find her pretentious and shallow. Alan Greenspan? You like talking to him when you two are alone and then only about economics. Mary Ann? When have you ever had anything to say to her? Edith? You enjoy her intelligence. Is that the same thing as truly liking the person? You tell me. Elayne and Harry? Well, they're different — they're family." She went on to name a few other people who had come into our life. "Come on, you know what I mean. You enjoy them all — to a point. But if any one of them were not here, would it make a difference to you?"

I felt what she was saying was true, but not necessarily the whole truth. "Well, then, if you say I'm not that crazy about the Collective — who *do* I like?"

"Apart from Ayn? No one." This struck me as devastatingly true, at a very deep level of my being, and even with Ayn I —

"You *want* to like people," Barbara said with genuine compassion. "You really want to. And you would do anything you could to help any of our friends. All right, maybe you do like them, in a way, but — do they *excite* you?"

I asked her about her own feelings, and she answered, "I share your attitude to some extent, but I think I can enjoy people more than you can. Yes, definitely, I am more fond of the Collective than you are."

My perception was confused by the fact that on some occasions I would look around the room at our friends and feel love, or something very close to it — affection, benevolence, deep caring — and I would think: this is my family, not just Elayne and Harry, but all of them. They are good human beings; they are all struggling; they are decent, conscientious, dedicated. Look how far all of them have come.

Sometimes, by myself, I would be hit by a sudden attack of loneliness — I could not have said for what. There was an unfamiliar emptiness at my center. Once I had imagined that all loneliness ended with the arrival of Ayn in my life; now I knew that in some way that relationship was making the loneliness worse — perhaps because I did not feel fully free to be unhappy. But I loved working on *Who Is Ayn Rand?*, I loved giving my lectures, I loved the sense of building my own world — of which the projected newsletter was the newest facet — and these activities felt almost like a form of self-nurturing that helped me preserve equilibrium.

·   ·   ·

It was perfectly natural, I told myself as I approached the start of "Basic Principles of Objectivism" at the end of September, that I should be looking forward to seeing Patrecia Gullison again. She was attractive, she had a bright kind of energy, she was enthusiastic about Objectivism — she was a thoroughly *likable* human being. I enjoyed looking at her and talking to her. She was practically a child, twenty-one years old, ten years my junior; even if there were no Barbara and Ayn in my life, there would be no challenge in anyone that young. The frequency with which I reminded myself of her youth should have been a warning to me; it wasn't.

She arrived only a few minutes before the lecture was to begin and there was no opportunity to talk to her. When she looked at me throughout the lecture, I thought she was a little remote, a little pulled back, as if contemplating me from a greater distance. The class was an unusually large one, and afterward Ayn and I were surrounded by students eager to extend the question period. When I was able to look for Patrecia, she had gone. The following week she arrived early, as warm and open as she had ever been, and almost immediately we began to talk.

"You didn't wait to say hello last week," I said without reproach.

"I wanted to see what it would feel like not to," she answered cheerfully, as if the issue had no charge and there was no reason not to be truthful. While I groped for some appropriate response, she went on, smiling, "I heard you grew up in Toronto. I was born there!"

In answer to my questions, she told me that her family had moved from Toronto to California when she was seven; that she had a sister Leisha, who was an identical twin, a brother several years older, Ralph, and another sister who was older still, Anne; that her family had "pioneered" for a while in California, "in the middle of nowhere."

"The man who was supposed to build us a house and have it waiting when we arrived from Canada disappeared with our money, leaving us with this empty stretch of land; when I was twelve years old I helped dig for water: *it was so exciting!*"

Her father was a hairdresser and her mother operated a nursery school in Palo Alto, and they had divorced some years ago. Patrecia and her sister Leisha were both represented by the Eileen Ford Agency and sometimes did television commercials as twins. They had both come to New York from Palo Alto only at the beginning of the year, shortly before Patrecia came to my first lecture.

"You mean there are *two* of you," I could not help exclaiming.

She laughed. "Well — not really. Psychologically, Leisha and I are very different. I don't know if I could ever persuade Leisha to come to lectures like this. I'm going to try."

Her eyes were the most beautiful shade of blue; they had such abundant life in them. Her forehead was broad; I recalled a line of Victor Hugo's that Ayn had once quoted, to the effect that a lot of forehead in a face was like a lot of sky in a painting.

"Why do you like the lectures so much?" I asked her.

"It's what Miss Rand and her novels — and now you — represent to me. *Sanity.*"

Sanity. Just what I had once told Ayn she gave me.

"Patrecia, you're an interesting person."

"So are you," she announced, and I could not tell whether I saw a touch of humor in her eyes.

In November I learned that she had begun dating a fellow NBI student, Lawrence Scott, who had heard Ayn's speech at Yale and had become interested in Objectivism. He and I exchanged a few sentences and he struck me as a thoroughly decent and attractive man, intelligent and serious. Still, Patrecia continued to look at me as she had always looked at me.

That fall Ayn received an invitation to speak at Ford Hall Forum in Boston. She fell in love with this particular organization and would speak there every spring until the year of her death, with only one exception when illness made an appearance impossible.

At first she had been reluctant to accept the invitation because she associated Ford Hall Forum with the political left; but she was treated royally by her hosts, drew enormous crowds from her first lecture onward — admirers came from all over the country to hear her there — and this prestigious institution became her favorite lecture platform.

Her first lecture, delivered on December 17, 1961, was "America's Persecuted Minority: Big Business." Early that day, to the surprise and delight of the people at Ford Hall Forum, lines formed around the block for tickets. Here is how her speech began — which I quote because it captures the typical emotional quality of an Ayn Rand lecture:

> If a small group of men were always regarded as guilty, in any clash with any other group, regardless of the issues or circumstances involved, would you call it persecution? If this group were always made to pay for the sins, errors, or failures of any other group, would you call *that* persecution? If this group had to live under a silent reign of terror, under special laws, from which all other groups were immune, laws which the accused could not grasp or define in advance and which the accuser could interpret in any way he pleased — would you call *that* persecution? If this group were penalized, not for its faults, but for its virtues, not for its incompetence, but for its ability,

not for its failure, but for its achievements — would you call *that* persecution?

If your answer is "yes" — then ask yourself what sort of monstrous injustice you are condoning, supporting, or perpetrating. That group is the American businessman.

Most of the Collective had driven to Boston for this event and everyone was thrilled and excited by the overflow crowd, the enthusiasm of the audience, the crackling tension of the question-and-answer period, the thunderous applause that refused to stop. To us it was another sign that Objectivism was on the march.

In *Atlas Shrugged* Ayn had portrayed the American businessman at his best. She had also written an indictment of the pro-statist businessman who is often mistaken for a representative of capitalism, the type who prefers government protection to free trade, political privilege to competition, and legislation that gives them special favors denied to others. This latter type is in fact the chief villain in the novel. And yet Ayn had no real interest in business or businesspeople as such — "just as I had no significant interest in architecture, except as a vehicle for *The Fountainhead*." Business was a symbol; in her writing it stood for free trade and free minds, for productive achievement, for the material means of human survival, for the glory of life on earth.

Certainly big business did not support her or her work in any way: did not buy and distribute *Atlas* in quantity, as one might imagine it would; did not champion her publicly; did not write her letters of appreciation; did not invite her to address boards of directors. I suspected that for most businesspeople she was far too radical; she advocated *total* laissez-faire. Then there was her stand on religion. And the business community's fear of controversy — any kind of controversy.

My impression was that her message was better received by small- and middle-level business than by big business, which was more invested in the status quo. Taxes on corporations, for instance, tended to protect older, more established businesses against aggressive, talented newcomers for whom capital accumulation was made much more difficult. Old money rarely favored laissez-faire. Those who *consistently* support the separation of state and economics are a minority in any economic group.

I said to Ayn, "One day I really ought to write an article entitled 'Big Business Versus Capitalism.' "

"I'm afraid you're right," she answered.

"What you've given us in *Atlas* is business 'as it might be and ought to be.' "

"And *sometimes* is. What is realistic is my presentation of the *process* of industrial achievement; what is romantic is that I created characters who match that process."

Ayn's penchant for seeing life as a great novel in which good and evil are locked in combat was very central to her psychology (her treatment of business was only one example). This was very evident in *Atlas Shrugged* and was no less evident in her personal communications. There was a strain of Manichaeism in her outlook — not the literal dualistic Gnostic religion first preached by Mani, of course, but rather the tendency to see good and evil as essentially separate and opposed principles, and to interpret all human experience in terms of their confrontation. Mani had taught that the mixture of good and evil in the world was itself a manifestation of the evil principle at work, and in secular terms Ayn thought similarly.

My own tendency was to think more biologically — to see life as a struggle for adaptation, so that behavior was best understood in terms of survival strategies and coping processes, which may be more or less appropriate, more or less in accord with the individual's actual long-term interests. The term *biocentric* (life-centered) had not yet entered my vocabulary, but its meaning was already present in my thinking. I compared the concepts of good and evil to the concepts of health and illness; they had no near-religious charge for me; they merely designated that which was beneficial and harmful to our physical and spiritual-psychological well-being. The notion of sin was relatively absent from my thinking, whereas in Ayn's, on some level it was still very active. When I saw behavior I did not admire, or strongly disapproved of, I was still inclined to wonder: what is this person trying to accomplish?

Of course I pronounced moral judgments; but I was never the passionate moralist — or moralizer — that Ayn was. In retrospect, I would say that in emotional terms I had achieved far greater separation of morality from any religious connotation or influence; to me, "immorality" was a bad strategy chosen when one could have chosen better. Not that Ayn would have said otherwise about the literal meaning of immorality; but she had a need to make severe moral pronouncements on every conceivable occasion, charged with heat and indignation. Ayn used the word *evil* frequently; I used it too, but sparingly.

We were aware of our differences but did not attach much significance to them. Ayn was satisfied that I was passionate about my values and convictions, even if my form of expression was different from hers. "Your perspective comes from being a psychologist," she said. "It's not a fundamental difference between us."

As I reread the articles we wrote for *The Objectivist Newsletter*, this difference in our focus struck me as very apparent, in spite of the inappropriate moralism sometimes present in my writing. Ayn's pieces were far more filled with the language of moral contempt. In my post-1964 articles, when *The Objectivist Newsletter* became a magazine, *The Objectivist*, I see the difference as more apparent still, no doubt reflecting shifts in my thinking that were not yet fully conscious.

Nonetheless, there was a streak of Objectivist puritanism in all the Collective members that at times drove out normal human warmth; the zealous concern with being morally irreproachable, combined with a tendency toward emotional repression, often inhibited spontaneity and natural affection. My own affectionate impulses, when they were not blocked entirely, often took the form of psychological encouragement, or pats on the head, or an occasional squeeze of an arm, which rarely closed the distance between the other person and me. In other moods, I could project an austerity that, I was told, could be intimidating and anxiety provoking. The paradox was that, just because Ayn took her irreproachability for granted, she was often the freest in communicating positive feelings toward her friends; in some moods she was kinder and more emotionally expressive than anyone else in our circle.

The tendency to stiffness and formality was noticeable in many students of Objectivism, especially when more than two people were present. "Two Objectivists by themselves can sometimes have a good time," someone said to me, "but as soon as you add a third person, everyone gets very self-conscious. And parties are often a disaster. No one wants to be thought 'mindless.' "

There were wonderful exceptions. One was a baseball game held in Central Park between the "Attilas" and the "Witch Doctors," whose members included most of the Collective, plus various NBI students. What made the event so special and so enjoyable was that all matters of intellectual rank vanished and only baseball mattered. I smile whenever I remember the unconstrained laughter of that very atypical afternoon.

Many smaller Objectivist circles had formed throughout the city and throughout North America. Many friendships, marriages, love affairs, job opportunities, and business associations were born out of these meetings. Ayn and I enjoyed the idea of our own ever-expanding subculture.

Occasionally word would reach me of someone being "excommunicated" from one of these groups because of some betrayal of Objectivist standards. It seemed to me that some of these students were more severe than Ayn or I in their condemnation of infractions. "They're more royalist than the king," Ayn would comment wryly. "I guess all intellectual movements have to cope with one aspect or another of the 'true believer syndrome,' " I remarked once. Some years earlier Ayn had discovered Eric Hoffer's *The True Believer* and had recommended it to Barbara and me. "Because of our emphasis on rationality and independence," Ayn had confidently forecast, "this won't be a problem for us." I now knew that she was overly optimistic so far as our followers were concerned; I did not yet recognize that she was mistaken even about the inner circle.

Allan and Joan had their own private sphere where, I heard, they did reign like king and queen. Some members of their group were former therapy clients of Allan's — or current ones. After initially resisting the idea, Allan had allowed Joan to persuade him that it was appropriate for him to ask some of his clients to pose as models for her. The central focus in this circle was the arts. Barbara and I wondered about the fact that so many of the men in the group were homosexual. A member of the circle subsequently told me, "We got the message that Joan was supposed to represent well-realized femininity, and through her we might learn to understand women better."

Since I had sponsored him, I was happy when people communicated to me that Allan had significantly helped them. On the other hand, I was uneasy about a joke that began to circulate, to the effect that if Howard Roark had gone to Allan Blumenthal for advice, Allan would have told him not to be so pretentious and to give more serious thought to being practical and earning a living. "A lot of these people have no sense of reality," Allan said to me by way of explanation. "They're grandiose. They all imagine they're geniuses." I understood this phenomenon, of course; I had seen it myself. It did not occur to me then that in his zeal to discourage grandiosity, he might also discourage legitimate ambition, much as his own dreams had been discouraged — that his mother's voice might speak through him to his clients.

"When Allan told me I was a social metaphysician," one of his former clients said to me, reminiscing about these years, "he conveyed not only a verdict of moral condemnation — all of you did that when you spoke of social metaphysics — but also a more personal distaste, almost a wrinkling up of his nose, a kind of fastidious pulling back, as if I had an odor. And yet, what drove me crazy at the time was, if I understood the concept at all, if it meant surrender to the minds of others in some fairly basic ways — how could you or Allan or anyone maintain that *he himself did not fit the diagnosis*?"

Ayn had observed that in the main the lectures on Objectivism had made "better people" of even our least promising students; but she had not defined what she meant by "better people." She could have said, correctly, that they were inspired by the ideal of rationality as a way of life; inspired by the ideals of independence, honesty, justice, and productiveness; committed to self-responsibility. All of this, we saw, had positive consequences for their behavior.

What they would not have learned from us was the importance of listening to their own inner signals, those messages from the organism which are not encoded in conceptual language. If anything, they would have learned to be almost ritualistically suspicious of the nonverbal or the subconscious. This, we did not see — or, if we did, did not perceive as a problem. Certainly our students would have learned nothing of "the wisdom of the body"; many of them would be reinforced in alienation from the body. We did not see this, either; did not see that an adequate psychology had to address the entire organism, not merely the neocortex.

Neither would our students have learned anything about kindness or compassion; they learned only an intellectualized kind of "benevolence," which had little to do with real encounters between real human beings. Yet if "Man's Life" is the standard of value, then in a world in which accidents, misfortunes, and disasters are real and continuing possibilities, kindness and compassion have survival value. Granted it is an error to treat them as the most important virtues, above rationality or integrity (which would make suffering the most important part of life); but they *are* virtues nonetheless. I am not speaking of self-sacrifice or of "compassion" coercively engineered by a government, but of private, voluntary mutual aid, and generosity, and good will. These traits and practices are life-supporting. A society whose members value them is more adaptive biologically than one whose members do not. If life is the standard of the good, then kindness, compassion, and a spirit of mutual aid are virtues to be cultivated. This was a logical implication of our own ethics that we did not grasp. Some of us were kinder and more compassionate than others, but that was, in effect, a psychological matter, not judged to be philosophically significant.

Meanwhile, the requests for our lectures came streaming in from all over the world. We began hearing of Objectivist study groups as far away as India and Australia. We were besieged with requests for more information about the philosophy.

"I really must write a comprehensive treatise on Objectivism," Ayn said many times. I sat through hours of hearing her think aloud about this project, knowing it would never happen because the emotional energy to do it was not there.

·　　·　　·

As planned, *The Objectivist Newsletter* began publication in January 1962. The lead article, written by Ayn, was entitled "Choose Your Issues," and dealt with the importance of not allowing the enemy to choose the terms of the battle, and of knowing what is essential and what is not.

> Neither a man nor a nation can have a practical policy without any basic principles to integrate it, to set its goals and guide its course. Just as the United States, having abandoned its own principles, is floundering aimlessly in international affairs, is unable to act and is merely *reacting* to the issues chosen and raised by Soviet Russia — so, in domestic affairs, the "conservatives" are unable to act and are merely *reacting* to the issues chosen and raised by the statists, thus accepting and helping to propagate the statists' premises.

Barbara wrote a review of Ludwig von Mises's *Planned Chaos,* introducing Von Mises to what was to become a new and ever-widening audience. The entire Austrian school of free enterprise economics was to gain a much broader readership in consequence of our reviews and recommendations. Alan Greenspan wrote a piece entitled "The Crisis Over Berlin."

> Over a piece of real estate scarcely the size of Rhode Island, the Russians have brought the world to a state of war. . . .
> History rarely offers so controlled an experiment in rival economic systems as has been seen in Berlin during the last decade. In the late 1940's, when the rest of Western Europe was sinking under a morass of socialistic experiments, West Germany, including West Berlin, turned instead to free enterprise (at least predominantly). The results were dramatic: from a country defeated and devastated by war, it rose to become spectacularly prosperous. Meanwhile, East Germany and East Berlin barely emerged from the rubble.

I wrote on the relationship between reason and emotion. In the months ahead, while I occasionally wrote in other fields such as ethics and economics, I tended to favor psychological themes. Leonard, Edith Efron, and Robert Hessen, a young historian who had joined our circle and worked at NBI, contributed to future issues.

Ayn began writing a weekly column for the *Los Angeles Times,* and subsequently went into national syndication. Her ability to remain surprising was always in evidence: for one column she wrote an unusually moving piece on the death of Marilyn Monroe; in its sensitive appreciation of what the actress stood for in the minds of a great many people, it revealed yet another aspect of Ayn's complex personality. But a little more than a year later she abandoned this project, in part because it required too much reading of and attention to current events.

In 1962 NBI began publishing Ayn's lectures and essays, as well as those of Barbara, myself, and a few other people, in pamphlet form. An essay of Barbara's, "The Moral Antagonism of Capitalism and Socialism," was adapted from a radio talk she had given. Eventually we established NBI Book Service to sell these pamphlets by mail along with the books we were recommending to our students. NBI had moved out of our apartment and now had regular offices, shared with *The Objectivist Newsletter,* and an expanding number of employees. In this environment Barbara seemed to flower; she became an excellent administrator and handled the daily flow of business with cheerful competence. I loved watching her in this arena; she was most alive here; I felt validated in the sense of connection I still felt with her. She had said, "Give me a barricade!" and in our offices she seemed to have found it. Here she was a crusader, and she felt in her element. If we both had a need for a great moral adventure, which was central to our motivation during those years, it was fulfilled by Objectivism; the happiness this provided allowed many other frustrations to be tolerated far longer than they otherwise might have been.

Once I said to Ayn, "I see us all as children of the Enlightenment, very much part of that historical tradition — life on earth to be transformed through education."

Who Is Ayn Rand? was scheduled for publication in June 1962. I wanted Ayn to be pleased with the final result, and she said she was, but sometimes when we discussed the book I noted some reserve. When I asked her about it, she said, "The book is wonderful. But you and Barbara shouldn't have had to write it, not my own students; it's almost humiliating. It should have been written by an outsider." I quoted this to Barbara, who sighed. "I wish — just once — Ayn could be completely satisfied about something."

"There's someone at the lectures you two should get to know," Joan said to Barbara and me one evening. "Her name is Patrecia Gullison. Her boyfriend is Larry Scott. Allan and I think they're a really nice couple."

"Patrecia is a very unusual girl," Allan agreed enthusiastically.

"In what way?" I inquired carefully.

"Well, she —" Joan began eagerly and then broke off. "You'll have to see for yourself. She's just different. It's hard to explain."

I did not know whether Barbara noticed the looks on their faces, something young and attractively vulnerable that I was not used to seeing. Barbara said that she would look for Patrecia at the lectures.

"The clearest thing I can say about her," Joan added, "is that when you're with her, you like the way you feel about yourself."

"I think Patrecia and Larry are engaged," Allan remarked.

When Patrecia and Larry had coffee with us, Barbara agreed with the Blumenthals that they were an appealing couple, although she did not share their particular reaction to Patrecia. As far as I could tell, she found her "nice" but unremarkable. I consciously chose to focus most of my attention on Larry, who kept raising philosophical questions that I enjoyed answering, knowing for whom I was showing off.

They informed us that they planned to be married in June. I congratulated them both, thinking idly that Larry was the same age as I, which meant he was ten years older than Patrecia. But they looked very attractive together; he did not seem too old for her. If someone had asked me what I was feeling, I would have said that I was happy for them, in a detached, benevolent sort of way, and I would not have found significance in the numbness that felt like a general anesthetic to my body.

One evening, after a lecture, Patrecia announced, in a state of high excitement, "*Miss Rand invited Larry and me over for a visit!*"

Later, when I asked Ayn about it, she told me she was impressed by them both; she saw them as serious, idealistic. "I think I agree with Joan; Patrecia has a lightness of spirit that's very interesting, not ordinary. Of course she's very young; we'll have to see what she grows into." Then Ayn chuckled and announced, "I invited myself to their wedding. All four of us will be getting an invitation." The feeling of numbness deepened. "Terrific," I said.

Barbara and I had learned that Larry was quite a good amateur photographer, and we asked him to take our pictures for the jacket of *Who Is Ayn Rand?* He came with Patrecia to our apartment on an afternoon in May. When the photographic session was over Larry had to leave for an appointment, and we invited Patrecia to stay on for a visit.

I wanted Barbara to like her, to appreciate her as I did. When I saw Barbara warming to Patrecia's bright energy and unself-conscious openness — as Patrecia talked about her life, about what *The Fountainhead* and *Atlas Shrugged* meant to her, about the modeling profession, about her admiration for Larry — I felt a quiet exhilaration. I also felt that I liked Barbara more in this moment, because she was conveying a friendliness and good will that matched my sense of the occasion.

Patrecia made no attempt to disguise her pleasure at being in our apartment and answering our questions and being the focus of our attention. In her eagerness to make herself known to us, her words sometimes tripped over each other, her voice rose in uncontrolled excitement — "Oh, God, listen to how loud I'm getting!" She had a youthful vulnerability that made her totally unlike anyone else we knew.

Something Patrecia said prompted Barbara to ask if she ever felt bored, for example, if she were on a date with an uninteresting man. Looking surprised at the question, Patrecia answered that she never felt bored. "I think people who get bored easily are people who are boring themselves, part dead inside and looking to others to make life interesting. There's always ways to make an evening entertaining, if you're not passive." I asked her how, and she said, "This will probably sound crazy, I don't know if I can explain it, but there's a kind of music inside of me, and I can bring that music to anything I'm doing — and sometimes I can draw music out of whoever I'm talking to, at least while I'm talking to them."

Barbara smiled blankly, pulling back a little. "I understand you perfectly," I declared, ignoring Barbara's puzzled glance.

It was time to take our dog, Muttnik, for a walk, and I asked if the two women would join me. Barbara said, "I'm a little tired. I feel like reading for a while. Why don't the two of you go?"

On the street Patrecia said, "I'm afraid I don't express myself very clearly sometimes. I wish I were more articulate. I think I might have been a bit intimidated by Barbara; she speaks so well." I asked her if I intimidated her. "Oh, no," she answered. "Because I always know you're going to understand me; so I'm not afraid of how I'll sound; so I speak more clearly."

I complimented her on her candor in naming her fear; she shrugged and said easily, "Why shouldn't I name it? Everyone is afraid of something, at one time or another. I'm not afraid to admit it; a lot of people are. That's not just fear, it's cowardice. I'm not a coward."

A young boy went sailing past us on his bicycle, an expression of rapture on his face, and pointing to him as he went by, Patrecia said, "Oh, look. Isn't his face perfect? There's something so innocent about a young boy. His bicycle is his spaceship."

I told her that I had felt that sometimes when I was a boy, and she answered, as if uttering an obvious truth, "One of the best things about you is that you're friendly with that side of yourself." I did not think I had a single friend who would have made that statement or even agreed with it.

I was very conscious of how she moved; she had a superabundant energy that seemed to spill out of her gestures and steps, like a torrent of life. This was combined with a gracefulness that at one moment made me think of the movements of a dancer and the next of an athlete; it was the gracefulness, I realized, of a person for whom the body is experienced as the primary vehicle of self-expression; the body as soul-in-action.

"You have a way of moving that projects a magnificent enjoyment of life," I said casually.

She received this with delight, as a precious compliment. "When I was sixteen, I wanted to be a dancer. I danced all the time." When I asked her why she didn't pursue it, she answered, "It wasn't mental enough. I knew in the end it would be frustrating. I wanted an outlet for my mind." I asked, "What might that be?" For the briefest of moments I saw sadness touch her eyes, as she said, "I don't know yet."

Then, without transition, she began speaking of how much she liked Ayn's treatment of man in her novels. "To me, that's one of the most important things about her as a writer." I had the sense that she took some pleasure in leaping from subject to subject unexpectedly, challenging me to follow. "Can you believe there are readers who are surprised when they learn Ayn Rand is a woman? Is that stupid? Only a woman could write her novels; only a woman could have her perspective on the male characters. The passion for the shape of a man's body, for example. Her kind of man-worship. When I read it, I felt, '*That's me*. That's the way I feel — about man the ideal, the abstraction.' Not most of the actual men one meets, of course. When I first read *The Fountainhead*, I was excited from the very beginning — the description of Howard Roark standing on the cliff — in love with Ayn's angle of vision, the way she looks at things. It felt like coming home to myself."

We walked silently for a while, with Muttnik pulling forward on the leash. Patrecia was grinning, as open in her happiness as the boy on the bicycle had been. I liked the absence of any attempt to appear poised or sophisticated. With my peripheral vision I contemplated the purity of the lines of her face, her look of spiritual cleanliness, as her steps blended with mine. She asked, in a manner of buoyant, youthful trust, "Do you know how *thrilling* this walk is for me?"

"I think she's a remarkable person," I said to Barbara later, wanting to believe that Barbara's values and mine were aligned; wanting not to hide my enthusiasm from her but to share it.

Barbara shrugged noncommittally, as if the matter were of no importance, and I did not press further.

Patrecia's twin sister, Leisha, now attended my lectures. The resemblance was truly startling. At thirty feet I could still mistake one woman for the other, although Patrecia's features were slightly finer. Even close-up, some people were confused.

Leisha elicited in me none of the feelings Patrecia inspired. She conveyed anxiety and a desperate desire to please, eager to be perceived as "good." She could hardly have been more conventional in her values, I thought. Where I saw Patrecia as active, assertive, independent, I saw Leisha as passive, accommodating, dependent — by conventional standards, more feminine. She had initially been reluctant to come to the lectures because Patrecia's enthusiasm had scared her a little. "In the modeling field," Patrecia mentioned once, without rancor, "most people like Leisha more." Reflecting on the difference in my response to the two women, I thought how much more important the spiritual was than the physical in terms of what draws one human being to another.

I learned that Patrecia, the younger of the two, had spent the first eleven days of her life in an incubator. And yet from infancy onward, her parents perceived her as the most aggressive member of the family, the most exploratory and adventuresome. "I always felt Leisha was closer to me," her mother had told her, "because Leisha was more timid, more afraid. I could understand that. To me, you were always a teeny bit of a stranger."

One evening at NBI, I saw Patrecia talking to Joan Kennedy Taylor, and I joined them. Joan lived a considerable distance from the hotel where I lectured and I offered to give her a lift home; I had never done this before. Casually I said to Patrecia, "Come along with us. I'll drop you off too."

I drove Joan home first, then headed south again, through Central Park, toward Patrecia's apartment on the East Side. It was a warm night and the top of the convertible was down.

We did not speak. Patrecia sat with her head thrown back, her eyes closed, her face lifted to the night. The delicate, sculptured planes of her face projected, not sensuality, but near-transcendence. She looked ecstatic.

It was the shocking suddenness of my own response that stunned me: in the next instant I was aware only of the slenderness of her body under her summer dress, of the line of her legs and hips, and for one terrifying, intoxicating moment I thought that my hand was going to reach down to take possession of her — simply, as a right — certain that it was what she wanted. But I was Nathaniel Branden, rational being, and this was clearly an aberration that had no place in the structure of my life.

When she got out of the car, across the street from the apartment she now shared with Larry, I called, "See you at the wedding!" and drove off.

The next time I saw her, May 31, she was walking down the aisle on her father's arm. Larry stood waiting for her, smiling proudly and happily, and Barbara sat on one side of me, Ayn and Frank on the other.

"She looks beautiful," Ayn whispered. I was unable to answer or to move — because, now, for the first time, the thought was clear and unmistakable in my mind: I do not like this. I do not like Patrecia marrying another man.

The intensity of my reaction was shocking: it was if I were experiencing a personal violation, as if my most private possession were being taken from me. The questions my reactions raised were terrifying — except that I did not feel terrified, I felt excited, agitated, absorbed by my own passion.

Standing in line behind Ayn, Frank, and Barbara, waiting to congratulate the bride and groom and their families, I thought that in this context it would be permissible for me to hold her for an instant and to kiss her, and I felt reckless about what she would or would not sense in my touch.

Then we were off to the restaurant where the wedding party was being held — and I could feel nothing but the memory of her skin and her mouth. From a great distance, I was astonished to notice that I continued to talk and act normally. But inside, I was completely out of control. I moved from person to person, unable to concentrate. I chatted with Leisha and with Patrecia's mother and father, Elsie and Raymond. Raymond had read Ayn and admired her, and tried to talk to me about it; I heard nothing. Then Patrecia broke through the crowd and asked that Ayn, Frank, Barbara, and I pose with Larry and her for wedding pictures. The experience was disorienting: how could she seem happily in love with Larry and at the same time look at me in that special way of hers that caused the ordinary context of my life to vanish? Next day they were scheduled to depart for a honeymoon in Europe.

Later that evening, alone with Barbara in our apartment, I told myself, All right. Back to reality.

In early June, a few days after the wedding, Barbara and I stood together on Fifth Avenue, looking at the prominent display of *Who Is Ayn Rand?* in Brentano's window.

Since the age of fourteen, I had known I wanted to be a writer. Now, seeing a dozen or more copies of my first book in Brentano's window, I felt transported. My problems with Barbara and Ayn vanished; Patrecia was a pleasantly distant memory. Nothing existed but the books in front of me.

The expression on her face told me that Barbara felt as I did. We held hands. We knew why we had come together and why we had remained together: for the values that had led us to this moment. We were where we belonged.

Or so I told myself.

Neither Barbara nor I was prepared to face how far apart we had drifted. Not fully. We might acknowledge the feeling sometimes but not its wider implications. We could not imagine an alternative to the life we were living. We thought of happiness not in terms of our personal lives but in terms of the progress of Objectivism. We had been euphoric, for example, when Ayn had received a letter from L. Quincy Mumford, Librarian of Congress, in which he had written: "Among the most widely discussed philosophies of our time is that associated with your writings. In your fiction and essays you have made the Objectivist philosophy an issue affecting many levels of public discourse. When the history of our time is written, your work will have a prominent place. In order to insure that your work will be the subject of informed study, I invite you to place your manuscripts and personal papers in the Library of Congress." Our shared pleasure in events such as this was our substitute for the fulfillments of a real marriage.

Another such pleasure, in the fall of 1963, was our trip with Ayn and Frank to Lewis and Clark College in Portland, Oregon, where Ayn was to receive an honorary Doctor of Humane Letters. The entire student body and faculty was to read *Atlas Shrugged* and there would be two days of discussions, some led by Ayn, some led by the two of us together. Ayn and Frank were in high spirits. For two days I forgot every problem of my life and was simply and uncomplicatedly happy.

Barbara and I thought of progress in terms of the sales of Ayn's books, the lecture invitations, the radio broadcasts, the articles on Ayn's work now appearing with increasing frequency, the student enrollment at NBI, the number of cities across the continent where our lectures were offered, the people who were entering our lives as a consequence of their response to *Atlas Shrugged*. We watched the flow of new people with passionate interest.

What looked like an important friendship had developed between Ayn and John Hospers, a professor of philosophy at Brooklyn College. He had heard Ayn speak there and had been greatly impressed in spite of the fact that his orientation was radically different from hers in virtually every sphere. He later wrote several widely used textbooks and was destined for a distinguished career. Reading *Atlas,* he became wildly enthusiastic. He visited Ayn regularly to discuss philosophy, and became a total convert politically and a partial convert ethically;

their enduring differences centered on epistemology, metaphysics, and aesthetics. Hospers was more sympathetic to logical positivism and linguistic analysis, although not a pure exponent of either; he found many of Ayn's criticisms persuasive. More important to both of them, however, was the passion they shared for philosophy; I saw that Ayn enjoyed talking to him as she enjoyed few outsiders; she found him unusually intelligent and fair-minded, and on more than one occasion addressed his classes.

Their friendship came to a painful ending in October 1962 when, at Hospers's instigation, Ayn addressed the annual meeting of the American Society for Aesthetics at Harvard University. Her topic was "Art as Sense of Life," and Hospers was to comment on her paper. He offered to show her his comments in advance but she declined, saying that she was confident of his friendship and his integrity and that she knew the event would be what she called "civilized." After her talk, Hospers proceeded to challenge her viewpoint, not with the good-natured demand for greater clarification or specificity she expected, but with the kind of gentle sarcasm professors take for granted and Ayn found appalling. To her, it was an enormous, unforgivable betrayal. When she responded to Hospers's critique with her own brand of sarcasm, I sunk deeper into my seat, knowing that disaster had struck. Afterward, while Ayn went back to the hotel with the rest of our group for a party in our suite, I was assigned to bring along Hospers in a separate car and in effect to read him the riot act. I went through the motions, feeling thoroughly miserable. At the party, no one acknowledged Hospers, no one spoke to him, and Ayn acted as if he were not there. I whispered to Barbara, "If Ayn is really through with him, she owes it to him to say it to his face." Barbara nodded, sharing my discomfort. But Ayn said nothing to him, and their relationship ended that night.

Years later, when he was teaching philosophy at the University of Southern California, I talked with him one evening about the meaning of Ayn in his life. He spoke of her with passionate admiration, telling me that the memory of those wonderful philosophical discussions was still precious to him as one of the highlights of his intellectual career. "You know," he said gently, "when Barbara interviewed me for *The Passion of Ayn Rand,* and I began to talk about the past, suddenly — so many years later — I found myself weeping. Isn't that remarkable?" I answered sadly, "That was how Ayn could affect people."

During this same period I formed a friendship that was to enjoy a somewhat longer life than Ayn and John's. Robert Efron, Edith's brother, was a research neurophysiologist at the Veterans Administration Hospital in Boston. I was greatly impressed by one statement he had made about *Atlas*: "This is the work of a great biologist." We visited each other's cities and had many long discussions about biology, psychology, and philosophy. I found him to be among the most brilliant of the new people we were meeting. I noted that, although their relations were cordial, Ayn never quite shared my enthusiasm. Like his sister Edith, Robert Efron was not a "worshiper" of the kind Ayn was used to in the Collective; he was older by the time he met Ayn and more formed; he exhibited a certain detachment that I thought made Ayn suspicious, although she never said so. She would subtly rebuke me sometimes when I told her I was going to Boston for the weekend. "Do you really find him more worthwhile than the Collective?" she would ask. I would answer, "He's got more to say that interests me right now; that's all I can tell you." "What kinds of things do you talk about?" "Oh, lots of things. Evolution, for instance." She would shrug and drop the subject. I knew it was not the Collective she felt protective of, but herself; she was jealous of any interest of mine she could not share. The unspoken between us was, time spent with Robert Efron was time taken away from her.

I was fond of Edith, and sometimes Ayn was tense about that, too. There was an irreverence to Edith, and a streak of anger and sarcasm. I did not like the anger or sarcasm, but I did like the irreverence. Once Edith told me indignantly that she had telephoned Joan and said "What's new?" Joan had answered, "Nathan and Barbara bought a new living room rug." To me Edith protested, "Isn't that *preposterous*? I asked Joan what's new in her and Allan's life, and she tells me about you and Barbara acquiring a rug! Talk about living through others! Talk about dependency! Isn't Joan's own life worth talking about?" Later, treating the matter almost as a joke, I recounted the incident to Ayn, whose response startled me. "Edith is always making trouble. If you and Barbara are heroes to Joan, and what you do is important to her, what's wrong with that? Why criticize her for it? If her own life is less exciting than yours and Barbara's, so even small details of yours are meaningful to her — well, what's wrong with hero worship? I don't trust Edith."

Within a few years, Edith was excommunicated, and Barbara and I met with her alone to deliver the sentence. We would both regret our loss, agreeing that, with her brother, she was among the best minds we had met. We reproached ourselves for our complicity in banishing her. In 1981, about a decade and a half later, I asked Barbara one day, "Why were we angry with Edith Efron? Why was she expelled?" Barbara sighed and answered, "I haven't the foggiest idea."

We met attorneys Henry Mark Holzer and his wife, Erika, and Henry Holzer became Ayn's and my lawyer, doing work both for *The*

Objectivist Newsletter and Nathaniel Branden Institute. Occasionally we wanted strong letters sent to someone on our behalf, and Holzer's zeal in such matters was intense in those days. He had a style that made even Ayn appear tame by comparison.

We met screenwriter Al Ramrus and television producer Ted Yates; economist Martin Anderson, later to become an adviser to two presidents; theatrical manager Ralph Roseman; drama coach Phillip Smith; his actress wife, Kay Nolte Smith, who later became a gifted writer of psychological thrillers; Spanish artist Jose Capuletti, whose work Ayn first saw at the Hammer Gallery on Fifty-seventh Street and greatly admired; psychologists Roger Callahan and Lee Shulman; and Lee's future wife Joyce, who would also become a psychologist. Roger, Lee, and Joyce became particular friends of mine, along with Ralph Roseman, and remain so to this day.

I met Lee and Joyce through Roger Callahan, who I met as a consequence of his enthusiasm for the chapter on psychology in *Who Is Ayn Rand?* At that time, Roger and Lee more or less shared the ideas of psychologist Albert Ellis, and a result of our association was a shift in their thinking in my direction — to the annoyance of Ellis who seemed to feel they had been "stolen."

I had met Ellis some years earlier, in 1958, when Mike Wallace had done an interview with me in the *New York Post*. Ellis dropped me a note complimenting me on it, which led to a lunch at his institute. We soon discovered that although we both professed to be advocates of reason, agreed that irrational beliefs played a central role in understanding emotional problems, and shared a disdain for psychoanalysis, the differences in our ideas were profound. Ellis was a materialist, an advocate of logical positivism, a moral relativist, was very antagonistic toward any notion of certainty, and was especially antagonistic to my concept of self-esteem (which he has not stopped misrepresenting in print to this day). Our relationship at that time was cordial but distant.

The parties Barbara and I threw got bigger. In addition to our new friends and acquaintances, my sisters Reva and Florence in Toronto, and their husbands, Sholey and Hans, sometimes came to New York and were included in social events. Roger, Lee, and Joyce, all of whom then lived in Detroit, also visited us in New York periodically. "You have truly created your own society, darling," Ayn said to me. "With all its imperfections, it's a magnificent beginning." I knew that in a different mood she could speak of our friends very differently. But for the moment I was glad to hear her say it.

One day Joan telephoned and invited Barbara and me to a New Year's Eve party. I asked if anyone outside the Collective was coming.

I did not deceive myself about why I was asking, or for whose presence I was hoping. Joan answered, "Bob Efron and his wife, from Boston. Al Ramrus. Larry and Patrecia Scott. Oh, I don't know who else — I'm still calling people." In that instant Joan felt to me like an infinitely precious human being.

When Ayn, Frank, Barbara, and I arrived at the New Year's party, on December 31, 1962, we acted out our ritual. Everyone rose to greet Ayn. She turned around, like a child preening, and waited for people to admire her outfit. Praise was instantly forthcoming. Then people complimented whatever Barbara was wearing. (I do not recall that anyone else's appearance was ever commented on.) Then Ayn pulled out a cigarette holder and lit up. Then Barbara did the same. Then the party proceeded.

Tonight I did not pay attention to any of this. My eyes searched the room. But she had not yet arrived. I wandered around, feeling restless.

When the doorbell rang and Patrecia and Larry entered, I deliberately held back until they had said their hellos, then walked over and shook their hands warmly. They greeted me exuberantly, as if I were their closest friend.

I thought impersonally that they looked well together; both were tall and held themselves confidently; she had blue eyes and blonde hair, his eyes and hair were dark brown.

At some point I heard Patrecia say, "the two most rational men I know," and I knew she was speaking of Larry and me. She went on, looking directly at me, "Larry is the most rational man I know." She glanced at him with great warmth and affection, then her glance swung back to me. "You're next. I live with Larry and I know him, and I don't really know what you're like on a daily basis, so you're the second most rational man I know." I saw that she was playing with me and I was amused. She's full of herself tonight, I thought.

Larry was grinning at me with unreserved esteem. It was as if what Patrecia was saying and doing had his full understanding and blessing.

"Did I hear you call Nathan the *second* most rational man you know?" Joan asked Patrecia, chuckling.

"Oh-oh, look at his face," Patrecia said in mock fear, pointing at me. "He doesn't like that."

Suddenly I felt shy and slightly unnerved. Another part of me enjoyed the fact that she dared to tease me. No one ever dared to tease me.

She leaned forward almost intimately and asked, "You want to be first in everything, don't you — with everyone?" Her insinuation was so flirtatious that I wondered what those standing around would be thinking. Larry continued to beam. I could not help myself: I began to laugh, in self-protection.

Stepping still closer, in the manner of a detective trying to intimidate a suspect, she persisted, "Isn't that what you really want? To be number one, in every possible respect, with everyone, women in particular?"

It happened much too quickly and much too unexpectedly for me to assimilate the fact that what she was saying was essentially true; not about women in general, but certainly about her. It was a truth that was now throwing me off balance — because I had not known it or faced it until this moment. Just the same, I felt, it was not a fact to be announced in this manner and context; her youth and her exuberance had gotten the better of her judgment. "Have you been drinking?" I joked, knowing she did not drink.

Suddenly the humor vanished from her face and disappointment took its place. "You lack courage," she said wonderingly, as at a new discovery she had difficulty absorbing and was still not certain of. "Nathaniel Branden lacks courage. Can this really be possible?"

I knew that what she wanted of me a moment earlier was to acknowledge unapologetically the accuracy of what she was saying, to acknowledge it proudly, not to make a joke of it — while allowing the deeper meaning of her statement to remain silently understood between us.

The knowledge that, objectively, she was being inappropriate was swept aside by a rush of elation. *She was not afraid of me.* In the world in which I moved, I had been elevated to a larger-than-life status. In front of all my friends, knowing my position here, she had dared to say to me, "You lack courage." She stood there gazing at me, this beautiful, electrifying person, neither child nor woman, with the smile of a young girl and eyes that had looked upon the world for a thousand years. I felt joyfully transparent. I felt overwhelmed with admiration. I felt drunk.

"*Barbara,*" I called at the top of my voice. "Barbara! Where are you? You've got to hear this! *Patrecia says I lack courage.*" Habit drove me to share this moment with Barbara — habit, and the desire to avoid, until I could be alone, the deeper meaning of what had taken place. I strode into Allan's study where she was talking with a few friends. Eagerly I tried to convey what had just happened and what had so impressed me. Barbara smiled affectionately and indifferently and went on talking to our friends. Ayn, sitting next to Barbara, looked at me blankly.

When I returned to the living room, Patrecia was deep in conversation. For the rest of the evening her eyes sparkled with humor whenever she glanced in my direction — and periodically I would break into a laugh, unable to shake off the sense of intoxication and to return to normal consciousness.

I fell asleep thinking of Patrecia. I woke up thinking of Patrecia. All New Year's Day, I saw her face before me. That was how 1963 began.

FOURTEEN

"I'M COMING BACK to life," Ayn began saying with increasing frequency and urgency in the spring of 1963. "Can you imagine what these past years would have been like if you did not exist?" she asked during one of my visits, and I felt a familiar sense of heaviness. "Do you still love me?"

With only the briefest pause I answered, "Yes," knowing that the sense in which this was true was not the sense she meant or wanted.

It was the only answer that would not have precipitated an immediate crisis, the endpoint of which would have been the annihilation of our relationship. "I refuse to see myself as a nonsexual being," she had said to me. "If we're not a romance, we're nothing."

That she and I might be "nothing" was not a possibility I could accept. And in an impersonal way I approved of the way she insisted on seeing herself: as someone I *should* find desirable. I often experienced her perspective — and her pain — as my own. That was part of the trap.

She went on, "Do you think — ?" There was no mystery about the meaning of the unsaid; she wanted my reassurance concerning the eventual resumption of our affair.

I replied, "I need time. Life at home is more and more of a shambles. I've got to find a way to pull my marriage together."

She sighed. "I don't feel fully ready yet, either; I was just testing your attitude for the future. Can I help you with Barbara?"

Neither of us found such an exchange bizarre.

Long before my encounters with Patrecia, I had begun to feel increasingly distant from Barbara. Nothing essential had improved between us. Notwithstanding her work at NBI and for *The Objectivist Newsletter,* she continued to project a fundamental passivity that I found irritating. I knew it hurt her that this was how I perceived her,

since it was not how she perceived herself. Although I was not then
aware of the issue in these terms, our rhythms were incompatible: I
was naturally fast, she was naturally slow — in her movements,
speech, and responses. We got on each other's nerves: she felt rushed
by me, I felt confined by her. Our sexual relationship fluctuated between nonexistent and uninspiring.

I continued to be stunned by her declarations of the last two or three
years that she could not live without me. I felt that I loved her, and so
I was often touched — and yet I felt no closer to understanding her
responses to me than in the first years of our relationship.

And I did not fully understand myself, either, did not understand
the nature of the tie still holding me to her. It had never been easy for
me to decide that I loved someone; once I did decide, once I lifted the
barrier within me, it was as if I could never fully close it again. So
Barbara was *part of me*, fused at the level of identity.

Ayn once told me about an interesting comment that Frank had
made. "You know how fond of Barbara he is. And yet he said that
'Nathan has too much blood in him for Barbara — that's the basic
difficulty.' Isn't that a remarkable thing to say? That's what I love
about Frank — he finds ways to put things uniquely his own that
somehow go to the core." I nodded miserably. "It does go to the core.
That's how it feels."

I was now thirty-three, and Barbara was thirty-four. I did not fully
grasp the magnitude of her unhappiness. I did not know that in her
own mind she had decided that if our problems were not resolved by
the time she was forty, she would leave — leave me and leave Ayn if
need be, leave everything. She told me that years later; when I heard
it, I knew that in this respect she'd had more common sense than I.

Her unhappiness was not only with me but with our life — our
whole existence. She allowed herself to wonder about options and alternatives; my mind was closed to their possibility. Once, returning
home from an evening of dancing in the country, she said, hesitantly
and tentatively, "We had a good time tonight. We enjoyed the music
and dancing. It was fun. Ayn wouldn't have; wouldn't have liked the
music or anything else about tonight."

Immediately I felt defensive about Ayn and responded, "True, it
wouldn't have been her kind of evening, but . . ." I did not finish the
sentence because I did not know how to.

Quietly and persistently, Barbara said, "Nathan, listen — please listen. Ayn would see a difference of this kind as a gulf between us, a gulf
in our values." I did not answer. "Nathan, *what does that mean?*"

I sighed unhappily. "I don't know what it means." Barbara sank
back in her seat and let the subject drop. I felt immense compassion

for her; in remaining silent, I felt I was betraying her; if I had spoken my true feelings, I would have betrayed Ayn. Barbara was crying out for the right to have a youth, to be free and to be happy; I did not acknowledge that she was crying out for me to respond as well.

The entire structure of my life felt precarious — all of it resting as it ultimately did on a relationship that in one moment seemed indestructible and in the next, appallingly fragile. Deeper than any estrangement that had developed between us was my tie to Ayn at the most profound level: the thought of being without her was intolerable. I could not have said what benefits I now derived from our friendship; I was increasingly aware of feeling drained by it; yet I could not let go. Our relationship was the rock of my life. I had come to Ayn out of a void — and I imagined that without her a void was all that awaited me.

When I saw Patrecia and Larry together, they seemed harmonious. I liked the respect and esteem they conveyed to each other. With me, Patrecia was a shade more reserved than she had been in the past, which I thought appropriate. The experience of New Year's Eve had been, so I imagined, like the taking of a dangerously exhilarating drug; an experience enjoyed but not to be repeated, because it was too threatening to what I would have called the rational shape of my life. It was quite beyond my view of the universe to understand that the drug was striving to *liberate* my reason, not to overwhelm it.

When I was not thinking about my marriage or my future with Ayn, I was thinking about the book I wanted to write on self-esteem. But the chaos boiling inside me made concentration difficult. Life consisted of interruptions. If I was not having a quarrel with Barbara, I was called on some emergency by Ayn. If life was peaceful with them, I had to fly to another city to give the opening lecture on "Basic Principles of Objectivism."

On one occasion, all four of us flew to San Francisco for an opening night with several hundred students, and Ayn joined me in the question period. A short time later, we topped this event with the biggest opening night in our history: eleven hundred people in Los Angeles. The overflow crowd listened to the lecture in the foyer, through loudspeakers. A fire marshal came to inform me that the size of the audience was hopelessly in violation of the fire law; then he winked and told me not to worry, just to clear people out of the aisles a little. He was an admirer of Ayn Rand. His name was David Bergland, and one day he would be the Libertarian party's presidential candidate.

If my writing was not interrupted by problems, it was interrupted by triumphs — by the growth of NBI and the demand for more personal appearances. At the same time, I had to contribute an article each month to the newsletter. Gradually, I conceived the idea of writing psychological articles, which I later adapted for my book on self-esteem. First I prepared an outline for the book; then, from the outline, I projected a series of articles; then I scrambled the order in which I wrote them. It was the only way I could think of to get the book done.

To celebrate the success of our work and to expand further our vision of an Objectivist minisociety, Barbara and I decided to hold an NBI ball. Everyone in the Collective was enthusiastic — except Ayn. "Don't you think you should have asked my opinion in the matter before you said anything to anyone?" she asked me sharply. I replied, bewildered and slightly annoyed, that I couldn't have imagined that she would object. "Objectivism," she declared sternly, "is me — and I am not feeling particularly happy. A ball seems frivolous. NBI is an educational organization, not a social one." I sighed, thinking of what Barbara had tried to tell me the night we had gone dancing. I pointed out to Ayn that it was not unusual for schools and universities to hold dances; reluctantly, she agreed. Then, suppressing my anger, I asked her if she wished me to cancel the event. "No; I won't ask that. But thank you for making the offer. It was the right thing to do."

The event was black tie. Mike Wallace and his wife sat at our table, and his presence seemed to please Ayn enormously. She joked with him, "Do you suppose you will be publicly compromised by being seen here tonight?"

I danced with Barbara. I danced with Ayn. I danced with Joan. Then I felt free to dance with Patrecia.

From the moment she came into my arms, my defenses collapsed, as did hers. Our communication was in our silence. Holding her body, I felt that I knew it more intimately than I knew Barbara's or Ayn's. For the first time I allowed myself to know fully and consciously that I wanted her. When I danced with her again at the end of the evening, I saw Ayn watching us: it seemed to me that her eyes were angry.

Preparing for bed that night, I thought that I had received a sentence with no appeal: to live with this desire; never to act on it; never to acknowledge it to anyone; and to find a way to endure.

To my friends and students, I became still more aloof; there was nothing of importance within myself that I was prepared to share; I felt encased in ice.

That spring, neither Larry nor Patrecia attended any NBI lectures. They came only to a reading I had done of Ayn's three plays — *Night of January 16th, Ideal,* and *Think Twice.* Then they appeared at the end of the last lecture of the season.

"Just dropped by to say hello," Larry said. They looked radiantly cheerful, the perfect image of a happily married couple.

"Wait a while," I said. "We'll have coffee."

A television crew was there to tape an interview with me. Larry and Patrecia stood watching and smiling. I was conscious of the energy flowing from her glance.

The television taping took longer than expected. They could not wait. They waved and left.

I did not see her again for nearly four months.

Self-deception was a necessity of survival. By fall, I had locked away Patrecia in some specially sealed compartment of my mind — like one of those anomalous facts scientists neither deny nor affirm because it cannot be integrated into any known structure of knowledge and belief.

Barbara and I had moved into a new building at 120 East Thirty-fourth Street; we had a large apartment on the twentieth floor. On the second floor of the same building were the offices of NBI and *The Objectivist Newsletter.* I had an office in our apartment; I preferred it to working below, where Barbara and our staff worked. We now had a business manager: Wilfred, Barbara's old lover, friend, and sometime antagonist from Winnipeg. He had brought his family to New York in May 1963.

He himself came to New York approximately a year earlier, for reasons of his own unrelated to Objectivism or to Barbara. At some point he began helping NBI as an unpaid consultant. One day Barbara came to me and proposed expanding Wilfred's role at NBI to full-time employee. The fact that we could not pay him what he was worth did not matter to him. She conveyed that he had lost enthusiasm for his Winnipeg business and wanted to involve himself more deeply in the Objectivist cause. I thought about it for a while and then said, "Okay, let's give it a try." Her face was expressionless as she answered, "Thank you." Later, I said, "I know you and Wilfred will always care for each other. That's not a problem to me. I trust you completely."

I knew that they were spending a good deal of time together and had been for over a year. They seemed to be getting along better than they ever had before, which in no way troubled me. I did not think they were having an affair. In retrospect, I see myself as rather naive.

I felt detached. I told myself I should be concerned, but I wasn't. I continued to feel that our marriage was impregnable and indestructible, a viewpoint that Barbara consistently reinforced. "I will always love you," she insisted. "No other man or feeling can ever threaten that." Discussing Wilfred with Barbara, I was aware of forcing emotions I did not really experience, as if I were obliged to play the role of jealous husband. Barbara had suffered so terribly over Ayn, I told myself; let her have something of her own, but not an affair. An affair struck me as invalidation of everything Barbara and I had been trying to create. I suspected I was being completely unreasonable in my viewpoint.

One afternoon in October I met Patrecia on the street. She was carrying a huge black model's case in one hand and a handbag and book in the other. Our greeting was warm, cheerful, and unstrained. She mentioned that she was thinking of taking some classes at Hunter College. I mentioned a new course of lectures I was preparing on psychology. Then I said, "If you're ever in my neighborhood and feel like coming up for a cup of coffee, consider yourself invited." Her eyes shone with a child's excitement. "*Really?*"

I wondered how soon she would come. The thought of her visit flooded me with happiness.

When she entered my office, she walked carefully — almost, I thought, as if she were entering a temple. As she moved around the room, looking at objects, running her hand over a book or a vase or stack of paper, there was a suggestion of reverence in her touch. Her manner projected a deadly earnest joyfulness.

This was her theme, I thought, watching her, this was her sense of life: not joy exactly, but ecstasy; it shot into the world from her eyes.

"Can you believe," she said, sitting in a chair by my desk, "that when I saw you for the first time, at NBI, you struck me as much older than I? I was twenty-one that night and you were thirty-one; it seemed like such a great distance. Far greater than the distance between Larry and me, though you two are the same age. And then, that night we stopped by when you were being televised, last June, I thought for the first time, how young you look." I answered that I felt especially young whenever I talked to her and that I did not know why.

We both spoke with a kind of grim earnestness, devoid of flirtatiousness or sexuality, as if the occasion were too solemn for any hint of lightness. Only later did we relax and begin to smile.

I sat on the sofa, facing her, and asked questions about her childhood, wanting to know everything I could about how she had developed. She spoke of her early years as insane. "I grew up in a totally irrational universe." Her parents were some kind of eccentric Christian mystics who believed in spirits and demons and supernatural forces, and they had terrified their children with these notions. On one occasion, when Patrecia and Leisha were still very young, they watched their father attempt to strangle their mother. When the whole family was in the car, sometimes he expressed his rage and frustration by driving at full speed toward the edge of a cliff, braking only at the last possible moment. "Many times I was certain we were all going to die." Yet at other times, her father played with his children, entertained them, made them laugh, was loving and affectionate. Her mother had tried to inculcate both girls with her own distaste for men and sex. "She didn't succeed. In spite of the terrible things he did, I felt sympathy for my father. I thought my mother treated him terribly. She starved him sexually and tried to squeeze the life out of him." I asked, "What did you learn from all that?" and Patrecia answered, "I learned, very early, that most of the terrible things people do, they do because they are afraid. No, not because they are afraid; because they won't *admit* they are afraid."

I admired the serenity with which she spoke. She did not seem eager to discuss her childhood, but she answered my questions willingly. She told me of the most appalling incidents without a trace of bitterness or self-pity; she did not see herself as anyone's victim.

"Pain," she declared at one point, "is unimportant. People are too afraid of it. It's only a feeling — right? I don't deny pain or repress it; I accept it, but then let it pass through me without my hanging on to it. I believe that's why I have no bitterness. I don't like people who are bitter, do you? They feel sorry for themselves."

I thought of my friends in the Collective, all of whom were older than Patrecia. There was not one of them who lived what she has just said, and I thought that she did. "You seem so untouched," I said, wanting her to see my appreciation and respect. "Looking at you, one would never guess that you were brought up in the kind of madhouse you describe."

That's what she was proud of, she told me. She thanked me for understanding that about her. How had she accomplished it? I wanted to know. She asked me if I remembered the time she had spoken of having music inside of her, and I told her I did. "The music helped me," she said. I felt totally disoriented. No one I knew spoke this way. I was profoundly moved and at the same time suspicious of my own feeling. As if reading my thoughts, she added, by way of explanation, "I mean, the conviction that something better was possible — my own sense of life, you could say."

We began to talk about *Atlas Shrugged* and *The Fountainhead* and their meaning to her. Here my critical antenna was fully up. Her statements were impeccable; she seemed to understand the spirit and vision of those books with her whole being, even if she did not yet fully grasp some of the more technical philosophical issues.

"This is so *wonderful*," she said suddenly. "I am so *happy* to be here. I've always wanted a chance to talk to you like this."

Then she proceeded to tell me, guilelessly, that sometimes when she was alone in her apartment she danced to me, that is, danced around the room while imagining that I was her audience and that she was speaking to me not with words but with the motions of the dance. I searched her face for any hint of seductiveness; I saw only innocence and pleasure at the memory of what she was describing. "Sometimes, when something was troubling me, you helped me." Did she do this only when she was troubled? I asked. "Not at all," she answered with the faintest suggestion of a smile.

Toward the end of the afternoon she expressed concern that she had talked too much. "I think I really wanted you to know me," she said. I asked why that was important to her and she replied that perhaps she wanted validation. "From you that would mean something."

When Barbara came home I told her about the visit, reporting a good deal of what had been said; I did not mention the part about Patrecia dancing to me. Nor did I mention the exhilaration that was tearing through my body like fire.

A week or two later, Patrecia returned. This time she entered my office with the carefree manner of someone who has decided to be daring. She walked to the chair behind my desk and sat down. "I want to see the room from your perspective," she explained. Then she stood up. "Was that improper?"

"Absolutely not," I heard myself saying. "Please sit down again. I like seeing you there."

I felt such a rush of sexual excitement that I flung myself down on the sofa, hoping she would not notice.

We talked: about philosophy, and modeling, and her sister Leisha, and the people she had met at NBI, and why some students seem to use Objectivism in ways that enrich their lives while others merely turn into robots. She mentioned how kind Allan and Joan had been to her. "Joan once said she wanted to adopt me," Patrecia said, laughing. This was an aspect of Joan quite unknown to me, and I was intrigued. "When you're alone with Joan," Patrecia was saying, "and she drops her phony way of talking, she gets open — and lovable."

Joan? I thought, but said, "You must bring that out in her."

"Yes," she said matter-of-factly, with no hint of boasting, "I know how to do that."

When I went into the kitchen to make coffee, Patrecia accompanied me. I did not turn on the light and the room was in half shadow; light came only from the broad expanse of living room window. She stood in the center of the room, her back to me — and I broke. I put my arms around her, wordlessly, holding her as if my life depended on it, as if I were struggling in an invisible sea and her body was my only support. She leaned against me. Her head was against my cheek, and I saw that her eyes were closed. I felt despair.

After a moment I stepped away and resumed making coffee, concentrating on keeping my movements steady. I was not prepared to speak of what had happened, and I saw her accept my decision. We returned to my office and continued our discussion, our eyes saying everything that our words did not.

I did not see her again for two weeks, until early December. It's not love, I told myself insistently, it's some kind of incredible fascination. I felt my world disintegrating.

There could be no question of confronting Barbara or Ayn with what was happening and asking them to understand what I did not understand myself. On one side, Barbara, with whom I had been building a relationship for fifteen years; my wife; my comrade-in-battle. On the other side, Ayn, whom I admired more than anyone on earth and who spoke of me as her lifeline to the world, without whom her existence would be unbearable. Against that — a twenty-three-year-old girl at a far lower level of philosophical development, who earned her living as a fashion model — and with whom I felt an affinity, an aliveness, an *awakening* that was as terrifying in its intensity as it was incomprehensible to my rational mind.

I knew the essence of my attraction to Patrecia was spiritual, and the sexual, while supremely important, was only a consequence. However, I could not yet identify of what the spiritual connection consisted; I experienced only its overpowering presence.

I believed that, whatever my mistakes with Barbara or Ayn, I had always striven to conduct each relationship with honor. Was I about to forfeit my integrity for a passion I could not justify? I refused to consider an affair. Yet the idea became an obsession.

What I needed, I thought, was time; time to sort out my feelings, to see what was happening in rational perspective — as I taught others to do — time to cut myself free, not from Barbara or Ayn, but from Patrecia.

On the day of her third visit it was snowing. She wore a fur coat and hat, and looked unbearably beautiful, the light in her eyes wiping every thought from my mind but one. I pulled her against me, her arms rose eagerly around my neck, and our mouths crushed each other as if this first kiss might also be our last. Her hat fell to the floor.

Then I stepped back, helped her take off her coat, and led her into my office. We fell into each other's arms again. Her face reflected only pure, guiltless enjoyment, with none of the pain that sometimes shadows ecstasy.

We did not have sexual intercourse. Neither of us was ready for that. So I was not yet committing myself fully; I might still find a solution that would not lead to disaster.

A long time later, when we were able to talk, she whispered, "I love you. I've loved you since I was twelve years old, when I first thought that one day I would find a man who would see in my face what I saw in his. Do you think our souls are in our faces? I do. When I was twelve I thought, someday I'll be free from all this, free to find my own kind of life, my own world."

I was not prepared to say that I loved her. I had said those words to only two women in my life. I did not know what Patrecia was to me — other than oxygen, and that for years I had been moving through a world without air. I held her face in my hands, breathing in her being.

I asked her why she had married Larry. She said that she had believed I was unattainable, and she had admired him more than any other man she had met. She felt that she did love him in a way; they seemed to share so many values — Ayn's world and everything it meant to both of them. Larry had wanted to get married, and although she knew she was not ready, she allowed herself to be persuaded because she did not want to lose him. "Larry was the opposite of everything I had seen as a child; he was solid and consistent. That meant a lot to me. He married me, knowing how much I care for you. He cares for you, too, very deeply. That's one of the things I admire in him. You don't have to tell me that I've probably made an insane mistake; it's insane to get married when you're not a hundred percent certain; cruel to Larry and cruel to myself."

Overcome by the reality of our present circumstances, I said miserably, "Then what are we doing now? This is completely wrong."

"Yes," she said sadly.

I saw the way she was looking at me, the trust in her eyes. "Patrecia, will you give me time to think? There are things about my life you don't know. It's all much more complicated than you can imagine."

Patrecia could never have guessed that I was thinking about Ayn. She said she knew how much I loved Barbara, that was obvious, and she expected absolutely nothing of me. Today might be the beginning and the end between us; but if we were to continue together in this manner she would not deceive Larry, she would tell him the truth; he had a right to know the facts and to decide whether he wished to go on living with her while she worked out her relationship with me. "He does not deserve this," I agreed sadly, thinking that in whichever direction I looked there was only suffering. I asked Patrecia if she would be willing for a while longer to say nothing, until I had time to think the situation through more carefully, and she said yes.

Alone in my apartment, I paced the living room, swinging between feelings of exultation and torment, struggling with the question of what to do. I had once asked Barbara to endure my affair with Ayn. I could not now ask her to accept *another* woman in my life, and one whose meaning to me she could not possibly accept. I knew she would be devastated. I felt that my life depended on what I was now experiencing with Patrecia — this sense of freedom and aliveness — but that I could not justify this to anyone, not in light of my other commitments and values. I told myself that I was now doing to Barbara and Ayn what Barbara had once done to me, and this made me a total scoundrel — but if I was a scoundrel, why did I feel cleaner and more like myself when I was with Patrecia than at any other time? I felt that if I confronted Barbara and Ayn with my confession, I would hurt them beyond repair — Ayn in particular, who was far from recovered — and in so doing I would betray every value I espoused; and if I didn't confront them with the truth, I would betray myself. I saw two roads — and each seemed to lead to moral treason.

Speaking of Kant, whose philosophy she did not like, Ayn had once said to me, "I don't think in such terms, it's a too malevolent view of reality, but I accept the principle, 'If the truth shall kill them, let them die.'" I told myself that the principle was right, but it was a principle to which I now felt unequal, and I was ashamed. The truth was, it was I who did not wish to die.

Later that week, I fought to keep my face and manner impassive when Barbara asked that I give my consent to her having an affair with Wilfred. She had been seeing a great deal of him. It would change nothing between us, she said — just as Ayn had said it in another context long ago. I thought that if I gave my consent it would be the final nail in the coffin of our marriage, my final acceptance of the death of the dream I had had when I was eighteen years old. It seemed that everything was falling apart: my marriage, my relationship with Ayn, my personal integrity, my vision of what my life was to be. And in the name of the values I was still trying to hang on to, I told her — totally irrationally — that I couldn't give her what she wanted. In truth, I did not care if she and Wilfred slept together; it was my *consent* I could not tolerate. If the crash was to come, it would not have my blessing.

I did not want to know that I was fighting a battle that had already been lost; that it was too late; that we were already living a life of obsolete fantasies. I looked at her hurt face across the dinner table and thought: now we're even; now I have given you the right to despise me because I am truly a hypocrite.

Throughout December I visited Patrecia in her apartment and she visited me in my office, and the passion of our time together went on escalating, until she begged me to make love to her, saying that right and wrong and long-range consequences no longer mattered to her. I knew this was not true; I knew how proud she was of her own honesty.

I knew that to make love to her would be to embrace the greatest joy of my life and at the same time to enter a nightmare worse than any behind me. She loved me, trusted me, looked up to me, counted on me to know what I was doing — and all I was prepared to offer was two choices of pain: the pain of our being lost to each other or the pain of being together under dishonest conditions. The third option was not one I was prepared to consider: giving up my world — walking away from Ayn and Barbara and NBI. I loved the world I had created, I was proud of it, I could not abandon it. Objectivism was still the central passion of my life.

When Patrecia came to my office early in January, I took her in my arms, I kissed her eyes, I held her tightly, and I said, with agonizing happiness, "I do love you. Of course I love you." I felt as if I were holding my own soul in my arms, in the person of a woman.

"You must think very carefully about what I am now going to tell you. If we are to have an affair, you must agree never to tell Larry; never to tell anyone. There are reasons and I will tell you about them — soon — but not today. You must give me your word of honor that unless a day comes when I release you from your promise, whatever happens between us will be secret."

"*Never* tell Larry?" she asked uncomprehendingly. "*Never?* And you're not going to tell Barbara?"

"No. But Barbara is not the primary problem." This was more bewildering still; her eyes searched my face for some indication of what I could mean. I told her that I knew what I was asking and what she would be doing violence to within herself. "Don't agree simply out of desire, because you'll regret it later." She looked at me almost contemptuously and replied that if she agreed it would not be out of desire but out of love.

In the second week of January 1964, knowing I could not allow her to proceed without fuller knowledge, I met her in Central Park and told her the whole story of my relationship with Barbara and with Ayn. The affair with Ayn did not surprise her. "Do you remember," she said, as we sat on a bench overlooking the half-frozen lake, "the night at NBI when, in answer to some question, Ayn said that any fully rational woman who shared her philosophy would be in love with Nathaniel Branden, if only abstractly? You looked so shy and uncomfortable standing there, trying to appear nonchalant. I wondered then: what was Ayn saying about herself?" When I went on to speak of Ayn's suffering and of her lifelong struggles, Patrecia listened with tears in her eyes.

"I cannot deliver a new blow to her," I stated. Patrecia nodded her head, whether in understanding or in agreement I could not have said. "I can't. And I can't accept losing her, either — she's too important to me. Since I was fourteen years old, this woman has been at the center of my thoughts and my values and everything I admire. You said once I lacked courage. Maybe you're right." Patrecia's look was silent compassion — for me, for Ayn, for all of us, herself as well, perhaps.

"As to Barbara," I went on, "I'm still trying to make the marriage work. I'm not ready to give up and walk away. But there's another consideration: if I tell her the truth, then I put her in the position of having to join me in lying to Ayn. Is it right to do that? The torture is, I don't know what's right any longer."

"That's what's killing me. I didn't think a problem of this kind was possible. I thought I would always know what was right. I was so proud of that."

"And there are still other factors. I know Ayn. If, at this point, I were to tell her not only that my feeling for her is no longer romantic, but that her rival is a girl of twenty-three — it wouldn't matter who the girl was — that would be the end of not only our relationship, but the end of NBI, the end of *The Objectivist Newsletter,* the end of everything I've been trying to build since Ayn and I started. I can't let it go. I need to be honest with you. I can't let it go. I don't want to. *I love it.*"

"Are you sure," Patrecia asked wonderingly, "Ayn would react that violently?"

"You would see an explosion such as you cannot even begin to imagine."

She asked why she could not at least tell Larry about us, and I answered, "Because for any of this to make sense, you would have to tell him about my affair with Ayn. Ayn has said over and over again how adamant she is that no one ever know. Some part of her is still a nineteenth-century Victorian, or the Russian equivalent. I just can't take a chance on Larry talking to somebody else, out of his own pain, perhaps. I've betrayed Ayn in enough ways already. I know what terrible burdens I'm putting on you, so, before things go further, be sure, Patrecia, please be sure . . ."

Looking at me as if she were still unable to absorb what I was asking of her, she said, with a heartbreaking effort at clarity, "Then I guess the only choice is . . . to give each other up . . . or to take whatever we can have, for as long as we can have it, or until we find an answer . . ."

I saw my best, highest vision of myself fading before me — and I felt a violent, desperate, rebellious rage: against Ayn, against Barbara, against my sense of invisible chains, against myself for being unable to think my way to a solution that matched my values. I told myself: don't transfer any part of the blame to Ayn or Barbara; the guilt is yours.

I taught people that if, for any reason whatever, they placed another value higher than their self-esteem, they would pay for it — and the price could be worse than they had the power to imagine. I thought of that now, looking at Patrecia. And I thought: so be it.

A week or so later I again visited her apartment — and we made love for the first time. I told myself that whatever lay ahead, whatever the cost, would be worth it. Holding her in my arms, the happiness I experienced lifted me beyond any level of fulfillment I had ever known. It was an answer to every frustration, every heaviness, every moment of suffering, of the past fourteen years. "Patrecia and Nathan," I said to her exultantly, and she answered from somewhere inside her music, "Nathan and Patrecia."

Twelve or thirteen days later, in the first week of February, recognizing that my stand on the subject of Wilfred had become ludicrous and unconscionable, I gave Barbara my consent to their affair.

When I thought of the lies and deceptions to which I was now committed, I felt self-hatred. When I thought of the man beginning to awaken within me, I felt pride. The ascent into liberation, the descent into hell, had begun.

FIFTEEN

PATRECIA AND I were driving along the Henry Hudson Parkway in the late winter of 1964. I had no more passionate wish than to remain in this space forever, cut off from the past and the future, with reality reduced to the sensation of speeding motion, the sight of snow and naked trees against a slate sky, and Patrecia beside me, her face alive with excitement and happiness, her legs stretched comfortably forward, her hand resting on my thigh.

"This is the way I like to see the countryside," I said, "as a backdrop to your face."

"This is the way I like to see the world," she answered, "as a backdrop to your face *and your body.*"

I tried to tell myself that what I was now experiencing with Patrecia was immoral. It was impossible: I could say the words, but I could not make them real. I was betraying Ayn, I was betraying Barbara, I was betraying what I taught my students — and what I was experiencing was a sense of spiritual uplift. How was it possible, I wondered, to be a liar and an adulterer and yet to feel that I was passing through some rite of purification?

I was learning to lie expertly, as I became a master at inventing reasons to be away from the office. If I had only an hour, I would drive to Patrecia's apartment, make frenzied love to her as if I were never to see her again, and leave, sometimes without our exchanging thirty sentences. She had begun to forgo work, in order to be available whenever I called. We would talk endlessly on the telephone. There were days, like today, when I would steal four or five hours; sometimes we would spend them in bed, in her apartment, and sometimes we would spend them driving in the country.

I existed in a constant state of joy and frustration. If we spent our time making love, I was desperate for conversation; if we spent our time talking, I resented the time taken from lovemaking. If I spoke at too great length, I was desperate for the sound of her voice; but if she spoke at great length, I felt frustrated about all the unexpressed things I wanted to tell her. I wanted to stand looking at her from a distance, to contemplate her as a being in the world apart from me — and I wanted there never to be space between her skin and mine.

Now, racing through the countryside, I remembered a shocking moment in Ayn's study a few days ago, when Ayn had shown me a photograph of Patrecia she had stowed in her desk. She had handed it to me, grinning. Straining to sound casual, I had asked, "How do you happen to have that?" "I asked her to give it to me," Ayn had answered brightly, amused by my reaction; she always loved to shock. "I told you I like her physical type. She's very American-looking. You couldn't quite imagine her from any other country. You know, that kind of cheerful energy." My God, are there sides to you I still do not understand, I had thought, telling myself that I was living in a world with Ayn, Patrecia, and Barbara that I would never be able to explain to anyone, including myself. Mentioning the incident to Patrecia now, I said, "What must you have felt when Ayn asked for the photograph? It must have been awkward for you."

"It was *very* awkward."

Patrecia began to question me, gently and tactfully, about the evolution of my relationship with Ayn. I could see that a part of her understood perfectly how and why an affair had developed, while another part of her felt distaste. I thought, in her heart she does not approve. "You're offended — aesthetically — aren't you?" She squeezed my arm and said only, "The present situation has got to be very hard for both of you."

She had never questioned me about my marriage to Barbara, she waited for whatever I was prepared to volunteer, and I had adopted the same policy with regard to Larry.

Nor did she ever ask me about the future. But at our last meeting she had stunned me by saying, "I'm hoping we'll have six months." My voice strangling, I had asked, "Six months? What are you talking about?" She had answered, "The differences in where we are in life. I'm so far behind you. There's so much I have to learn. You're set on your course; I haven't even found mine yet. You think that doesn't matter, but it will, eventually." *Six months* — it had the sound of a death sentence.

Now Patrecia said to me, "You're driving very fast. If you get a ticket, you might be asked when and where and how you got it."

I answered, "You didn't mean that, did you — about six months?"

"I don't know. At this moment, I see us going on indefinitely. When

I'm alone and I think about your life and your work, I know that you have other loyalties that have to be respected. And I think of where you are and where I am — oh, I don't know — I get confused. We'll have to wait and see what happens." Then she shook her head, as if to dispel thoughts of anything but the present moment, and smiled a brilliant smile that demolished pain. "And appreciate what we have," she said.

During one of my visits to her apartment, before the affair began, she had said to me, "There haven't been many women in your life, have there?"

"Just two," I had answered. "How did you know?"

"I knew from the beginning that you were a man who had never been promiscuous."

"But how?"

"You have a special kind of sexual intensity that one wouldn't see in a man who plays around — almost a kind of sexual fanaticism — that I associate with purity."

I had intuitively known what she meant but expressed my surprise that someone so young and relatively inexperienced herself would know it.

She had answered, "There are certain things — if you're conscious — you just know; experience doesn't have much to do with it."

Now, in the car, I reminded her of that conversation; I asked her what else she knew about me that she hadn't yet told me, and she answered, "I know you like a lot of distance between yourself and almost all other people, such as your students. It's almost funny, watching you come into the room at a lecture. You have a way of striding toward the platform that says to everyone, loud and clear, 'Don't approach me; don't speak to me.' You scare people. They don't want just to learn from you, they want to feel they're important to you, that their admiration and appreciation matters to you — and it doesn't, not in the way they would like. It reaches you, but in a fairly superficial way; you're really off somewhere else. Sometimes I think it wouldn't hurt you to be a little kinder and friendlier with them, but another part of me likes your detachment — I think I would feel a greater pressure to nurture them in some way — and I envy your lack of concern."

I told her that sometimes my sense of distance from my students bothered me, too. "Sometimes I'm more curt than I intend and then I reproach myself later. You know, in the NBI world I'm sort of a public person, and if you don't protect yourself, people will swallow you up — their needs don't ever stop. Everyone seems to want something, more than I've got to give. I haven't yet learned how to find the right balance." She nodded in agreement and said, "That's one of the things

I think is awful about being other people's fantasy figure. When you're up on the lecture platform, you give them everything you've got. Do they have a right to expect more than that?"

"What else do you know about me?" I asked, and she answered, "I know that when we walk down the street together, and I imitate your way of walking, very aggressive, almost a kind of march, with that grim look of a professor very busy thinking about something — you like to see me do it; I make you laugh." It was true; she was an excellent mimic and she did make me laugh.

"I love you," I said to her.

And yet a voice inside my head would not relent: *Is this reality?*

In the beginning I did not know what she would come to mean to me. I thought of our relationship as an extraordinary adventure in love, a unique experience outside the normal orbit of my existence. I imagined that somehow my "normal" life would continue, essentially undisturbed. I wanted to believe that. Yet Patrecia's recent statement about our affair lasting six months continued to nag at me.

If I'd had greater respect for my emotions, enough to have examined them more carefully — if I had lived less in a world of abstractions — I would have understood far sooner the depth and permanence of my involvement. I would have known that from the moment Patrecia came to my office, my life with Barbara and Ayn had ended — and that if I wanted roots I would have to create them anew.

The actual end did not come quickly. It took four years and eight months. Like the process of a long, protracted death, it came with agony and with periods of deluded hope and apparent remission.

It happened against the background of one advance after another in the sphere of work.

For the spread of Objectivism, the 1960s were one long rocket explosion of growth. This itself contributed to my emotional disorientation. I ran from the home I shared with Barbara to Ayn's apartment to the offices of NBI and *The Objectivist Newsletter* to Patrecia's apartment — while watching in astonishment the nerveless skill that I possessed, that of an emotional juggler. While our personal life was spinning increasingly out of control, the success of Ayn's, Barbara's, and my working life kept gathering momentum: we were gaining adherents in escalating numbers, expanding our professional activities in all directions, broadcasting our message to the world in ever-widening waves of impact. The structure I had wanted to create for myself was growing stronger and more deeply entrenched just at the time when my need became greatest to break free.

I recall my gratification sitting in Barbara's office at NBI and listening to her reports on the stream of requests for our lecture series pouring in from Europe, Africa, Asia, and Australia. I loved the anecdotes she or other staff members would bring to me. An Indian psychologist came to the United States on a fellowship to complete her studies at a university in Boston. Shortly after her arrival, as one of her first questions about America, she asked her hosts, "Can you tell me, please, how to contact the Nathaniel Branden Institute, so I can hear the lectures on Ayn Rand's philosophy?" Soon she was enrolled in the Boston tape series. Incidents like this were reported to me almost every week.

Writing in the leftist *New Leader* (September 26, 1960), one antagonist warned his readers: "Objectivism, unlike most other past and present right-wing movements in this country, has more of an intellectual than an emotional appeal and is consequently attracting young people to its ranks." We laughed gleefully at comments of this kind, even though we did not like the designation "right-wing," nor any other designation that suggested conservatism, and even though the rest of his article was filled with inaccuracies. "We are making people nervous," I told Patrecia at our next meeting, showing her the article.

In another publication, of a similar political persuasion, *New University Thought* (Autumn 1962), a teacher of English wrote about the danger of Ayn Rand's influence on college students.

For the past two or three semesters, no other author, not even the Luce-touted J. D. Salinger, has threatened to upset Miss Rand's commanding popularity. At first, I thought my students' enthusiasm was hardly representative, but just recently I had an opportunity to talk with several other college teachers, from various parts of the nation, and many of them informed me that they too had been troubled by Miss Rand's appeal.

Some of the commentators on Miss Rand's popularity have tended to play down Miss Rand's apparent popularity, but I am not ready to do so, and I am genuinely disturbed by the similarity between my student's enthusiasm and the eagerness to talk about her books and her ideas which Gore Vidal noted when he was campaigning for Congress. She was "the only writer" the voters he so futilely wooed were acquainted with and were eager to talk about; it is dismaying to contemplate the possibility that Ayn Rand is the single writer who engages the loyalties of the students I am perhaps ineffectually attempting to teach.

All the students I talked with struck me as intelligent (three of them are in the honors program of my school), and most were quite able to verbalize the reasons of their admiration for Miss Rand.

At Yeshiva University I spoke with a teacher of English, Professor Henry Grinberg, who reported the same trend. At the start of the semester he had given his freshman English class the assignment of writing a paper on the book they had read during the past year which they had most enjoyed and which had most impressed or influenced them. "Twenty-five percent of my students wrote on one or another of Ayn Rand's novels. When I was a young man, the students who experimented with new ideas were attracted predominately to socialism and communism. But Ayn Rand seems to be capturing young people with *anti*-altruist ideas."

Although Objectivism was attracting people of all ages and from all backgrounds, it was logical, I thought, that its major following should be among the younger generation, and, most particularly, among college students. This group was the one most likely to be open to new ideas, most eager for a rational, intelligible view of life, and most dissatisfied with the intellectual and cultural status quo.

John Chamberlain, reviewing *For the New Intellectual* in *The Wall Street Journal* (March 24, 1961), wrote:

> Seated about in booths in college-town snack shops, the young Randites talk about their intellectual leader as their fathers and mothers a generation ago talked about Karl Marx, or John Maynard Keynes, or Thorstein Veblen. . . .
>
> Whether [Objectivism] amounts to a rear-guard action that is destined to universal defeat, or whether Ayn Rand possesses in her own intransigent head the philosophy of the future, will be hotly argued. Nevertheless, she has been gaining many followers among the young. And it is normally a matter of two decades before the young take over the seats of power in the name of what they have learned to believe 20 years ago.

The mail we received at NBI and *The Objectivist Newsletter* provided interesting insights into what was happening around the country. "I heard some people arguing about *Atlas Shrugged* at a dinner party — the book sounded interesting — so I went out and bought it." "I first read *Atlas Shrugged* because people told me it was an evil book no one should read." "After fighting with my professor for a month, I finally obtained permission to do my term paper on Objectivism." "I first discovered the works of Ayn Rand when they were recommended in a course on psychology." "At the end of the first class, my professor of philosophy suddenly announced, without explanation or context, when no reference had been made to the subject, that if anyone turned in a paper on Objectivism, that student would automatically fail." "Can you recommend additional readings to supplement our discussion of Objectivism in an ethics seminar?" "I first heard about Ayn Rand when Galt's speech was quoted in a political science class."

"When our bank mailed out a reprint of Francisco d'Anconia's speech on 'the meaning of money' from *Atlas Shrugged,* I went out and bought the book." "My psychiatrist recommended I read *The Fountainhead* and *Atlas Shrugged* as a helpful adjunct to psychotherapy." Increasingly at NBI we heard of students who had been advised to take our courses by psychiatrists and psychologists.

All through the country Ayn Rand study clubs and Objectivist study clubs were appearing on college campuses. We had no official connection with such clubs; they arose spontaneously, on the initiative of students we did not know. Ayn was sometimes apprehensive about such groups speaking as if they had her personal endorsement, and more than once she had Hank Holzer write a cautionary letter. She was obsessed with protecting the purity of her system against the distortions of confused or irresponsible admirers. On occasion she shrieked about her fans "exploiting" her work. Sometimes Barbara or I would complain to Ayn about the gratuitous severity — or hostility — of Holzer's written communications, and sometimes we succeeded in toning them down. But sometimes we wrote bullying letters ourselves. We insisted that people call themselves "students of Objectivism" rather than "Objectivists."

As the operations of NBI continued to grow, we created a publishing division, NBI Press, which issued a favorite novel of Ayn's, released early in the century and now long out of print, *Calumet "K,"* and Victor Hugo's *The Man Who Laughs,* almost unknown in this country. Ayn wrote introductions for both novels. And in addition to NBI Book Service, which sold our books and pamphlets to the people on our rapidly expanding mailing list, we established NBI Art Reproductions in order to sell prints of paintings by Frank, Joan, and a portrait of Ayn that would subsequently replace photographs on the jackets of her books, painted by Ilona (Ilona Royce Smithkin). "My God," said Ayn, "you really are building an empire."

Who Is Ayn Rand? was published in softcover in June 1964, with a first printing of one hundred thousand copies, and went through several such printings throughout the balance of the decade.

A year earlier, Robert Hessen and I visited Ayn to propose that she publish in book form a collection of the essays on ethics she had been writing for *The Objectivist Newsletter.* The idea was Robert's, so we knew Ayn would resist since she had not come up with it first. But after some discussion Ayn agreed and she assembled a book entitled *The Virtue of Selfishness.* First published by New American Library in softcover in 1964, its success led to a hardcover edition — followed, in 1966, by another collection, *Capitalism: The Unknown Ideal.* I contributed a number of essays to both books and in the second book there were also articles by Alan Greenspan and Robert Hessen.

I had urged Ayn to expand on her ethical theories when she wrote for *The Objectivist Newsletter,* instead of merely commenting on current events, as she was often inclined to do — and I was gratified to see her more philosophical essays pulled together and made available in a single volume. I was especially pleased to see in print for a wider audience the elaboration of her ideas concerning individual rights, which were the foundation of her political thinking. She included her essay on racism, a piece I had suggested for the newsletter, against her initial reluctance. "Of course, racism is evil, but the leftists have made it their issue," she had protested. I had argued that that was precisely why we should come out with our own analysis of the problem, not to surrender the field to the opposition, and that it was important that the piece come specifically from her. In the end, after several months of discussion, she had agreed and had written a powerful article branding racism as biological collectivism, totally incompatible with an individualist philosophy, and explaining why a free market best serves the interests of all races, reiterating her theme that the smallest minority on earth is the individual and that the rights of minorities can have no other base.

Much as I liked *The Virtue of Selfishness* as a total, I was uncomfortable with the first sentences of her Introduction to the book:

> The title of this book may evoke the kind of question that I hear once in a while: "Why do you use the word 'selfishness' to denote virtuous qualities of character, when the word antagonizes so many people to whom it does not mean the things you mean?"
>
> To those who ask it, my answer is: "For the reason that makes you afraid of it."
>
> But there are others, who would not ask that question, sensing the moral cowardice it implies, yet who are unable to formulate my actual reason or to identify the profound moral issue involved. It is to them that I will give a more explicit answer.

This was a typical example of Ayn Rand in the respect I liked least. Why begin the book with an insult? What was accomplished by sounding a note of abusiveness on the first page?

This was a mild version of the angry behavior she displayed during the question-and-answer periods at my lectures, and it troubled me there, too. The result of this policy was that our students became afraid to ask her questions, alarmed at the prospect of what she might announce about their psychology or moral state. I knew that Ayn saw her position as one of moral intransigence; I had seen it that way once; now I was beginning to see it as bad temper and displaced rage.

The question she addressed at the start of her Introduction was not irrational and did not necessarily come from fear; it could equally come from bewilderment. It would have been more appropriate and more persuasive to begin her response benevolently, especially since she had something genuinely new to teach. When I suggested this to her, she became impatient, launched into a brief lecture about not yielding an inch to the enemy, and dismissed my comment as if I had a sudden aberration, best forgotten.

As its title suggests, *Capitalism: The Unknown Ideal* discusses issues in political economy and the moral basis of a free society. Ayn was especially fond of her lead piece, entitled "What Is Capitalism?" My own favorites were a piece she wrote on "The Roots of War," which I still wish would be required reading for anyone genuinely devoted to peace, and a devastating analysis of the student protest movement, entitled "The Cashing-in: The Student Rebellion." In her critique of the current educational system, she was ahead of her time. Only in the 1980s would many of her ideas begin to be properly understood and appreciated.

It was during her work on *For the New Intellectual,* a few years earlier, that Ayn had first realized how thoroughly she enjoyed nonfiction writing. "All I have to think about is clarity and logic. The arguments don't have to be integrated with emotion, story, and suspense." Ayn lacked the motivation to write an entire book from scratch; but thanks to the newsletter and then, after 1966, to its successor, *The Objectivist,* a new collection of her essays would be published in book form every two or three years. I felt proud of my role in helping to bring this about.

Smiling one day at what must have been my grin of self-satisfaction, she chuckled. "You're an intellectual entrepreneur, and I'm one of the factors of production you're organizing. That's all right — go ahead — I don't mind." She expressed gratification at the salary she was receiving from *The Objectivist Newsletter.* "I always wanted a source of income apart from my books. Without the newsletter, I wouldn't have that, and without you, I wouldn't have the newsletter. I would never have started it on my own." I listened gratefully, wanting to believe that contributions of this kind somehow offset what I was unable to give her — and knowing I was deluding myself.

The Virtue of Selfishness and *Capitalism: The Unknown Ideal* were published by New American Library, which now published in hardcover as well as softcover, because Ayn had broken with Bennett Cerf and Random House. She had offered Bennett a collection of her essays, of which the lead piece was to be "The Fascist New Frontier," based on a lecture she had given at Ford Hall Forum, in which she drew parallels between the ideology of fascism and that contained in the speeches of John F. Kennedy, emphasizing the common demands for personal "sacrifice" on the altar of "public good." At first Bennett gave evidence of being enthusiastic about the project and reported excited responses from the bookstores; then, less happily, he began reporting opposition from his own editors; then, finally, as if this had always been his viewpoint, he refused to publish the book unless Ayn withdrew the piece on Kennedy. Of course Ayn would not withdraw it. From the farewell notes they exchanged, it was obvious that there was a good deal of sadness on both sides. Ayn said grimly, with a conscientiousness that touched me, "I'll always give Bennett credit for the ways in which he did support my work." She would not acknowledge how deeply hurt she was personally; her discussion of the issue was entirely philosophical. "When you deal with a person of mixed premises," she declared with stern detachment, "these things happen." One more pillar had collapsed, and the weight of my responsibility for Ayn's happiness felt correspondingly heavier.

By late 1964, NBI was offering courses in fifty-four cities, and plans were under way to offer taped programs in Munich and the Marshall Islands in the South Pacific — and also somewhere under the Atlantic Ocean, in a Polaris submarine.

By the end of 1965, we were approaching eighty cities. We had been asked to make my course on "Basic Principles of Objectivism" available to soldiers in Vietnam, and we were also making plans for Greenland and Pakistan. Barbara had hung a large map of the world in her office, with flags pinned to locations where the lectures were offered, displayed proudly for visitors.

"Do you ever feel like we're on an express train?" Barbara asked, paraphrasing a line from *Atlas,* in one of those rare moments of happy intimacy still possible to us. I grinned and nodded.

We were on an express train. But up ahead, the bridge was out.

In April of 1964, near the time of my thirty-fourth birthday, NBI held its second ball — which again led to an explosion of temper on Ayn's part. "You have no emotional time for me or our relationship, but you do for a dance?" she shouted.

This was said during a period when I spoke to her at length every day on the telephone, still visited her twice a week, and spent at least one full afternoon or evening a week with her. What she now wanted was the resumption of our affair, and I kept inventing reasons to hold that issue at bay. Ayn was now fifty-nine. "When, if not now?" she asked. At the ball I danced with her a good deal. I danced with Patrecia briefly and carefully. And yet to hold her in my arms publicly, even under these circumstances, felt like a justification of the entire event. In the midst of all the important people of my life, this was the one encounter, the one interaction, that felt *right*.

"Ayn's blindness on some issues is incredible," Barbara remarked, and I froze, wondering what she meant. "Any other woman I can think of, seeing how you behave, would conclude that the fire is gone, the affair is past history, and all you can be now is friends. Watching how you are with her from the sidelines, I think it's all so obvious. How is it possible that she doesn't understand that?"

Relaxed now, I answered that I still felt a kind of love for Ayn, at times very intense, and I showed this plainly, and therefore I was responsible for maintaining Ayn's confusion. "Yes and no," was Barbara's comment.

In other moods, more empathetic to Ayn, she said, "You've got to find a way that won't devastate her to help her see the truth. Not that Ayn would ever admit to being devastated. Poor Ayn. Poor Nathan."

Barbara seemed happier; her affair with Wilfred seemed to have brought her new contentment. She informed me that whereas she and Wilfred had not been sexually compatible as teenagers, they were now very compatible. I noted with mild astonishment my indifference, recalling the suffering I had once experienced over her other men, as well as over her lack of response to me.

Our own quarrels and conflicts had not abated, but had escalated. Most of our disputes were over trivia, the content of which was usually forgotten within a day. I was too fast, she was too slow; I was too cold, she was too maudlin; I was too impatient, she was too dreamy — that was how we saw each other. I found I had less and less desire to talk with her apart from the office. I did not resent Wilfred; I liked him, enjoyed our relationship, and appreciated the important contribution his business skills made to NBI. When Barbara complained to me about something he had done that had hurt or disappointed her, my sympathies were often with Wilfred.

Barbara verbalized her unhappiness over our marriage more than I did now. For me, there had been too many years of her nonresponsiveness; now my reaction to marital frustration was withdrawal and silence. She complained, not without justice, that she felt unaccepted and unadmired by me. "You *think* you love me," she would declare insistently, like an accusation, "but you don't." She would point out that I did not really feel comfortable with her sense of life, disliked some of her deepest artistic tastes, and did not find her stimulating. As always, her reproaches were mixed with an unspoken plea for my compassion and concern. "There's always been another woman in comparison to whom I've been found wanting. First, it was Ayn's heroines. Then Ayn. Now, God help me, a twenty-four-year-old *child*." This last was said in response to my evident admiration for Patrecia, which I displayed openly; I had not yet told her about the affair. Barbara was now thirty-five.

At first, I resisted fiercely her statement that I did not love her, still fighting to see us as we were in our youth. After a while, I began to wonder if she might be right; the possibility still had the power to fill me with sadness. My passion for her had gone, but something within me still found it difficult to let go. She could not yet let go either. Perhaps because, as teenagers, we had given each other what neither of us had ever received before, we remained in each other's mind as an irreplacable resource, a point of support not to be relinquished.

When Barbara and I discussed our marital difficulties with Ayn, we tried to focus on the incompatibilities that seemed intrinsic to our relationship for many years; Barbara did not tell her about Wilfred and I, of course, did not tell her about Patrecia. I thought that with Ayn's extraordinary powers of analysis I might acquire some new, deeper understanding of why and how Barbara and I had gone wrong. I still cared enough to want to understand that. The chief result of our sessions was to drive me closer to the conclusion that the marriage had been a mistake and that no happy solution could ever be found. I doubted that, at this point, Ayn very seriously wanted it to be found.

It was wrong, I knew, to solicit Ayn's help with our marriage while withholding information about Wilfred and Patrecia. Barbara did not seem troubled by her deception, and when I asked her about it, she announced, "Wilfred is irrelevant to our problems." Fine, I thought; so is Patrecia — knowing that my resentment and guilt were speaking, not my intelligence.

I did not communicate to Ayn my growing certainty that my marriage was finished, because I knew that it would only heighten her desire for a resurrection of our romantic relationship. One of the values of the marriage was that it operated as a shield against Ayn's emotional expectations. What I wanted was for Ayn herself to grasp that our time as lovers had passed, and that now, after fifteen years together, we should be the best and closest of friends.

There are other bonds no less powerful than romantic love. I felt bonded to Ayn with a symbiotic intensity; a cable of steel connected our souls; life with her was rarely happy any longer, except for brief, exhilarating flashes, but life without her continued to feel like death.

I did not want to be in the tradition of Leo: I did not want her to experience rejection. If she were the one to lead me to the conclusion that a romance no longer fit our circumstances, I reasoned, her pride would be protected and there would be hope for our future together.

I *wanted* that future; I wanted Ayn's friendship, I wanted the Objectivist world we had created together, and I wanted Patrecia — and my deepest conviction was that, in reason, I *should* be able to have it all. I had to find a way to make Ayn see that.

I knew that the deception in the manipulation I was attempting was in conflict with my own convictions about human relationships. I paced the floor of my office for countless hours, trying to think my way toward an alternative that would not result in the total collapse of the life I had built. I could not find it. I knew that absolute truthfulness would mean the end of everything. Check your premises, I kept repeating like a mantra, but the torment remained: *which* premises?

An angry voice within me would demand: Have *they* no responsibility in any of this? Barbara doesn't love me; she's in love with Wilfred; why doesn't she leave me? What's her payoff for remaining in a life she says is intolerable? And at the start of our affair Ayn herself said it would be absurd to imagine we would have more than a year or two. "Can either of you see me as an older woman, a few years from now, pursuing a younger man? It would be contemptible." She had said that to Barbara and Frank. Why did she not have the honor and sanity to remember it now, and to act accordingly? And if she was hurt and appalled by my behavior with her, and did not choose to accept me as only a friend, did she not have the option of withdrawing, without turning my lack of sexual responsiveness into a moral issue of cosmic dimensions? And Frank — did he not have any responsibility? If he was suffering in his marriage with Ayn, wasn't it his obligation to say so? Then I would tell myself that all of that was irrelevant. Their actions were their moral responsibility. I had to be concerned with mine.

And yet, I would ask myself, how do I know my feelings are not irrational? How do I know this is not all some once-in-a-lifetime emotional storm that will disappear suddenly? Are there not moments when I love Barbara, desire Ayn sexually, doubt my feelings for Patrecia? How am I to act boldly and place everything in jeopardy when my brain is chaos and I am in an agony of confusion? *Do* I lack courage? Then why does courage in other arenas come so easily to me?

Is it rational to give up Ayn and Objectivism? No. Is it rational to give up Patrecia? No. *Then of what does rationality consist?*

All the years of mangling, denying, "transcending" my emotions, were now taking their revenge. By too often forbidding myself to feel, I had denied myself access to much of my inner life and to many of my most intimate values; I had undermined my ability to think — in just

that area where thinking was now urgently needed. My sense of helplessness kept building.

During the first year, I rarely felt guilt when I was with Patrecia. The
intensity of what I experienced with her wiped out the reality of the
rest of my life. But by the fall of 1964, the weight of my self-reproach
was becoming excruciating, like a great rock crushing self-respect out
of my body.

Never before had I been so troubled by a conflict between what I
wanted to do and what I thought was right. I had tended to look on
such conflicts with scorn. Never before had I known such tension, dismay, and anxiety. Now, my own torment felt humiliating.

One day I returned from Patrecia's to find Allan Blumenthal and Leonard Peikoff waiting for me in my apartment; Barbara had let them in,
then gone downstairs to the NBI offices.

"Nathan doesn't love us anymore," Allan announced to Leonard in
mock solemnity; he looked mischievously forlorn.

Bewildered, I asked, "What's this about?"

They proceeded to explain that I had become inexplicably kinder in
my dealings with them; I had withdrawn all demands and expectations
concerning Objectivism; I projected that I merely wanted them to enjoy life. They spoke in the exaggerated manner of describing a tragedy.

The change in me they were describing had begun almost immediately following the start of my affair with Patrecia. Some of the cause
was my own happiness, some came from my feelings of guilt. *What
moral right have I — now — to expect anything of anyone?* was the
conscious thought in my mind.

Leonard shook his head in half-mocking, half-serious regret, and
declared, "You've lost respect for us; there's no other possible explanation. You've given up on us; that's why you've become so pleasant
and easygoing. Since you no longer think we're able to amount to
much, you figure we may as well be happy."

"I can't win with you two," I answered, feeling a mixture of amusement and sadness, feeling also that what I was saying was true.

If my relationship with Allan had its ambiguities, my relationship
with Leonard had even more. One afternoon, about a year earlier, I
had dropped by Ayn's for a visit, and Leonard was there, being coun-
seled by Ayn about a personal problem — and Ayn had asked him to
repeat for my benefit what he had just said to her. She had been trying
to raise his self-esteem, not too successfully, and he had confided in
her that, "Whenever I begin to feel better about myself, whenever I
begin to feel pride, I see Nathan's face, and I imagine I see scorn and
contempt, even though I've never actually seen that look on his face in

reality, and my good feelings about myself collapse." I was stunned. Then Ayn had protested, "But Nathan is your champion. He's the one who most often defends you when I'm angry at you." Leonard had answered miserably, "I know. I know." Ayn had gone on, "Perhaps it's the fact that I'm a woman — and you want the esteem of a man. Nathan is the man you most admire, the man you most want to be like." Then Leonard had said, "It isn't that I feel he despises me, but that deep inside I feel he *should*, if he really knew me." "Oh, Leonard." Ayn had sighed, while I had stood looking at the two of them, feeling as alienated as I had ever felt in my life. What does he want of me? I had thought. What do they all want of me?

Now, grinning cheerfully, Allan declared, "You're becoming mellower and gentler. Can a mellow and gentle Nathan still be Nathan?"

I knew that underneath this banter was a curiosity and a wonder about what it all meant.

"Old chaps," I said, because there was nothing else to say, "you drive me nuts."

Within a year Leonard made Ayn angrier than she had ever been with him before, and he was exiled to the University of Denver, where he had been offered a job teaching philosophy. His offense, as always, involved some failure to support and defend Ayn and her work in his dealings with other people. His assignment was to redeem himself in Ayn's eyes, to prove somehow that he could be a good Objectivist, perhaps by his proselytizing in Denver. He would accept this verdict as he accepted all of Ayn's verdicts, as reasonable and appropriate justice. I was chief prosecutor at his trial, and afterward I had a special dispensation from Ayn to be kind to him privately, within limits, so that his suffering did not drive him past a point of no return. The anxiety level of the entire Collective went up after this event: if this could happen to Leonard, it could happen to anyone; and if it did, every friend in the group would be aligned against one — as they were now aligned against Leonard.

Looking at the Collective, on the night of Leonard's temporary expulsion, I thought: if I were to tell Ayn the full truth and she were to react as I know she will, is there one of you who would not fall into line behind whatever she might then choose to say about me? There was not a person in our group whose intelligence was not above average; but in this issue, their intelligence would be useless.

People spoke to me about Patrecia as if she were their personal discovery.

In the summer of 1964, Florence's oldest son, Leonard, came to New York City for a visit. Then sixteen, with a remarkable intellectual capacity, he was tall, athletic, intellectual, exuberant, and with enough energy for three teenagers. I was very fond of him.

Leonard went with Joan and Patrecia to the New York World's Fair. He had known Joan before, but he was meeting Patrecia for the first time. Later he said to me, "Patrecia is *fantastic*. Has she got energy! She can keep up with me! Have you ever noticed how physically strong she is? Watch how she moves! And yet she's so slender! Isn't she *something*?" Grateful for the opportunity to talk about Patrecia with someone, I asked my nephew what else he liked about her. "When she looks at me," he answered with deep feeling, "she *sees* me. Adults don't do that with kids. She asks about my life and what I'm doing, and she's *interested*, she really *listens*. She makes me feel *respected*."

Patrecia and Edith Efron became friends. This intrigued me, since Edith, who was a few years older than I, was among the more cerebral members of our group and was usually contemptuous of nonintellectuals (as well as most intellectuals). "With Patsy I can *play*," Edith announced cheerfully. "With Patsy I can be *young*."

When Joan visited me in my office, she said earnestly, "You still don't know Patrecia very well, do you? You really should take the time. I don't know anyone else like her. I don't even know how to explain this — she reaches me. That's all I can say. She reaches me." I saw that there were tears in Joan's eyes; this was totally unlike her. "She has a special kind of goodness that makes you feel good when you're with her. As if she sees in you what no one else sees, something intimate and precious." In that moment I wanted to embrace Joan and tell her how well I understood; instead, I listened impassively. I said only, "I like Patrecia very much. And I like what comes out of you when you talk about her." When Joan had gone, I realized that in a sense she had been speaking not about Patrecia but about herself, and how she wanted me to see her, and how she wanted to experience herself, and I regretted that my personal involvement with Patrecia had diverted me from the deeper intent of her communication.

I thought that there was something very important that Patrecia gave to people that I wanted to learn.

"It's my sense of life," Patrecia said, when I spoke to her about it.

No, I answered, it was more than that.

"Then I'll tell you what it is," she said thoughtfully. "When I'm with someone, often I don't pay much attention to the self they show the world. I always try to find their best self, even if it's buried deeply, even if they don't know about it, and I try to speak to that part of them, as if that's the only part that really matters."

"But isn't that faking reality, in a way? — I mean, to ignore all the rest?"

She answered that she did not ignore all the rest, that she saw it, but chose not be controlled by it in her responses. "I admit I don't see everything you see. But that's one of the things I want to learn from you — how to see everything, without letting that kill my ability to respond as I do." She said many times and in many ways, "I want to learn what you know, but I don't want to lose who I am." It took me a long time to understand what she meant.

Part of what she meant, although she did not have the words to tell me then, was that she wanted to master a higher level of linear, analytic, conceptual functioning, without weakening her strongly developed intuitive capabilities. But that was not all. "Ayn's writing," she said, "makes you very aware of how much evil there is in the world, how much irrationality and cruelty, and it's important to be aware of that. But a lot of NBI students — that's all they see. They may talk about a benevolent sense of life, but they're really very malevolent, always looking for evidence that the world is an evil place. And when your sense of life is malevolent, you become mean and cruel yourself — never mind what you say philosophically. I wish Ayn would write more articles that stress the positive in life, like the best parts of her novels. I don't dare say this to anyone in the Collective because they would all say I was crazy — what does a twenty-four-year-old model know? — but I can say it to you. Sometimes when I'm with the Collective, I'm afraid. It's not just NBI students, it's the Collective as well — something has got to them. A deadness. I don't want it to get to me."

On an impulse that I knew was a mistake even as I did it, I attempted to relay this conversation to Barbara. Her response was to ask me if I didn't think Patrecia was inclined to be hysterical.

"Patrecia," Barbara announced, "is a very strange girl. She never reads newspapers. She knows absolutely nothing about current events. She doesn't know things that *everyone* knows. After a lecture one night, a few of us were talking, and she said, 'Who's Chiang Kai-shek?' You don't find that eerie?" I thought, but did not say, One day, when she learns that such things are worth her attention, Patrecia will know who Chiang Kai-shek is; but will you ever know what Patrecia knows?

In October, Patrecia and Larry moved to a new, larger apartment, the penthouse of a building one block away from where Barbara and I lived. From my bedroom, I could look east on Thirty-fourth Street and see the penthouse and imagine that behind those glass windows Patrecia was looking back at me. Almost every morning, while Barbara was still sleeping, I got up and stood looking out from our window for a long time.

"Is it possible to be in love with two people at the same time?"

This was one of the most often asked questions following my lectures. At first, I was surprised; I could not imagine why so many people would be interested; gradually I gathered that many people felt this issue touched their lives. "In the realm of human relationships," I typically answered, "I suppose we must say that almost anything is possible. Two people can each embody our values, or perhaps slightly different aspects of our values, in so profound a way that we cannot help but feel love for both of them. And yet, I have to add that sustaining a love for two persons and integrating that love into the everyday structure of one's life has got to be almost terrifyingly difficult. Sooner or later, one relationship tends to lose out to the other; and the danger is that the person who tries it will make a mess of both."

I was acutely aware of Ayn sitting beside me as I spoke, aware of the faintly superior smile on her lips, and knowing what she would stand up and say when I had completed my answer. "It's a project that only giants can handle properly," she always added. "When average people talk about it, they mean something much more casual than love as Mr. Branden and I discuss it. If you really mean a serious passion, if you mean romantic love, the highest kind of rationality and integrity are demanded. And even then, it's a very rare phenomenon, nothing that happens every day, nothing that most people even need to think about." Our students would listen as if we were discussing life on another planet, and I wondered: is it possible they don't hear what she's saying? To me, it sounded like a public announcement of our relationship — or what our relationship had once been.

Another question we often heard was, "Can heroes such as Miss Rand writes about actually exist?" Ayn would always insist on answering that question herself. Inwardly I would cringe, knowing what was coming. "You're looking at two of them," she would say, pointing to me and herself. Pointing to Frank and Barbara, she would add, "And there are two more." This would effectively end the discussion.

On one occasion someone asked a question about some viewpoint of Ayn's and I launched into an answer, then stopped and apologized for speaking for her when she was present in the room. "You can speak for me any time you wish," Ayn announced, "on any subject whatsoever." Turning to the students she stated, "There is no subject on which Mr. Branden is not qualified to speak for me."

Notwithstanding the growing tensions between us, Ayn continued to pay me the most unreserved compliments on every possible occasion. Feeling uncomfortable and fraudulent, I would tell her, "Ayn, I am *not* John Galt."

"Yes, you are," she would insist, "except for a few blemishes."

When I recall my erratic behavior with Ayn during this period, my absentmindedness, my elusiveness, my coldness — alternating, as always, with expressions of passionate devotion — I am inclined to think that at least some of it was motivated by a subconscious desire to be seen realistically, to jolt Ayn out of her fantasies, to get a message through that I was not prepared to convey in words.

At the height of my arrogance I had not imagined I was John Galt, but by the end of 1964, every time I mounted the NBI lecture platform, I felt less like Nathaniel Branden.

In 1960 I had become interested in hypnosis. I had discovered the papers of Dr. Milton Erickson, a psychotherapeutic genius, the most innovative figure in the history of hypnosis. I became keenly interested in what hypnotic phenomena could teach us about the nature of the human mind.

Over the next several years, I did hypnotic demonstrations for the Collective and various other friends — from the induction of positive and negative hallucinations, to time distortion, to posthypnotic suggestion. Ayn was suspicious and borderline hostile. "It's a fraud," she insisted initially. The very notion of trance seemed incompatible with her view of an ideally rational consciousness — whereas I, in contrast, saw altered states of consciousness as capacities of mind that could sometimes be highly useful. Today, of course, there is much wider appreciation of the ways hypnosis can be helpful in all the healing professions.

One evening I did a demonstration of age regression. I used as my subject one of our secretaries at NBI who I knew to be an excellent subject. I had regressed her to the age of thirteen, and she was doing splendidly, but I saw that a few of my friends, and especially Ayn, continued to look skeptical. Allan Blumenthal, who was most in tune with what I was doing, got a sudden inspiration and handed me a ballpoint pen, motioning me to show it to my subject. When I did so, she frowned in unmistakably genuine puzzlement. "What is this?" she wanted to know. "It's not a pen and it's not a pencil. *What is it?*" Ayn gasped as understanding hit her: when this young woman was thirteen, ballpoint pens did not exist. "You win," she muttered reluctantly at our next meeting. "I have no explanation of how it's possible, but obviously hypnosis is something real." Not three months later, I heard her announce to a visiting professor in her living room, "Hypnosis is a fraud." In response to my request for an explanation, she said only, "I'm just not convinced."

Thereafter, hypnosis occupied a strange status between us: neither real nor unreal, neither a fact nor a nonfact, just my private eccentricity, to be indulged by her because of who I was. I recall the disconcerted look on her face during some of our discussions, torn as she was between the impulse to declare hypnosis nonsense and her reluctance to suggest that her "intellectual heir" had lost his mind. Occasionally she would make passing reference to this interest of mine as evidence that we were drifting apart.

Almost any new interest of mine could now lead to an unpleasant conversation. I tried to persuade her to read Arthur Koestler's superb book, *The Ghost in the Machine,* explaining that while I did not agree with some of his conclusions, his treatment of evolution was brilliant and very important psychologically and philosophically. When I attempted to explain non-Darwinian theories of evolution, she nodded with perfunctory interest, then quickly became impatient with me. "You have time for everything but you and me," she declared, "hypnosis, Koestler — what next? Extrasensory perception?"

When I tried to tell her of some new research that suggested that certain kinds of depression had a biological basis, she answered angrily, "*I* can tell you what causes depression. I can tell you about rational depression and I can tell you about irrational depression — the second is mostly self-pity — and in neither case does biology enter into it." I asked her how she could make a scientific statement with such certainty, since she had never studied the field; she shrugged bitterly and snapped, "Because I know how to think." Evidently she interpreted my comments about biology as undermining her idea of free will, which was not my intention.

I was astonished at how closed she typically was to any new knowledge that seemed to clash with her familiar paradigms. Outside the territory where she felt in full intellectual control, she was utterly lacking in a spirit of openness or adventure. Where my work was concerned, she made it abundantly clear that my task as a psychologist was to develop knowledge that would support her work as a philosopher. She was instantly on the attack about any line of inquiry that had even the *appearance* of challenging her notion of "the rational." She projected herself as the commander of an eternally beleaguered fortress.

In her grandiosity and suspiciousness, her behavior bordered at times on paranoia, although that is not a thought I would have permitted myself. The worst I would have accused her of were the slight excesses so often typical of genius.

I did not attach significance to the fact that, since her late twenties, she had been taking amphetamines daily, on the advice of a physician, for weight control; I do not think the discovery had been yet been made that a protracted use of amphetamines can precipitate paranoiac reactions — a discovery that would have horrified no one more than Ayn. Nor was I aware that her single-track obsession with her own frame of reference, her reflex suspiciousness of anything foreign to it, almost went with the territory of being a major innovator: such blinders often have functional utility for the creative process, whatever the cost in terms of an out-of-balance psyche. Freud and Wilhelm Reich were two examples in my own field. Milton Erickson, I would one day learn, was another; Erickson, I am told, tended to speak as if no other work in psychology but his own could possibly be worth studying.

A tendency already in evidence when I first met her grew much more pronounced during the 1960s: regarding her personal likes and dislikes in art, literature, and music as being very close to laws of nature. If, for example, she regarded Rembrandt as "a talented draftsman, nothing more," if she was antagonized by Shakespeare's "fatalism," if she detested Beethoven's "malevolence" — then anyone who spoke admiringly of Rembrandt, Shakespeare, or Beethoven might very well be met with spoken or unspoken contempt. "Not my kind of person," she would say, "not my sense of life." Similarly, if someone failed to enjoy Victor Hugo, or Dostoevsky, or even Mickey Spillane, that person would be watched carefully for other signs of deficiency. In March 1966, she wrote an article for *The Objectivist,* entitled "Art and Sense of Life" (subsequently reprinted in *The Romantic Manifesto,* 1969), which she concluded with these ominous words: "When one learns to translate the meaning of an art work into objective terms, one discovers that nothing is as potent as art in exposing the essence of a man's character. An artist reveals his naked soul in his work — and so, gentle reader, do you when you respond to it." The use of words like "expose," "naked," and "gentle reader" could have no other purpose than to intimidate — to scare hell out of — her audience. I can still see the angry, gleeful grin with which she read that paragraph to me.

To our more fanatical and conformist students, Objectivism did not signify merely the body of abstract philosophical propositions and arguments that we wrote about and taught. Its meaning was expanded to include every personal like and dislike of Ayn's. They absorbed and embraced Ayn's implicit dictum, "Objectivism, *c'est moi.*" These students proved they were good Objectivists by their skill at mimicking Ayn's viewpoints down to the smallest detail — re-creating Ayn, as it were, within themselves. They further proved it by watching one another, suspiciously and critically, for deviations; if they could not match Ayn in intellect, they could at least match her in harshness. They scourged one another mercilessly for any signs of "social metaphysics."

Patrecia had always spoken of Ayn with great affection and regard, but one day I asked for her first impressions when she saw Ayn at my lecture, and she answered, with some hesitancy, "I was disappointed. I didn't like those slashes of bitterness in her face. And her eyes — to tell you the truth, now please don't become upset, I felt I was seeing madness there. Enormous anger. Something out of my childhood. Of course later I came to see her as a wonderful person, but still —" I took a long breath, to control myself and to give me time to think. Part of me felt indignation against Patrecia — how could she say this of the author of *Atlas Shrugged* — while another part felt admiration for her courage, for the unfrightened way she looked at me as she spoke, even though she knew how her words would impact me. I heard Ayn's voice roaring in my brain: *if you are who you say you are, you will now walk away from Patrecia and never look back.* I looked into the steady blue eyes watching me across the lunch table, as if she could track my thoughts, her face lifted in acceptance of whatever I might now choose to say, and I knew that no power on earth could make me abandon this woman. "Patrecia," I said, "please don't ever say this to me again. I understand that you're only describing what you felt in that first moment, but it's not something I wish to hear about Ayn Rand." She nodded gravely, without apology, and answered, "I understand." The terror at the root of my response was the not-to-be-admitted knowledge that I had seen in Ayn's eyes precisely what Patrecia had seen. To think of Ayn as mad in any respect whatsoever was to plunge my universe into chaos. If there was a streak of irrationality running through Ayn, what did this mean about my entire life? What did this mean about me?

And yet at some level I, too, was aware of something wrong in Ayn, an explosive rage that did not fit my more exalted view of her. I wanted to get Ayn out of my question-and-answer periods, for example, because I was appalled by how she sometimes abused our students. Since Ayn did not enjoy these sessions, it was simple enough to thank her for her past help and to say that NBI was sufficiently well established that her participation on a weekly basis was not necessary. "Thank God," Barbara muttered as Ayn began to come less and less frequently.

· · ·

"Larry and I are fighting a lot," Patrecia told me, in the spring of 1965. "And it's not his fault. What he wants is reasonable — he wants a wife in the full sense, and he has a right to expect that — only I don't have it in me to give."

My own marriage was moving toward collapse. Barbara and I were quarreling almost constantly. One moment she was violently angry toward me, the next, hurt and bewildered. One moment I was projecting warmth and affection, the next, a deadly chilling remoteness.

Toward the end of summer, we agreed to a "trial separation." That was how we named it. "I can't stand how miserable we both are," Barbara said. "I can't stand fighting all the time." I do not know what she thought silently, but I felt that once I walked out the door of our apartment with my bags under my arms — once I experienced life apart from her — I would never return to our marriage. Perhaps that was why I initially resisted her tearful, angry suggestion of a separation.

I took an apartment on the third floor of our building, telling our friends that I needed the office space, not wishing to make the break public until Barbara and I definitely decided what we wished to do.

We discovered that, living apart, we could often be kinder to each other. "There might still be hope," Barbara said to me tenderly.

I asked her if she had ever thought of marrying Wilfred, in the event that he would leave his wife. "You don't understand," she said wistfully. "You are the only *husband* I ever wanted."

When I told Ayn of the decision to separate, she breathed what looked like a long-suppressed sigh of relief. "Now, darling, perhaps there will be a chance for us to be in love again."

SIXTEEN

I want to see real, living, and in the hours of my own days, that glory
I create as an illusion! I want to know that there is someone, somewhere, who wants it, too! Or else what is the use of seeing it, and
working, and burning for an impossible vision? A spirit, too, needs
fuel. It can run dry.

These lines are spoken by Kay Gonda, the heroine of *Ideal,* a play Ayn
had written in 1934, during a time of difficult professional struggle.
Ayn referred to the speech often, applying it to herself. "A spirit, too,
needs fuel," she would say, "and I am running dry; I am running dry."

Gonda is a beautiful actress who projects such a quality of glory that
she comes to stand as a kind of symbol for the values and ideals of her
admirers; her quest in the play is to discover whether their professed
worship in fact has any meaning — a theme that was a lifelong preoccupation of Ayn's. Gonda appears in the life of a number of her fans,
seemingly in great danger, and they are challenged to help her at considerable risk to themselves. Only one man, Johnny Dawes, passes her
test and dies tragically and unnecessarily in order (he believes) to save
her.

The play was never produced. After Ayn's death, Leonard Peikoff
published it in a collection entitled *The Early Ayn Rand.* The play is
bitter, anguished, radically unlike her future works in its emotional
quality, although traces of that quality are present in all her writing.
It is clearly the cry of a soul that feels itself wounded. It illuminates an
aspect of Ayn's psychology that was to become increasingly and ca-
lamitously central to our relationship.

In the story, Kay Gonda has spread the rumor that she is wanted by
the police for murder and that she is trying to escape arrest. Not one
of her admirers is willing to help her, until she meets Johnny Dawes,

a young man alone and utterly alienated, a man "who cannot live to-day," with whom the actress has the following exchange:

GONDA. What do you dream of?
JOHNNY. Nothing. Of what account are dreams?
GONDA. Of what account is life?
JOHNNY. None. But who made it so?
GONDA. Those who cannot dream.
JOHNNY. No. Those who can *only* dream.

The play was not meant to be "realistic," in that Ayn did not really believe that people should be willing to put their life on the line for an actress they loved but did not actually know. Yet in the story Johnny does redeem Gonda's view of humanity by dying for her, and Gonda accepts his gesture when she has the power to prevent it.

There was a parallel between the play and the relationship of everyone in our circle to Ayn. What Ayn made overpoweringly clear to us was that the ultimate test and proof of one's idealism was one's loyalty to her work and to her personally. We absorbed this view profoundly, the consequence being that our self-esteem was intimately tied to our support of Ayn and to her positive regard of us. The "trance" in which we existed permitted this.

It was one of my most disastrous errors — that I overidentified "loyalty to my values" with "loyalty to Ayn's happiness." This dangerously undermined my reason when I attempted to resolve the conflicts building to a climax between us.

"Do you still love me?" Ayn would ask.

"I still love you," I would answer, without permitting a moment's hesitation. *Ayn, see me; see our context realistically; come out of your dream.*

"Am I still a sexual being to you?"

"You will always be a sexual being." *Listen to the form of your question. What answer can you expect?*

"I am not just an older woman chasing a younger man, am I?"

"The younger man is chasing you." *Now I am collaborating in your self-deception. I do not want to cause you more pain than the world has caused you already. But in the end I am going to, because lies do not work.*

"I believe that if I were eighty years old, I would still have the right to see myself as a woman."

"You *should* see yourself as a woman, as long as you're alive." *I cannot abandon you.*

"I'm not ready to grow old gracefully."

"Why should you grow old gracefully?" *Can you not sense what my answers cost me, as I sense what your questions cost you?*

"Why can't you always be as wonderful — and *present* — as you're being right now?"

"I don't know, Ayn. I don't know." *You are the greatest mind on the planet. Wake up. Wake up.*

Ayn and Frank moved from their apartment on Thirty-sixth Street — into a newer, more spacious apartment on the sixth floor of our building at 120 East Thirty-fourth. Now we were all on different floors of one building: Ayn and Frank, Barbara, the offices of NBI and *The Objectivist Newsletter,* and I — and Larry and Patrecia were a block away. I recalled the title of a novel by Anaïs Nin: *House of Incest.*

One day Patrecia came to my apartment, obviously wanting to talk yet acting strangely shy and reticent.

Finally she declared, "I've decided what I want to do professionally. I want to be an actress." She looked at me as if she anticipated a negative reaction.

She was not entirely wrong. It was one of the rare times I did not want her to see what I was feeling.

On hearing her announcement, my spirits crashed — not because I doubted she could be a good actress; I knew she could be — but because I regarded the profession of acting as one in which great suffering was almost inevitable. Failure bred one kind of pain, success bred another.

I felt afraid for Patrecia and afraid for our future.

"What do you think?" she asked nervously and challengingly.

It was axiomatic to me that I would give her choice my full support. "I'm thinking that if this is what you want, what's the best way to proceed? Tell me, why are you so tense?"

"I've always disliked everything I've ever heard about acting and that whole world. I've always thought of it as phony, unreal, crazy. I thought you might think I'd lost my mind. I remember some producer saying that he had rarely known a happy actor and never a happy actress. Still — it's what I feel myself drawn to, it's what I want to do, and I believe I can be good. I've been weighing this for a long time. I know it's a horrible sort of life — probably."

I thought of my friend Ralph Roseman, who had come into my life some years ago when he wrote Ayn an enthusiastic letter about *Atlas Shrugged*; he was a successful theatrical manager and a sometime teacher of acting. I proposed a meeting between them.

"I was the first person you and Patrecia spoke to about her interest in acting," Ralph would recall years later. "After working with her for a while, and having many discussions about the theater, and being impressed by the questions she asked, I thought her potential was enormous. She brought to her lessons qualities that actors spend years developing, such as emotional openness and a sense of daring. She took direction very well. Her one fault, which is common with talented beginners, was that she threw herself into a role with such relish that she failed to relate fully to the other actors. Later, when she studied with Rose Schulman, I saw that this trait was being corrected. Rose shared my opinion of Patrecia's potential. The one performance that I saw her in — in 1966, in Philadelphia — was Lorraine Hansberry's *The Sign in Sidney Brustein's Window*. It was her first stage performance, I believe. She was marvelous. Her energy and spirit excited the audience. Her appearance, of course, was beautiful. One would never have thought this was her first job. She had something that was electrifying. Vulnerability and raw power."

In the late afternoon of November 9, 1965, the lights of New York City went out, in the famous power failure that would remind many people of *Atlas Shrugged*.

I knew that Barbara was in the office of NBI and that Ayn was in her apartment. When I tried to telephone Patrecia's apartment and couldn't get through, I became alarmed, for no reason I could explain. I ran down the stairs to the street, then down the street to her apartment building. With the power out, the elevators were not working. I ran up twenty flights to the penthouse. Discovering that she was not there, I returned to the street, which was now dark, and began searching for her. Eventually I gave up and went to Ayn's apartment.

Within a few minutes, Patrecia appeared with a flashlight and Frank. Their spirits were festive. Like a number of other people, Patrecia had been helping those on the streets or in darkened buildings find their way to their destinations. Encountering Frank, she had offered to escort him home. "Aren't you a guardian angel!" Ayn exclaimed. "Frank's rescuer! Oh, thank you, darling!" Within an hour or two, we were all there together: Ayn, Frank, Patrecia, Larry, and Barbara and me — eating and talking and laughing by candlelight. "Isn't this like a wonderful scene in a novel?" Ayn said cheerfully. Later, I was stunned and pleased to hear her say to Patrecia, "You have such an air of benevolence; that's why I love you." I reminded myself that for Ayn this was only a moment's mood. As absurd as it seems, that evening I felt supremely contented.

One month later, in December, Barbara and I decided to make our separation public and official. We had not yet decided to initiate divorce action, but we wanted to end our pretense of being a happily married couple. Among the first people we told were Elayne and Harry, and Allan and Joan; all four took the news badly.

Not long after that, Larry and Patrecia informed Allan that they had decided to separate and divorce. He asked them to withhold a public announcement for several months — "because Barbara and Nathan are just about to announce their separation, and we don't want people thinking the two events are related. You know how gossip and rumors start." They agreed to his request.

I learned that Patrecia's sister Leisha was also separating from her husband. Patrecia remarked, "It's funny. All my life, Leisha has followed me in whatever I've done. If I took up a sport, she took it up. When I got engaged, she got engaged. When I decided to go to Hunter College, Leisha decided she wanted to go. Now I wonder if her breaking up with Randy is just another imitation. God, she makes me feel suffocated sometimes. Being someone's identical twin can be difficult." A short while later, Leisha announced that she had decided to pursue a career in acting.

Barbara and I denied to everyone that any other romantic interest was involved in our decision to separate. "We're just incompatible," we said. "We're just not able to be happy together." I was astonished at the distress we caused our friends and families, for whom our marriage evidently had meant more than I had appreciated. That we chose not to take anyone into our confidence as to the real nature of our problems only increased the sense of distance that Barbara and I experienced with everyone; we both suffered over that.

I wanted to tell Barbara about Patrecia and me; there was now no reason not to — except for Ayn. To tell Barbara was to ask her to lie to Ayn, as I was doing, and I decided this was unacceptable. So while I became progressively more open about my feelings for Patrecia, I did not yet tell Barbara the full truth. Barbara was now quite open in her jealousy of Patrecia, which mystified me. I wondered why she cared. She kept questioning me about Patrecia's and my relationship and I kept describing it — unconvincingly — as a friendship.

Even though Barbara's and my separation was now official, and she and Wilfred were accordingly much freer to enjoy their affair, she continued to convey that it would somehow be a tragedy if we did not find our way back to each other. Occasionally I found myself wondering if she could be right, but not often. I gathered that many of the old tensions between Wilfred and her had once again begun to trouble them.

Many years later Barbara declared in her biography of Ayn that by the summer of 1965, exhausted by our relationship and in love with another man, she was intent on obtaining a divorce. In fact, for a long time after that she was still requesting a reconciliation. In May 1966, about eight months after I moved out, she went on a world cruise — "to be by myself, to think about the future and what I want out of life, perhaps to find a solution to our relationship" — and she wrote several almost lyrical love letters, which invariably began, "Nathan Darling" or "My Dearest Love." In one of these letters, she asked, "Did I ever tell you why I love you?" — and proceeded to tell me in passionately complementary terms, and to inform me that I provided the inspiration for the hero of a novel she had begun to think about. In another letter she stated, to my confusion, that she now knew that everything she had ever wanted out of love was possible, and that it was I who had made it so for her. "I will always love you," she wrote. She proposed that I fly over and meet her in London; I declined. I did not call the ship on her birthday, May 14, because I wanted to impress upon her the full reality of our present state. Then I proceeded to feel self-reproachful, knowing she would be hurt, and subsequently wrote to her rather more warmly than I felt.

Even though the Scotts had not yet publicly announced their separation, Patrecia moved out of the penthouse and into a studio apartment a block away, 165 East Thirty-fifth Street, where Barbara and I had once lived.

"I think one of the most important bonds between us," I remarked to Patrecia one evening at dinner, "is our excitement. With you I don't have to sit on anything. Our energies are the same. We love and enjoy each other's excitement."

"Yes!" she exclaimed. "With other people I often feel like I'm too much. But never with you."

"Patrecia, I think this issue of shared energies and shared excitement is important to an understanding of the dynamics of love."

"Another very important bond between us," she said to me during one of our drives in the country, "is that we both formed the idea early in life that adults were crazy — frightened and irrational — we both have that sense of somehow creating ourselves out of a nightmare — or in reaction against it — I don't know how to say it — and we both decided we wouldn't let other people get to us, we wouldn't accept their view of life or become like them — and so much of who we are and how we developed came out of that decision." Again I nodded in agreement.

One evening, at a party at Wilfred's, Patrecia sat quietly beside me in a corner of the living room while Allan Blumenthal, who had joined us, unexpectedly began to talk about how much I had contributed to his and Joan's life, and how much everyone in the Collective had been helped by me. I struggled between wanting to appreciate his words and finding his manner obsequious, subtly self-abnegating, and sycophantic. "You gave me my career," he was saying. "You taught me to believe in myself. You made my marriage to Joan possible. You contributed so much to our happiness. I hope you know how appreciative I feel. I can't think of a time when, if we asked for help, you weren't right there. Look around this room: think how much you've given to everyone here. You gave us Ayn's world. You gave us our best selves. Not one single person would be as happy as they are now if it had not been for you. You must feel very proud. You ought to." At some level I was aware that he was reaching out to me, seeking some kind of response from me that was not forthcoming and perhaps never had been. I felt an intense desire to escape. I thanked him and squeezed his shoulder, and he moved away. When I glanced at Patrecia I was astonished by the odd mixture of protectiveness and severity I saw on her face. "It must be very uncomfortable for you — so often receiving what they think are compliments from people who are so frightened and insecure. I wanted to tell Allan to go away. To him I'm sure you looked polite and compassionate. To me you looked young and lonely."

I felt more loved by Patrecia than I had ever felt loved before, in the terms that mattered most to me. I also felt better understood, in just those respects I now most badly needed.

I did not feel blindly worshiped; she was completely unsentimental and straightforward in calling me on my faults any time she believed I was thoughtless, unfair, unkind, or self-indulgent. I felt absolutely supported by her; but when she looked at me, I saw a consciousness that was not afraid to see what she saw.

Perhaps because of her youth, perhaps because that was what she was most sensitive to in people, Patrecia seemed especially keyed in to the younger part of me, the part untouched by my experiences with Barbara or Ayn, the part most open, receptive, and unarmored. In all our interactions it was as if she were constantly calling me back to that younger self, as if to remind me of an identity I had allowed to become submerged. "At times," I said, "I feel almost as if you have been sent to me — don't ask me by whom — to help me remember who I truly am."

"Isn't it funny?" she remarked. "You draw out the most adult side of me — and I draw out the youth in you."

"We give each other what each of us most needs right now," I answered.

In the past, when I had thought about the basic attraction in romantic love, I thought in terms of basic affinities, of shared values and sense of life. Now, without denying the importance of these affinities, I be-

gan to appreciate the role of complementary differences. With Patrecia, I simultaneously felt a profound sense of mutuality, a sharing of
basic attributes — and a sense of challenging and exciting differences
that stimulated each of us in the direction of greater balance.

My verbal-intellectual skills were more finely honed than Patrecia's;
she was more developed in the intuitive area. Patrecia lived far more
"in her body" than I did, and awakened my physical consciousness.
She was in far better touch with her feelings; her emotional openness
and willingness to be transparent facilitated the process of my own
deepening contact with my inner self; I began to learn the power of
vulnerability and receptivity. She, on the other hand, began to acquire
a taste for more intellectually demanding pursuits, as evidenced in the
philosophical questions she would raise and the books she wanted to
read. I put her in touch with her disowned ruthlessness; she put me in
touch with my inner child. I was more oriented to the single-track purposefulness of work and career, she to the nurturing of a relationship;
we learned from each other and began to cultivate our subdominant
side. All these processes began slowly and subtly; they became evident
only over time.

I did not have the words or the understanding to name what was
happening; it happened primarily at the level of feeling and implication. Without words, concepts, explanations, I felt powerless to defend
or justify my choices and actions. I knew only that I was fighting for a
happiness of a kind I had never known before, and that happiness was
not all I was fighting for — something deeper was involved — I was
fighting for my *self,* even if I could not explain in what way or why.

The joy I experienced with Patrecia was paid for in guilt, anxiety,
and depression. My worst crime was that I obliged Patrecia to pay too.

"Run for your life," I once burst out to her. "Run away from me
and from this world. Your kind of spirit can't survive intact here. I'm
sinking into horror and I'm afraid for you." She shook her head calmly
and said, "I love you." "What am I doing to you?" I cried to her. And
she stroked my face and said simply, "I do not admire what you are
doing — I hate what *I* am doing — but I admire everything about you,
and I will stand by you, I will stand by us, as long as I can."

"It keeps getting harder," she said to me in the summer of 1966. "I
never really believed that the secrecy would go on this long. It bothers
me that I still have not told Larry the truth, even though our marriage
is finished. It bothers me, every time I see Barbara or Ayn, to smile and
be friendly and know that everything I say and do is a lie. I feel awkward whenever I'm around anyone in the Collective or at NBI. I act
strange. I exaggerate being young and confused to cover up what I'm
really feeling, and then I see Joan or Barbara looking at me oddly, and

I know they're thinking how immature I am, and it's so humiliating, but I don't know what else to do. I'm no good at lying. I don't feel like myself anymore. Sometimes I'm so angry with you, I want to run away. Or else I want to give you an ultimatum: either you announce the truth publicly or I will leave you. Only I'm afraid to give you an ultimatum because I don't think you're ready, and I'm afraid of losing you. I love you so much — you're everything I ever wanted. I can't leave you; I don't want to. I ask myself which is the real courage: to leave you, taking a chance that one day we might be together again — or to hang on, to absorb everything and give up parts of who I am, as the price I have to pay for having you."

On another day and in another mood, she would fling her arms around me and assure me that I did not have to worry about her, that she could handle whatever she had to, and that she knew I would find a solution. I would shake my head and tell her, "I'm behaving despicably — and you're trying to cheer me up. The truth is, I don't know if I'm going to find a solution. I'm lying to other people; I don't ever want to lie to you. *I don't know how this is all going to end.*"

I could see tears in her eyes and feel tears in my own.

When I finally told Barbara of my relationship with Patrecia, there was no drama and no shock on Barbara's part. I told her because it had become intolerable not to. "It was obvious and inevitable," she said, her voice subdued and noncommittal. "Do you expect it to last?" she asked, and I said that I did not know. "It won't," she declared flatly. She agreed that Ayn must never know about Patrecia, "because you're right, that would be the end of everything."

She felt strongly, some of the time, that Ayn should be told once and for all that a resumption of our affair was impossible. The rest of the time Barbara retreated into uncertainty, shuddering and saying things like, "God knows how she'll handle the rejection. God knows what you should do. What a mess."

Barbara continued to bewilder me. When we met she would invariably turn the subject to our future and to her conviction that it would be a tragic mistake if we did not reconcile. "We had everything," she said to me. "We mustn't lose it all." My sister Elayne told me that, a few years earlier, on a day when Barbara had been out walking with Joan and her, Barbara had declared, "I have everything I ever wanted. A beautiful apartment in New York. Exciting and important work. Wonderful friends. And marriage to a great man." In spite of everything that had happened, in spite of Ayn, Wilfred, and Patrecia, some part of Barbara still seemed to be clinging to that vision. I had moments when that vision still had power over me.

She continually reminded me of the life we had shared, at its best, as if our staggering incompatibilities required only good will to be resolved. Gently, almost compassionately, she continued to insist that, whatever the short-term rewards of my relationship with Patrecia, I was inviting long-term calamity, even without Ayn in the picture. I let her plead her case, out of some last, lingering notion of fairness and objectivity.

Vanity too played its part. Vanity and old pain. My eighteen-year-old self enjoyed having Barbara pursue him, try to argue him back into a relationship. Our conversations were predominately tense, even anguished, but there were times when I found her behavior seductive, as I was meant to. On a few occasions, we even made love.

"You have to," said Patrecia, to whom I told everything. "You have to know once and for all whether there's still anything between you." I saw no trace of jealousy or hurt, only a matter-of-fact realism and a serene, fearless dignity.

After much indecision and turmoil, I agreed to go away with Barbara for a weekend in the Poconos, a resort area in Pennsylvania. "Let's give ourselves this last chance," Barbara had implored, knowing at the same time, deep in her heart, that the marriage was at an end — and should have ended long before. "Go," Patrecia had ordered. "You haven't said good-bye to each other yet anyway. So I hope you give each other your best. Then maybe you'll know more clearly where you are."

At the resort, holding Barbara in my arms, I knew it was obvious that I had no enthusiasm for what we were doing. This seemed to drive Barbara to greater frenzy, as if she were determined to bring everything to this one sexual encounter that she had withheld through the length of our marriage. Then, suddenly and violently, Barbara began to cry, in great moans of pain beyond anything I had ever heard from her.

"I can't stand it!" she sobbed. "I can't stand it! I'm going to die! This is too much!" Utterly bewildered, I begged her to tell me what was the matter. She then cried, "*I can't stand the idea of your sleeping with Patrecia! It's killing me!*"

Her wails were devastating; I felt almost as if my own sanity were slipping away. Where had this explosion come from? I implored her, "What are you talking about? Please calm down and help me to understand what you're saying."

She kept repeating hysterically that she was tormented by mental pictures of Patrecia and me making love. "The pictures are unbearable!" She was weeping and holding herself.

Finally I said the only thing that seemed relevant: "Barbara, why do you care? I was never what you wanted — not sexually. Why do you begrudge my being happy?"

She said that she loved me and that she would never resent my happiness, but, oblivious to the contradiction, that she could not bear the idea of my sleeping with another woman.

"What about my sleeping with Ayn?"

Barbara answered, her voice rising, "That was different! Ayn was different! Ayn was another world — much older and a great genius — I couldn't think of rivalry with Ayn — and besides, Ayn never meant to you sexually what Patrecia means to you! Don't you suppose I know that?"

Again I asked helplessly, "But why do you care?"

And then — at last, after eighteen years of a tortured relationship — she finally told me, in a voice broken by sobs. "Because I know what sex means to you! Because for you it's almost a religious act! You don't understand how rare you are in what you bring to it! How could you know? But I know the look on your face and I can't stand you're giving that to anyone else!"

I thought of all the nights of all the years of lying in bed, my fists clenched, in an agony of frustration and loneliness, while Barbara lay beside me reading a book.

I thought of one night in particular — long ago in Los Angeles, when we were still at UCLA — the night she confessed that when I showed any suffering she felt uncomfortable and disappointed.

I told myself that I deserved all the pain I had endured in our marriage — because I had not left her then.

Now, looking at her tear-streaked face, I felt mystification at her jealousy but also indifference. I thought that probably I would never understand her and that I did not need to. And I proceeded to comfort her as I would comfort a child, feeling nothing except leaden tiredness.

Driving back to New York, I thought: There really is no mystery. It's an issue of self-esteem. Are you not the man who teaches that all roads lead to self-esteem? Hers was tied, in part, to what I brought to our bed — even if, as a woman, she wants a different kind of man.

I asked Patrecia if in any sense she had known what would happen.

"No," she said. "I thought you might discover you were still in love with her."

"Patrecia, you are a brave person."

Barbara and Wilfred's breakup had been coming for a long time, as the frictions that had plagued their relationship since they were teenagers surfaced in new forms with increasing frequency and heat. They were clearly incompatible at the core.

However, a long time later I learned that Barbara made an extraordinary statement about this breakup. "We were overwhelmed by what appeared to be Nathaniel's magnanimity and benevolence toward us; it was an attitude that was fatal to our relationship." So if I had *not* given my consent to their affair, if I had remained hostile to it, their relationship would have had a better chance at surviving. By realizing the unfairness of my initial intransigence and by reversing my position, I evidently victimized them both. This was what she was now claiming.

Happily for Barbara, almost immediately she fell in love with another man.

I was glad to see Barbara in a happier state. She became more serene, more whole. And she no longer talked about the redemption of our marriage.

In a muted, cautiously restrained way, we had settled once again into a comrades-in-battle friendship. I had come to think of her almost as if she were my fourth sister, connected by blood, which transcended liking or disliking in the ordinary sense.

When I told Ayn that Patrecia was to appear in *The Sign in Sidney Brustein's Window*, in Philadelphia, she immediately responded, as I had known she would, "We must go to see her."

Ayn was fond of Patrecia and it was a fondness I intended to cultivate. I was convinced that if Ayn grew to know Patrecia before discovering that my feelings were romantic, she would see in Patrecia what I saw. My goal was to be with Patrecia openly and to integrate our relationship into my Objectivist life. I was convinced that my desire was a rational one and I hoped that in the end Ayn's own rationality would assert itself. But it was imperative that Ayn come to this conclusion on her own. I wanted her to accept that age had become an insurmountable barrier to our romance, that our time as lovers had come and gone. I wanted her old benevolence and basic sanity to come back to her. I wanted her to grasp that I had to have a private life apart from her, and that this life included a woman who was my contemporary. And I wanted her to be the one to *tell me* these things.

I hated the calculations and manipulations this strategy entailed, but I felt that my back was to the wall and that my survival was at stake. Another, previously unrecognized self had emerged within me: not the younger self that Patrecia had reawakened, nor the adult, masculine self that had fallen in love with her, but someone ageless, androgynous, and utterly ruthless, who had no other purpose than to assist me in realizing my aims and who was willing to blast through any obstacle or impediment. I will call this part my survivor-self.

This self smiled pleasantly at Ayn and said, "Yes, of course we must go to see Patrecia's play. It might be fun."

On the stage Patrecia was, as Ralph Roseman would say, "electrifying," a being of energy, light, and devastatingly innocent sexuality, who projected a stylization that clashed with the naturalism of the other performers and made it impossible to look away from her.

I sat between Ayn and Barbara, with a number of our friends around us, plus a number of NBI students who had driven down for the event. "She's wonderful!" Ayn said with great excitement, whispering in my ear. "Oh, this girl is an actress!"

Later, backstage, Ayn threw her arms around Patrecia and proceeded to praise her in terms that even I found extravagant. But this was like Ayn: nothing in moderation. Everyone crowded around, congratulating Patrecia, whose face was flushed with somewhat dazed happiness. Then Ayn said something astonishing and preposterous: "Patrecia, what is magnificent is that you have taken the philosophy of Objectivism and applied it to the art of acting!" I saw the blank expression on Patrecia's face. Her glance said to me silently: what has Objectivism got to do with this? But then the moment was swept away as more people forced their way into the room to extend praise and good wishes.

"Now I see more clearly why you say she is someone very unusual," Ayn announced to me as we drove back to Manhattan. Frank, who had aged enormously in this past decade, and whose faculties were already beginning to slip — a result both of his drinking and of early senility, neither of which anyone grasped — muttered, "Marvelous. Marvelous."

A few weeks later, Patrecia and I stopped by Ayn's apartment, declaring that Patrecia had sought my guidance in a scene she was preparing. This was accepted by Ayn and Frank as normal and unalarming, as I had calculated it would be. That evening, Patrecia and I had in fact been working on scenes from Ibsen's The Master Builder — simply for our own pleasure — and, at their prompting, we read one of those scenes now. We were all in relaxed high spirits. Then Ayn hurried into her office and came back with the script of Ideal. She asked us to do a dramatic reading of the climactic scene between Kay Gonda and Johnny Dawes. After two or three faltering attempts, Patrecia succeeded in locking onto Gonda's psyche and persona, and all three of us sat back watching her and listening, mesmerized. "How did you do that?" Ayn demanded afterward. "What did you do to capture her?" There was something almost intimidating in Ayn's intensity and I saw Patrecia freeze. I knew that she could not explain her own internal processes in doing Gonda, not now, neither to Ayn nor to herself, and I also knew that — because the person asking her for an explanation was Ayn — she would blame herself for her inability. As she stammered and groped for words, unable to say much more than "I just *felt* her," I saw some of the eagerness and warmth disappearing from Ayn's eyes, and I saw Patrecia noticing it too, but there was nothing I could say and no way I could help. "You must do better than just talk about feelings," Ayn said to her, and Patrecia replied with awkward conscientiousness that she was trying to learn. "I think you were magnificent," Frank said abruptly, loudly, and defiantly. The evening ended on a note of emotional flatness.

Since her marriage to Larry, Patrecia had worked professionally as Patrecia Scott. Now she discovered that there were at least six Patricia Scotts in New York in the worlds of modeling and acting, and she decided to change her last name. One evening, discussing the question of names with Ayn and a few other of our friends, she asked for an opinion of several alternatives she had been considering.

"If I can make a suggestion," Ayn said, "how about Patrecia Wynand? I think it has a very good sound, don't you?"

"After Wynand in *The Fountainhead*?" Patrecia said thoughtfully; then she nodded. Professionally, she became Patrecia Wynand.

I never explicitly discussed with Patrecia the strategy I was pursuing with Ayn. It was understood between us wordlessly. But I knew that to put the issue fully into words would only make her more self-conscious in Ayn's presence. "It will take a long time," Patrecia informed me solemnly, "to recover from all the consequences of what we are doing now. Even if we end up together, we won't come out of this undamaged. I hope you think about that." I knew there were times when she resented me enormously for the position in which I placed her; I did not blame her; my guilt for doing so dwarfed any other guilt I felt.

As 1967 approached, Ayn asked me what we might do on New Year's Eve. No one was in the mood for a large party. "I don't feel like spending New Year's with Barbara and her boyfriend at a Collective event," I told her, knowing that was a feeling she would have to respect. "And I don't want an evening alone with you and Frank; it'll be hard on me, and I'll drag you both down." I was determined to spend New Year's Eve with Patrecia.

I said that I was feeling rather depressed and not really in the mood for festivities. I had been complaining of depression a good deal; it was obvious to Ayn that I was often unhappy. I was attributing this to the breakup of my marriage; to the exhaustion of overwork; to an odd sense of deadness that made it exceedingly difficult to think of resuming a romance with her; to the lingering trauma of her past devastating reproaches; to the lack of any kind of personal pleasure in my life apart from work — all of which were intended to account for my moodiness, withdrawal, and the very real despair moving through my body like a sickness.

"I have an idea," Ayn said brightly. "Why not ask Patrecia to be your date? Perhaps Alan Greenspan could ask Leisha, and the six of us could have an evening together?" After considering her proposal carefully for a few minutes, searching Ayn's face for any sign of a trap, I said that it might be a good idea. "There's only one thing you must be careful about," Ayn said. "I suspect Patrecia already has a little crush on you. You must watch yourself not to encourage her. You don't want to hurt her."

We celebrated New Year's Eve at the Plaza hotel. As if in rebellion against the insanity of the occasion, Patrecia decided to enjoy herself, to be simply and openly who she was, without weighing her every statement. She did not retreat behind her usual protective facade of semi-inarticulate teenager; she allowed herself to be a confident twenty-six-year-old woman and to treat me in every sense as her date of the evening. If I sat too long at the table in deep conversation with Ayn, she would grab my arm possessively and cheerfully and say, "Let's dance!"

Ayn and Frank seemed truly to enjoy themselves, as if they too were glad to be away from the somberness of what our Collective parties had deteriorated into.

Dancing with Ayn, I told her, "This was really a good idea."

"Yes," she replied, "both girls are very pleasant to be with, don't you think?" Frank was dancing with Leisha and Alan was dancing with Patrecia. "I think Alan likes Patrecia more than Leisha," Ayn said. "Do you suppose it could develop into something?"

I shrugged. "Who knows?"

A week or two later, in an irritable mood — perhaps because her subconscious mind had registered a signal her conscious mind had missed — she stated angrily, "There's not a single person in the Collective who would dare to interrupt, if you and I were talking, and ask you to dance. I'm afraid Patrecia is pushy. That's not the way an idealist behaves."

Although Ayn's desire for greater emotional intimacy was unrelenting, she was still reticent about the resurrection of our affair. She felt that it was premature to think about sex until the distance between us, so incomprehensible to her, was closed. Our conversations focused more on what was wrong with me, why I was so emotionally repressed, into what dimension I had disappeared.

Our personal life aside, we were as much in alignment as we had ever been. She could not doubt the enormous esteem in which I held her mind and her achievements, nor my dedication to fighting for Objectivism. Nor could she doubt that in some sense I loved her, even though the erotic component could hardly have been more absent. "You're here but you're not here. You're elusive. You act like a man in love one day, and on the next you're withdrawn and you have no explanation of why. Do you know what kind of torture this is for me?"

We'd had eighteen years, filled with wonderful memories. I had built my life around this relationship. Had I been merely indifferent toward her, or had my emotions been principally negative, I would not have been able to keep us both in a state of suspension for as long as I did. It was not romantic love, but it was love; I did not doubt it then and do not doubt it now. I still worshiped her as a goddess of reason. And yet the thought clearly present in my mind, but not yet manifest in words, was: if Ayn's philosophy holds that I am morally wrong to be in love with Patrecia, and that I am a traitor to my values for not romantically desiring Ayn, then at least in these respects *her philosophy is wrong*. This was not a position I yet knew how to defend.

What I told myself consciously was that there had to be a way to fulfill Ayn's emotional needs without romance or sex, and when she and I discovered it — when Ayn accepted that our relationship was of minds, not bodies, as it had started out to be — the road would be cleared for an emotional renaissance.

"Do you realize," I said to her, "that I've known you half my life?"

She looked at me silently and suspiciously.

I went on, "A year after I left home, I acquired a new one — in a manner of speaking. You might say, I've never been really on my own. Sometimes I wonder if that's healthy."

"Getting tired of a serious, philosophical life?" she asked sharply. "You're on your own now, in every way that counts. Unless you mean — you want to be free of me?"

"Free of you? I want us to be friends forever."

"*Friends* is not what I'm talking about! What new irrationality is this? Do you think I would have dedicated *Atlas Shrugged* to a *friend*? I've told the whole world that *you* are Objectivism. Do you think I would say that about a *friend*? What's the matter with you? Don't you attach meaning to the words you speak? *Where has your mind gone?*"

We had "psychological" conversations in which she struggled to "help" me with my seeming depression and confusion, and I looked for opportunities to drop the hints that might grow in her mind toward the conclusions I desired.

"I can't see myself spending my future as the third person in your marriage to Frank," I would say, and she would answer, alarmed, "Are you asking me to leave Frank and live with you openly?" "No," I would say, "but I want you to understand how difficult our situation has become." She would respond indignantly, "You want a life with a *lesser* woman just because it's *easier?*"

We had adopted the term *psychoepistemology* to designate the study of cognition from the aspect of the relationship between the conscious and the subconscious, the volitional and the automatic, as well as individual differences in methods of cognitive functioning. We spoke of a person's psychoepistemology as rational or irrational, reality-oriented or emotion-oriented or people-oriented. "Something has happened to your psychoepistemology," she would say. "Clarity was always your strongest trait. What's happened to it? Do you realize how much chaos you permit yourself?"

When we were not discussing our personal relationship, my mind functioned as it had always functioned. Throughout 1967 there were many occasions when we were as exquisitely attuned as we had been at our best. At such times Ayn would both become optimistic about the future and announce that no problem could possibly resist our combined brains. "Haven't we been soul mates since you were fourteen years old? Think of what we have already been through together!" It was still possible for us to be happy together, to hug and laugh and say that we lived in a benevolent universe.

"Remember," she would say, sometimes cheerfully, sometimes threateningly, but always as a warning, "without you the Collective loses its meaning for me. They're the tail, but you're the comet. If anything goes permanently wrong between us, I'm finished; *everything* is finished; you're my lifeline to the world and to any chance at happiness I'm ever going to have." What she projected — and this was the judgment I dreaded — was that if I failed her it would be tantamount to a sin against the Holy Ghost, deserving of total damnation. A part of me shared her view: that was the trap.

My attachment to NBI and to the world I was building was another trap. Yet another was the comparison I made between my devastating experiences with Barbara, when I was barely twenty and had my whole life ahead of me, and what I suspected I was now doing to Ayn when she was in her sixties, after a lifetime of her feeling battered by an uncomprehending world.

Beginning in 1966 and continuing into 1967, Ayn was engaged in writing the last major assignment of her career, a monograph entitled

Introduction to Objectivist Epistemology, published in monthly installments in *The Objectivist* (later published in book form by The Objectivist Press and subsequently by New American Library). In this monograph she brilliantly addressed one of the great issues in philosophy: the nature of concept-formation. This work is one of her most original and important achievements. I was grateful for the opportunity to discuss its ideas with her, not only because of my enthusiasm for what she had done, but also because it was a way to be close to her in safe territory. During one of our "honeymoon periods," as Ayn called them, she laughed and said, "I don't know whether it's good or bad, but for you my brain really is an aphrodisiac!"

In September 1967 — less than a year before our world was to shatter irredeemably — Nathaniel Branden Institute leased eight thousand square feet of office space on the lower level of the Empire State Building. We were now offering lecture courses in eighty cities, and people all over the world were asking us to bring our courses to them. Wilfred negotiated a fifteen-year lease; it was the biggest financial commitment I had ever made — almost half a million dollars. *The Objectivist* moved in as our subtenant. It was here that we began to hold our Saturday-night dances.

"Are we *crazy?*" Barbara said to me apprehensively. "Everything can explode at any minute! It's only a matter of time until you have to tell Ayn the truth; we both know that. Wouldn't it be better to tell her *before* signing the lease?" Eight thousand square feet in the Empire State Building to house all of our projects: I wanted that. "I am going to find a solution," I said. I did not grasp that by now I was almost totally out of control.

I felt anxiety at the knowledge of how many of my own principles and convictions I was violating. I felt the rage of an animal pacing a cage and roaring impotently.

I had not felt effective with Barbara since the first months of our relationship, I no longer felt effective with Ayn, and I was failing the one person with whom I did feel effective.

But when I looked at the doors of our new offices and saw the gleaming letters, NATHANIEL BRANDEN INSTITUTE, I felt I was still the man and the mind who had launched a philosophical movement. I looked at the stage, the auditorium, the conference room, the glass partitions, the desks, the filing cabinets — I thought of my first letter to Ayn and of everything it had taken to come from that day to this sight — and I thought: I can't walk away from this; I can't give this up. Why should I have to? There is so much I want to accomplish. I love this battle; it's the crusade I always wanted. Am I damned because I want Patrecia as my reward?

Sometimes Patrecia and I came to NBI late at night, when the staff had gone, and we would walk through the rooms together, and one time I stopped in the middle of the auditorium where I lectured on philosophy and psychology, and I cried to her, "Patrecia, what I want is *right*! I want you and I want all of this! *And I have a right to want it!*"

I was shocked by the expression on Patrecia's face: it revealed a depth of anger I had never seen in her before. It was a look of the most profound moral indignation. "Nathan," she said, her voice shaking, "I have always loved and admired Ayn and I have always felt compassion for her. But what I saw that first night at your lecture was real — the twisted side of her. In this issue, the issue of *you,* Ayn is totally *out of her mind*. She's as irrational as any of those mystical loonies who scared me in childhood. She is *insane.*"

I did not cut her off, did not forbid her to speak as I once had. I did not answer. But this time she knew I had heard her.

Early in 1967 I received a phone call from psychologist Albert Ellis, founder of rational-emotive therapy, who explained that many of his followers were pushing for a rapprochement with Objectivism because, they believed, there were so many points of agreement between us. "You and I know, of course," he said, "that our differences are much more meaningful than our apparent similarities. When we talk about the importance of reason, for instance, we do not really mean the same thing. I propose that we stage a public debate — Rational Psychotherapy [this is what he called his system at that time] versus Objectivist Psychology. This should make the facts of life clear to everyone." After some hesitation, I agreed. I was not an enthusiast for debates, but I felt this would be an interesting experience.

Ellis proposed that each of our institutes sell tickets to our respective followings, and we would each keep our own proceeds. On Friday evening, May 26, approximately eleven hundred people crowded into the New Yorker hotel. Ellis had sold about two hundred tickets, NBI had sold about nine hundred. Our mutual friend, psychologist Lee Shulman, was moderator.

Although I was pleased with our large ticket sale, I did not like the fact that the room was weighted so heavily in my favor. This made Ellis the underdog, a role I much preferred for myself when intellectual combat was involved. Several times I had to join Lee in requesting that the audience show more courtesy to Ellis, whom I thought generated antagonism almost instantly by a kind of provocative abusiveness and haranguing that seemed to be the trademark of his lecture style.

At one point, when he attacked the "unrealism" of Ayn's heroes and heroines — in a radical departure from the subject of the debate — Ayn leapt up from her seat and shouted, "Am *I* unreal? Am *I* 'a character who can't possibly exist?' " It took Lee some time to restore order.

For Ellis, it was not a good evening. He became angrier and angrier as the event progressed, inspiring the audience to laughter. It was after this debate that Ellis began attacking Objectivism and my psychological ideas with unfailing regularity.

While I hardly appreciated this at the time, I came to see that some of his concerns about the attitudes and behavior evident in the Objectivist subculture — fanaticism, dogmatism, oppressive moralism — were justified, his misrepresentations of Objectivist theory aside.

At a gathering at Ayn's after the debate, everyone was euphoric. I was hailed as, in effect, the consummate intellectual warrior. Ayn, typically, chastised Lee for being too gentle with Ellis, but Lee pointed out how essential it had been to remain absolutely impartial, and Ayn conceded his point.

Of our various projects at NBI, none gave me as much pleasure as a new venture I had initiated, NBI Theatre. Patrecia's involvement in acting had reawakened my early love of the theater, and I wanted to produce a series of plays and to write for the theater myself. Ralph Roseman was guiding and coaching me in the various business aspects of production. Barbara had written an excellent stage adaptation of *The Fountainhead* (Ayn told me she liked it more than her own movie adaptation), Phillip Smith was to direct, we were talking to agents and actors, and we aimed for a fall 1968 opening.

By that time, I projected, *The Psychology of Self-Esteem* would be finished. I had a contract for the book with World Publishing, a house owned by Times-Mirror, which also owned New American Library. Ayn had promised my editor that the book would be good and, given Ayn's importance at NAL, that had been enough, and he did not request to see any part of the book as it was being written. It was promised for delivery this year.

I was behind schedule. I was also late with many of my articles for *The Objectivist*. I found it difficult to concentrate on my writing. Today it is difficult for me to believe that it was during the agonizing chaos of this period that I was writing my central chapters on self-esteem.

Ayn was often late with articles herself, yet reproached me constantly for not delivering mine on time, blaming my preoccupation with the stage production of *The Fountainhead*. "I would never have given my consent to that project," she spat at me, "if I thought it would get in the way of your writing for *The Objectivist*. Nothing should come ahead of your articles. Nothing matters more."

Ayn did not want to pursue me; her self-concept demanded that I pursue her.

"Tell me what's wrong. If I ask, you say you love me, and sometimes you act like a man in love, but there's no consistency to anything you do. If our romance is over, say so." When I made the most tentative move in that direction, she would immediately respond with an explosion of wrath that would last for hours.

During calmer times she would say, "Is it my age? I could accept that."

No, you couldn't. I tried to tell you more than once, and even the hint sent you through the roof. How can I say to you, "Yes, you're too old for me. I can't go to bed with you anymore"? "It's more exact to say that I would like the chance to build a life with someone who is a contemporary and with whom I could have a complete relationship."

"Where will you find a contemporary who is my equal?"

"You have no equals at any age." *Is love only a contest of philosophical grandeur?*

"Well, then, what are you suggesting? Do you want to be like Goethe or any of those so-called geniuses who marry a nothing hausfrau? You know the type I mean; I despise them. Do you wish to be a hero in public life, but not in your private life?" Each word was a thunderbolt of moral condemnation.

"Ayn, the world consists of more than you and hausfraus."

Her voice rose. "The man to whom I dedicated *Atlas Shrugged* would never want anything less than me! I don't care if I'm ninety years old and in a wheelchair! This will always be my view! If you are a complete and utter fraud, at least have the decency to say so, and we'll go our separate ways and you'll be out of my life for good and I'll be out of my misery! I won't have to see or speak to you again — ever!"

In her despair, Ayn was beginning to confide in Barbara, who she sought as an ally to her cause. Barbara said to me, "Ayn insists that it's you who keeps pressing for a continuation of the romance. She says she knows perfectly well that she may be too old. If she's offering you a chance to withdraw, why aren't you taking it?"

I told that I did not think she understood what Ayn meant by offering me a chance. When Barbara declared that I could not let Ayn suffer this way and that I should tell her the truth, I asked if she meant that

I should tell Ayn about Patrecia. "No. Not about Patrecia. The idea that she was being rejected for Patrecia would kill her." When I pointed out that Ayn was not being rejected for anyone, that my feelings for her changed years ago, long before I ever met Patrecia, Barbara observed, correctly, "That's not how Ayn will see it."

If Ayn is "insane," I told myself, I have contributed to it. By giving her contradictory signals. By not letting her know the limits of my feelings for her at the start of our affair. By not holding her to the original agreement of "one or two years at the most." By feeding her grandiosity from the day we met.

Sometimes, when I saw the enormity of Ayn's pain, my anguish and self-reproach were overwhelming. Other times I confronted another truth within myself, no less real: an attitude of cold indifference toward a suffering I was less and less able to respect.

At NBI on Saturday nights, I danced with Ayn, with Patrecia, with a few of our friends, and struggled to maintain the appearance of normalcy while wondering why the actual facts were not obvious to everyone. I would later learn that parts of the truth were obvious, at least to some students, who suspected a relationship between Patrecia and me. Years later, reflecting on "the old days at NBI," screenwriter Richard Danus remarked, "Seeing you and Patrecia together, it seemed very natural, very logical, that you two would be in love. You fit, somehow. It was Barbara and you that never fit; at least, I never thought so, and I know I was not the only person who had that viewpoint. Patrecia and you were not the puzzle. Barbara and you were the puzzle."

At Ayn's, we discussed my psychoepistemology, my mysterious emotional repression, my difficulties with the triangle of Ayn, Frank, and me, the question of my real values. And I twisted my brain to let Ayn have the truth in every way but explicit statement — and failed.

Her conflicts with Frank were also worsening. Frank's mind was continuing to deteriorate, although no one yet grasped the onset of arteriosclerosis. He would erupt against Ayn in violent rages, often in my presence, and I would see a look of helpless bewilderment on Ayn's face. "Frank, darling, are you *angry* with me about something you haven't told me?" They would have interminable talks about his psychoepistemology. Ayn did the talking and Frank listened silently, except for an occasional muted response. "Do you have any suggestions," Ayn asked me, "on how I can encourage Frank to speak to me more?" I suggested that Frank might have a great deal of stored anger and resentment against her. Later she informed me, "I asked Frank about that and he says 'Absolutely not.' You're wrong."

At one point, some years earlier, Ayn had suggested that Frank consult Allan Blumenthal for treatment of a possible emotional disorder. Among other complaints, Frank had lost interest in sex. To Allan it was obvious that since Ayn was a supremely rational human being, it was irrelevant to examine Frank's behavior in the context of the family system in which he lived.

Frank had his own studio apartment by that time, where he painted — and drank. Years later, after his death, "when his studio was discovered to be filled with empty liquor bottles," Elayne would tell me, "Ayn refused to admit that he had become an alcoholic; she said the bottles must somehow have been used by him 'to mix his paints in.' She saw what she wanted to see."

In the early spring of 1968, still another aspect of Ayn's psychology came into focus — and that was her disposition to use people in the most cold-blooded and hypocritical way. As our relationship continued to deteriorate, she turned to Barbara more and more for help, often pouring out her suffering in a way that Barbara found heartbreaking. At the same time, she often spoke to me of Barbara with utter lack of respect, as if Barbara were a person of no particular importance. Neither her moments of affection toward Barbara nor her contempt could be taken at face value; one had to know what purpose they served in the moment — or in what mood Ayn happened to be on a particular day. When, for example, she focused on the history of my marriage, she said it was clear that Barbara had not been the right woman for me, "not strong enough, not purposeful enough;" but when she suspected that I might be attracted to Patrecia (which I denied, and yet whose virtues I could not stop praising), she declared that Barbara was the only "other woman" in my life she could accept. Then she virtually embraced Barbara as a spiritual sister. Barbara's guilt at deceiving Ayn, by protecting my secrets, began to rise.

She was obliged to listen in increasing distress, while Ayn spoke of her suffering. Ayn confided that she felt my objection to being the "other man" in her marriage was only a rationalization. "If he feels for me what he says he feels, and sees in me what he says he sees — he'd be willing to be part of a harem. Doesn't he know that the great proof of my love for him is that I chose him *despite* a happy marriage and the difference of our ages?" Ayn had made this remark about a harem to me, too.

Once, when I expressed to Ayn my desire for a personal life apart from NBI and our work, she immediately answered, "You mean, a personal life *apart from me?*" This was sufficient to throw her into a lengthy, impassioned, and indignant speech. "You have *no right* to other concerns. I placed my life's work in your hands. I told the world you were my 'intellectual heir.' I have not gone through the hell of the past forty years, I have not fought and fought and fought, and endured and endured, so that *you can profit off my blood*! I am not going to retire gracefully and let you reap the rewards of my agony! You have no right to casual friendships, no right to vacations, no right to sex with some inferior woman! Did you imagine that I would consent to be left on the scrap heap? Is that what you imagined? Is it?"

Such tirades had become commonplace.

Throughout the spring of that year Barbara had been pressing me to tell Ayn that I was not in love with her. At no point did she suggest that I tell Ayn about my relationship with Patrecia, perhaps partly because she still imagined Patrecia was one day going to vanish from my life.

I knew that my agenda with Ayn had failed. She was becoming increasingly suspicious and hostile toward Patrecia, as my feelings became more obvious, and looked for every opportunity to find fault with her. Where she had once spoken positively of Patrecia as a possible mate for Alan Greenspan or Leonard Peikoff, she now conveyed that such an idea would be inconceivable and denied that she had ever thought differently.

"Don't ever permit yourself to think, even for a moment" — she said to me once, her voice shaking with suppressed violence — "that Patrecia or some equivalent is going to cash in on my ambition, mind, and achievement. I have not lived as I have lived in order, now, to hand you over graciously and lie down and die."

Returning from a drive in the country, where we had gone to talk, Barbara said, "You look terrible. I've never seen you so unlike yourself. You look so haggard. God, how did we all get into this?" We pulled into the parking garage of our building and my head fell on the steering wheel in total despair and misery. "I've got to tell Ayn the truth about *everything*," I said. "I can't stand this any longer. The whole situation makes me sick and I make myself sick. I've got to tell the truth — and let everything collapse, as it's going to anyway." Now it was Barbara's turn to be frightened. She whispered gently, urgently, that I did not know what I was saying, that I was overreacting out of emotion, that I needed to think more clearly and move slowly. There was a subtle note of hard, practical calculation behind her words. "Give up NBI?" she said, as if we were discussing the end of the world — *her* world. "Give up everything we've created? Just walk away from Objectivism? Walk away from NBI? How can you possibly do that? You can't. You'd never respect yourself again." I nodded in exhausted acquiescence; but my survivor-self contemplated Barbara as from a great distance, thinking: So. Well, well, well. We are all operators, it seems.

When I saw that I felt like a fraud when facing my own students; when I realized that no aspect of my work gave me pleasure any longer; when my meetings with Ayn were reduced to long, drawn-out sessions made of nothing but pity, rage, guilt, and mutually inflicted pain; when I knew that there was no longer an ounce of dignity between us; when I heard Ayn scream her suspicions that I was falling for a "chorus girl"; when I heard Patrecia tell me, after returning from the run of a play she had done outside New York, "I missed you, but I was glad to be away, away from everything, away from this madhouse" — I knew that I could not remain passive any longer, that I had to act, to bring some reality back to Ayn's and my relationship, no matter what the consequences.

I had to communicate — clearly, explicitly, unequivocally — that a continuation of the romance between us was impossible; that the love affair was over.

I decided to write a letter, which I would give to Ayn personally, so that she could read it in my presence. I knew that if I attempted to *tell* her my thoughts, I would not have a chance to finish; there would be an explosion within the first seconds. I was no longer afraid of her anger; I had faced it too many times, and in any event the letter would hardly spare me that; but I was afraid of never having the opportunity to be heard and understood.

A letter also allowed me to select my words carefully, to say exactly what I meant to say with no possibility of ambiguity or misunderstanding — tactfully, lucidly, lovingly. I was a writer; I knew how to express myself on paper. This was the most challenging writing assignment of my life. My purpose was to communicate that our time together as a romance had passed, and that my most fervent wish was that we be passionate, loving friends and intellectual comrades. I worked on the letter with more care than I had ever brought to any other project. I wanted Ayn to understand that I had to have a life of my own. When Barbara read it, the expression on her face was of fear and horror.

She told me that it was "a good letter, or as good as such a letter can be," and that she felt "petrified" at the thought of Ayn's reaction.

She made an unexpected statement, the full truth of which I recognized only later. "I don't for a minute think you really expect this letter to work. The idea that you and Ayn are ever going to be friends after this is a joke. Some part of you already knows there is absolutely no way for you to save the situation and have everything you want. I think your intention is to precipitate a crisis. I think you know exactly how all this is going to end and that you're orchestrating it."

On an evening toward the end of June, Ayn came to my apartment
for dinner. When she entered and took one look at me, she embraced
me with concern and said, "Darling, what's the matter? You look so
tortured!"

I told her that I needed to speak to her. We decided to try to eat first,
but it was impossible. Alarmed by my manner, Ayn became her most
caring, sympathetic self. I told her that I had written a letter in which
I attempted to convey my understanding of the core problem in our
relationship. As soon as she heard these words, the warmth disappeared from her eyes and I knew it would not return, not toward me,
not ever again. "Have you written that you're not in love with me?"
she demanded harshly. I handed her the letter.

It was several pages long. In it, I apologized for not conveying to her
sooner the truth of my feelings. I acknowledged the great joy and love
I had experienced with her over the years. I spoke of feeling that I was
an outsider in her and Frank's marriage, as I properly had to be, and
of my need for a personal life entirely my own. I said that the twenty-
five-year difference in our ages now made sex with her impossible for
me. And that I wanted us to be again the great friends we had once
been.

Within ninety seconds she was screaming at me, with a violence that
exceeded my worst projections. "You *bastard*," she kept shrieking,
"You bastard, you bastard! You nothing! You fraud! You contemptible swine!" Then she leapt up and said, "I don't want to be alone in
the same room with you! I want Barbara here! I want Barbara to know
about this *obscenity*!" She ran to the telephone, called Barbara's apartment, and said, in a trembling voice, "Come down at once and see
what this monster has done!"

When Barbara arrived, Ayn held up my letter — her entire body
now shaking — and asked, "Have you seen this *vile thing*?" Professing
bewilderment, Barbara said that she had not and asked what it was. I
felt indifferent to her lie. When she finished reading it, she nodded her
head at Ayn with an expression that could have meant anything, and
gave a long sorrowful sigh.

I looked at them — two allies. I was in a numb stupor.

"Everything you have ever professed to be," Ayn stated, her face
twisted in hatred, "is a lie!" My love of *Atlas Shrugged* was a lie, she
informed me. My dedication to Objectivism was a lie. My idealism
was a lie. Even my work in psychology was fraudulent. "Everything
was stolen from me. When did you ever have an original idea of your
own?"

In my horror I realized that I was hearing nothing I should not have expected. My mind flashed to other examples of Ayn's rewriting of history regarding other people.

No matter how tactfully my letter was worded, the basic message that came through to her, and all that she would register, was that she was too old to inspire romantic feelings in me. All of her energies were now being mobilized to deny her suffering. The intimately personal meaning of what was taking place between us, the devastation she was experiencing, was ferociously swept aside. It was easy to track her internal process: since I was a bastard and a scoundrel, clearly I could not have the power to cause her pain; therefore, what she was feeling was not pain; it was moral indignation. I had witnessed this kind of rationalizing in Ayn before, when I had not been personally involved; I was thoroughly familiar with the defense mechanisms by which she disowned her feelings and protected her self-concept.

She paced the room, while Barbara and I sat silently, watching her. Her first impulse was to break with me totally and on the spot. "I will denounce you in *The Objectivist*!"

Deeper than my anguish, I felt a strange, almost lightheaded calm. I had been right, I told myself; I had been right. I had understood Ayn correctly. She did not yet know about my love affair with Patrecia; all she knew was that I did not want the continuation of a romance with her — and she was prepared, on the basis of that information alone, to repudiate me publicly, to deny the value of my work, and to tell our followers, as she now announced to Barbara and me, that I was a "traitor to Objectivism" and "a complete fraud."

"What am I going to do?" she moaned, almost as if we were there to help her. "I've given him my public sanction. I've dedicated *Atlas* to him. If he can do this, he's capable of anything. How do I know what he might say or do publicly that will embarrass me?" I had the sense that her greatest fear was that I would retaliate against any attack by disclosing the secret of our affair. "If I can't have some guarantee that I am going to be protected from him, I'll disgrace him, I'll ruin his name — it doesn't matter what happens to him now — *I've got to protect myself!*"

I did not attach literal meaning to any of her words; even in my state, I thought them ludicrous. I also knew that sooner or later a more practical-minded side of her would make her aware that, in order to denounce me to the world at this point, she would have to say what my letter had been about. Looking at Barbara, I imagined that she was having the same thought.

When Ayn began to speak of canceling all plans for the stage production of *The Fountainhead*, I listened almost indifferently, as if she were referring to some project that had mattered in some other life-time.

She had begun to calm down and it was obvious that she had real-ized the practical difficulties in denouncing me publicly at this time. She could hardly say to the world that she repudiated Nathaniel Bran-den as a spokesman for Objectivism because he failed her romanti-cally — he refused to sleep with her. If the denunciation was ever to happen, she would have to find other grounds.

Almost incoherently, she spoke to Barbara — as if I were not there — of "giving him one more chance." Our personal relationship, she announced, was ended, but perhaps "he can show me that he is still competent and trustworthy to represent Objectivism." How I was to establish this to her satisfaction, she did not say and I did not ask.

When they had gone and I was alone in the apartment, my most urgent desire was to talk to Patrecia. But she was away from New York, working in summer theater. I clung to her image in my mind: a sole point of support in a collapsing world.

I was in agony. And yet — in the midst of remorse, anxiety, and the worst suffering I had ever known — I was glad this evening had taken place, glad I had given Ayn the letter. And passionately sorry I had not done so years earlier.

It was the first step toward a confrontation that would be far more terrible than the one tonight. But it was also the first step toward a return to reality and the rebuilding of my self-esteem.

After that night, Ayn and I spoke infrequently and almost always about business concerning *The Objectivist* — until the day we saw each other for the last time.

During the month of July, we had a few working sessions, awkward and somewhat formal. Our exchanges about my mental and emotional state were detached, strained, impersonal. After eighteen years of in-timacy, we had lost the art of talking easily and naturally together.

When we met, our eyes were dry. We did our crying alone. We ac-knowledged this once to each other. I was touched by Ayn's candor in admitting that she, too, wept, even though there was a total absence of emotion in her voice when she said it.

"How are you feeling?" Ayn asked once, and I answered that I was in hell. "But a better, cleaner hell than I was in a month ago." She nodded in understanding, and I said, "And you?" She answered, "Just as you see. In hell." We spoke dryly and factually, like two accountants comparing the figures in our ledgers.

I saw that there were times when, in response to her own pain and mine, Ayn wanted to reach out to me. I saw also that she needed me to make the first move, to make it easier for her to melt against the resistance of her official intellectual position. But I was still withholding the truth about Patrecia, and I knew that soon that truth would have to come to light. Until it did, to allow further warmth between Ayn and me was a fraud I was no longer willing to tolerate. If we were ever to be close again, I wanted that closeness to be based on honesty.

Ayn needed time, I told myself, to absorb and accept the fact that I was not in love with her. I hoped that our relationship could restabilize in this new context; then I would tell her about the affair I had been having with Patrecia for the past several years, and hoped she could make peace with these facts.

I could not relinquish the idea that a happy conclusion might still be possible. My deepest feeling was that I was rational and right in wanting to continue my work with NBI and *The Objectivist,* to have an intimate friendship with Ayn, and to have my life with Patrecia; and I felt as if we were all trapped in some vast, tragically unnecessary mistake. Yet a voice within me said that this embittered woman sitting opposite me on her living room sofa was not the person I had fallen in love with when I had first read *The Fountainhead,* and that Ayn Rand no longer existed.

I sensed a corresponding conflict within Ayn: moments when she looked at me with hatred, and moments when her dark, pain-filled eyes said, *But this is Nathan! This is the man with whom I shared everything!*

To Barbara, she said, "There is nothing for me to look forward to, nothing to hope for in reality. My life is over. He has forced me into a permanent ivory tower. He took away this earth."

When I heard from Barbara that Ayn believed I had "rejected her as a person," I protested, "I did *not* reject her as a person! What's the implication of what she's saying? That she owns me? That my life belongs to her?"

Ayn said that I obviously needed to talk to someone who would would be emotionally uninvolved in the problem. She suggested Allan Blumenthal. I agreed, not because I imagined that Allan could help me "clarify my thinking," but because I thought that if he knew the actual facts, he might be able to influence Ayn in a saner direction. I knew that whatever I said to Allan would go directly to Ayn. Both Allan and Ayn communicated this to me at the outset. No one suggested that I should have the right to privacy and I did not ask for it.

Ayn gave me permission to discuss with Allan all the details of our affair. She recognized that there was no way Allan could participate effectively without this knowledge.

I recall the first moment of entering Allan's apartment. Allan and

Joan looked at me with eyes guarded and noncommittal. Joan's expression conveyed a hint of satisfaction. For some months past the Collective had sensed the presence of trouble; no one could imagine what it might be, only that it involved some conflict between Ayn and me. Now, Joan's eager anticipation at learning the nature of the conflict seemed palpable. I recall thinking, with indifferent astonishment — as I walked with Allan into his study — that Joan's accumulated resentment toward me had to be enormous and all her protestations of undying gratitude were empty and meaningless, and if I had been paying attention I would have known it sooner.

I had to keep myself from laughing when I saw the involuntary, fastidious wrinkling of Allan's nose, so typical of him when his sensibilities were offended, as I related the story of Ayn's and my relationship. It was obvious that he did not approve of the affair. When I observed his growing sympathy and concern for me, I allowed myself a flicker of hope.

"But this is monstrous!" he finally exclaimed. "What's the matter with Ayn? How can she not see how irrational and unfair she's being? Ayn should never have allowed your affair to begin in the first place! She's twenty-five years older — it was her responsibility to know better at the start! Disaster was inevitable! And never mind you, look what she's done to Frank and Barbara!"

When I protested that I was hardly an innocent victim, the impatient gesture of his hand brushed my statement aside. "Oh, Nathan, you're so naive!" He went on to express the view that for some time he and Joan had been troubled by Ayn's near-paranoia, violent temper, and general blindness to any context but her own. He insisted that he was prepared to take my side and do whatever he possibly could to help Ayn see reason. He said that we had to "save her" for her own sake as well as mine.

"My heaven," he said, "and to think that sometimes Joan or I faulted you for being tense or abrupt or insensitive! I think it's incredible that you've been able to function at all, to do all that you've done, carrying the weight of these ridiculous burdens all these years! I'm more in awe of you than ever now!"

It was not awe that I needed from him now, but strength. Our meeting took place on a Sunday and I knew that tomorrow, Monday evening, he had an appointment with Ayn to hear her version of our relationship. When he repeated that I could count on him absolutely, I pointed out that he had not yet spoken to Ayn. He drew himself up in his chair and said, as if he imagined I would find his words encouraging, "You can trust me and I'll tell you why. I'm more afraid of you than I am of Ayn."

I did not hear from him on Tuesday morning, when he had promised to telephone, so I called him. His first words were, "Now, I know you're going to think I've been brainwashed" — and then I knew that he had been. I listened, with the old, familiar sense of heaviness, as he said, "Ayn gave me an entirely different picture of the situation. I had no idea that it was you who has been chasing her all these years, when she gave you plenty of opportunities to withdraw from the romance. To tell you the truth, I'm shocked at your cruelty! You obviously do have very serious psychological problems!"

At our next meeting, I told him that I had not been chasing Ayn as she had declared to him, although this was a fantasy in which she was heavily invested, and I explained the actual progression of events and the nature of my complicity. His own knowledge of Ayn's psychology inclined him to believe me, he said. He suggested that of course Ayn had her own biases and blind spots and the truth was no doubt more complicated than either she or I appreciated.

I wanted to tell him about Patrecia — first, because she was an essential element of the full context, and second, because I thought his own regard for her would make it possible for him better to understand me. The problem was, I was not prepared to ask Allan to deceive Ayn on my behalf. Barbara agreed. "You can't put Allan in that position." I decided to communicate my love for Patrecia but not the affair.

I began by telling Allan the story of my relationship with Barbara, because in a sense that was where it all began, and I spoke of the years of loneliness and sexual frustration, both before and after the romance with Ayn. "The trouble with you, Nathan," Allan informed me, "is that you attach too much importance to sex."

Why am I telling this eunuch anything? I thought in revulsion. But then, impatient for some kind of resolution, I proceeded to acknowledge the depth of my feelings for Patrecia.

"You'll have to give her up," he announced, as if it were self-evident. If I did, I asked him, would that make her importance to me go away? He shrugged. "You'll have to solve that on your own."

When I remained silent, and Allan realized that it was not a foregone conclusion that I would be as submissive as he had expected, he said, "Otherwise, what do you imagine will happen? You're absolutely dependent on Ayn; your whole reputation is as 'Mr. Objectivism,' and for that you need Ayn's sanction. How will you earn a living?"

I smiled inwardly and wondered: does he really think I'm trapped? For the past several summers, I had been spending six weeks in California, lecturing in Los Angeles and San Francisco; I had developed a fondness for Los Angeles and recently I had begun to think of moving there with Patrecia, if I could not rescue the situation in New York. At the same time, the thought of leaving this city was painful. I answered, "I will move to L.A., and open a practice in psychotherapy."

Allan looked at me as if I had abandoned all reason. "But Nathan, *Ayn won't let you.*"

It was not Allan for whom I now felt contempt but myself: for sanctioning Allan as a psychiatrist; for imagining that he could ever be any sort of ally in a battle of this kind; for crediting him with any significant amount of independence or integrity. I felt thoroughly worn and battered, but I could not control myself; I said, "How do you think she will stop me?"

When Allan told Ayn of my love for Patrecia, she immediately announced that under no circumstances would she ever speak to me again. I was informed by both Allan and Barbara that Ayn had now ascended to a higher level of rage. "You don't want to know what Ayn is now saying," Allan told me. We discontinued our meetings as we recognized they had no purpose. All further communications to or from Ayn, Barbara said, were to be channeled through her.

"Judgment day is coming," I told Patrecia, and when she asked what I meant, I answered, "The day when everything will be out in the open." Patrecia observed that when I said it, I looked relieved. "Judgment day is coming for all us," I added. "For everyone involved. Ayn likes to say, 'Judge, and be prepared to be judged.' Fair enough. I guess every day of our life is judgment day, and our own ego is the judge. That's my theory of self-esteem."

As a condition of continuing to support NBI, Ayn demanded a letter from me in which I admitted I had behaved inconsistently with the principles of Objectivism. Indifferently — in a note consisting of one or two sentences — I obliged. To acknowledge that I was not a perfect Objectivist had no importance to me at that point; my letter mentioned no specific act or person; I saw myself as calming Ayn's paranoia, placating her morbid fantasies that I would do something to disgrace her and Objectivism — as if my note could protect her or mean anything to anyone but her.

I listened passively as Barbara informed me of Ayn's newest "terms," which included that I now devote my life exclusively to Objectivism, forswearing all other interests and goals, and somehow persuade her that my mind was still reliable and that I could be trusted to represent her. I gathered that neither she nor Ayn was struck by the absurd contradiction of a man teaching Objectivism while practicing the kind of *selflessness* Ayn demanded. Abandon my ego and preach the morality of egoism? If my sin had been hypocrisy — was atonement to consist of a new form of it?

"You need to know," Barbara said, "that Ayn is not enthusiastic about your continuing the work for NBI under any circumstances. She says she thinks it's imperative that she denounce you in *The Objectivist*. But on what grounds — that you're in love with Patrecia? That's the truth, but she can hardly say it. All that's protecting you is Ayn's fear for her own reputation. Right now, your relationship with her is hanging by a very slender thread."

I recognized finally and irrevocably that any hope of a reconciliation with Ayn had been foolish self-delusion, another instance of refusing to see what was staring me in the face. I felt bitterly ashamed of my own blindness and failure to act decisively. I knew that the next step was to announce to Ayn that Patrecia and I had been having an affair. I did not take it. I was afraid — and I could not have said precisely of what; afraid of Ayn's wrath, to be sure, but that was not all; afraid most of all, perhaps, of facing finally and inescapably that I had betrayed myself for nothing. I felt crushed by the humiliation of what I had allowed to drag on for so long — four and a half years of lies and deceptions. It was difficult even to recall the reasons that had once made my choices seem imperative. All shreds of context or history vanished from my mind.

I was beginning to hear the first rumors of new charges against me, originated by Ayn and now beginning to spread among our friends, which struck me as so preposterous that I felt my whole world had become a madhouse, sinking deeper and deeper into a waking nightmare. Leonard Peikoff, now returned from his exile in Denver and proudly reinstated with Ayn, looked at me tensely as if I were an unpredictable disaster that could happen at any moment. Other members of our circle spoke to me carefully, tentatively. I looked like hell, I told myself, and that was responsible for at least part of their response.

I thought more and more about breaking with everything and leaving with Patrecia for a new life. However, Patrecia was not particularly eager to leave New York; she loved the stage and saw the East Coast as the center of theatrical activity. It was primarily Leisha's interest in acting that made a move to California tempting for her. "Leisha and I have talked about it," Patrecia told me. "Since we're identical twins, we both can't hope to make it here. Maybe we'll divide up the country; she'll try to succeed in New York, I'll try movies and television in California. If it comes to that."

By early August I knew that it would come to that; I merely did not know the specific steps that would make it happen. I watched a progression of events I felt powerless to alter or stop, and waited for the inevitable to unfold.

One day Barbara announced, "Ayn is wondering if I could run NBI without you." She did not say this as if it were a prospect she especially relished. I suspected she was already having her own daydreams of escape. "Of course I was," she told me later. "I saw what your 'glory' cost you."

"Run for your life," I said to Patrecia, as I had said it before, and she answered, "Not now and not ever." I had not allowed anyone — not Ayn, not Barbara — to see the depth of despair I disclosed to Patrecia. I wanted her to see the worst, to see me at my lowest, with every possible illusion stripped away. She said, "We are going to survive." She did not attempt to influence me in any particular direction; it was as if she too were merely a spectator of a drama unfolding before her. "The only choice I have to make right now," she said, "is the one I've made: to stand by you — and to wait. I love you. Do what you have to do. Your job is to get through this. When it's all over, I hope you'll condemn yourself less than you are doing now."

I spent long, tortured hours of self-examination in my study, looking out the window, leaving to Barbara and Wilfred the daily business of NBI.

On an evening in August, Barbara came to my apartment, visibly shaken. "I've reached the end," she stated. "Ayn is about to make me her heir." Up to that time, I was the beneficiary in Ayn's will, after Frank, just as I was the beneficiary in Frank's will, after Ayn. Ayn had informed Barbara that she had made an appointment with her lawyer to change her will. "Ayn intends for me to inherit everything!" Barbara said, as if it were a disaster. "I can't live with that. The guilt is too much. And it's too late for you to tell her the truth. She refuses to speak to you now, under any circumstances. *I* have to do it."

At least give me a chance to save myself, she was saying, and it was a request I could not deny. There was nothing to discuss or argue about.

I knew that if I told Ayn I had something important to say to her, she would have met with me. I did not care to do it — or I did not have the courage to do it. It would accomplish nothing. The outcome would be the same regardless of what action I took.

Now this moment seemed inevitable. From the night I had given Ayn my letter and listened to Barbara's suggestion that my goal was to precipitate a crisis, some part of me had known precisely what I was doing and how all this was meant to end, and all the rest was just wishful thinking and self-deception.

"Tell her," I said.

Barbara did not act immediately. She waited another two weeks, perhaps to gather her courage. Then she telephoned Allan Blumenthal and asked him to accompany her. They went together to Ayn's apartment on the sixth floor while I waited in mine on the twentieth.

Barbara proceeded to tell Ayn that I had been lying about my relationship with Patrecia, that we had been in love and having an affair since 1964, and that for the past two years Barbara had known about it and collaborated with me in deceiving her. This, Barbara explained, is why I had been in such a bad way for such a long time.

They talked for less than an hour when, leaping furiously to her feet, Ayn demanded that I be summoned at once.

It was Allan, Barbara told me later, who advised Ayn against the confrontation, declaring that my state was so terrible, my remorse so profound, that no one could be as hard on me as I was already being on myself. Barbara supported Allan in this position. "Don't think Allan took pleasure in what happened," Barbara told me later. "He was very concerned for you. More than once, when I was telling Ayn the story, he ran into the bathroom to throw up."

"*Get that bastard down here!*" Ayn hissed.

It was Allan who telephoned me. "Nathan, Ayn wants you to come down."

Riding down in the elevator, I felt my mind dividing, felt part of my consciousness splitting off from the exhausted and battered rest of me, to observe what was about to happen and to guide me through it.

I entered and looked at them — Ayn, Frank, Barbara, and Allan. Ayn and Barbara sat opposite each other on the sofa. Frank lay stretched out in a chair, looking a little more present than usual. Allan let me in and returned to his chair.

"I don't want you in my living room," Ayn said, standing to face me, her body trembling. She pointed to a straight-back chair between the living room and the dining area, halfway to the door. "Sit *there*.

"What a loathsome creature you are!" she said, and I watched her carefully as the tirade began, and she poured abuse on abuse, drowning her suffering in self-righteous anger. "*You* have rejected *me*? *You* have dared to reject *me*?" I watched and I listened and I thought: There is nothing I need do now, only sit, and wait, and endure, Everything has been set in motion — now let it play itself out. Let her say whatever she needs to say. I owe her that.

I cannot say what I felt as I watched and listened. I was beyond feeling. In moments of great crisis, the organism protects itself by moving into a state feelings cannot reach.

"Do you *begin* to know what you've done?" Ayn was shrieking. "Do you *begin* to know what you've thrown away? May you be damned to the hell you put me through! You rotten hypocrite!"

And I thought: Patrecia, I *am* guilty. Guilty for what I put you through — for the sake of protecting my relationship with the people in this room. Ayn is right, I do warrant condemnation, only hers aren't the reasons, not the most important ones. . . . What does it matter, the pain Barbara, Ayn, and I caused one another? We're all crazed animals, anyway, and none of us have clean hands, but you — you never brought me anything but good, and I betrayed you, by not shouting my love for you aloud from the first day I became aware of it. . .

Listening to Ayn, I experienced a combination of pity and contempt for her beyond anything I had imagined possible. The sounds of her denunciation went on, as if she wished her words could turn to blows. It took all of my energy to hold my body erect in the chair.

I noticed that, even now, it was important to Ayn that I agree with her, that I share her verdict, that I see myself as the "depraved monster" that she insisted I was. "Do you realize — ?" Her sentences began. "Do you admit — ?" I thought, if I really were the rotten human being she was describing — if, as she claimed, I had no sense of moral principles — her rebukes would mean nothing to me. And if I were willing to give my sanction now to what she was doing, wouldn't my willingness be the very error she cautioned against in *Atlas Shrugged*? The "sanction of the victim," she called it — the error of granting moral validity to the premises of one's own adversaries and thus collaborating in one's own destruction.

"You are an irredeemably rotten human being," she was saying — but if I was, why was she telling it to me? Was she not still counting on a virtue she would not admit I possessed?

"Objectivism never meant anything to you! Not *The Fountainhead*, not *Atlas Shrugged*, not any value you pretended to share with me! You passed yourself off as my soul mate, God damn you, and you're less than Peter Keating or James Taggart! You've damaged me worse than any of my enemies ever could!"

I thought that in a sense that last sentence was true. Barbara had said to me, "She had weapons against her intellectual adversaries, but you hurt her as a woman, hurt her at the point of her greatest doubts and insecurities. She never liked her body or her appearance, she hates the fact that she doesn't resemble her heroines — so what do you imagine she will feel, visualizing Patrecia?" Was that the image that was driving her now to wilder and wilder frenzy?

"Your whole act is finished! I created you and I'll destroy you! You won't have your career or money or prestige! You'll have nothing! I'll stop the publication of *The Psychology of Self-Esteem*! I have the influence at New American Library to do it! I'll remove your name from the dedication page of *Atlas Shrugged*! You would have been nothing without me and you will be nothing when I'm done with you!"

Suddenly, in the voice of a five-year-old, tears rolling down her cheeks, Barbara began to cry, "I'm *proud* I could never really respond to you! *Proud* I never gave you what you wanted!"

Poor Barbara, I thought. Look at what you are now doing to protect your self-esteem, to rationalize this insanity, and to survive.

I told myself: Do not argue, do not fight. Study these people and learn, once and for all. These are the people you have not wanted to let go of all these years; these are the people to whom you sacrificed Patrecia and your own integrity.

My attention shot back to Ayn when, at the edge of my vision, I saw a new thought hit her consciousness. Taking two steps closer to me, she asked ominously, "Did you tell Patrecia about our relationship?"

I answered that I had and that I'd had to, in order to help Patrecia understand my context and my requirement of secrecy.

Ayn gasped as if she had been struck — and then it was she who struck out, at me, slashing her hand twice against my face, while screaming, "God damn you! God damn you!"

It would have been easy to avoid her blows; I chose not to; I wanted her action to stand there, unobscured.

I felt my body straightening and my shoulders relaxing. I leaned forward almost eagerly, as if an important revelation about Ayn were in the process of disclosing itself.

"Oh, well," she said, and chuckled grimly, "what does it matter? No one is going to believe you, anyway. Not when I am through with you. It won't matter what you say or to whom. The whole world will brand you as a liar — I'll see to that."

But in this matter I would be telling the truth, if I chose to talk, and Ayn knew that, and everyone in the room knew it, and the truth about Ayn and me did not matter to any of them, only the protection of the Ayn Rand image and the destruction of me.

Lies had been part of our life — *at Ayn's insistence* — since the start of our affair, when I was twenty-four years old. And Ayn was about to embark on a new campaign of lies to conceal from her friends and from the world the real cause of our break. Everyone in the room knew that. And if Leonard or the rest of the Collective were ever to learn the truth, it still would not matter to them: they would twist their brains into pretzels of rationalization to protect their vision of Ayn.

Frustrated by my long silence, Ayn demanded, "Well? Do you have anything to say?"

"I am sorry," I answered truthfully, "for the pain I have caused you."

"Well *I* have one more thing to say to you!" Ayn stated. And then she left me her final legacy. "If you have an ounce of morality left in you, an ounce of psychological health — you'll be impotent for the next twenty years! And if you achieve any potency sooner, you'll know it's a sign of still worse moral degradation!'

I welcomed the long moment of silence that followed. I wanted everyone in the room to hear what she had just said.

I looked deliberately at Allan. I thought: You are a psychiatrist. How do you assess the mental and moral state of a human being who would say what Ayn had just said? This is the person you have now chosen to stand by.

I looked at Barbara; she was still crying.

I looked at Frank; his eyes were open, staring at me, revealing nothing. Would anyone ever know what all this meant to him? Would he permit himself to know?

"Now get out!" Ayn ordered.

I got up and walked to the door. I turned, knowing this was the last time I would see her.

I thought of the night Frank had greeted me at the door, more than eighteen years ago, when I had entered their home for the first time, then waited for Ayn Rand to walk toward me. "How do you do, Mr. Blumenthal."

I thought of her reminiscences of that evening, and of her saying to me, her eyes intense with happiness, "Walking into the living room, seeing you for the first time, I thought, 'He's got my kind of face,' and then I told myself, 'Don't start that again,' meaning, 'Don't start hoping.' I'd met too many alleged admirers who seemed intelligent and serious in their values, and who turned out to be phonies. But, you see, this time it didn't end in disappointment. This time I was right."

"Good-bye, Ayn," I said, standing at the door. I nodded to Frank. Then I left.

SEVENTEEN

AYN FORGAVE BARBARA.

She told Barbara that while it was wrong to deceive her, it was an understandable mistake in that Barbara legitimately had conflicting loyalties. "You chose the man you had married," Ayn had told her. "I can understand that. And eventually you did come to me with the truth."

After reporting their reconciliation, Barbara presented me with Ayn's new demands. Ayn wanted me (1) to withdraw from any and all participation in NBI and its various affiliates; (2) to turn over, without compensation, full ownership to Barbara; (3) to transfer, without compensation, my fifty-percent ownership of *The Objectivist* to Ayn; and (4) to inform all our friends, as well as the NBI and *Objectivist* staff, that I was doing so, and that Ayn was breaking with me, because of immoralities I had committed.

If I agreed to these demands, Barbara told me, Ayn would write only a brief statement in *The Objectivist* — "a single paragraph stating that because of moral failures on your part she has terminated your personal and professional relationship, and that you no longer speak for her or for Objectivism." If I did *not* agree to these demands, Barbara said, "Ayn will create a public scandal."

Even in the depths of my misery, I could not help smiling at the foolishness of this threat. *I* had no fear of a scandal, *Ayn* had. Did Ayn really think the world cared if Nathaniel Branden slept with a woman who was not his wife? Did Ayn not appreciate that the very next question in everyone's mind would be: why is Ayn Rand so interested in Nathaniel Branden's sex life? If the full truth about our conflict was revealed, Ayn — by her own statement — had the most to lose, since it was she who was obsessed with protecting her reputation.

Barbara knew the threat of scandal meant nothing to me, and that the only power Ayn had over me was moral — made possible by my own feelings of remorse. She said that she, too, thought the scandal threat was nonsense. Nonetheless, she believed that I should agree to Ayn's demands.

In a detached, impersonal voice that revealed nothing of her own emotions, she pointed out that it was to my advantage to sign over NBI because my lease with the Empire State Building still had fourteen years to run, and without the rent payments of *The Objectivist,* even if I tried to operate a more modest NBI on my own, I would not be able to meet my monthly obligations. "You'll be stuck with an enormous debt," she observed. "We're offering you a way out."

And you and Ayn will receive the benefits of all my work of the past ten years, I thought, without it costing either of you a nickel. I did not say it, because I truly did not care. If they wanted NBI, they could have it; it meant nothing to me any longer. A fair trade, I told myself; I will have my freedom and Patrecia; and *you,* God help you, will have Ayn and all the burdens of NBI.

On August 25, the summer of 1968, Barbara came to my apartment accompanied by Wilfred and Hank Holzer. It was evening. My sister Florence, whom I had telephoned in Toronto, was with me; she had flown to New York at my request, knowing I wanted someone outside the situation to talk to. Hank, Barbara, and Wilfred had been sent to my apartment by Ayn; they had brought the papers transferring to her my half interest in *The Objectivist.* I said to Hank, "As my lawyer, are you advising me to sign these papers?" He answered that he could not continue to act as my lawyer. He handed me a letter of resignation. I said, "Without notifying me in advance that you had resigned, and without counseling me to get a new attorney?" Only Florence looked shocked. Barbara and Wilfred gave no sign of finding the situation abnormal. In this and in everything that followed, it seemed clear that Hank was presenting Ayn's idea of the arrangement.

I felt sick with contempt. Whatever my past errors, I knew that this whole situation — Ayn's demand and their complicity — was despicable. On the other hand, what was *The Objectivist* to me now? Let Ayn have it, I thought; let her have whatever she wants. I prepared to sign — and then I stopped.

I remembered the copyrights to my *Objectivist* articles. As a matter of convenience, Ayn's and my pieces were all copyrighted in the name of the magazine, with the understanding that each of us retained full rights to our material. So long as we were co-owners of *The Objectivist,* we had never felt the need to put that understanding on paper. But now? I said that I would not sign the transfer papers until rights to my articles were assigned to me in writing. Hank telephoned Ayn and she told him that she agreed that my articles would remain my property but wanted *The Objectivist* turned over to her this night. "You have Ayn's word," he urged. "You have my word in front of witnesses. What more can you ask for?" I looked at Barbara. "Sign, Nathan," she pleaded, "sign. Ayn is still Ayn; she would never renege on a promise of this kind." Barbara is right, I told myself; such a betrayal would be too much for Ayn, even in her present state; I was thinking of her respect for property rights. "Sign," Wilfred urged. "We had to talk Ayn out of wanting to send Bob Teague up here with us *to make you* sign." Teague was a man who worked for us; he had a brown belt in judo. Involuntarily I laughed and asked, "You mean the idea was that Bob would *strong-arm* me into signing?" Looking miserable, Barbara and Wilfred nodded. Somehow, this idea did not lower my spirits, it raised them; in this moment, all four of them, including Ayn, struck me as absurd. Seeing my hesitation, Hank then began talking about "financial improprieties." These comments struck me as being as ludicrous as Ayn's idea that Bob Teague might use physical coercion to obtain my signature. I felt swept clean of every other emotion but contempt. To Florence's silent horror, I took the documents over to the dinner table and signed them.

The next evening, I was visited by my two nephews, Florence's sons, Leonard and Jonathan Hirschfeld, twenty and eighteen respectively. I had asked them to come. Both had been brought up as Objectivists, raised to the sound of my lecture voice on tape in the basement of their home, where Florence held NBI classes in her capacity as NBI's Toronto representative.

For the past year or two, Leonard had lived in New York and attended NYU, and Jonathan, who had only recently arrived here, was to begin at NYU this fall. I was very attached to them both and deeply concerned about the emotional impact my break with Ayn would have on them. I felt it imperative that I discuss it with them personally.

When I interviewed Leonard for this memoir, he remembered this about the evening: "We arrived at six o'clock. No lights on in the apartment. You looked worn and altogether wrecked, as if you had been crying or in horrible pain for a very long time. It was shocking to see you that way. Could this be my *uncle Nathan*? But I thought it made you look more vulnerable, more human. You said that you had very bad news, that you had committed immoral actions, betrayed your Objectivist principles, and that Ayn had broken with you. I was touched by the fact that you cared that much about how we would be affected; you seemed very protective of us. You didn't want us to lose our idealism or become disillusioned. I can't remember how many of the facts you told us that night and how many I learned over the next several weeks. I think you told us about Patrecia. That made me happy: I thought she was a fantastic human being and — I didn't care about anything else — I was glad she and my uncle were in love. Later, when I heard the things people were saying about you, I thought they had gone crazy. Nothing you did justified what was said. That was the hardest for me to absorb: not what you did, but how people reacted — how cruel and hysterical they became." Leonard subsequently wrote a long, detailed letter to his parents in which he dissected the irrationality of Ayn and her various spokespersons with a lucidity and insightfulness truly dazzling for a person his age.

Jonathan recalled: "You told us that you had done something immoral, that you had betrayed Ayn. You seemed most concerned that the break between you and Ayn would lead us to doubt the validity of Objectivism. None of it made any sense to me — I am sure I was in shock. . . . You were the embodiment of virtue; it was impossible for me to grasp that you had been lying about your relationship with the woman you loved. Throughout my adolescence I had eagerly awaited my departure for New York, the center of the world, the center of Objectivism. I was eighteen, I had just arrived, and this world with you at the center had crumbled. I was far less concerned with Ayn's behavior or the justice of the attacks on you than I was with my own overwhelming disappointment. In the end, I did ask the necessary questions of your enemies and then they betrayed themselves and my perspective changed, in your favor." Jonathan, too, wrote a letter to his parents, profoundly moving in its depiction of his feelings of personal letdown and betrayal by the uncle he had so much admired; rereading it two decades later, I am still moved to sadness by its quiet dignity and luminous anguish.

For more than a year, my nephews would be at odds with each other over their conflicting perspectives. Since Jonathan and I deeply cared for each other, our estrangement was painful for both of us.

Leonard, Florence, and Hans rallied to my support. Leonard did so fully and immediately, which created a unique bond between us which continues to this day. Florence and Hans did so with some ambivalence at first, although I believed that their basic instincts were with me. Some of their hesitation in opposing Ayn was due to the fact that they admired her enormously and had learned a great deal from her. Also, perhaps, they were influenced by the fact that their younger son was very critical of me; as his parents they wanted to be open to both sides. However, whatever she was struggling with internally, Florence was very protective of me, very indignant about the growing lynch-mob atmosphere, and very helpful in our discussions. Of my three sisters, she alone stood by me. She persisted in asking questions until she was satisfied she had the truth.

A crucial turning point for Florence was a meeting with Ayn. After several hours of evading questions about whether she had ever had an affair with me, Ayn finally lost her temper, under the pressure of Florence's questioning, and shouted, "If Nathan were the man he professed to be, he would be in love with me and not with that harlot!" At this same meeting, Ayn vigorously denied that I had ever made any contribution to her on a personal level; yet years earlier Florence had heard her say more than once that in the period following the publication of *Atlas Shrugged,* I had saved her life. Ayn's denial of this, following our break, struck Florence as particularly graceless and ugly. Thereafter more vehement in championing me, Florence too became a pariah in the eyes of Ayn's supporters.

Increasingly outraged by the dishonesty and malice of these supporters in their campaign against me, she said to Jonathan, "No sense in you and I arguing about this. Go talk to Allan and Joan, Leonard Peikoff, and Ayn's lawyer. Listen to what they've got to say and decide for yourself if they're people you want to stand with."

I did not expect Jonathan's sympathies for Ayn and his antagonism toward me to last, and they didn't. He was repelled by the demands of Ayn's supporters for the blind acceptance of her pronouncements and their resentment toward almost any questions, which they took as evidence of "irrational hostility."

On August 28, five days after my final meeting with Ayn and two days after my meetings with my nephews, I assembled the staff of NBI and *The Objectivist* for a formal announcement of the break. My chief concern that was their work on behalf of Objectivism continue; I knew that many of them would be devastated by the news of my withdrawal and my repudiation by Ayn. I did not want them to collapse into disenchantment and cynicism. Also, I wanted to take responsibility — openly and honorably — for the mistakes that I had committed. "I have taken actions I know to be wrong," I said. "I have failed to practice the principles I taught to all of you. Ayn is fully within her moral rights in severing our relationship. But I ask you to remember that a philosophy is not to be judged by the behavior — or misbehavior — of any of its exponents. Objectivism is as worthy of your support as it ever was."

"Even while you were speaking to our staff," Barbara told me later, "inside something was screaming that this was a mistake. You gave Ayn and the others a terrible weapon that they all used again and again. 'Nathaniel Branden himself admits he acted improperly,' they said. 'What else do you need to know? He stands convicted out of his own mouth.'"Florence, who was also at NBI the day I made that state-ment, shared Barbara's apprehension. "I wanted to shout to you," she said, " 'Nathan, don't do this.' "

Word of the break shot through the Objectivist subculture in New York, and then across the country, virtually overnight. The problem was, no one knew what I had done wrong. Was I a secret drinker? A drug addict? A child molester? What did Nathaniel Branden do that was so terrible as to be beyond redemption? There was no way to stop — or answer — the rumors that were now spreading like wild-fire.

Although I was prepared to share the full truth with members of my immediate family and a few friends, I had no intention of disclosing to the world the story of my past affair with Ayn and its relevance to our break. However, without that information, my affair with Patrecia was merely a personal issue without significance to our following. An extramarital relationship might be questionable, but hardly a sin of major magnitude. If nothing more was said by Ayn or me, our break would remain essentially unfathomable to people. I do not know what was in Ayn's mind; evidently she imagined that her admirers would require no more information than that she had repudiated me and that I had admitted to doing "something wrong" — and that on the basis of no more than this, I would become persona non grata, a moral out-cast, among them.

So far as the Collective went, Ayn's assumption was correct; no one was willing to talk to me or to hear my response to any charges. Elayne and Harry were an exception; I did discuss the situation with them briefly. They informed me that I was entirely responsible "for getting into this mess" and their allegiance was to Ayn and Objectivism. When I informed them of my affair with Ayn, explaining that it was the back-ground of the entire conflict, they were clearly shocked and appalled; but it made no real difference to them. I was unable to communicate adequately the context in which I had made my choices — or they were unable to hear. "Why didn't you come to us sooner?" they de-manded. "Why didn't you ask for our advice and help?" I could not make them understand that I had been sworn to lifelong secrecy by Ayn and that I had felt bound by that. It was obvious that they were deeply hurt that I had not taken them into my confidence years earlier. I thought it possible that, if I had, they might now be responding dif-ferently. I would never know. Having worked with Ayn at close quar-ters, through her work for *The Objectivist*, Elayne was already dis-enchanted with Ayn, although I was not aware of this at the time; nonetheless, she felt that Objectivism represented the best hope for the future, and that, to build a better world, the work must continue, and this meant that Ayn must be supported. Harry held this viewpoint even more strongly.

In Toronto, Reva and Sholey communicated that they stood with Elayne and Harry, although with less heat. My father had died some years before; on the last days of his life, he had been showing *Who Is Ayn Rand?* to the nurses in the hospital, and boasting about his son's work. Hearing that Ayn and I had severed our relationship, my mother was bewildered by snatches of information she could not grasp and kept asking questions no one wanted to answer. Seeing the issue exclusively in terms of family solidarity, she tormented Elayne with phone calls and reproaches: "Why are you still working for that woman?"

When I had my first opportunity to tell my brother-in-law Hans the full story myself, he made a comment I have never forgotten — one that shocked me profoundly, because he said it about Ayn Rand and because I knew it was true. Referring to Ayn's desperate desire to hang on to me romantically, and her virulent antagonism to my love for Patrecia, he exclaimed, "But it's so *antilife!*" This spoke to the core of my own deepest feelings. Nothing could have been more helpful for me to hear. I shall always be grateful to Florence and Hans for what they gave me during this period: emotional support and sanity.

When I told Patrecia of the response of Elayne and Harry, and Reva and Sholey, she was incredulous. "*Your own family?*" she said. "Two of your own sisters and brothers-in-law have repudiated you because you weren't honest and aboveboard about our relationship? Nathan, *what's happening to people?*" I replied that if there were other, additional reasons, they had not spelled out what they were.

For years I had done every kind of violence to myself, because I could not let go of the vision of my youth. I saw that they could not let go either.

Meanwhile, Barbara and Wilfred were working long hours to prepare a plan for the restructuring of Nathaniel Branden Institute without Nathaniel Branden. I had not yet signed over ownership to Barbara nor had she pressed me to do so. Her first step was to gain Ayn's approval of the plan. I was not surprised when Barbara told me later, "Even while I was working on the project, I wanted to fail. I did not want to remain in that world. I wanted to be free."

Initially Ayn agreed to the plan Barbara and Wilfred proposed; then — evidently frightened of allowing any organization again to use her name — she announced with great agitation that she wanted no part of it.

In the days that followed, she reversed her decision about writing only a single paragraph about our break. She decided to publish a long denunciation that would completely destroy my reputation.

To destroy me, Barbara later told me, had become Ayn's obsession; she spoke of little else. How will she do it, I kept wondering, when she's terrified of anyone learning about our affair?

Barbara was particularly distressed to hear Ayn mention, once again, her intention to stop the publication of *The Psychology of Self-Esteem,* through her influence at New American Library. "He'll never be published!" Ayn raved.

Having heard Ayn praise my book as a "work of genius," Barbara was stunned by Ayn's vindictiveness. "Over that issue more than any other," Barbara later told me, "my view of Ayn crashed."

Ayn's attacks against me were becoming more and more frenzied. New accusations were materializing daily. Barbara confided her growing alarm to a couple of friends, expressing concern both about the state of Ayn's mind and the risk of my "professional destruction."

Barbara's worries were instantly transmitted back to Ayn, and Barbara was summoned, via Hank Holzer, to appear before Ayn and a few members of the Collective to answer charges of having made false and immoral accusations against Ayn. Barbara telephoned Ayn and told her, "I am willing to discuss with *you* anything you care to discuss. I am not willing to appear before a jury of my peers to answer charges." Ayn's only response was to ask whether Barbara was coming to the meeting. When Barbara answered "No," Ayn slammed down the telephone. Their friendship of eighteen and a half years had ended.

When Patrecia asked me if I was surprised that Barbara and Ayn had broken their relationship, I answered, "Not for a minute. Barbara has been too close and seen too much. She would not have the stomach for what's going to be happening around here from now on."

Some weeks earlier, when I saw that my own relationship with Ayn was spinning toward final dissolution, in precisely the way that I had foreseen, I telephoned Allan Blumenthal and told him, "Here is what is coming next. I want to go on record for saying this now — before it begins. Ayn will soon be saying, and then the rest of you will be saying, that I never originated anything, never contributed anything, that every idea of mine is really Ayn's." Allan answered, "Don't be paranoiac, Nathan. That's ridiculous. No one has ever denied that you're a clever fellow." I was not yet impervious to shock. I said, "A *what*? 'A clever fellow'? Is that what the party line now says I am? I'm too late for a prediction then. The process of rewriting history has already begun."

Patrecia and I were making plans and arrangements for our move to Los Angeles. Barbara told me that she and Bob Berole, the man she was planning to live with, were also going to relocate there. Shortly after that, I learned that Wilfred and his family were planning to do the same. Patrecia was not especially happy at this news. "Are they *following* you to California?" she asked, concerned that we might become a West Coast mini-Collective. I assured her that they all liked Los Angeles for reasons that had nothing to do with me. Patrecia did not dislike any of them, but she wanted a total break from the kind of life we'd had in New York.

The task of liquidating NBI entailed selling off equipment and as much of our stock of books and art prints as we could. Wilfred performed heroically at this project. He found someone who would take over our lease with the Empire State Building and he handled all the negotiations. Because we had kept pouring almost all of our earnings back into the expansion of NBI, we did not have large cash reserves; at the end, the corporation had only about $45,000, and Wilfred, Barbara, and I divided it equally. That was what was left of ten years of work. I had no other personal savings.

Throughout September, students kept rushing into the NBI offices, desperate to learn what had happened. They arrived in anger, they arrived in tears, they arrived in agonizing bewilderment. No more NBI? It was as if their world had shattered. Ayn Rand and Nathaniel Branden no longer together? It was as if their mother and father had divorced, violently. No intelligible explanation as to why? It was as if their worst fears about an irrational universe had come true. Witnessing their suffering was very hard.

One day, when Elayne and Holzer were in the office, supervising the removal of some files and equipment, I shouted to her, "Do you think our students are *stupid*? Do you think they will never figure out what this conflict really concerns? Do you think you people can go on spreading lies about Barbara and me without our fighting back? What is Ayn counting on? If I'm the monster she says I am, *how come she's so certain I'll remain a gentleman, keep silent, and protect her reputation?*" Several of Ayn's people heard me shout this; now a new story circulated: "Nathaniel Branden is showing evidence of having a nervous breakdown."

Ayn went to our literary agents, Curtis Brown, and demanded that I no longer be represented by that firm. Alan Collins had died, and the new head was Perry Knowlton. Gerry McCauley, who represented me at Curtis Brown, announced he would quit if any writer was allowed to exert such pressure. As Gerry told me, there was never a question in Perry Knowlton's mind — or in anyone else's — of yielding to Ayn's demand.

With New American Library she was evidently more successful. Its sister company, World Publishing, informed me that my contract was terminated, shortly after I passed the promised deadline without submitting a completed manuscript. All but three chapters of the book were finished, and no publisher would normally terminate at that point, without even asking to see any of what I had written.

I watched the flow of events, sometimes feeling pain or indignation and sometimes feeling numb and disoriented. I was able to think ahead to my life in California; I found it difficult to concentrate on the events in New York.

Barbara came to me in dismay, reporting that when she passed people on the street whom she had known for a decade or more, they turned and looked away — people who once would have felt happy to spend five minutes in her presence. I would tell her some new horror I had just heard rumored about me. But I rarely felt horror; more often, I felt pain, lethargy, anger, sadness, or detachment. All my life I had enjoyed abundant energy; none of it now seemed available for this battle.

"You've got to understand," Barbara beseeched me, "that *Ayn wants you dead!* The Ayn out there now is not the Ayn you were in love with! The craziest, worst side of her is now totally in control! You've got to get this through your head! You've got to fight back! You've got to defend yourself! Ayn wants you dead! That's all that's moving her now!"

On that night long ago — March 2, 1950 — when I had sat facing Ayn for the first time, I had thought, *I'm home, I'm home, I'm home.* Now I asked my brain to absorb the fact that the woman who had been my idol was plotting my annihilation.

A friend who was particularly helpful to me during this period was psychologist Roger Callahan. Roger had moved to New York from Detroit, because he wanted to learn what Objectivism had to offer, philosophically and psychologically, and because he wanted to deepen his association with me and with our circle.

I did not know how he would react to the news of Ayn's and my break, because about two years earlier, some time after the dissolution of his own marriage, he came to my office one day and began to confide his feelings of love for Patrecia. I had not known of this and I sat listening in considerable distress, wondering if he would feel betrayed by me when he found out, as he would eventually, that Patrecia and I were lovers. It was an excruciatingly difficult meeting.

"What's going on, Nathan?" he asked, when the first rumblings reached him, and I told him the whole story. There was not a beat of hesitation; instantly he was totally committed to defending me — not only against my critics but also against what he regarded as my overly severe judgment of myself.

"Your own sense of morality is being used against you," he said indignantly. "You're still not thinking clearly. It's admirable that you don't want to evade responsibility for your mistakes, but your attitude is blinding you to the seriousness of the mistakes the other side is making. Granted you didn't handle Ayn and Patrecia as you should have; granted it would have been better if you had told the truth from the beginning, regardless of consequences. But there were reasons why you didn't; there were mitigating circumstances. For one thing, you knew exactly what you would be up against. The mistakes you made were not evil. But trying to block the publication of *The Psychology of Self-Esteem,* taking *The Objectivist* from you the way it was taken, lying about your achievements, literally trying to destroy you — *is* evil. They accuse you of betraying Objectivism. What is your 'betrayal' compared to Ayn's and the others'? What is your deception compared to the multiple deceptions they're all conspiring in right now? Can't you see that? Is this some kind of perverse egoism on your part that makes you place your vices — if that's what you call them — above everyone else's? If the great Nathaniel Branden does something wrong, that makes him worse than anyone? Wake up, Nathan. For Christ's sake, *wake up.*"

That conversation took place more than twenty years ago. I am still grateful for it.

Roger's practice as a psychotherapist was fed largely by students of Objectivism. He knew that, in supporting me publicly, he would draw enormous antagonism. Nonetheless, he invited me to guest-lead several of his therapy groups, and gave me a forum to answer his clients' questions about my break with Ayn. And, he lost a sizable percentage of his practice. Anyone who went to him was labeled a "traitor to Ayn Rand and Objectivism." When I expressed appreciation, and concern for his loss of business, Roger answered, "I've had a large practice for many years without referrals from Allan Blumenthal and the others, and I will again."

When my psychologist friends Lee and Joyce Shulman, from Detroit, came to New York for a visit, I filled them in. Lee telephoned Ayn to ask for a personal meeting; he felt very strongly that Ayn was on the verge of making a colossal mistake that would damage both her and the Objectivist movement. He intended to urge her not to go public with our conflict but rather to settle it privately, without scandal. As soon as he told Ayn about his concerns, she told him to talk to Allan Blumenthal, who was authorized to speak for her in this matter.

When Lee and Joyce met Allan and Joan for dinner, they were told that Ayn absolutely must repudiate me publicly. Then they proceeded to make the same accusations against me that Ayn would subsequently publish. They urged Lee and Joyce to join them in condemning me. When the Shulmans declined to do so, Allan said, "You're trying to judge a situation about which you don't really have full knowledge." Why, Lee wanted to know, is a judgment *against* Nathan without full knowledge acceptable, but a judgment *for* Nathan wasn't? Allan's response was to lean on Ayn's authority. "You must choose between Nathan and the author of *Atlas Shrugged*."

As an example of my alleged immorality, Allan and Joan told the Shulmans that Larry and Patrecia had been marriage-counseling clients of mine and that during this time I had engaged in an affair with Patrecia. "So, ethically," Allan announced, "Nathan has disqualified himself to practice psychology."

This story was typical of the lies being circulated about me. Twenty years later, this slander circulates widely among students of Objectivism. I encountered it when interviewing former NBI students for this book. The Blumenthals told it to my own sisters who, not questioning me, accepted it as the truth for nearly two decades.

When I met with Larry Scott in 1988 to discuss this memoir, I told him about the Blumenthals' story. Larry wrote Allan and Joan a letter:

> There are rumors . . . that Patrecia and I consulted Nathaniel for marriage counseling and that during the same time Nathaniel and Patrecia were engaged in an affair. If it is true that you have been telling people this, you need to know that the story is untrue. Patrecia and I were never marriage counseling clients (or any other kind of clients) of Nathaniel. . . . The notion that Nathaniel was guilty of unethical professional behavior toward Patrecia and me has no basis in fact. Since a story of this kind can be slanderous and unfair as well, I would hope that you will make it a point of contacting the people to whom you told the story and please retract it.

Larry invited a response from them. It is reasonable to assume that if Allan and Joan had been operating in innocence and ignorance, they would have been quick to answer Larry and to take corrective action. Larry has not heard from them. And I have heard no word of any retractions.

Ayn refused to release the rights to my articles in *The Objectivist*, which I needed for *The Psychology of Self-Esteem*.

When I told Barbara and Wilfred the news, I waited for one of them to acknowledge some regret for their role on the night I signed over to

Ayn my interest in the magazine. Neither of them said a word, not then or at any time since.

Ayn had *not* refused to release my copyrights, declared Hank Holzer, but there were "conditions." Hank sent me a memo stating her terms: (1) that neither Barbara nor I ever answer the charges in "To Whom It May Concern" (Ayn's denunciation of us in *The Objectivist*); (2) that we never discuss Ayn Rand, or our relationship with her, with anyone; (3) that he never be charged with unprofessional behavior in his dealings with me. There were other demands, but these were the main ones.

I refused. I knew that this was plain, undiluted evil.

"What happened to property rights?" I asked. "Either the articles belong to me or they don't." The answer was that Ayn's offer was the only deal I was going to get.

And the answer that came back to me, via the Objectivist grapevine, was that "Normal standards are inoperative when dealing with a moral criminal such as Nathaniel Branden."

"This," I said to Patrecia, "is what all their talk of reason, justice, and integrity comes to. This is what their ideals mean in the real world. And this is what they will have to live with, and lie to themselves about, from now on — all those who know Ayn's demands and still choose to stand by her."

"They were your friends," Patrecia said sadly. "They were your family. What must you be feeling?"

"Horror. Revulsion. And gratitude that it's over."

"Can they really keep your rights to those articles and prevent the publication of your book?"

"Hell, no. The first thing I'll do when we get to California is find a lawyer who will blast through all this garbage. Then I'll find a new publisher. I promise you: nothing will stop the publication of *The Psychology of Self-Esteem*."

One evening Barbara burst into my apartment, highly agitated. "I've been on the phone with Peter Crosby," she said. Peter and his wife, Jan, were our Los Angeles representatives, in addition to being personal friends. "Leonard and the others are already busy on the telephones, coast to coast, spreading the word that no good Objectivist should deal with either one of us. We are officially declared 'enemies.' Since everyone is afraid of what you might choose to tell — I don't just mean Ayn, I mean other people too, because you know where a lot of bodies are buried — the strategy is to spread the word that Nathaniel Branden is a confessed liar and is not to be believed on any subject."

I told Barbara that except with the die-hard true believers, I did not think the strategy would work. "Ayn had always had such contempt for her own followers. She thinks they'll believe anything she tells them. I think she's wrong."

Barbara expressed surprise at my seeming lack of anger. I shook my head sadly. "Barbara, I would never have done what these people are doing now — but still, how angry can I get? I'm Dr. Frankenstein, and they're my goddamn monsters."

"But you *are* angry!" said Patrecia when we discussed it. "You're *furious*! And you should be!" I knew she was right and I said so. She went on, "If there's one thing I hate in this world more than I hate anything else, it's malice — and malice is what I see everywhere. These people worshiped you — and never forgave you for the fact that they were never as important to you as you were to them! Now we're seeing the envy and hatred that's the other side of adulation! I've always sensed this and it's always made me wary of any kind of fame. It's not just Ayn who thought she owned you, it's *all* the people who are now going berserk."

"Patrecia, I set myself up for it."

"*No, you didn't.* I was at NBI too. I saw and heard the same things everybody else did. I never thought you owed it to me never to do anything I might think was wrong. You are a human being. You are entitled to struggle and stumble and do whatever you have to do. I love you. But I never thought you were a Divinity."

I knew that she was suffering her own shocks, as friends of years withdrew from her. I did not know if she was aware of the things being said about her by the other side — by Joan Blumenthal, for example, who had once spoken of her love for Patrecia with tears in her eyes; or by Ayn, who had told her the night of the power blackout, "You have such an air of benevolence; that's what I love about you"; I guessed that she wasn't. And yet, at another level, she would have to have known; not the concretes, not the specifics, but the gist of their accusations.

I watched her handle the pain. I admired and wanted to understand how she did it. She did not fight her pain; she did not repress her emotions. She *accepted* the pain, relaxed into it, was not afraid of it. "Pain is only another feeling," she would say. And because she did not resist her suffering or deny it, she was not controlled by it, she could rise above it when she needed to. Pain did not become as a poison inside of her. Her soul seemed to be untouched by it. I knew I was watching a form of integration and transcendence I did not fully comprehend, but knew was important — and I wanted to attain it within myself.

Catching me studying her once, she said, "I watch you watching me. Whatever you love, you *merge* with psychologically. That's one of the ways I see you learn and grow. That's what you did with Ayn also." I asked her how she felt about that, and she answered, "I like it. You make me feel extremely visible."

I held her in my arms, I pressed her head against my face, I thought of what still lay ahead, and I told myself, just hang on a little while longer.

But already, like music growing louder and louder, the feeling of liberation was rising within me, towering above pain, rage, or any sense of loss — towering above the whirlwind of madness, rising in greeting to the future.

It would be coming in the next issue of *The Objectivist*, Ayn's definitive statement to her following — and to the world — about her break with Nathaniel and Barbara Branden.

It was in the May issue, which actually appeared in October, because we had fallen so far behind in our schedule. Through an acquaintance, we obtained an advance copy, directly off the printing press, two weeks before publication.

"To Whom It May Concern" was six pages long. It began:

This is to inform my readers and all those interested in Objectivism that Nathaniel Branden and Barbara Branden are no longer associated with this magazine, with me or with my philosophy.

I have permanently broken all personal, professional and business association with them, and have withdrawn from them the permission to use my name in connection with their commercial, professional, intellectual or other activities.

I hereby withdraw my endorsement of them and of their future works and activities. I repudiate both of them, totally and permanently, as spokesmen for me or for Objectivism.

Following this introduction, Ayn proceeded to launch a long list of accusations, primarily against me and secondarily against Barbara. It seemed obvious to Barbara and me that the article was libelous.

One of the charges against me was financial malfeasance — which stunned Martin Coblenz, the man who was the accountant for both NBI and *The Objectivist* and who knew every detail of our financial life. "I can't believe this," said Mr. Coblenz, "I can't believe I am reading this. *What has happened to Miss Rand?*"

Ayn's article ended with the following statement:

FOR THE RECORD

We, the undersigned, former Associate Lecturers at Nathaniel Branden Institute, wish the following to be on record: Because Nathaniel Branden and Barbara Branden, in a series of actions, have betrayed fundamental principles of Objectivism, we condemn and repudiate these two persons irrevocably, and have terminated all association with them and with Nathaniel Branden Institute.

> Allan Blumenthal
> Alan Greenspan
> Leonard Peikoff
> Mary Ann (Rukavina) Sures

Our judgment that Ayn's article was libelous was supported by George Berger, an attorney in the Louis Nizer office, whom we consulted. He had never heard of Ayn Rand, but halfway down the first page of her·article, he turned to me and asked, "How old is Miss Rand?" At the bottom of the page, he asked, "And how old are you?" After reading a paragraph or two of the second page, he said, "A woman scorned." Barbara and I flashed astonished glances at each other. Was it that obvious to an outsider?

He encouraged us to initiate a lawsuit. "I promise you, this will be one of the easiest cases I ever had to try. I would love to have Miss Rand explain in court, to impartial listeners, how she justifies the things she says in this piece. I don't understand how her own attorneys ever allowed her to do this."

After some reflection, Barbara and I decided against the suit. The thought of spending the next two years of my life in the sewer of a libel action appalled me; I wanted to get on with my future in Los Angeles. We decided instead to write a detailed answer to Ayn's accusations. I would answer the charges against me, Barbara would answer the charges against her. Since Ayn's attacks were so ill reasoned and ill founded, and since we saw them as easy to refute, this seemed the most rational course of action. We would send our answer to all the people on the NBI/*Objectivist* mailing list.

I experienced extreme distaste at the thought of writing about my affair with Ayn, although I knew that if I did not communicate the actual nature of our relationship, people would never understand the conflict. I did not realize the extent to which I had internalized Ayn's obsession with secrecy. I could not fight her at that level, I told myself, and I did not think I needed to. The thought of the shame and embarrassment I would cause her and Frank was repugnant to me, in spite of everything that had happened. I was relieved when George Berger advised me not to disclose the affair in my published "Answer," but rather to address Ayn's charges, point by point, in their own terms. "But what do I do about this?" I asked him, pointing to a paragraph in Ayn's piece about an "irrational" and "offensive" written statement

of mine which had compelled her to break off our association. Ayn
was referring to the letter in which I explained that a resumption of
our affair was impossible for me. But she gave no indication of the
content of my letter. Many people would later comment on how incomprehensible they found this omission. "My advice," said Berger,
"is to follow Miss Rand's lead and say the minimum possible. Answer
this point briefly, stating only the *content* of the key paragraph she
found so 'offensive.' " After a long process of reflection, I decided to
accept his counsel.

After answering Ayn's various accusations — which included loss
of serious interest in philosophy, financial improprieties, and vague,
unspecified intimations about my "sordid" personal life — I ended my
answer with this statement:

> I believe it is apparent, to any thoughtful reader of Miss Rand's ar-
> ticle, that whatever the truth or falsehood or any of her specific
> charges, the real and basic reasons for her condemnation are not
> given in that article. . . . A major part of the story is obviously miss-
> ing.
>
> She does provide one indirect clue — and I must confess I am as-
> tonished that she chose to include it.
>
> She writes: "About two months ago (at the beginning of July), in
> an apparent attempt to terminate the discussions he himself had ini-
> tiated, Mr. Branden presented me with a written statement which
> was so irrational and so offensive to me that I had to break my per-
> sonal association with him."
>
> In writing the above, Miss Rand has given me the right to name
> that which I infinitely would have preferred to leave unnamed, out of
> respect for her privacy. I am obliged to report what was in that writ-
> ten paper of mine, in the name of justice and of self-defense.
>
> That written statement was an effort not to terminate my relation-
> ship with Miss Rand, but to save it in some mutually acceptable form.
>
> It was a tortured, awkward, excruciatingly embarrassed attempt
> to make clear to her why I felt that an age distance between us of
> twenty-five years constituted an insuperable barrier, for me, to a ro-
> mantic relationship.

The charges against Barbara chiefly had to do with alleged financial
exploitation — completely disregarding the fact that it was Ayn's announced intention to make Barbara her heir that prompted her to tell
Ayn the truth. Barbara's written response was devastating in its quiet
dignity and in the facts she marshaled to counter Ayn's accusations.

We knew, however, that for many of Ayn's followers this would not
be a trial of facts, evidence, or logic. Someone said to us, "Regardless

of what Ayn Rand or you say or write, roughly one-third will take Miss Rand's side, one-third will take your side, and one-third won't take sides." We thought that this was probably true.

If students could not accept Ayn's charges merely on the basis of her written statement, they were told sternly by Ayn's fervent supporters, "You are challenging the judgment of the author of *Atlas Shrugged*." When one of Allan Blumenthal's therapy clients expressed a desire to meet with me and hear my side, Allan informed him, "After Miss Rand's article, there are no sides." I began to hear of clients expelled from therapy with Allan because they refused to agree that Ayn Rand was entirely in the right. I heard similar stories about Hank Holzer's clients, including draft cases he was defending. "You are asking," people said to Holzer and to Allan, "that I condemn a man without any hard, objective evidence — a man who has made a gigantic contribution to my life." "You are asked," they were answered, "to demonstrate your loyalty to Ayn Rand and to Objectivism."

Anyone who professed any reservations about Ayn Rand's rightness in the matter of her conflict with Nathaniel Branden, was declared an enemy. Friendships of decades-long duration shattered over disagreements in this matter. Marriages and families broke up. Former lovers no longer acknowledged each other.

I heard the rumors from various sources. "Separated from Ayn Rand, Nathaniel Branden will now disappear into oblivion." "Ayn Rand says Nathan was a gigolo." "Branden is an embezzler." "Branden was only in Objectivism for the money." "Branden hurt Ayn Rand; that's all anyone needs to know to condemn him." "Branden will become a bum; he's finished." "The only moral thing Nathan can now do is commit suicide."

"*No one should discuss the situation with Nathaniel Branden or Barbara Branden.*" This was the word sent down by Ayn, passing to Leonard Peikoff, Allan and Joan Blumenthal, and Henry Holzer, then to our students, our readers, and on to an ever-widening network. Some people obeyed. Others did not; the latter came to me and I answered their questions as best I could. I did not tell them about my affair with Ayn. However, when I told them what they would later read in my published "Answer to Ayn Rand," many of them guessed.

When people asked me if I minded if they talked to the other side, I urged them to do so. I especially urged them to talk to Leonard Peikoff; he was so hysterical now in his defense of Ayn and in his denunciations of me that I knew he would win converts for me. This happened again and again. People said to me, "If they had a good case, foam wouldn't be coming out of Leonard's mouth." I laughed when I heard this, and said to new inquirers, "Don't just hear my side. Talk to Leonard Peikoff."

"This war," I said to Patrecia, "is going to split the Objectivist movement in two. The setback is going to last a long time. It may take two decades, and a whole new generation of readers, for the movement fully to recover, assuming there's anyone competent to focus it then."

"Why do people care so much?" she asked. "Why are they so tortured about it?"

"Because to them, Ayn and I were the proof that the Objectivist vision is possible. We were the evidence that it was not just a dream. Now they will either have to stand by Ayn as uncritical, conformist true believers — or they will have to rethink the philosophy on their own, without mother and father figures to make it easier, and make a new judgment about its validity. For them also, this is judgment day."

"What do you think will happen to the Objectivist movement?"

"Short-term, I think it will go into something of a decline. Long-term, I think it will have a major impact culturally and politically and that its biggest growth will happen after Ayn's death."

" 'After Ayn's death' . . . what do imagine you'll feel?"

"I'm already feeling it."

We talked about the Collective and my predictions for its future. I said, "For a while, everyone will be closer and nicer to each other. Ayn will be especially warm, securing everyone's loyalty. Some of them will scramble to win points with her by dredging up any bad memory about me or Barbara they can to prove Ayn right. There will be endless discussions of my psychology, and every kind of theory you can imagine will be put forth, principally by Ayn; then, whatever the idea is, she will discard it a week later for some new idea. Eventually she will drive the Collective crazy with her psychologizing."

Years later I learned that this was precisely what happened. She spent many hours speculating about my psychology with the Collective. I heard that she wrote many papers to herself on my "psychology" and "psychoepistemology." She was obsessed with such questions as: Was Nathan always evil or did some strange transmutation occur during the course of our relationship? If Nathan had always been corrupt, how had he been able to fool everyone? How could he master Objectivism so well if he did not really care about ideas? Yet at no time did she tell the Collective the truth about our relationship. Knowing Ayn as well as I did, I knew that in her private notes, not meant for the Collective's eyes, she would be rewriting the history of our relationship in order to explain and justify her own "errors of judgment" and to account for my "collapse into evil."

I said to Patrecia, "I don't know how long anyone will last, but the Collective will not stay together. One by one, for one reason or another, they will leave or be thrown out. Holzer won't last; he's too abrasive. The Blumenthals won't last; they're too timid and too conventional at the core; they never belonged in that environment in the first place, even at its best. Elayne and Harry won't last; sooner or later their basic sanity will rebel. Maybe one day we'll be friends again. I don't know whether Mary Ann Rukavina will remain with Ayn or not. I can't see Alan Greenspan breaking with Ayn, or Ayn with him — Alan is too artful at avoiding confrontations; my guess is that after a while he'll simply fade away without ever severing the connection officially. But Leonard Peikoff will last. Because he truly has no identity apart from his relationship to Ayn."

I made this forecast publicly on more than one occasion, because I wanted to be on record. It all came true.

One afternoon toward the end of October, shortly before Patrecia and I were to leave for California, I received a phone call from a man I did not know in Dallas, Texas. I gathered that he was a fairly wealthy businessman with intense convictions about the importance to civilization of the Objectivist message. "You *can't* retire and withdraw from all this, Mr. Branden. My friends and I are prepared to put up any amount of money you think you need to start up a new organization, anywhere in the country, to teach the Objectivist philosophy."

I was stunned and touched. "Haven't you heard," I asked, "that Miss Rand has repudiated me as a spokesman for Objectivism."

"I never admired you in the first place because Miss Rand told me to. I don't plan to stop admiring you now because Miss Rand tells me to. I won't presume to speculate about what's gone haywire with that woman, although I do have my own, private opinions, but you were the greatest teacher I ever heard and the job you started out to do is still waiting to be done."

I thanked him and said, "I've got a life of my own to pursue now that goes beyond Ayn Rand and Objectivism. I agree about the job that needs to be done, but — it's not my problem any longer."

"What do you want for yourself now?"

"A private life."

I was not concerned about re-establishing myself professionally or financially. I would contact the people on the NBI mailing list within commuting distance of Los Angeles and inform them that I was opening a psychotherapy practice; I knew that very quickly my appointment book would be filled. Nothing Ayn or her supporters might attempt would really matter. John Hospers, now head of the philosophy department at the University of Southern California, had already arranged a job for me there, lecturing on the philosophical foundations of the biological and psychological sciences. My mind was filled with plans for future books.

The primary challenge awaiting me in California was not economic but intellectual and spiritual. I faced the task of rethinking my philosophical convictions down to their base, and of redefining myself and my goals outside the context of my relationship to Objectivism and Ayn Rand. I knew I would need time. At the age of thirty-eight I had to create a new foundation for my existence and a new direction. I felt excited and inspired at the prospect.

On the morning of October 31, 1968, I rode with Patrecia down the elevator at 120 East Thirty-fourth Street for the last time. A car was waiting to take us to the airport.

I stood on the street looking up. Six floors above was Ayn's apartment, and fifteen floors above that was Barbara's. I thought about everything I was leaving behind, and I was aware of feeling immensely solemn — and of experiencing the sense of a vast, ecstatic emptiness within me, an emptiness of unlimited possibilities.

I got into the car and took Patrecia's hand. She was smiling. There was earnestness in the total stillness of her body, and in a quality of serenity and strength that seemed to flow from her spirit. I thought of what she had given me. I felt gratitude and love. I knew that she read in my face the same thought I read in hers: *we're free.*

I paused to reflect: what were the appropriate words for this occasion? Signaling the driver to go, I said, "Thank you for waiting, Patrecia."

EPILOGUE

IT IS SEPTEMBER 1988, twenty years since I left New York to begin a new life.

Out of the complex experiences of the past two decades, I will confine myself to a few essential developments and a few final reflections that will complete this story.

During our first year in Los Angeles, free from outside conflicts or pressures, Patrecia and I had the opportunity to explore and deepen our relationship, confirming and strengthening our earlier assessments and intuitions about each other. My feelings of being connected to her, more deeply than I had ever felt connected to anyone, grew even more powerful.

On November 7, 1969, a year after leaving New York, Patrecia and I were married. We decided not to invite anyone to the wedding. The ceremony was a height we wanted to experience alone. I remember the breathless solemnity of our mood, the touch of Patrecia's hand in mine as we rode back to our hotel suite. I remember thinking that my strength had come back to me in full and that I needed nothing more to guarantee our future.

"I want us to grow old together," I said to Patrecia. I felt very sure that the worst was behind us. Our life was exquisitely simple, organized around our two cardinal values: work and love. "No more obstructions," I declared. "Now we're free to concern ourselves only with what matters."

I was instantly busy with my new office practice, and my economic recovery was as rapid and relatively effortless as I had predicted to Patrecia. Nine months after arriving in California, we moved into the house where I still live. For me, the house was the symbol of our freedom and of my victory over the past. Standing in our glass-enclosed living room, we looked at the city and the sky stretched out before us.

"What a fool I was," I said, holding Patrecia in my arms, "to hang on to the past so long. Now, everything is ahead of us."

I would awaken in the morning eager to begin the day and conscious of feeling none of the weight of duty and obligation to which I had become accustomed in New York. I did not have to wonder how Ayn was feeling or if she needed me for anything. I did not have to think about Barbara. I had no organization for which I was responsible, no staff, nor large overhead. I did not have to spend time with people I did not like. I felt the tension of years draining from my mind and body.

The simplest outings — a drive down to the ocean for lunch, a walk through Beverly Hills, a day's visit to Santa Barbara — were occasions of great exuberance. To sit at my desk and think of nothing but my own work felt like a magnificent luxury. To anticipate an evening with Patrecia and to know that our time was ours to spend in any way we wished felt intoxicating.

When working as a model in New York, Patrecia had lightened her hair to blond; now she allowed it to return to its natural brown, which I preferred; as she stood in the swimming pool in our backyard, it glistened in the sunlight, showing faint traces of auburn. I flung my arms around her and lifted her body out of the water and into the air, shouting "Patrecia Branden!" And she shouted back, "Nathaniel Branden! *My husband,* Nathaniel Branden!"

Inevitably there were times when we were hit by pain, anger, or depression about the past. Some mornings I would wake up with my jaw tightly clenched and the heavy awareness that my dreams had taken me back to Ayn and my life in New York, and I felt consumed by rage. When these attacks came, I did not fight them; I accepted them, knowing they were inevitable and that Patrecia and I both needed time to heal. During the first year or two, we talked about the past a great deal. The bad periods never lasted. There was too much to be happy about.

The Psychology of Self-Esteem was published by Nash Publishing Company in the fall of 1969, then was subsequently sold to Bantam Books. Two decades later, in its twenty-seventh printing, it continues to sell actively in its Bantam edition. The central importance of self-esteem to human well-being, so ignored and neglected when the book was first published, is today widely accepted as incontrovertible.

With *The Psychology of Self-Esteem* completed, I was eager to begin another book. I was pure energy, searching for outlets. In 1970 I published *Breaking Free*. It explores the childhood origins of negative self-concepts, illustrated by brief case studies. It reflects the beginning of my interest in the developmental aspect of psychology, which I, and everyone else in the New York circle, had largely neglected. With this book I began thinking, more deeply than I had before, about the role of parents in nurturing or subverting the growth of healthy self-esteem.

During this period people asked me, "Do you still consider yourself an Objectivist?" I answered, "If, by an 'Objectivist,' you mean someone who agrees with every idea or position Ayn Rand takes, then I emphatically am not an Objectivist. If, however, you mean someone who agrees with the *essentials* of her philosophy — the supremacy of reason, and opposition to any form of irrationalism; an ethics of rational or enlightened self-interest, in contrast to the advocacy of self-sacrifice; individualism as against collectivism; inalienable rights, political and economic freedom, laissez-faire capitalism, as against any version of statism — then I am an Objectivist." Sometimes I laughed and said, "You must understand that Ayn Rand would say that I am definitely *not* an Objectivist. Perhaps I am a *neo*-Objectivist." I was thinking of the continuous refinements and modifications I made in my philosophical convictions.

Over the years I encountered many men and women who, in the name of idealism (Objectivist or otherwise), crucified their emotional life to conform to their professed values. Inevitably, this entailed massive self-repudiation, which students of Objectivism are appallingly expert at, notwithstanding their talk of "selfishness." Hearing their stories, I thought of my own history and of what I had learned from it. In my therapy and lectures, I said, "No one has ever evolved to a higher level of development by repudiating and damning what he or she is." I had come to see how supremely important self-acceptance was to healthy self-esteem.

Writing and teaching have always been my path to self-understanding and self-healing. *The Disowned Self,* published in 1972, is an examination of the widespread problem of self-alienation, in which an individual cuts himself off from his deepest emotions and highest possibilities. This book, which stands as a kind of sequel to *The Psychology of Self-Esteem,* represents a shift in emphasis from the purely cognitive aspects of self-esteem development toward a wider focus that embraces feelings, emotions, and the problem of self-disowning via the mechanism of denial and repression; it was intended not to replace but to supplement my early book. It illustrates, far more than the previous two books, the kind of therapy I was practicing during the 1970s. Writing it, I was acutely aware of my former students at NBI; it was them in particular that I felt myself addressing; it was almost as if I were writing them a letter. In offering them a more lucid understanding of emotion than I had provided in the past, and in emphasizing the supreme importance of self-acceptance, I hoped to undo some of the harm I might have caused them.

During this same period I went back to school and, in 1973, I received my Ph.D. from the California Graduate Institute.

When I reflect on the early years in Los Angeles, the memory that remains most powerful with regard to my own development is that of awakening to an internal sense of efficacy far greater than I had ever experienced in New York. In addition to the joy and satisfaction I found in writing, I loved the practice of psychotherapy, loved experimenting with new and different procedures, and was excited about the results I was achieving. Nothing seemed more interesting to me than the process by which human beings *change*.

After *The Disowned Self*, although I continued to write for myself, I did not publish again for seven years. "I am learning so much so rapidly," I told Patrecia, "that I don't want to publish for a while because I feel that by the time I finish a project I will have already moved too far beyond it."

Apart from my theoretical work in self-esteem, and of course in Objectivism, I became known for a technique I developed for self-understanding, self-exploration, self-acceptance, and self-healing — a sentence-completion procedure I first wrote about in *The Disowned Self*, then brought to a higher level of sophistication which I taught in my seminars. Many years later, I elaborated on the technique in *If You Could Hear What I Cannot Say* (1983) and *To See What I See and Know What I Know* (1986). The basic idea is to give a client an incomplete sentence, a sentence stem, and ask that it be repeated aloud again and again, each time with a different ending. The art consists of knowing which stems to select and how to build a structure from one stem to another, often in a very long chain, pursuing a course that may be subtle, complex, and indirect, utilizing subconscious associations along the way, toward the goal of accessing knowledge and resources of which the client may be quite unaware. I received many invitations to demonstrate and teach the particular ways I worked with this method. Almost every week, in one or another of my therapy groups, I would have visiting psychologists or psychiatrists who had asked to sit in and observe. It delighted me to see their amazement at what the sentence-completion technique could accomplish. It remains the simplest and fastest instrument I know for rapid access to blocked or disowned aspects of the self. The procedure can be integrated into virtually any therapeutic approach.

I did not miss the world I had left in New York; but sometimes I missed the intellectual intensity of that world. I did not miss Ayn as a person; but sometimes I missed the stimulation of our philosophical conversations at their best. I did not miss the Collective; but sometimes I missed the sense of community we had shared.

When I thought of Ayn, it was rarely with anger. I saw her as a great, enraged animal lashing out impotently, and at times I felt pity. When I thought of the woman I had once been in love with, it was as if I were thinking of someone who no longer existed.

Remembering the Sunday afternoon, on Father's Day so many years ago, when I had written on my first published article, "To my father, Ayn Rand," I saw that one of the motives that had held me to Ayn long past the time when I should have left was the subconscious longing for someone who would give me what my own father never had. I had wanted an older person who would teach me things, help make life and the world understandable, be a point of security and stability while I was forming my own identity. I had wanted a hero to admire. I had not known I had wanted that; growing up I had told myself that I did not need anyone; and because I disowned the need, its power over me became all the greater, blinding me to dangers in my relationship with Ayn that I might otherwise have seen.

In the early years in California, Barbara reproached me for not condemning Ayn as she had. Although Barbara's attitude toward Ayn later softened enormously, in the period following the break she took the position that Ayn was a monster, utterly destructive in her dealings with people. "You don't realize what a victim you were," she told me repeatedly. I said that I did not think that I, or she, or anyone else in the New York circle, was Ayn's "victim," and, in any event, that I was far more interested in understanding the roots of my own behavior than in focusing on how terrible Ayn was.

I argued that so far as Ayn's philosophy was concerned, the challenge was not to throw out the baby with the bathwater, not simply to rebel against everything we had learned but to take the time to re-think our ideas, so as not to lose what was valuable. I was concerned about this; I saw students of Objectivism, hurt and disillusioned by the divorce of their philosophical parents, rebelling against philosophy as such, discarding any serious interest in ideas, and collapsing into bitter cynicism.

In retrospect I would say that Barbara and I each had a valid point. I was slow to appreciate fully the destructive side of Ayn's character and to see that, by her own code of morality, she merited the most stern condemnation for her hypocrisy, dishonesty, and megalomania. But I was also right in insisting that self-examination should be our number-one priority — and in warning of the danger of backing off from philosophy.

Contrary to what Barbara says in *The Passion of Ayn Rand,* where she suggests that not long after the break her feelings of anger at Ayn faded and her love reasserted itself, she and I remained at loggerheads over this issue for eleven years. On an evening in 1979, in the living room of my home, Barbara began to speak with great pain and anger — once again — about how Ayn had almost ruined her life. Losing patience, I said sharply, *"Stop seeing yourself as a victim!"* I had long ago confronted what my own rewards were for remaining with Ayn (I have discussed them throughout this memoir) and I hoped Barbara would at last do the same about herself. We had an intense discussion in which, to her credit, she finally did acknowledge the payoffs: the position she (and I) occupied as leaders and teachers; the adulation she received; with the ego-intoxicating conviction that she was participating in history; the sense that in the Objectivist cause her existence had unique moral meaning; and the fact that, quite simply, she enjoyed the personal friendship and confidence of a woman she regarded as one of the greatest thinkers in the world. Thereafter, she spoke of Ayn more sympathetically and much less angrily. She still lapsed into her old perspective, but less often.

More than once during the 1970s Barbara and I came close to abandoning our attempts at friendship. Many of our old temperamental differences reasserted themselves. An additional source of strain between us was that I increasingly experienced negative feelings over the financial settlement made at the time of our separation. Wanting to be legally free as quickly as possible, and being poorly advised by my attorneys, I had signed an agreement that gave Barbara a significant claim on my earnings for the rest of my life. Barbara subsequently acknowledged that the settlement might not be fair or appropriate, but resisted my efforts at new negotiations. Not until 1981, following a rather unpleasant battle, did we reach a revised agreement. After that, we spoke only rarely.

Sometimes, when I talked with Patrecia about the future, I saw the faintest suggestion of a shadow flicker across her face. When I asked her about it, she said, "I don't know. All my life I've fought against that feeling of doom my mother raised us with, the sense of some terrible catastrophe — an earthquake or a war or some other cataclysm — that will devastate everything. God, how I hated hearing about that! Sometimes, when I'm very happy, as I am now with you, that old message comes back just for a moment, like something cold and evil chasing after me. Then it's gone and I'm all right again." This was an aspect of Patrecia I had not seen before and I did not know what to think of it. I held her in my arms to create an island of safety.

But those brief moments seemed to vanish almost immediately, and she was her fast-moving, high-energy, laughing self again.

"I love you so much," she said often, "it's frightening." I knew what she meant; the intensity of what I felt sometimes frightened me, too. I had never been this happy. But I would laugh and say, "What is there to be frightened of?"

I never ceased to reflect on Ayn's philosophy and the aspects I was convinced needed rethinking. I found myself dwelling on the inadequate attention she paid to benevolence, mutual aid, generosity, and simple kindness as ethical desirables. If life was the standard of the good, these issues were not marginal but important. These issues deserved a more prominent place in Objectivist doctrine. I knew many Objectivists who understood this and practiced it in their personal lives and took it as self-evidently implied by their philosophy even if Ayn had remained too silent on the subject. Had this theme been developed fully and explicitly by her, I think it would have made it easier for people to understand what she meant by "rational selfishness."

I thought about Ayn's concept of justice. One of the most significant things she had to say on this subject was that we should not think of justice only in terms of dealing with the guilty but also in terms of appreciating the good, of acknowledging and rewarding the virtuous and admirable. In *Atlas* this theme is central. However, Ayn also urged her followers *not* "to withhold contempt from men's vices," witness the violently abusive language with which she and her followers characterized actions of which they did not approve. After our break I came to understand, more deeply than I had before, that even if what people are doing is wrong, even if they are being irrational and errors of morality are involved, we do not lead them to virtue and rationality by projecting contempt. We do not make people better by telling them they are despicable. If the goal is to inspire positive change, a better strategy than scorn and abusive condemnation is required.

Asked constantly by people to discuss my current perspective on Ayn's philosophical system, I began to realize that in the full sense Ayn had not formulated a philosophical system — she had sketched the outlines of one. Some of the elements were filled in rather specifically, while others remained vague or entirely missing. What she provided was an overarching vision of man's place in the universe, man's relationship to existence, and some brilliantly argued support for certain key ideas — such as her views concerning concept-formation, or her metaethics, or the morality of self-interest, or her justification of natural rights — and some dazzling insights on a wide variety of philosophical issues — such as the nature of sensory perception, the irrationality of conventional ethics, the value and meaning of art, and the virtues of freedom and the evils of statism.

Viewing her writing as a whole, I thought she was right far more often than she was wrong. I thought her work abounded with philosophical wisdom, even if I was sometimes antagonized by her form of expression. I thought it contained the ingredients and the clues out of which a true philosophical system could be developed, if her followers had the mind to do it. These are still my convictions today.

On a Sunday afternoon in 1975, in the living room of our home, I was sharing these ideas with a group of students who were interested in Objectivism. I said, "Ayn Rand knew far more than she wrote. Having participated in hundreds of philosophical discussions with her, and having been present at her discussions with gifted professional philosophers, I know she could have argued far more cogently for her ideas, and answered many more objections, than she ever did in print. I think she was a far better philosopher than almost anyone fully knows. She believed that all she had to do was fling her inspired thunderbolts into the world and that any decent mind could do the rest. Her achievements are enormous. But in the sphere of technical philosophy, she needed to give more than she gave, if her purpose was to leave behind a comprehensive system. However, I do not believe that was her purpose; her purpose was to formulate only what she needed for *Atlas Shrugged*."

Someone asked how I felt about the fact that Ayn had instructed her publishers to remove all references to me in *Atlas Shrugged* — the dedication at the front of the book, and the statement at the back about my being "as rational and independent a mind as I could conceive of," and "my intellectual heir." I answered that I would always remember my joy and excitement when Miss Rand first told me of her intention to dedicate *Atlas* to me — and that her subsequent repudiation felt less important to me. "Just the same, it's difficult to think of Miss Rand without sadness."

When they had gone, I stood with my arm around Patrecia on our garden terrace, overlooking the city. "I'm happy," I told her simply. "I'm really happy. When I was a teenager, I had two ambitions: to be able to earn my living doing work I cared about, and to have the woman I loved. Ever since *The Disowned Self* was published, I've felt that life doesn't owe me anything; I mean, I hope there will be many more books and more great years together, but if I had to die now, I don't feel I've missed anything."

"I wish I could feel that." She sighed. "I do feel that about you, but not about work. I still feel unsettled about what I'm going to do with my life. The most important thing I've learned since coming to California is something I knew before, but I know it better now, and that is that love is not enough, living through you is not enough, nothing will ever be enough until I know what to do with my energy, until I have an outlet, a way to use what I am. Will I achieve that in acting? I don't know. . . . What's the most important thing you've learned since moving here?"

I answered, "How utterly irrelevant Ayn is and was to my self-esteem. Whatever it was that made me write to Ayn, and that knew how to talk to her when I was not yet twenty years old — whatever launched me into the affair with her, with all of its madness, and that gave me a particular kind of certainty — whatever made it possible for me to create NBI, and to accomplish whatever I've accomplished in psychology — I had all that long before I ever met Ayn. Her great gift was that she helped me to see it. Back in New York, she tried to take it back — to make me forget it. I suppose what I've been doing, since we came to California, is reconnecting with that force within myself, reowning it."

"You are today," Patrecia answered, "as I saw you in that first moment at NBI — only much more relaxed and cheerful."

One day that fall, as I walked from my office to the elevator, a voice inside my head told me, It's time to telephone Ayn.

"Tell me what you hope to accomplish by calling her," Patrecia said to me that evening at dinner.

"In one sense," I answered, "I don't hope to accomplish anything. I don't think Ayn will be willing to talk with me. In all likelihood, she will hang up on me. When I think of all the years in New York when I could have been fully truthful with her and wasn't, I have to face the fact of my fear. I am not afraid now. I don't know whether calling is the right and rational thing to do, or whether it would be wiser not to call, to let the past remain the past. But if I have to choose without full certainty, then at least I'll know it's not fear that's motivating me this time. It feels important to do it — important for my self-respect, important for my self of those years — and how Ayn reacts is really not the point. This is between me and me."

"What would you like from the conversation, ideally?"

"Not a resumption of our relationship, but a better ending — one with more honesty and dignity between us."

I telephoned Ayn on a morning in January 1976, during a week when I was in New York to conduct a psychotherapy workshop. Here is the conversation, verbatim.

"Hello?"

"Hello, Ayn. This is Nathaniel." To my ears my voice sounded relaxed, almost gentle, as if to soften any shock.

"Who?" I smiled at the sharp intake of her breath.

"This is Nathaniel."

Now in the tone of a prosecutor, a tone I remembered too well: "To whom am I speaking, please?"

"Nathaniel Branden."

"Well, you didn't really think I would speak to you, did you?" That old familiar contempt, the contempt reserved for enemies.

"I didn't know. But I think it would be a loss for both of us if you refused to. I feel there are things we need to say to each other. So I hoped we could talk."

An ugly chuckle. "Well — no. Good-bye." She hung up.

I began to laugh. I got up and began to dance around the hotel suite. I felt as if birds were flapping their wings in my chest. I felt the absence of some enormous weight. I pulled out some hotel stationery and wrote down what Ayn and I said to each other. I called home and told Patrecia what had happened. "How do you feel?" she asked.

"Just as I sound — wonderful! It was odd, even as I was dialing her number, I was feeling absolutely serene, almost light-headed, as if I was going through the motions, because I needed to, just to finish something once and for all, but it was already finished — I had felt that, but I wanted to be certain — and this was the final confirmation."

"I'm glad you called her. Hurry home. I'll pick you up at the airport."

That was not the end of my reflections on Ayn or my efforts to understand my behavior in our relationship. Increasingly I saw to what extent my personality had become distorted through our association. It was sometimes a difficult struggle to sort out my own thoughts, feelings, and responses and to differentiate between those that were authentically mine and those that were, in effect, Ayn's voice speaking through me and influencing me in old ways. I came to appreciate the importance of separation and individuation, not only in infancy and childhood, but at each and every stage of development. I did not rebel against that which seemed to me to be valid and important in Objectivism, but I learned to ask, "And what else is true?"

I felt the presence of changes within me that were difficult to articulate. They had less to do with conscious philosophical convictions than with a growing experience of my relatedness to the natural world. I felt almost childlike at times, wanting to say to Patrecia, "God, I love this earth," without knowing clearly what I meant. Yet when I did say it she nodded in a way that told me she understood.

I felt the emergence within me of a spirituality that had nothing to

do with religion and everything to do with love: a love of life and of
the life-force that I saw manifested wherever I looked; a love for the
world as a place of wonder and enchantment and unlimited possibilities; a love for Patrecia's face in the first light of morning when I
thought how lucky, how incredibly lucky, I was; a love for all the simple daily activities that supported our existence.

On an evening in 1975, Patrecia and I were having dinner with Dale
Wasserman and his wife. I was talking to her, and Dale and Patrecia
were discussing theater. My attention was divided between my own
conversation and eavesdropping on the one I was missing, since both
interested me. Whenever Dale reflected on plays he had written, such
as *Man of La Mancha* or *One Flew Over the Cuckoo's Nest,* or difficulties on the way to production, I was always intrigued. Dale sometimes conveyed that he was not overly enthusiastic about actors and
actresses as a group; he was, however, always warmly supportive of
Patrecia. She had been talking for a long time, very earnestly, when he
said to her, "Are you sure you want to be an actress? For an actress,
you think too much. The way your mind works is more that of a writer
or a director."

A month or so later Dale telephoned to say that the Los Angeles Free
Shakespeare Company was staging a production of *Macbeth* and suggested that Patrecia audition for the role of Lady Macbeth. As she had
no background or training in Shakespeare, she was flattered and at the
same time taken aback. When she protested that she did not think she
was qualified, Dale said with great authority, "Patrecia — just do it."
He gave her the name of the director, David Alexander, whom he
knew, said he would make a call on her behalf, simply to introduce
her, and then she would be on her own.

Patrecia was called back to audition for the part three times. David
Alexander and his associates were impressed by her work but wondered if they would not be wiser to go with a "name." After the third
audition, they told her the part was hers.

The production was well received and Patrecia was praised for her
performance. Seeing her on stage, I knew that with Shakespeare, Patrecia had found herself as an actress. I recall a professor of English
literature raving to me about the depth and originality Patrecia had
brought to her interpretation and wanting to know where she had received her Shakespearean training.

Later that same year, we read that a major production of *Macbeth*
was being staged at the Los Angeles Music Center, with Charlton Heston and Vanessa Redgrave in the leads. It was scheduled to open early
in 1976. Before Patrecia could check out the possibility of auditioning

for a smaller role, her agent at William Morris telephoned to say he had already been contacted by the producer's office about Patrecia auditioning for Lady Macduff as well as Redgrave's understudy.

She was quickly hired. John Ireland played Macduff. The director was Peter Wood. We heard later that Redgrave was known to get sick during performances, and that Patrecia had been hired specifically to take over the role of Lady Macbeth when and if necessary.

Several weeks into the production, it happened. On a Wednesday morning in February, Patrecia received a call instructing her to come to the theater immediately to prepare for the Wednesday matinee: Redgrave was ill and Patrecia would be going on as Lady Macbeth. I wanted to cancel my therapy appointments so I could go that afternoon, but Patrecia asked me to wait for the evening performance, saying she would be more in control by then, and, not wanting to add to her tension, I agreed. Immediately after the performance on Wednesday afternoon, she telephoned in a state of unreserved rapture and told me the show had gone beautifully, not a single problem, everyone was excited, Heston and the rest of the cast were enthusiastic and complimentary, and Peter Wood was looking very pleased.

Sitting in the theater that evening, watching the authority and passion of Patrecia's performance remains to this day one of my most thrilling memories. All my life the longing to admire had been powerful in me, nowhere more so than in the context of romantic love, and that longing now felt supremely fulfilled. I love you, I said to her silently, feeling the emotional sum of all the steps from our first meeting at NBI in New York to the performance in this theater tonight.

When we were alone after the performance, I told her what I was feeling while she was on stage. "I am so proud of you. I felt awe at what you were doing. Your certainty was magnificent. You brought a quality of ecstatic consciousness to everything you were doing, down to the smallest gesture, it was there underneath your scenes of worst suffering — just as you bring it to your life. I love you so much."

Redgrave did not return for the balance of the week and Patrecia played Lady Macbeth through Saturday night, then resumed the role of Lady Macduff. The critics had been invited back to see her, and although Charles Champlin of the *Los Angeles Times* had reservations about the production as a whole, he compared favorably Patrecia's performance to Redgrave's.

I wondered, sadly, if she would ever again have an opportunity to play so satisfying a role — and what she would be feeling when next auditioning for the typical movie or television female role that was then being offered.

She too had been thinking about her future. She was keenly aware of the emotional cost, to her personally and to our relationship, of her pursuit of an acting career. She did not feel optimistic about finding satisfying work in Los Angeles and she did not want to seek work elsewhere in the country, because she did not want us to be separated for any length of time. "I feel totally boxed in," she said. Prior to the recent production of *Macbeth,* she had decided to enroll at Antioch College, first to complete a B.A., then to obtain an M.A. in psychology. Ever since New York, she had dreamed of one day completing her education. *Macbeth* had not changed her mind.

Once I asked her, "What does acting mean to you?" She thought for a moment, then said, "Ordinary reality is *too slow.* In art, everything is condensed, stylized, reduced to essentials; so, when I'm acting, I'm in a world where nothing is accidental, everything has a purpose, every gesture and word has to count, life is speeded up, everything is much more intense, and that intensity feels like my natural state."

On November 7, 1976, we celebrated our ninth wedding anniversary. It was almost sixteen years since we had seen each other for the first time. "I looked at you," she said, smiling, "and I thought: I will never have him; he will have to remain an abstraction." "I looked at you," I answered, "and I felt I had stepped out of ordinary reality into a dream."

In February 1977, Patrecia was contacted by the Old Globe Theatre in San Diego, notified of the Shakespeare festival being planned and invited to audition. She had been waiting for this event for a year. The central conflict of Patrecia's life came into focus most sharply at this point, the conflict between love and career. If she was accepted, she would have the opportunity to do Kate in *Taming of the Shrew* and Gertrude in *Hamlet,* plus a smaller role in a third play, the prospect of which filled her with rapture. However, the commitment entailed being away from Los Angeles for six months, five months in San Diego and one month in Scottsdale, Arizona.

We both felt it imperative that she audition. "If you get the job," I said, "I'll drive to San Diego on weekends. We'll manage. This is important to you." She spoke to Antioch and was assured that, if necessary, she could take a leave of absence without academic penalty.

Meanwhile, I was on fire with a project of my own.

From the beginning of my career, the central focus of my interest was self-esteem. Since coming to California, I had been researching what might be accomplished working with groups — and in the spring of 1976, I began to think about the possibility of conducting a therapeutic-educational program that could accommodate as many as one to two hundred participants at a time. Its purpose would be to generate psychological growth, particularly in the area of self-esteem. The workshop, to be called an "Intensive," would be spread over three and a half days.

I saw this as an opportunity to create an event that would combine didactic elements — straight teaching — with participatory, experiential learning, psychological exercises, and processes aimed at raising consciousness, stimulating self-awareness and self-acceptance, and leading to increased self-expression, self-assertiveness, and personal integrity. I wanted to take the participants on a journey that would reflect some of the key elements of my own evolution.

At first, I both resisted the project and was drawn to it. I knew that if the Intensives succeeded, I might again be obliged to create an organization, and I liked the simplicity of my life with an office and one secretary. I was afraid the Intensives could become the center of my professional life, by the logic of their own momentum, demanding more of my time than I wished to give. But they represented a challenge difficult to resist. Could psychological truths of the kind that interested me be effectively transmitted in the context of an Intensive in such a way as truly to change lives? Could I create the kind of experience I imagined, that would draw on everything I had learned?

When I thought of "Self-Esteem and the Art of Being" and what I wanted the program to contain, I thought of my own struggles since leaving New York to free myself of old perspectives that no longer served me, to free myself of pain and anger, to be more sensitive to my own needs, more empathic in my dealings with others, more balanced as a total human being. Never for a moment did I delude myself that the process was finished. I still carried too much tension, still was too impatient, still too remote when I didn't intend to be, still not in a harmonious relationship with my body. I thought that in giving this Intensive, I would advance my own development as well as that of my students.

On the evening of March 17, 1977, I conducted "Self-Esteem and the Art of Being" for the first time in Los Angeles. The class consisted of about one hundred seventy-five students. The assistants scattered around the room were all psychotherapy students of mine. Patrecia and her father were sitting among the other students. The Intensive was very powerful emotionally for everyone, including me. I felt I had attained a new height of effectiveness in working with people and generating change, and I was thrilled by the many demonstrations of honesty, self-confrontation, and personal growth I was witnessing. It works! I thought triumphantly.

"What an incredible breakthrough this Intensive is!" Patrecia said happily at the end of the weekend. "I feel as if I've taken the most fantastic leap in my own development — as if I've risen to a higher level of autonomy."

Two students who had known me at NBI came over to tell me how much they thought I had changed. "You have all your old power," one of them said, "but now you're *human*."

"He certainly is!" Patrecia announced.

Next morning, while she was still in bed, I sat down beside her and said, with unexpected tears, "Whatever I became that allowed me to do what you saw at the Intensive, I saw that Nathaniel Branden reflected in your eyes when you were twenty-one years old at NBI. You gave me that vision and helped me to achieve it all these years. You said once that I've been your protector. Do you understand that you have also been mine?" She listened with an expression of quiet gratitude and pride that matched my own feeling.

A week later, some friends of ours invited us to join them for a few days of skiing at Aspen. At first I was going to go alone, because Patrecia was running late on some school assignments. At the last moment, she decided she would come with me — it would be a long time before we would have another vacation if she got the Old Globe job. Between her studies at school and her preparation for the audition, she was exhausted; her eyes had the bright intensity of having pushed herself past her limits. She was now anxiously awaiting final word from the theater, which would not come for another week.

Flying to Aspen, I smiled when I saw her writing in her diary. She kept diaries all her adult life, and she kept one throughout our relationship. To my surprise, in our lodge that night she volunteered to show me a few pages, which she had never done before. "Nathaniel, stretched out, peaceful and serene, soon to fall asleep into his own private bliss. The touch of his hand holding firm on my leg, will soon be slipping off . . . I have work to do and it *will* get done, but I didn't want to sit alone in my big empty house, longing to be with Nathaniel. . . . 'The hand' has slipped off. I miss its warmth. I shall pick it back up and do with it what I will." I pulled her into my arms and told her how happy I was that she had decided to come with me.

For some years we had known that she had a mild epileptic condition, possibly a consequence of slight oxygen deprivation during her eleven days in an incubator. On three occasions in the past decade she had seizures and lost consciousness for a minute or two; that was the only symptom. We had been told that the condition was easily controllable with medication. On the second day of our trip, I saw her looking at a medicine bottle with some concern. She had taken her last Dilantin; in her unexpected rush to leave Los Angeles with me, she had not noticed that the bottle was almost empty. Neither of us was aware that if you have been taking Dilantin regularly, it is dangerous to stop abruptly, because this can lower the seizure threshold in anyone. Incredibly, we had not been told this and I learned it only much later.

In the day we skied and in the evening we talked. Patrecia was a faster skier than I was and on difficult slopes would go down first, then wait below waving her pole and smiling, as if to say encouragingly, "Nothing to it!" In the evening we talked about Intensives, the Old Globe, and Patrecia's studies at Antioch. I saw that the strain that vanished from her eyes on the ski slopes reappeared when we focused on the future.

We arrived home on Wednesday, March 30, and went out for dinner. We were both exhausted from skiing all day and talking most of the nights. I recall that we could hardly hold our heads up in the restaurant. Patrecia remarked that first thing in the morning she would refill her prescription. I could see that she was strained and tense: tomorrow was the day she expected to hear from the Old Globe. I encouraged her to talk about her feelings, but she was uncharacteristically reticent. "What can I say that you don't know?" she said. Next morning she seemed in better spirits. We lay in bed for a long time, holding each other. "How is it possible," Patrecia said, "that after so many years I still love you so much?" I shook my head in wonder. "I don't know," I answered. "I look at you now and I feel as I felt when I saw you fifteen years ago, as if you were a miracle that had been sent to me. For fifteen years, whenever I see you, the lights in the universe grow brighter."

At 2:30 that afternoon she telephoned me at the office. I remember the hushed, solemn quality of her first words: "Well, Nathaniel, I got it." She had just heard from the Old Globe. She reported to me the compliments she had been paid on the quality of her work. The quiet happiness in her voice had a quality of muted intensity; I thought how much I loved the sound of her voice. "Oh, Patrecia," I said, "I am so glad that you are getting the appreciation you deserve. I am so happy for you." She answered, "I wish you were home right now. I've got classes at Antioch. I don't know how I'll concentrate, but I've got to go. See you around seven-thirty or eight." We said we loved each other and hung up.

Later, someone who saw her at school that day at 4:30 would report, "She looked so happy, she looked like she was going to blow a fuse."

Driving up the winding road to our house at 7:15, I wondered whether, in her excitement, Patrecia had remembered to feed our dog, Takara. We usually fed her each day around 5:30. When I pulled into our driveway and saw Patrecia's car, I smiled and thought: she couldn't stand to be in classes today; she's come home early.

Inside the house I shouted, "Patrecia!" When she did not answer I called her name again. I moved through the house, looking for her. When I stepped into her study and saw her bag lying on the floor, I felt sudden alarm; she never went anywhere without her handbag. Then I became aware that Takara was in the room, jumping up on me, but how was that possible? If Patrecia were not home, Takara would be locked outside. Then I saw that the door to the yard was open, and I ran out, my eyes rapidly sweeping the area.

When confronted with unbearable reality, the brain sometimes tries to protect itself. Looking into the swimming pool, for some small fraction of a second I wondered how a part of a tree could conceivably have fallen to the bottom of the pool. Then, in a moment of unspeakable horror that has never left me, I grasped that it was not a tree. Through the dark water, I discerned the shape of Patrecia.

I shouted, flung myself in, dived beneath the surface, and grasped her body in my arms. I pulled her to the side of the pool and struggled to resuscitate her, searching my mind desperately for everything I knew about treating drowning victims. No response. I went on trying, pleading with Patrecia to come back to me. No response. Her eyes were open. Her face had the peacefulness of absolute emptiness. Patrecia was not there.

I do not recall the details of the next sequence. I know I shouted for help and tripped the house alarm to summon the police. I know I kept returning to the body, fighting to give it breath and life, weeping like a child and begging Patrecia to wake up. At some point I felt a neighbor's hand on my shoulder and heard his voice saying, "It's no use. She's dead."

I prowled through the house like a wounded animal, moving from room to room, shouting *"Patrecia!"* Then I collapsed on the living room sofa, whispering her name again and again, like a prayer never to be answered.

What could have happened? Why and how did she die? For a brief moment the thought flashed through my mind that Patrecia had somehow had a seizure and lost consciousness while standing too close to the pool; what other explanation could there be? My next thought was that if she had *not* had a seizure, she had been murdered — by someone from "the old days" who imagined he would be avenging Ayn Rand.

Later there was an autopsy and the coroner's verdict was death by accidental drowning. Patrecia had evidently left school early and come home. Following normal routine, she was feeding Takara by the swimming pool around 5:30 in the afternoon. At that time, the bright sun would have been pouring down into our yard through leaves and branches, reflecting off the glass windows of our home as well as the water in the pool, toward which Patrecia would have been facing. The result presumably was a "flicker phenomenon," a pattern of change in the frequency of light, hitting her eyes, triggering electrically unstable brain cells, and precipitating a seizure. Had she been feeding Takara a foot or two back from the pool, she would merely have lost consciousness. All this was conjecture, the most logical explanation anyone could produce and the one most in accord with the evidence. Later I learned that a "psychological autopsy" was also performed, checking into details of Patrecia's life, to discover if, conceivably, her death had been a suicide, difficult as suicide would have been in a swimming pool; this possibility was ruled out entirely. Murder also had had to be considered, but there was absolutely no evidence of foul play — although my nephews Leonard and Jonathan, on hearing of the death, found themselves wondering, as I had, about some lunatic from our past. The only rational interpretation of events was that Patrecia had died in a freak accident, caused by the interaction of several factors including running out of Dilantin, photic stimulation from sunlight, physical exhaustion and emotional stress, and proximity to the swimming pool.

The night of her death, Thursday, March 31, 1977, I lay in my bedroom, dreading to fall asleep because I dreaded to wake up, dreaded the first moments of consciousness in a world in which Patrecia no longer existed. Trying to make my brain absorb what it could not absorb, I said aloud to the empty room, "I found my wife's body in the swimming pool. I found Patrecia's body in the swimming pool." I kept repeating these sentences, in a voice I had never heard before, pleading with an indifferent universe for some response. Everything inside of me seemed to be disintegrating, as if the entire structure of my mind and body were crumbling and I was falling endlessly through space. I had no center; I was only endless falling.

That was eleven and a half years ago.

I shall not attempt to describe the agony of the long mourning process. Nor shall I attempt to describe the terror — and the miracle — of falling in love again. I briefly address both these issues in *The Psychology of Romantic Love*, published three years after Patrecia's death, in 1980, and then again in a book that I wrote with my wife, Devers, *What Love Asks of Us* (originally titled *The Romantic Love Question-and-Answer Book*), published in 1982.

The struggle to rebuild my life after Patrecia's death — and Devers's heroic support of me through this process — is not part of this memoir. But I will not end my story here, as I do not want to leave my memoir a tragedy.

In the fall of 1980, Devers and I were flying to New York to give a new Intensive, "Self-Esteem and Transformation." An hour into the flight, I was reading and she was sitting silently, thinking. Occasionally I glanced up to look at her profile outlined against the window. I thought that I was blessed beyond what a man has a right to expect of life.

I have been given another chance, I thought. Against all probability. It is three and a half years, and there are still times that are very difficult; but I am learning to be happy. The strength of my love for Devers helps break through the barriers.

Watching her now, I thought of how we met. She came to my office for a job interview, shortly before the accident. I had been looking for a person who could take responsibility for the promoting and marketing of the Intensives as well as the day-to-day administrative work, and an acquaintance called to say he wanted me to meet a woman who might be right for the job. Her background was in business, sales, and management. She had an unusual work pattern; she typically moved into a new field for two or three years, worked as an efficiency expert or ran an office or got an ailing business on its feet, trained her own replacement, then took a sabbatical for several months, then moved on to a another field entirely.

She was tall, with long brown hair that fell straight back, and she possessed the quiet unstressed authority of a business executive. It was difficult to assess her age; physically, she could have been in her early thirties; only her quality of mature assurance suggested someone older. She was slender, strikingly good-looking, with a somewhat angular face and a bearing that reflected natural, unboastful pride. She held herself like a woman who knew her own value and had no need to flaunt it.

I was astonished when she said that she was forty-three; she easily looked a decade younger. I was then forty-six. I was still more astonished when she mentioned that she had two grown daughters whom she had raised alone; she had been widowed at the age of twenty-four. "That's when I went into the business world. I had to find a way to survive."

In the spring of 1977, after the accident, Devers began sitting in on all my therapy groups and attending all of my Intensives, then launched into a comprehensive reading program in psychology, with an aim to mastering every aspect of my work with people, which she did with a speed and proficiency that far excelled that of any student I'd ever had. She took many programs and workshops offered by psychotherapists of other schools, and displayed the same skill at rapidly assimilating their work. She brought to the world of psychology and psychotherapy the same luminous intelligence and self-assurance that previously she had brought to the world of business. I learned that, for two years in her thirties, she took troubled teenagers into her home and worked with the juvenile authorities. Now, in 1980, she was beginning to co-lead Intensives with me and to teach my approach to mental health professionals. She was already innovating and introducing new therapeutic procedures of her own.

When I looked at her, I saw energy, self-confidence, an absolute commitment to the vision of life as joy, and a quality of balance and internal harmony I had never seen in a woman before. I admired these qualities enormously. What I found extraordinary about her from the beginning was the degree to which the various aspects of her were integrated — the career woman, the lover, the inner child, the mother, the healthily selfish, the generously compassionate, the feminine and masculine parts of her personality. *Balance,* she said often, was her cardinal value. I was drawn to the serenity and excitement that united at the center of her being. The unspoken between us in our early encounters was: "You're my idea of a woman." "You're my idea of a man."

Later, as our relationship deepened and I knew how much I loved her, I said, "Do you know how I see you? You're the kind of woman I would like to be, if I were a woman." Devers answered, "That's how I feel about you. You're the kind of man I would like to be, if I were a man." "Perhaps," I said, "that's why we experience such a sense of completion with each other."

I enjoyed the fact that she was so often full of herself. She had more energy than any human being I had ever known. "No one," she told me once, "has ever been able to handle my energy except you." I was keenly aware of how much her energy had helped me during the hardest struggle of my life.

I recalled my incredulity when she informed me she was a grandmother. She had two daughters, Vicki and Lorin, and Vicki had had a son — who she named Brandon! — shortly before Devers and I met. How could this beautiful woman who moved through the world like a slightly impatient dancer be a grandmother? "Very easily," she had answered. "By having Vicki when I was not yet eighteen." I learned that her maiden name was Israel and that her ancestors had emigrated to Greece from Spain; her family was Sephardic.

Leaning back in my seat in the plane, I allowed my mind to drift. I recalled the day of our wedding, December 10, 1978. I felt absolutely sure of myself and of what I was doing. I knew I was not free of pain, but I loved Devers totally and without reservation, and I wanted the commitment to her, through marriage, to establish the reality of a new beginning for me. I would need time, because I was still grieving for Patrecia, the spiritual companion and climax of my youth. With Devers I felt I was embarking on the great love affair of my full adulthood.

Now on the airplane I became aware of Devers looking at me. "What are you thinking about?" she asked.

"I'm thinking that I have been graced by a miracle."

"We both have," she answered.

"There is such joy in you, and such joy for me in looking at you. You're like a walking affirmation of life."

Remembering the many nights Devers had watched me while I slept, my body shaking with dreams about the accident, remembering the long tortured process by which I had slowly came back to life, I said, "We've been through some tough times together."

She reached over and hugged me. "It was worth it. I love you very much."

"I love you — and I don't think I would have survived without you."

"You would have made it with me or without me. But I'm glad we went through it together."

She reminded me that she had been single for almost sixteen years when we met. "I've known men I liked and respected, and even one I felt a love for, but I never expected to fall in love again, not like this. I enjoyed my work, my sabbaticals, and my freedom, but what I wanted most was to feel absolute and total passion for a man. Now, for the first time, I'm able to feel everything I've always wanted to feel."

When she picked up a book and began to read, I sat thinking for a long time, my mind going back to the years in New York. An hour or so later, I noticed her putting her book down and I turned and said, a little meditatively, "So much of my life has been focused on work and long-range goals. There's been so little time for play."

She laughed. "Look at what you've had in your life. You're a man in love with drama, and look at the last thirty years. What do you think you've missed?"

It was then — for the first time — that I saw the plot-structure implicit in all that had happened since the day I picked up *The Fountainhead* at the age of fourteen. When I told Devers what I was thinking, she said instantly, "You must write it." I felt a rush of excitement. This was not the first time I had thought of doing a memoir; but her enthusiasm was the final catalyst.

My mind flashed back to an afternoon in October 1978, when I had pulled a notebook out of my briefcase and proceeded to write the following:

> This is the beginning of an experiment. Whether it will lead anywhere, I do not know. I am going to keep a journal. Keeping a diary has never interested me. Now it does. I cannot say why.
>
> I am lying on my bed in the Brown Palace Hotel in Denver, here to lecture and do some radio and television interviews in connection with my Intensive on "Self-Esteem and the Art of Being," which will be offered here in a few months. Devers is in Los Angeles. I have a few hours to myself.
>
> I live in this strange double reality. I can't really explain it to anyone. Part of me in hell, mourning the loss of Patrecia. Another part falling more and more deeply in love with Devers. Struggling to absorb and assimilate it all, everything that's happened, all the conflicting feelings.
>
> Knowing for an absolute certainty that Devers is the woman for me — loving her so passionately. The sense of beginning all over again.
>
> There's so much I want to understand.

Then I began to write about the night of Patrecia's death, then about the preceding week, then about the beginnings of our relationship so many years earlier — interspersed with accounts of my feelings for Devers, the growth of our love, my concern about what I was inflicting on her, our plans for the future. As I continued writing in my journal, after returning to Los Angeles, I found myself drawn deeper and deeper into the past, as counterpoint to the increasingly happy events in my present life, trying to achieve an integrated vision of the total. I had gone through all of Patrecia's diaries, notebooks, and letters, and incorporated elements into my journal. I reread my letters to Ayn and hers to me, my letters to family and friends about all my experiences since first meeting Ayn. I listened again to the forty or fifty hours of Barbara's and my tape-recorded interview with Ayn. I listened to the dozens of hours of conversations Patrecia and I had taped. (Patrecia loved diaries, journals, records of every kind. So she liked to tape anything she thought was important.) All of this, transformed by the inevitable intellectual and emotional process, found its way into my journal, alongside journal notes on the deepening of my love for Devers, my plans for new Intensives, and observations for future books. I did not yet know what impulse was driving me — only that writing had always been my way of understanding, and that I wanted desperately to understand the experiences through which I had lived. I did not know that all of this was preparation for the writing of *Judgment Day*. I date the beginning of the memoir from that October afternoon in the Brown Palace Hotel in Denver.

A day or two after our arrival in New York, out for a walk, we stood in front of 120 East Thirty-fourth Street, the building I had made a prison for so many years. "Here it is," I said to Devers. "Here is where so much of it happened. Six floors up — 6G — is Ayn's apartment, where she still lives. And look down there, that white brick apartment building on Thirty-fourth and Third — on top is the penthouse where Patrecia and Larry lived . . ."

"Ayn is alone now."

"Yes. Frank died two years ago."

"What do you feel, standing here?"

"I feel . . . where is he, the Nathaniel of then? The man who didn't want to let go of Ayn — or Barbara. I don't pretend he's not part of me, but — I feel as if I'm in a different incarnation."

"You are."

"After everything that has happened — after so much pain and struggle — I'm an incredibly happily married man. It's still very frightening at times — how much you mean to me. I'm so aware of our mortality."

"And when you were younger?"

"When I was younger, I thought we were all indestructible."

I glanced at my watch. Time to move on. We had a date for dinner with my sister Elayne and her husband, Harry. The reconciliation had happened at the time of Patrecia's death. A day and a half after the accident, Elayne and Reva had appeared at my home, with Florence, and our old conflicts suddenly seemed unimportant. Not long after that, Elayne and Harry terminated their relationship with Ayn. Devers asked me how I felt about seeing them tonight. "I wish our reunion had happened in different circumstances," I answered, "but I'm glad we're friends again."

Elayne telephoned me, some months later, in December 1981, to say that Ayn was very ill and that her death was imminent.

"Ayn never fully recovered from the conference in New Orleans at which she spoke last month," Elayne said. The event to which she referred was the annual conference of the National Committee for Monetary Reform, an organization whose aim was the reestablishment of the gold standard and public enlightenment concerning the benefits of a free market. Ayn had been the star speaker. Her political ideas were better understood by the world in 1981 than when *Atlas Shrugged* was originally published. (In the years ahead, her profound, if largely sub-terranean, impact on the culture would be still more evident. Her influence was present and acknowledged to be present, for instance, in the explosive renewed appreciation of capitalism in the late 1980s. And beyond the arena of politics and economics, the lengthened shadow of *The Fountainhead* and *Atlas Shrugged* appeared, socially, in a growing respect for self-fulfillment as a proper goal of life. The vision of her books and of my youth seems slightly less controversial today.)

"She was ill coming home," Elayne continued. "I think she caught a cold. Anyway, she developed cardiopulmonary problems. When she checked into New York Hospital last month, it was obvious that she didn't have long to live. There was nothing more the doctors could do. So, at her own request, she was allowed to go home a few days ago, with round-the-clock nurses. The most she's got is a few months. I thought you'd want to know."

I sat in my office for a long time, talking about my feelings with Devers. "I'm seeing the two of us as we were in January 1955 — when the affair began. I was twenty-four and she was forty-nine. Why couldn't we have had the courage to be kinder to each other? And why are questions like these usually never asked except at a time of death? Why did we both behave so goddamned stupidly?"

On the afternoon of March 6, 1982, Elayne telephoned again — this time to tell me that Ayn had died a few hours earlier.

Now they were both gone: Patrecia and Ayn. I knew it was not true, but that night I felt that finally and irrevocably my youth had died.

Later that night, sitting in my study with Devers, I said, "I'm thinking of what Ayn's and my world was really about. There's a profound need that psychology has never adequately studied — the need to ex-perience an ecstatic state of consciousness. An experience that shatters the ordinary walls of reality and lifts a person to another plane and another level of feeling entirely. Some people seek that experience in religion and in the promise of union with God. Others seek it in sex or in passionate love affairs. Some seek it in drugs; or in military battle; or in music; or in creative work; or in an athletic performance that seems to break the bounds of the possible. Ayn heard the most ecstatic music inside her own head — and she never fully learned what to do with it here on earth, except through her writing. Nietzsche says some-where, 'I love those who know not how to live today.' That was Ayn. And that's why I made too many allowances for her — because some part of me struggled with the same problem. Not just Ayn and me, but all of us — we were ecstasy addicts. No one ever named it that way, but that was the key. No one can understand Ayn, or her appeal to people, or the force that held all of us together back in New York, who doesn't understand that there exists in human beings that need for an ecstatic state of consciousness. That's what Ayn transmitted through her novels, and that's what we fell in love with and fought against leaving, because it was through her that we first entered that other plane. It was a spiritual hunger. A hunger that inspired the best in us, and sometimes the worst. My impression is that when people became disillusioned with Ayn, they turned also against the hunger in themselves — which is a mistake. I knew that the task, after breaking with Ayn, was to find other forms of fulfillment for that spiritual longing — not to disown and renounce it. I have: in my work — and with you. In the intensity of what we have together. And in the simple fact of feeling each day the preciousness of life."

We had bought a home in Lake Arrowhead, a beautiful mountain area two hours drive from Los Angeles, and it was there that I did my writing. It was an ideal atmosphere in which to think, away from the world, and where Devers and I could have a lot of time alone together.

Years ago I had thought: I want to be the champion of human self-esteem. Now I wanted to complete that assignment.

Over the next several years, in addition to the two books on love, I wrote and published *If You Could Hear What I Cannot Say, To See What I See and Know What I Know, Honoring the Self,* and *How To Raise Your Self-Esteem.* These last two books represented my effort to sum up the essence of what I had learned about self-esteem over three decades.

After *How To Raise Your Self-Esteem* was finished, toward the end of 1985, I knew that I was ready for the memoir. I began working my way through a complete filing cabinet full of documents I needed to re-read as preparation for the writing.

In February 1986, Devers and I flew to Scotland. Her daughter Vicki had moved there with her son, Brandon, and had remarried. He was now nine years old and I wanted to introduce him to skiing. He was not ready for the lift, so I pulled him up the hill by his poles while he yelled, "Faster, Grandpa!" He evoked feelings in me I had never experienced before. "How much does Grandpa love you?" I would ask him and, spreading his arms wide, he would shout, "A whole skyful!" I watched him shooting down the slopes like a runaway train, aimed straight at Devers, who was waiting for him at the bottom, and I laughed a good deal.

"You have given me so much," I said to Devers, "and one of the wonderful things you've given me is today. This is not a role I ever saw myself in. The paradox is, being Brandon's grandfather doesn't make me feel old — it makes me feel young."

Later, back at the house, Brandon looked at me a little wonderingly, almost wistfully, and said, "You laugh so much, Grandpa. I love the way you laugh."

Devers was standing beside me when he said it. When I looked at her, I felt tears in my eyes — tears of triumph. I felt I had just been paid a great compliment and that I had earned it.

Devers and I often talked about the greatest challenge of life — the challenge to remain vulnerable. To remain open, receptive, feeling. Not to retreat with our bruises into a shell. To remain responsive to life and to the possibilities for joy. The meaning of Brandon's statement to me was that this was a battle I was winning.

On the plane home, Devers said, "Well, Grandpa, how are you enjoying life on earth?"

I would soon be celebrating my fifty-sixth birthday. Devers's daughter Lorin was pregnant and in a few months would give birth to a girl who her parents would name Ashley. Devers and I looked forward to being present at the hospital for the birth.

I answered, "If I had tried to tell Nathaniel Branden, age thirty, that one of the best experiences of his life would be being a grandfather — I wonder what he would have said. How am I enjoying life on earth? I feel that everything is just beginning."

I was thinking with excitement that when I returned to Los Angeles I would begin writing *Judgment Day*.

To tell the story of Barbara, my first experience of love; of Ayn, my friend, my idol, my mentor, my lover, my enemy; of Patrecia, who set me free . . .

"Do you realize," Devers said, with love and a hint of humor in her eyes, "that right now everything in life is absolutely right. No major conflicts for us, no drama, no theater anywhere in your life. Can you stand that? Have you had enough of the other? Can you just relax and surrender to being happy?"

I looked at the face that was the center of my universe. I marveled at the capacity of ectasy to regenerate itself.

"Yes," I answered.